Marketing Library and Information Services: International Perspectives

Marketing Library and Information Services: International Perspectives

Edited on behalf of IFLA

by

Dinesh K. Gupta
V. M. Open University, Kota (India)

Christie Koontz
Florida State University (USA)

Àngels Massísimo
University of Barcelona (Spain)

Réjean Savard
University of Montreal (Canada)

K · G · Saur München 2006

Bibliographic information published by Die Deutsche Bibliothek
Die Deutsche Bibliothek lists this publication in the Deutsche Nationalbibliografie; detailed bibliographic data is available in the Internet at http://dnb.ddb.de.

♾

Printed on permanent paper
The paper used in this publication meets the minimum requirements of American National Standard – Permanence of Paper for Publications and Documents in Libraries and Archives
ANSI/NISO Z39.48-1992 (R1997)

Printed in Germany

Printed / Bound by Strauss GmbH, Mörlenbach

ISBN-13: 978-3-598-11753-4
ISBN-10: 3-598-11753-1

TABLE OF CONTENTS

INTRODUCTION

Matching, adapting, executing and optimizing organizational resources, services and facilities which are best suited to satisfying customers, is the basic *mantra* of modern marketing. Marketing, applied and practised systematically, becomes the central focus and force of every successful organization, whether profit-making or non-profit making. The organization's success depends on its effectiveness in meeting identified customer wants and needs, both explicit and implicit. *Customers* are people whose behavior we want to influence and with whom we want to develop long-term loyalties for our library's offering.

Delivering satisfying products and services for library customers is an *art* in itself. And to this endeavour, we must capitalize upon our experience as well as gain knowledge from other professions, which consider customer loyalty and satisfaction central to their mission. The turn of the 21st century brings forth new trends in marketing from cradle to grave. And our profession must be cognizant of these trends and ready to employ them.

Our profession's offerings include libraries, library and information professionals, and library and information goods and services. Our offerings represent a sacred store of human mental efforts for centuries. Successful libraries are influenced by the application of marketing. Marketing is necessary to: offer benefits, users want; reduce barriers to use and access; persuade and inform our customers; and carefully plan to satisfy their needs. *From a set of techniques to a mindset* - the more we delve into marketing, the more useful it is for daily planning, execution and outcome.

Marketing today spreads its wings within library services and is described in new categories such as relationship marketing, internal marketing, interactive marketing, technological marketing, emotional marketing and experiential marketing. In libraries, (no matter what category we call it) it is ideal to use marketing to promote behaviour change.

To streamline a growing plethora of thought and viewpoints of the library and information profession on this topic of marketing, we gathered voices in this volume of experts/educators/practitioners from across the world, who contribute provocative and stimulating viewpoints, endeavors and case studies.

The volume is divided into six sections. The first section begins with an elucidation of the concept of marketing, highlighting its relevance to modern libraries. Marketing is described as a broader umbrella concept which includes: promotion, public relations, publicity, advocacy, campaigns. The next section offers a detailed analysis of activities, efforts and programmes of marketing library and information services in various countries from Norway to Kenya! We hope this sharing of experiences will lead to more comprehensive analyses of problems in common areas. The third section reviews the value of library associations in marketing libraries. The fourth section emphasizes the importance of the addition of the marketing into library and information science curricula. Various universities initiated library science not only as a subject within a course, but also as a separate field of study. The fifth section details the awarding of "best practices" in marketing of libraries in different countries. The last section reviews databases of marketing information and literature, which increased manifold in the past few years.

We as editors felt the utmost need to make these sections of this volume rich as any person referring to any topic, whether known or unknown finds it necessary to be introduced to the catalogue of finest works in the field. We as contributors and editors of this book do not boast of a "comprehensive compendious catalogue" but do emphasize a hard work was put into collecting material available till date. We sincerely hope that the votaries of library science around the world would appreciate and recognize the relentless efforts put in.

We believe that the book shall prove helpful for both working librarians and future librarians to understand vital issues relating to marketing of library and information services at the local, national and international level.

The book calls for *"the mind shift as well as a paradigm shift"*.

ACKNOWLEDGEMENTS

We acknowledge the sponsor, the IFLA Management and Marketing Section which considered our proposal suitable to conduct such study. We stand deeply indebted for encouragement from the Section Chair Ms. Marielle de Miribel and Secretary Mr. Perry Moree at various occasions.

When we began this work, we never expected so much support from professional colleagues from every corner of the world. We have tried to cover many aspects of the LIS marketing in international perspectives. We would like acknowledging all contributors who have made excellent efforts in developing their papers and making this volume possible, we are grateful to them.

We also express our deepest gratitude to Ms. Deepa Chaturvedi, Lecturer in English, Government College, Kota who took care of the language part. She also put many useful suggestions to make this study cohesive.

Thanks are also due to Mr. K.B. Saxena, "Logo Computers" who did all data processing work of the volume in an efficient way.

Editors
2005

CONTRIBUTORS

Sueli Angelica do Amaral, University of Brasilia, Department of Information Science and Documentation, SQN 211 Bloco J Ap. 105, 70863-100 Brasilia-DF, Brazil, Samaral@unb.br

Kanwal Ameen, Lecturer, Dept. of Library and Information Science, The University of Punjab, Lahore, Pakistan, kanwal_ameen@yahoo.com

Gaynor Austen, Community Services Librarian, Library Division of Technology, Information and Learning Support, Queensland University of Technology, GPO Box 2434 Brisbane Qld 4001, Australia, b.ewers@qut.edu.au

John W. Berry (Past President & Chair, International Relations Committee, American Library Association), Executive Director, NILRC: Network of Illinois, Learning Resources in Community Colleges, 719 William Street, River Forest, IL 60305, USA jberry@nilrc.org

Antony Brewerton, Subject Team Leader (Arts, Social Sciences & Health Care) and Convenor of the Marketing Group, Oxford Brookes University Library, Headington Campus, Headington, Oxford. OX3 0BP,U.K, awbrewerton@brookes.ac.uk

Melinda Bukkei, Librarian, Biblioteca Centralã Universitarã "Lucian Blaga", Str. Clinicilor nr. 2, 400006 Cluj-Napoca, Romania, bukkei_m@yahoo.com

Chen Chao, Research Associate Professor and Director of Information Consulting and Research Center, Shanghai Library/ISTIS, Room 8501 No.265 YongFu Lu, Shanghai , P.R.China 200031, cchen@libnet.sh.cn

Barbara Clubb, (Member, IFLA Section on Public Libraries & President-elect, Canadian Library Association), City Librarian and CEO, Ottawa Public Library, 120 Metcalfe Street, Ottawa, Ontario K1Y 0K4, barbara.clubb@library.ottawa.on.ca

Kathy Dempsey, Editor, Marketing Library Services newsletter, Information Today, Inc., 143 Old Marlton Pike, Medford, NJ 08055, USA 609/ 654-6266, kdempsey@infotoday.com

Michael Dowling, Director of International Relations Office and Chapter Relations Office, American Library Association, Chicago, USA, mdowling@ala.org

Barbara Ewers, Queensland University of Technology, GPO Box 2434 Brisbane Qld 4001, Australia, b.ewers@qut.edu.au

Jorge Franganillo, Universitat de Barcelona, Facultat de Biblioteconomia i Documentació, c/ Melcior de Palau 140, 08014 Barcelona (Catalonia), Spain, franganillo@ub.edu

John Ganly, Assistant Director, Science, Industry and Business Library, New York Public Library in New York City, New York, USA, jganly@nypl.org

Audronë Glosienë, (Vice-president, Lithuanian Librarians' Association), Director, Institute of LIS, Faculty of Communication, Vilnius University, Lithuania audra.glosiene@kf.vu.lt

José-Antonio Gómez-Hernández, Universidad de Murcia, Facultad de Comunicacióny Documentación, Campus del Espinardo, 30100 Murcia, Spain, jgomez@um.es

Dinesh K. Gupta, (Member, Standing Committee, IFLA Section on Management and Marketing), Associate Professor, Dept. of Lib. & Inf. Sc., VM Open University, Kota-324010, India, dineshkg@sancharnet.in

Antonia Hermelbrach, Chair for Business Administration and Marketing, Bielefeld University, 33501 Bielefeld, P.O.-Box 10 01 31, Germany, ahermelbracht@wiwi.uni-bielefeld.de

Abhinandan K. Jain, Professor of Marketing, Indian Institute of Management, Ahmedabad -380 015, India, akjain@iimahd.ernet.in

(Late) Ashok Jambhekar, Former Librarian, Indian Institute of Management, Ahmedabad, India

Monique Jucquois-Delpierre, Media and Cultural Studies, Communication Science, Information Science, Heinrich Heine University of Düsseldorf, 40225 Düsseldorf jucquois.delpierre@skynet.be, juquois@uni-duesseldorf.de

Pan Jun, Senior consultant, Information Consulting and Research Center, Shanghai Library/ISTIS, Room 8902 No.265 YongFu Lu, Shanghai, P.R.China 200031, jpan@libnet.sh.cn

Istvan Kiraly, Senior Lecturer at the Faculty of Philosophy, Babes-Bolyai University Cluj-Napoca, Romania, philobib@bcucluj.ro

Christie Koontz, (Member Secretary, IFLA-3M International Marketing Award Jury) Research associate and Director of the GeoLib Program, Florida State University, Tallahassee, FL32306, USA, ckoontz@fsu.edu

Kathy Kunneke, Co-coordinator, Library Marketing Workgroup, Library Samuel Pauw Building 2-06, University of South Africa, PRETORIA 0003, South Africa, kunnekj@unisa.ac.za

Andrea Lapsley, Assistant Director, Marketing and Development, Houston Public Library, Houston, USA, andrea.lapsley@cityofhouston.net

Aira Lepik, (Member SC, IFLA Section on Education and Training), Professor of Librarianship of Department of Information Studies, Tallinn Pedagogical University Narva Road 25, 10 120 Tallinn , Estonia, aira@tpu.ee

G. Mahesh, Scientist, NISCAIR, Satsang Marg, New Delhi, India, mahesh7@hotmail.com

Angels Massisimo, Professor, Universitat de Barcelona, C/Melcior de Palau 140, 08014 Barcelona (Catalonia), Spain, amassisimo@ub.edu

Diane Mittermeyer, Associate Professor, Graduate School of Library and Information Studies, McGill University, Montreal, Quebec, Canada, diane.mittermeyer@mcgill.ca

Florence Muet, Information services management consulting, Information & Management, Associate professor ENSSIB, 69 Lyon, France, fmuet@information-management.fr

Muhudien Mohammed, Chief Librarian, Australian Islamic College, 11 Jamaica crossing, Langford, WA 6147, Australia, muhudien@yahoo.com.au

Julita Nawe, Head, Reference and Document Delivery Department and Training Officer, University of Dar es Salaam Library, P.O. Box 35092, Tanzania, jnawe2001@yahoo.com

Sissel Nilsen, (Member, IFLA Governing Board), Director, National Library of Norway, Oslo Division, Oslo, Norway, Sissel.Nilsen@nb.no

Niels Ole Pors, (Secretary, IFLA Section on Education and Training), Associate Professor, Department of Library and Information Management. The Royal School of Library and Information Science, Denmark., nop@db.dk

Roshan Lal Raina, Professor in Communication, Indian Institute of Management Lucknow , India, roshan@iiml.ac.in

T. P. Rama Rao, Professor in Computers, Indian Institute of Management, Ahmedabad, India, ramarao@iimahd.ernet.in

Pam Rollo, (President-Elect, Special Libraries Association), Collaborative Consultation Inc, USA, pcrollo@att.net

Mireia Sala, Cultural Programmes Department, Barcelona Library Consortium, La Rambla 99, 08002 Barcelona, msalaf@mail.bcn.es

Réjean Savard, (Chair, IFLA Management and Marketing Section 1999-2003), Professor, EBSI, University of Montreal, C.P. 6128, Succursale Center-Ville, Montreal, QC H3C 3J7, Canada, rejean.savard@umontreal.ca

Janine Schmidt, University Librarian, University of Queensland Cybrary, Australia J.Schmidt@library.uq.edu.au

Erik Senst, Projekt Conjoint-Analyse, Universitätsbibliothek Bielefeld, Postfach 10 02 91, 33502 Bielefeld Raum A2-139, Germany, Senst@ub.uni-bielefeld.de

Rajesh Singh, Department of Information Studies, Åbo Akademi University, Tavastagatan 13, Åbo-20500, Finland, rsingh@abo.fi

Linda M Smith, (Chairperson, Publicity & Public Relations Group, CILIP), Publications Manager, Libraries & Learning Resources, Nottingham Trent University, Dryden Centre, Dryden Street, Nottingham, NG1 4FZ , U.K., linda.smith@ntu.ac.uk

Tirong Arap Tanui, University Librarian, Moi University, Eldoret, Kenya, ttanui@mu.ac.ke

Verena Tibljas, Childrens Department Manager, Rijeka City Library, M. Gupca 23 51000 Rijeka, Croatia, verenat@net.hr

Sheila Webber, (Member SC, IFLA Section on Management and Marketing), Lecturer, Department of Information Studies, University of Sheffield, Western Bank, Sheffield, S10 2TN, UK, s.webber@shef.ac.uk

Mark Winston, Associate Professor, School of Communication, Information and Library Studies, Rutgers University, 4 Huntington Street, New Brunswick, NJ 08901, USA, mwinston@scils.rutgers.edu

Section - I

MARKETING CONCEPT : A CHANGING PERSPECTIVE

Section - I
Marketing Concept : A Changing Perspective

Today in the mayhem and maelstrom of life where reaching goals and objectives have taken a renaissance dimension, marketing comes as a soothing aid, a functional basis through which aims are attained in the most satisfactory way. The exact date when marketing as a scientific discipline insidiously entered our professional lives is difficult to demarcate but we can very effortlessly say that the last three to four decades have seen marketing rise not only as a necessary way of life but as a sole medium of life's *gravitas*.

The big ideas of the traditional and formalized concept of LIS marketing has been demonstrated in the following table:

Marketing Terminologies in use in Libraries Before 1970	**Marketing Concepts in use in Libraries After 1970**	
	Marketing term	**Major works/ Propagators**
Advertising Exhibitions Community relations Extension work Promotion Public relations Outreach Publicity Book talks Mobile libraries Display Bay guides	Marketing mix	Bellardo and Waldhart (1977)
	Marketing-planning	Wood (1984) Weingand (1987)
	Customer service	St. Clair (1993) Walter (1994)
	Future-driven marketing	Weingand (1998)
	Service quality	Hernan (1996)
	Relationships	Besant and Sharp (2000)
	Internet Marketing	Linda Ashcroft (2000)
	Digital Library Marketing	Jennifer Rowley (2001)
	Internal Marketing	Broady-Preston (2002)
	Integrated marketing	Gupta and Jambhekar (2003)
	The Visible librarian	Siess (2003)

The first column covers major marketing terminologies, used in librarianship for almost a century till 1970s. Greta Renberg (1997) traces the history of marketing in libraries during this time. The second column gives a rough idea of new marketing concepts as adapted in library literature and one or two major works undertaken on such areas, or mentions the propagators who made the new concepts popular in the library field.

These may not be complete lists and also not in any logical sequence, but, these marketing concepts have been used in libraries over a period of time. Traditional marketing approaches are mired in transactional muck; the numbers of items are calculated, the number of searches performed, the number of documents ordered and so on. The traditional marketing approach places the emphasis on quantity vs. quality; on the product rather than the customer. Modern marketing approaches emphasize customer satisfaction, retention and long-term customer relationship. Though there has always been a conflict of choice within the many of the terminologies.

Our contributors have here made grueling efforts to remove such conflict, bring the whole gamut of marketing definitions under one head, thereby giving a new revamping facelift to the concept over the decades.

Dinesh K. Gupta in the paper *Broadening the Concept of LIS Marketing,* gives a detailed description of the growth of the concept since its incubation period delineating its importance and seeks to bring out a synthetic view which is difficult to attain as the object as the medium and end of marketing is unstable and enriching - human.

Barbara Evers and Gaynor Austen in their paper *A Framework for Market Orientation in Libraries* in a fantastic discussion give importance to the market-oriented framework for libraries in the future by inculcating and applying the proactive proven methods of marketing research and planning.

BROADENING THE CONCEPT OF LIS MARKETING

Dinesh K. Gupta

Abstract *There are large number of definitions of marketing and some of those have been reviewed which are widely quoted in library marketing literature. Amidst the great plethora of definitions that exist on library marketing, elucidating, enhancing the great 20th century tenets. The valuations, judgments, evaluations which have hitherto been presented shall form the basis of a statement acquiring an essential essence of many studies shall form a part of this introductory chapter. It also gives a brief account of how marketing concept in libraries and information centers has grown and how LIS marketing has been changed over a period of time. It further discusses the nature of LIS marketing and details the scope of marketing which is broadening.*

WHAT IS MARKETING?

On first introduction to a subject, which hitherto belongs to another discipline, one should seek a clear and concise meaning of it. It is relatively difficult to define and conceptualize marketing in context of libraries as marketing has business connotation and library and information professionals take it with skepticism. Before starting discussion on the application, implication or orientation of marketing in libraries it would be appropriate to have the basic impression of what marketing is all about? Though, there is no single acceptable framework of marketing. Even library and information professionals find themselves uneasy with this situation and most of the time crippled with marketing jargons. Webber [1] shares such concerns, as there are almost as many definitions of marketing as there are marketing textbooks. Smith [2] considers that marketing is one of those rather abstract terms which is interpreted so differently and is almost impossible to apply in a consistent way. Some of the following are commonly cited definitions of marketing in library literature illustrates this variation:

"Marketing is the management process responsible for identifying, anticipating and satisfying customer requirements profitably"

(The UK's Chartered Institute of Marketing)

Marketing consists of individual and organizational activities that facilitate and expedite satisfying exchange relationships in a dynamic environment through the creation, servicing, distribution, promotion and pricing of goods, services and ideas"

(The American Marketing Association)

"Marketing is a social and managerial process whereby individuals and groups obtain what they need and want through creating and exchanging products and value with others"

(Philip Kotler)

The true essence of above definitions of marketing is that: there are human needs, wants, and demands for the offer (the product, service); the offers have ability to satisfy customer needs; the exchange of product or service is the primary activity for payment or making some efforts; there is always a need to create an edge over competitors; the identification of favorable marketing opportunities; that resources are utilized shrewdly to maximize a business's market position; and the aim to increase market share in priority target markets.

These themes are important, but there have been a lot of changes during recent years particularly in regard to consumers buying behaviour, consumption pattern, delivery mechanism, quality criterion, and so forth. Such changes have affected marketing vividly and necessitate the need to redefine marketing. An alternate paradigm of marketing is discussed widely that can account for the continuous relationships among marketing actors. The new information technologies are key enablers to this end. The new definition of marketing by American Marketing Association released recently addresses such concern:

"Marketing is an organizational function and a set of processes for creating, communicating and delivering value to customers and for managing customer relationships in ways that benefit the organization and its stakeholders"[3].

This definition sets many new dimensions to marketing concept. The emphasis is on that:

- Marketing serves as the overriding philosophy in conducting marketing task in the organization as a whole;
- It is a set of processes; process involves interactions among people, technology, methods, procedure, environment and material (information or information sources in case of libraries), by which any offer comes to the customer;
- Value is the basket of benefits or utilities which a user or customer gets while using a product or service. Value is clearly communicated to customers so that it can be understood easily;
- A long-term relationship is developed among customers and marketers through deep understanding, reciprocal dependency and mutual trust.
- Relationship is substantially beneficial to both the parties. From the organization's point of view, relationship is a tactical issue, but for customers, it is just a communication process.

It makes clear that marketing is a wider concept and marketing task continues changing. When marketing approach is considered as a way of doing business and a philosophy committed to customer satisfaction, every marketing driven library makes efforts to create substance between the customer and the organization. It starts with identification of customer and their needs and continues till such needs are met exceedingly. It goes through, with understanding customer needs with empathy and responsiveness; communicating effectively; and delivering the offerings efficiently.

LIBRARY AND INFORMATION SERVICES MARKETING: HOW IT HAS GROWN ?

Marketing is not new to libraries and it is as old as modern librarianship. The origin of marketing dates back to 1870s and the approaches and philosophies of library experts like Melvil Dewey, SR Ranganathan, and others were marketing oriented. Even today, Ranganathan's Five Laws have been seen in the light of today's marketing concepts. But, the development of formalized LIS marketing is tied up with the following assumptions:

- Libraries have a long history of being not-for profit institutions, and the development of marketing LIS has been greatly influenced with the theories of Philip Kotler, who formally propagated the marketing concept for non-profit organizations;
- Libraries are involved in services operations in the public sphere; services are different from the products, as the attributes of services are: intangibility, heterogeneity, inseparability and perishability. It makes services marketing different from product marketing.
- Libraries need to establish relationships with users, suppliers, fund providers, governments, parental organization, and so forth; as such they need to cater not only to need of users or potential users but also convince and satisfy others for efforts/ resources that are put to use for the benefit of the user community. Relationships between the stakeholders and libraries themselves and their economic and non-economic elements should be the useful way of stating what marketing is and a theory of LIS marketing should encompass. As such, relationship marketing has direct bearing on LIS marketing.
- Libraries are in information business. Information is inconsumable, untransferable, invisible and accumulative. Libraries are not the sole provider of information but there are others with which libraries compete.
- Internet has greatly influenced the concept of library and information services. It helps libraries to offer services anytime, anywhere, anyone.

Above assumptions have made marketing of library services a critical but interesting subject of study. More importantly, LIS marketing has the potential to draw together the different streams of marketing focus into an integrated LIS marketing, as shown in the following figure:

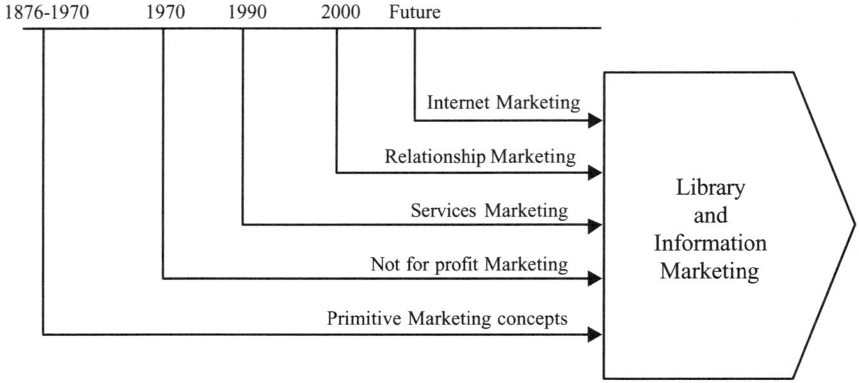

Fig. : Contributing Marketing Theories in Library and Information Services Marketing

These new theories have changed the nature and broadened the scope of LIS marketing. Although the concept of marketing of non-profit marketing, services marketing and relationships marketing is gradually developed in marketing literature. But, various marketing theories have different impacts according to their speciality and bases. These theories helped LIS Marketing to develop into an academic discipline in different time frame; the following are the basic tenets of such new marketing concepts that have bearing on library and information services:

Not-for-profit marketing	**Services Marketing**	**Relationship Marketing**	**Internet Marketing**
Marketing is equally important for libraries Adoption of practices from other sectors Exchange relationships Free services 4 Ps concept Segmentation, targeting, positioning	Internal marketing Service quality User empowerment Moments of truth Life time value to the customers One-to-one marketing	Customer orientation Customized products/services Long term transactions Customer loyalty High customer service emphasis Quality is concern for all	Network Marketing Interactive Marketing Self-service Round the clock service Database Smart Cards

LIS marketing draws heavily on social marketing but later theories vividly affect nature of present day LIS marketing. The later marketing concepts continually broaden the scope of LIS marketing. A very brief review of the development of LIS marketing is drawn below:

Prior to 1970:	In beginning, promotion, public relations of library services, was a prominent issue in librarianship widely debated in the late 1940s through the 1950s and 1960s. But the idea of using the marketing concept for libraries and information services started with Kotler and Levy's classic article "Marketing for non profit organisations" in the Journal of Marketing in 1969, which pioneered the idea of marketing non-profit organizations and accordingly library and information centers started taking interest in it. By this time only one of four, i.e. Promotion was mainly emphasized in libraries while marketing in discussion.
1970-1980:	During early years of introduction of marketing, it was thought that marketing is also applicable to libraries and traditional marketing techniques as useful for toothpaste and laundry will also be useful for non-profit institutions including libraries. Literature which originated during this period reflected this point of view. Public libraries were first among libraries which embraced the marketing concept.
1980-1990:	In this decade main thrust was on marketing planning in the framework of 4 Ps and greater importance was given to strategic planning as a means of marketing; promotion of emerging technologies; and new services reflecting the increased technology needs of library users. Of course extension of Four Ps in library marketing also has been noted. Academic libraries were leading in marketing in their services.
1990-2000:	By this time, library-marketing texts continued to emphasize traditional marketing strategies (i.e. recruiting new customers). Meanwhile, in addition to traditional marketing skills, the need for increasing employee's competence in customer satisfaction, service quality, and customer service started being realized. Special libraries greatly employed marketing to satisfy their users.

Presently, the focus of the library and information services marketing is on relationship marketing, internal marketing, branding, customer loyalty, internet marketing, network marketing and so forth.

WHAT LIS MARKETING IS ALL ABOUT?

There is still considerable misunderstanding within much of the library and information sector as to what constitutes LIS marketing. Though, there is much discussion as: what marketing is and what marketing is not. It is an issue that is discussed time and again in library and information circle but has never come to a conclusion.

'Marketing is marketing' [4], with common objectives, processes and tools, irrespective of the market in question. But, there are more than one marketing theories, having close proximity with library services. It would be interesting to know as to how library and information professionals themselves take marketing in libraries. The following are some marketing definition brought out in library literature:

" Marketing is a comprehensive, generic term dedicated to all the processes and interactions resulting in both satisfaction of users' wants and the information firm's requirement for profitable, growing revenues over the long term"[5].

"Marketing represents an integrated way of offering library services that includes adjustments to environmental influences, analysis of the needs and goals of current users and potential users, imaginative design of services, targeted communication, attractive and conveniently located facilities, and value of service that exceeds the user's cost of attaining it"[6].

"Marketing is about products/services you are trying to sell, or persuade people to use - assessing customer needs and designing products accordingly. Libraries operate a service and have customers - anything to do with promoting the library service and reaching out to engage readers in the community can be described as marketing"[7].

"The process of planning and executing the conception, pricing, promotion, and distribution of ideas, goods, and services to create exchanges that satisfy individual and organizational goals"[8].

Above definitions cover wide spectrum of marketing activities in libraries. But, definitions of marketing count for a little if businesses do not develop a process, culture and set of operational mechanism to actually "do" marketing. As, it is also considered as an important part of management philosophy, which is reflected in attitudes and approaches across the whole organization. The development of marketing thoughts and researches in LIS marketing has reached at a quite interesting stage. It is high time to pause and reflect upon what has been learnt. Towards this end, twenty three principles or big ideas of relevance and applicability of marketing in libraries have been identified from the library literature as listed below, though not in any particular order:

- Marketing is mindset[9].
- Marketing is a management framework which compels an organization or an individual, to answer a number of basic questions about the goal and functions [10].
- One major reason behind the growing interest in marketing is a pressure on managers to "prove the worth" of the library/ archive/information service [11].
- Marketing requires that you focus on what you do, why you do it, whom you do it for, how do you do it. If you want to be successful you must know these things, either by instinct, or by planning. [12].

- Marketing is a planned approach to identify and gaining the support of the 'community' and then developing appropriate services in a manner which benefits the users and furthers the aim and objectives of information services [13].
- Marketing is all about to support the library in its efforts to meet its goal by way of strategies which focus on consumer rather than the library's organization and content [14].
- Marketing is management style based on service philosophy [15].
- Marketing is all about a core management consideration and not just some optional add on [16].
- Marketing is all about being customer focus [17].
- Marketing does reap rewards for the library; it is fun and can be hard work, scary and exciting [18].
- Marketing is an attitude, a philosophy which influences the style of management [19].
- We must look at marketing, as a way of doing business and an approach that will help us manage better [20].
- Marketing is a continuous process and not a once-a month or once-a-year activity. Marketing is strategy, philosophy and a way of life for a successful LIC [21].
- A Marketing approach enables librarians both to understand and to reach their users. Librarians who use marketing techniques in their management of the library will be more efficient and effective. It is the terminology, not the techniques of marketing, which are unfamiliar to librarians to librarians [22].
- Marketing (in libraries) is more than a purely a practical function, done by people with a special label. It is a philosophy, a way of organizing and operating an entire library service. Like its close relative, quality, marketing should be a way of life for everyone, from top management downwards [23].
- Librarians may initially experience a conflict between their marketing role and their information role. Terminology may also reflect these despite the fact that, e.g. studies of user studies is still preferred term by many over market research, despite the fact that non-users are equally important [24].
- Marketing is a process that can help managers of library and information centers in achieving their objectives of improving access to their clientele, increasing the satisfaction of their clientele and reaching financial self-sufficiency [25].
- Marketing is 90% common sense [26]
- Marketing is fun. Marketing is about thriving in difficult times. But, above all marketing is about doing things [27].

- Marketing is not a one shot proposition. It is not something that you get right and then apply for all time. Your library will change. Staff changes and the mix of expertise and skills in various areas will change as people come and go. Users change, user needs change, and sources of information and means of delivery changes [28].
- Marketing is a management discipline, and equally it is part of management and organizational philosophy, which is reflected in attitudes and approaches across the whole organization. Marketing provides and illuminates the focus for successful organizations [29].
- Marketing in libraries is nothing but to evaluate their activities with the external environment, get in touch with users and their need, and integrate this analysis into every day operations of the library. It is a way of working, a way of living [30].
- Marketing is so basic that it cannot be considered a separate function within the library. Marketing is a central dimension of the entire library. It is the entirety of the library's operations and services seen from a point of view of its final result, that is, from the customers point of view [31].

Each of these profound statements is important and if, taken together are enough to evolve a new theory of LIS marketing. This needs for deep thinking from marketing perspective and is imminent to understand that marketing orientation in libraries is unlimited. To sum up, Marketing is:

A mindset	affected with values, behavior, assumptions of providers of the service.
A management style	staff manners, appearances, interior and exterior designs, language of the organization as a whole spoken with the customers, and the way service is delivered.
A set of techniques	that are necessary to formalize marketing into libraries.
A customer focus approach	customer is the pivot of marketing and all efforts must address meeting customer needs exceedingly.

A holistic approach of marketing will certainly improve the image of the librarians, will be helpful to attract more attention of the stakeholders and will be catalyst in meeting users needs happily.

IMPORTANCE AND SCOPE OF LIS MARKETING

Most Library and information professionals do not fully understand marketing's place in library and information services or how marketing is useful in their day-to-day operations and helps in managing these efficiently. For several reasons, interest of LIS professionals in marketing is rising. Some of the common reasons identified are: that the founding missions being found increasingly ill suited for the demands of the marketplace; budgets becoming tight while such units claiming for more support; the recruiting and fund-raising arenas having become extremely competitive; rising competition among similar information services providers, etc. There are some other reasons which require marketing orientation in library and information services, e.g. it helps in managing libraries better; it brings commitment to customer focus; publicizes the benefits of the library services and listening to customers needs; it helps in making users feel better that they use library again and again; and it improves the image. It is also essential to raise awareness about the resources and services available and creating desire to use these for the user benefits. Reasons, for applying marketing in any library is not to increase profit but to increase user satisfaction and increase of funding in turn. Because, increased customer satisfaction will result in increased willingness to use and pay for services offered. An enhanced perception of the value of the library will translate into increased level of support to the library. As such there is always a need for LIS staff to develop a more responsible attitude towards their customers and ensure credibility and a positive attitude to face new challenges and opportunities. There is always a greater need for appreciation and good understanding for marketing concept among librarians as what it can do for them.

The scope of marketing is extremely wide. It is further widened as one can see, based on the technology and database advances. The areas which marketing in traditional approach devolves: Collecting information, Forecasting trends, Consulting all concerned, Understanding markets, Formulating objectives, Implementing strategies, Evaluating strategies, Communicate with everybody.

Not only that a number of marketing decisions are made in libraries in day to day operations, which is evident with the following examples:

- Where should library be located?
- What opening hours are most suitable to users?
- How can the non-users be attracted to use libraries?
- Should the services be available free or any of the services should be labelled price tag or how different prices be for different users?
- What are the avenues and arrangements made in regards to participate in networks or consortia so as to widening up the resources base and optimum utilization of resources at the minimum cost?
- How are the needs of users are changing?
- How the resources, services and products, facilities can be better utilized?
- How to attract funds from donors and fund providers?
- How to rate the quality of services offered?
- Are customers happy with the level of service offered from the library?
- What are your customer's views about the service of the library?

- Is management aware of the poor or good services provided to customers and what attempts have been made to improve or benchmark the service?
- Are services user-friendly? Is it convenient to the customers?
- Do the customers have a clear expectation from library? Is that well understood?
- Is there a promise for customers? What are plans to meet them?
- Does every function in the library see itself as contributing to customer satisfaction?
- Is the concept of internal customer satisfaction works in the library? Is it measured?
- How circulation activities have been affected with the new service strategies supported with newer technologies?
- How much of the funding has changed over last couple of years? What are new avenues and strategies for further growth?
- What new initiatives have been taken up to raise awareness about the services and offers of the library?

Once a framework of responding such question is developed it would quickly be understood that marketing in libraries has an unlimited role. More important that, answer to these questions will not be similar and one can enjoy reading the different approaches for marketing from their own perspective. Such understanding often brings better results than the hard-core marketing always defined in marketing terminology mainly around marketing mix. Even the concept of marketing mix can be taken with some flexibility and open-ended approach while applying in libraries.

The marketing mix is commonly referred to the four P's of marketing – product, price, place and promotion. This is a simple, yet effective means of considering the key elements necessary and the emphasis to be placed on each, in order to effectively implement any marketing strategy. Some more concepts have been added over the years, e.g. Process and People. The mix still provides a useful framework for thinking about ways in which an organization's marketing strategy is implemented. The mix also considers a range of aspects concerning marketing and to reflect on how they interact with each other. However, there is a continual debate whether the marketing mix is relevant in present day times.

The most important mix in case of libraries is the product which can be offered to a market to satisfy a need in library and information set up. Product include *physical resources*, in the name of book, journal, available in print form or CD or on-line, in the name of *services* (both existing and potential) such as opening library for 24 hours, making reply to queries, bringing out newsletters, leaflets, library catalogue, indexes, organizing exhibitions, newsletters, bibliographies, current awareness databases, delivery of documents, consultancies, training in information use, *experiences* through the interactions with the people face to face, on telephone, fax, e-mail, etc., *facilities* such as furniture, atmosphere of the library, use of the computing and other equipment and the *information* itself.

Most of the time library and information professionals look at these aspects of products in segregation and not in integration, as marketing today embraces and integrated value proposition. This in effect, would mean that with making a decision about using a particular service or evaluating a marketing relationship, a customer not only looks at the product or value related to it, but he also evaluates in the process, the total transaction cost. To the customer, value is the benefit, received from the burden endured. Benefits may be product quality, personal service and convenience. Cost includes price and non-monetary cost as time, energy and efforts. Each library has its own niche! From that point of view, just the following areas are useful, to state the obvious, as whether: Focus is on the information itself; Focus is on the Library itself; Focus is on the function/services by the library; or the focus is on customers and meeting their need exceedingly?

Perhaps, libraries are the best candidates for marketing among non-profit service organizations. Here, the important thing is that can we see these benefits from the point of view of users and communicate in the way, they can understand. The public image of the library comes through experiences or moments of truth when users really come into contact. All promotion, advertisement, promises, will be wasteful if we are unable to transform these experiences into pleasant ones and that too from user's point of view. The deciding factors are our own attitude, our commitment to the community. Library staff that work in the library are the greatest marketing forces.

The next important marketing mix is promotion. All methods of communicating with users one-way and two ways, both are included in promotion. Whereas, people involved in marketing LIS need to do more than look inward- they must look outside the library to discover need of the many constituencies and respond to the needs of many constituencies or stakeholders to convince and attract funds.

Stakeholders are those persons who take an interest in the organization, or who have the capacity to influence its ability to achieve the objectives. A convenient way of identifying people whose opinions and activities will have a bearing on these issues is to draw a 'stakeholder map' of the organization. Any of these stakeholders can have an influence upon the organization's direction by impeding or facilitating the accomplishment of the library's goals. Some have more influence than others, but the library and information centers managers cannot afford to ignore any of them, and all need to be managed. This requires the library or information center managers to identify who they are, their level of influence and how each may politically, socially or economically affect the library's operations, functions and future plans. These actions form part of an environmental analysis or situation audit. It is also important that the library and information managers ensure that sufficient resources are allocated to deal with them. Good public relations with all stakeholders are a necessary part of marketing the library [32].

It is necessary to make it clear that many times different terms are used and employed for marketing communication in library and information centers, such as: advertising, promotion, public relations and publicity and advocacy. These refer to different-but related activities of marketing, to address the needs of users and convince the potential users and attract funds from sponsors, parental organizations or providers and decision markers, who are the stakeholders of libraries. A brief explanation of these concepts has been given below:

Public Relations	Influencing perceptions, attitudes, and opinion by transmitting information about the benefits of using the library's products and services.
Publicity	It is typically done with signs, brochures, direct mailings, e-mails, and personal contacts. Word-of-mouth is considered as most effective way of publicity these days.
Promotion	It aims to stimulate demand for the product or service. Exhibitions, display, library fair, are some of the examples of the promotion.
Advertising	A paid promotion through mass media such as newspapers, magazines, television radio, or Internet.
Advocacy	It is a planned, deliberate and sustained effort to address an issue before the people who matters for the development of library. It is a continuous process during which support and understanding of the issue are gradually increased over an extended period of time.
Lobbying	It is the interaction with politicians to secure specific objectives at an appropriate point in time in the legislative/ budget process. A part of advocacy

Successful marketing will require an integration of these activities, no matter by what name they are called. It is possible that more than one of these activities take place simultaneously, too, for:

- Informing existing and potential users about the existence of the library, its services, facilities, resources, and staff on service
- Making aware of benefits to be gained by using the library to the potential users. As libraries and information centers are under often under-utilized.
- Creating desire to use services/ products. Someone has said that marketing is the daily struggle to make people buy something they never knew they needed. I am joking, but if you have not felt that way before, you have not been a marketer.

- Informing and cultivating policy makers: Those who fund libraries want to know how well funds allocated to the library are being utilized to meet the information needs of users.
- Creating and enhancing public image of the library
- Understanding customer needs and meeting them satisfactorily.

Pricing is the most crucial issue of Marketing Mix in Libraries. Pricing of services in library and information centers is a strategic decision on a wide range of issues [33], such as:

- What are the costs that are involved in the generation of services and products? What factors/ parameters need to be considered in arriving at costs? Which of these factors can be overlooked or ignored for costing and why?
- Should the information services/products be given 'free' of charge? If so, to whom and why? What would be the impact in relation to value of product, if given free?
- If the services/ products are to be charged for, what should be the criteria for pricing? Full cost-recovery? Partial or marginal recovery? Should variable price based on ability to pay by the users be considered? Should a profit percentage be added to the cost in pricing?
- Who should be charged- internal or external clientele or both? What should be the impact on users in relation to pricing of products? Would they be willing to pay? Would demand fall and to what extent if products are priced?

While deciding for charging of fee the convenience, security, credit, speed, simplicity, collection procedure, and automation may all play a role in improving customer satisfaction. The following questions might help LIS managers in implementing price decision effectively: How much should be charged for? What should be the basis of pricing? Who should collect payment? Where should be payment be made? When should be payment made? How should payment be made? How should prices be communicated?

Place is the fourth mix of LIS marketing. Though, the future of the library as a physical 'place' has been a matter of considerable professional speculation and debate. As with greater dependence on information and convenience, libraries are also increasingly developing services available beyond the library walls such as enhanced electronic collections, virtual reference, and collaborations with services offered by other information providers. What will be the needs for physical and virtual library services when the concept of 'library without walls' 'e-library' 'digital library' already exists. Such new library distinguishes itself from what many libraries have done in physical space, or within the confines to a particular place. How library as a 'space' can be articulated to attract users in the library is an important question? And, how can we effectively plan for the future to balance collections, services and staffing between the physical and virtual library environments? With the great number of library resources and services available remotely, will physical library building be important? The physical library need no longer be just a warehouse of information, but can become a place for interaction, learning, and community. But there could be new and exciting ways library buildings focus on user needs such as an information commons, cybercafes, and self-services, etc.

The essential elements of the marketing mix must all be present, but in relation to the specific library, to individual product and services, at different times. The emphasis in parts of the mix will differ accordingly. Through four Ps of marketing mix in a library must define its activities and resource allocations for the satisfaction of customers, clients, patrons or stakeholders.

CONCLUSION

For a library that recognizes marketing concept and has orientation in its services will be closest to its users, as marketing starts with identifying customers and their needs and continues till such needs are met exceedingly with customer focus in all operations. As such, marketing must be understood and implemented in a comprehensive way. A perspective should reflect the raison d'etre of marketing, a perspective that is the common cause that no stakeholder (users, fund providers, government, or social critic, parent institutions) can question the existence of libraries in any time frame. Thus, there is a need to expand the understanding of marketing among library and information professionals and a broad, integrated framework of marketing needs to be employed in libraries.

REFERENCES

1. Webber (S). Marketing: A total solution? *Managing information*. 2 (10). October 1995: 23-24.
2. Smith (A). Marketing: What is it all about? *Aslib Information.* 21(9). Sept. 1993: 334-337.
3. Keefe (L M). What is the meaning of 'marketing'? *Marketing News*. 15 Sept. 2004: 17-18.
4. Fryer (P). Marketing at ASLIB. *Aslib Information.*19(2). Feb.1991: 42-44.
5. Weinstock (M). Marketing scientific and technical information services, In Kent (A), Ed. Encyclopedia of Library and Information Sc. vol.17, New York: Marcel Decker. 1976: 165-188.
6. Block (J) and Edzan (N N). Information marketing in Srilankan Academic libraries. *Malaysian Journal of Library and Information Science.* 7(2). Dec.2002: 87-100.
7. Botswana National Library Service: Advocacy and Lobbying Workshop, Botswana, 11th-14th June 2002. Facilitation and materials by Book Aid International.

8. www.ifla.org
9. Corfield (K). Marketing in libraries in the 2000s: Why do we bother? 11th National Library Technicians Conference, www.alia.org.au/groups/libtnat/conferences/2001/papers/corfield.html, dated 07.05.2004.
10. Savard (R). Guidelines for the teaching of marketing in the training of librarians, documentalists and archivists. Paris: Unesco. 1988.
11. Evans (G E), Layzell Ward (P) and Rugaas (B). Management basics for information professionals. New York: Neal-Schuman Publishers. 2000: 90
12. Hart (K). Putting marketing ideas into action. London: Library Association Publishing. 1999: 7
13. Yates (B), Ed. An assessment of marketing. *In*, Marketing of information. Canberra A.T.C.: National Library of Australia. 1983: 18-22
14. Dimick (B). Marketing youth services. *Library Trends.* 43(3). Winter 1995: 463-78
15. Amey (L). Marketing library services: Lessons from the private sector. *APLIS*. 6 (2). June 93: 69-76.
16. Ibid,7.
17. Athorton (B). Because you'are worth it. *SCONUL Newsletter*. 28. Spring 2003: 3-4.
18. Ibid, 9.
19. Ojiambo (J B). Application of marketing principles and techniques to libraries and information centers. *Library Review* 43(2). 1994: 46-51 (Online) available at http://www.emrald.com/brev/03543be1.htm
20. Gupta (D K) and Jambhekar (A). What is marketing in libraries: Concepts, orientations and practices. *Information Outlook*. 6 (11). 2002: 24-30.
21. Shah (P C). Marketing vis-à-vis revenue generation in libraries and information centers: An Indian experience. *Desidoc Bulletin of Information Technlogy*. 18(3). 1998: 21-28.
22. Keane (M). Marketing and librarianship: Yin and Yang, or uneasy bedfellows? *The Australian Journal*. May 1999: 116-126
23. Coote (H). Marketing matters-to you, your staff, your customers. *Aslib Information*. 21(9). Sept. 1993: 338-340.
24. Ibid,1
25. Jain (AK) et al, Eds. Marketing information products and services: A primer for librarians and information professionals. Ottawa: International Development Research Centre; New Dehli: Tata McGraw-Hill, 1999
26. Batchelor (B). Marketing the information service. *In,* Scammell (A), Ed. Handbook of Special Librarianship and Information Work. Ed. 7. London: ASLIB. 1997: 373-396.
27. Coote (H). How to market your library services effectively. Ed.2. London: ASLIB. 1997: 1.
28. Amey (L). Marketing library services: Lessons from the private sector. *APLIS 6(2)*. June 93: 69-76

29. de Saez (E). Marketing concepts for library and information services. London: LA Publishing. 1993: 3
30. Gupta (D K) and Jambhekar (A). On the link between marketing and quality. *In*, Savard (R), Ed. Education and research for marketing and quality management in libraries (IFLA Publication 99). Munich: K G Saur. 2002: 205-219.
31. Cram (J K). Marketing for non-school libraries:A guide to an essential management activity. Queensland: Department of Education. 1994: 1
32. Bryson (J). Effective library and information center management (Reprint). New Delhi: Jaico. 1996: 15-16
33. Seetharama (S). Resource generation in library and information centers: An overview. *In,* Seetharama (S), Ed. Libraries and information centers as profit making institutions. New Delhi: Ess Ess Publications. 1998:1-12.

A FRAMEWORK FOR MARKET ORIENTATION IN LIBRARIES

Barbara Ewers
Gaynor Austen

Abstract *Strategic marketing management is based on an organisation-wide marketing orientation that focuses strategic planning and management on the client; continuous market research; integrated activities and repeat business due to satisfied customers. Australian university libraries have been very successful in using the concept of market orientation to provide a framework for applying marketing principles to their management and service operations. This paper uses the seven Ps of services marketing to identify some strategies and operations that Australian university libraries have implemented as market oriented organisations. Issues discussed include market research, client segments, market positioning, product definitions, placement, processes, price, staffing and marketing communications.*

INTRODUCTION

University libraries need to survive and thrive in an on-line environment, where students find the ease of using generic search engines an attractive alternative to traditional library resources and services.

In order to do this, libraries increasingly need to adopt strategic marketing management, the process of creating and facilitating the exchange of products of value with others. Currently, the largest proportion of current library and information science literature on marketing deals with promotion and public relations, which is only a small part of the marketing mix. There seems to have been only a fragmented application of marketing principles in the management and operation of libraries, because most libraries have lacked strategies to translate marketing management into the functional management of their operations.

The concept of market orientation provides a framework for applying marketing principles to library management and operation. Market orientation means that the customer is the focal point of all organisational goals and integrates structure, management and operations[1]. Four elements underpin market orientation:

- Client orientation – satisfy customer wants and needs.
- Continuous market research – know your client and their wants and behaviours.

- Integration of all activities and systems–from management to front line staff, everyone must share information and the same client focus.
- Client relationship management – a repeat customer is an advertisement for others and sustains your business position.

In a market oriented organisation, "marketing" isn't pushed off to one side as promotion or public relations. Market orientation is an organisational management style and literature has shown that market orientation influences organisational performance[2].

Many Australian libraries are now cultivating a market orientation into their management style. Using the 7 P's of service marketing, this paper examines some examples of how they have done so.

MARKET ORIENTATION AND THE 7Ps OF SERVICES MARKETING

The 7 P's of service marketing are:

- Product
- Price
- Processes
- Place
- Physical Evidence
- Promotion
- People

As previously stated, the marketing concept is a management style or attitude. By looking at the 7 P's of services marketing, it is possible to break down the overall concept of market orientation into indicators against which organisational performance can be measured. An explicit market orientated focus will enhance management and operations as well as inform strategic vision, annual planning and organisational culture. Australian university libraries have been using this approach to maintain their "market share" in an increasingly challenging environment.

Market Research

To be market or client orientated, a library needs to understand its clients' wants and needs, the environment in which it and its competitors operate, its resources and strengths and the social factors influencing our clients. This requires the systematic collection of market research information.

Amongst libraries many mechanisms have been put in place to collect market data, including:

- Print and electronic suggestion boxes
- Client Satisfaction Surveys

- Staff feedback
- Client complaint handling processes
- Informal polling – exit interviews; small focus groups
- Statistics – peaks and troughs in demand
- Trends in higher education, management and information science literature
- Organisational statistics and planning documents – enrolment; staff numbers; client demographics; organisational goals
- Social and political environments

The data from these various sources provides information about clients' behaviour and product preference, demographic and life style factors; and client psychographics, that is their attitudes, values and motivations[3].

Market research is an ongoing function and, over time, can be used to predict resource priorities. For example, as a result of brokering undertaken by the Council of Australian University Librarians, one particular client satisfaction survey is currently conducted every two years in most Australian university libraries. This has enabled benchmarking of outcomes and identification of emerging sector wide trends.

Segment, Target, Position

Libraries always have many constituents or client groups and each library has to determine its main target market segments. Market research information allows the library to break the heterogeneous market place into smaller more homogenous market segments[4]. The clients of a university library may be segmented in many ways, such as:

- by type – academic staff as teachers and as researchers, community members; students; general staff
- by level of study – undergraduate, postgraduate
- by information seeking behaviours (coursework students vs research students)
- attendance – full-time vs part-time
- age – under 24; over 25 and under 34; mature age, etc.

The main criterion to be used in isolating market segments should be that which aligns the clients' need with your type of business. For example, the information seeking behaviour of university library clients is more meaningful than age; even though other demographic or life style factors may inform deeper understanding.

Segmentation is not only essential in identifying the different service requirements of each segment and appropriate communications strategies, but also in allocating resources appropriately[5]. A numerically large segment with homogenous needs will potentially be most demanding but will respond to economies of scale and technological intervention. Smaller politically important groups may need specialist services but their number allows for tailoring services with a minimum of additional resources.

Targeting is the process of deciding the most "critical" client segment and any other important niche markets. In most Australian university libraries it is evident that undergraduates are a primary client segment. Undergraduates are numerically our largest group and, in a university with strong teaching outcomes, they are an important segment to satisfy because of their political influence on decision makers. However, postgraduate coursework students have very similar information needs and behaviours and so many services directed at the main client group will also benefit the smaller market segment.

Most Australian undergraduate students are still young (under 24 years of age) and attending university full time. However, a large number now work at least part time in order to pay tuition costs and living expenses, and the demands of this external involvement is decreasing the amount of time which they spend on campus. As "Y Generation" students, they are highly technologically literate, "the connected generation", and, as they pay increasing fees for university tuition, are becoming increasingly discerning consumers of university and library services [6].

While undergraduate students are a primary focus, lecturing and research staff are important niche markets. Lecturers have a major influence on the information seeking behaviour and information skills development of students, through their teaching and assessment techniques. Therefore, many marketing strategies can be directed at these staff as a means to influencing the primary target segment. In contrast, research staff and students have quite different information needs for which tailored services and marketing strategies are required.

Positioning is about how an organisation wants their client segments to perceive it. It defines the bundle of attributes offered in relation to your customer and in relation to your competitors. This then becomes the core message and focus of marketing efforts. Positioning makes it easier for consumers to identify and remember a particular product/service provider. It strengthens the association of a product with one or more attributes of quality; and it creates a distinction between other products or services that may satisfy a customer's need.

Australian university libraries are attempting to position themselves as superior alternative sources of information, when compared to the chaos of the internet. At the Queensland University of Technology Library, for example, emphasis in communicating with clients is placed on the message "Search our Web!" This positions us with the attractiveness of our greatest competitor, the internet or WWW, and also against it by personalising the web as "our" web – the web within in the chaos. The word "Search" is intended as a direct positioning with the needs of the student. This statement serves as the message platform on which to base key communications with this client segment. Similarly, the University of Queensland *Cybrary* brand has been very successful and has endured for over ten years because of consistent and integrated reinforcement through all communications.

An organisation's position in relation to the client, if articulated within the library to staff, can also shape staff's perceptions about, and attitude to, their role and its relevance to clients.

PRODUCT

In their management structures many libraries organise their processes and performance by functional and line management sections. In a marketing oriented organisation, this should be overlaid by the library's product line, into which all the functional and management structures are integrated.

Library Oriented	Market Oriented
Acquisitions	Access
	- Web – 24/7 access
Cataloguing	- Opening hours
	- Learning and studying places and spaces
Web site development	- Borrowing
	- Document delivery
Collection development	- Reciprocal borrowing with other libraries
– print and electronic	- Resources sorted and catalogued
	- Classified and stored for easy retrieval
Document Delivery	- Navigability of web site
	- Course reserve (print or electronic)
Borrowing	
	Resources
Reference services –	- Selected for quality and relevance
information desks;	- Multimedia
reference service; liaison	- integration into study and teaching
services	
	High Tech/High Touch Relationships
Information literacy	- Service points – face to face
	- Reference desk service
Systems infrastructure	- Liaison librarians
	- Information literacy classes
	- Help and teaching documentation
	- Curriculum integration
	- Virtual reference - telephone, e-mail and chat reference service

The product line outlined in the right column of the table above is more meaningful to library clients than are the library's departmental structures. Some

Australian libraries have established organisational structures reflecting this product line by amalgamating computing, library and learning support staff into functional groups. However, where departmental boundaries are not changed, an explicit market orientated focus can foster more integration and cooperation between sections and thus a more seamless service to clients.

PRICE AND PROCESSES

Use of University libraries is not free. Students pay a price in terms of their time and also in terms of the kind of experience they have when using the library. Libraries try to ensure efficiency of users' time through:

- Reliable network and systems
- Cross campus services (most Australian university libraries operate on multiple geographically separate campuses)
- Minimal turnaround times for reshelving, document delivery, intercampus loans
- Navigability of web pages – the layout of the web page simplifies the complexity of the information environment
- Availability of Help – print and web documents are readily accessible at point of need; loans and information desks, e-mail and chat reference services, telephone assistance
- Reciprocal arrangements, both interlibrary loan and reciprocal memberships for students across all Australian university libraries
- Provision of collaboration services to extend client assistance outside normal library opening hours
- Self-service options – online renewal of loans; online placement of holds/reservations; self check-out units.
- Information literacy classes and orientation held on weekends and evenings as well as in business hours
- Problem solving procedures – missing item search; fast track cataloguing and processing
- Multi-skilling of staff, allowing them to move between work functions according to demand, and to act as front line problem solvers for clients
- Outsourcing "backroom" functions where feasible in order to focus staff time on client service

PLACE AND PHYSICAL EVIDENCE

Despite the expansion of online services in Australian universities, the majority of undergraduates still come to campus and need to find spaces for individual and group study, as well as socialising. Since library buildings are still, and will continue to be, an important resource for students, clients will continue to judge the quality of service partially by the physical environment available to them.

Even when not blessed with new buildings, old buildings can remain functional and attractive through innovative refurbishment. It is evident in Australian universities that students are wanting different spaces in libraries today such as group working environments, Information Commons, training rooms, lounges and eating areas. There have been major projects in many Australian university libraries in recent years to introduce such spaces through building renovation and in any new buildings constructed. Such details are also important for:

- A signage policy can ensure that both permanent and temporary signs are consistent and clear across all branches
- Promotional signs and library promotional publications should be professionally designed and displayed in purpose built display units.
- Facilities are maintained in a clean and tidy fashion.

PEOPLE

In service industries like libraries, staff are part of the production and delivery of the "product", as they are part of the service interaction. Customer service goes beyond a "cheerful attitude" to the key "moments of truth". Clients want assistance when needed; sympathy not indifference; resolution of a problem, not excuses; extra effort; individualised solutions; seamless assistance, not the run around. Training for staff needs to include:

- Skills training needs
- Customer service training
- Staff exchanges
- Study assistance
- Secondments

Regular Staff Reward and Recognition Schemes in many Australian university libraries are used to acknowledge and strengthen effective client service, by providing acknowledgement and reward to staff who exhibit high level client service skills. At Queensland University of Technology Library, for example, the Library's senior management personally funds an annual staff award for Outstanding Client Service.

PROMOTION

Marketing communication aims to build an awareness of what the library offers and to reduce the perceived and actual barriers to use of the library Marketing communication falls into two broad categories:

- A promotion for a specific or new service
- Ongoing promotions and communications about services

For both, you must use all the communication channels your target customer uses. No one channel will reach all clients.

Strategies for ongoing marketing communication used within Australian university libraries include the following:

- Web News – stories about new resources, services or focusing on a special topic on the front page of a Library's website
- Print Newsletters – circulated to academic staff and postgraduate students containing stories of new resources and services as well as more strategic concerns
- Web Page assistance – subject guides; database guides; help contextualised at point of need
- Personal selling – service points; librarians visits and e-mail contacts with academic staff
- Publications – appropriate publications; displays appropriately placed and attractive.
- Information included in other university publications.
- Self-subscribing e-mail lists – clients can, in many cases, subscribe to an e-mail list that sends a personal e-mail about any library news, ranging from new resources to service outages.
- Broadcast e-mails – at key times in the semester, e-mail students reminders of services they may need. For example, when the first assignments deadlines are nearing, send a reminder about information research classes.

Promotional campaigns in Australian university libraries usually focus on new services and use "ongoing" channels of communication as well as other promotional strategies such advertising, out-of-library posters and fliers, events or functions and sales promotion activities like give aways and merchandise. For such situations, an integrated marketing communication action plan, which sets out target audience, key messages, communication strategies and channels, time lines, responsibilities and costs, is a useful planning device.

Within Australia, a number of university libraries are now appointing specialist staff to manage their marketing and communication functions. Some of these are librarians, but others may be graduates in marketing and other business related disciplines.

At Monash University Library, for example, a position of Marketing and Communications Manager reports directly to the University Librarian. This role establishes and maintains a marketing and communications framework for the library. It initiates market research, develops appropriate library publications and web content, overseas signage, and manages the Library's "brand" and corporate image.

Royal Melbourne Institute of Technology Library employs a full time Marketing Coordinator who coordinates a cross campus publicity group and is responsible for publicity and promotional planning, publications, web publishing and client feedback mechanisms.

A similar role at the Queensland University of Technology is incorporated within the position of Community Services Librarian which reports to the Director, Library Services.

CONCLUSION

Market orientation is more than skin deep. It is a management style that focuses an organisation's planning and operations. By looking at the 7 P's of service marketing, libraries can cultivate a market orientated focus as a basis for its quality management frame work. Many Australian university libraries are marketing to their clients in just such a way.

The most important elements of such a strategy are:

1. Understand your client (Market research)
2. Identify your client market (Segment & target)
3. Identify your strengths as a competitive business (Position)
4. Know the product your clients want and where they want to use it (product & place)
5. Develop effective and efficient procedures & systems that facilitate outcomes for clients (processes)
6. Employ and train staff in both work skills and client relationship marketing (people)
7. Communicate the benefits and advantages of your product over competitors, such as the chaos of the internet (integrate marketing communication)

University libraries are being challenged as never before to maintain their relevance to their prime clienteles. Information quality may be a prime differential between resources offered through a library service and the "Google-mentality" of our new generations of students. However, only if university libraries market their services effectively to these users will they continue to hold a prime role in fulfilling the information needs of their universities. Australian university libraries are taking up this challenge with improved marketing strategies and techniques and integrated marketing communication.

REFERENCES

1. McKoll-Kennedy (J R) and Kiel (G C). Marketing: A strategic approach. South Melbourne: Nelson Thomas. 2000: 11

2. Langerak (F), Hultink (J) and Robben (H). The Impact of market orientation, product advantage and launch proficiency on new product performance and organisational performance. *The Journal of Product Innovation Management*. 21. 2004: 91.
3. Lam (M D). Psychographic demonstration. *Pharmaceutical Executive*. 24 (1). 2004: 79
4. Butscher (S A). Develop only what customers want, at their price. *Marketing News*. 31(6). 1997: 10.
5. Duncan (T). IMC: Using advertising and promotion to build brands. New York: McGraw-Hill. 2002: 17
6. Oblinger (D). Boomers, Gen-Xers & Millenials: Understanding the new students. *Educause Review*. July/Aug 2003: 38.

Section - II

MARKETING IN LIBRARIES AROUND THE WORLD

Section - II
Marketing in Libraries Around the World

No man, community, society can lead a solitary, confined existence in this world of globalization and interdependence. Whether we want or not, we need to collate our efforts and points of view to reach the common goals beneficial to the community as a whole. The cognizance to this fact of internationality is this collection of ours, where contributors from around the globe make it clear that LIS marketing is growing throughout the world in all kind of libraries and have shared their experiences which cohere in a conducive environment and try to reach the ideal state.

Niels Ole Pors in his paper entitled *Marketing Public Libraries in Denmark* shares his experiences about the marketing of libraries and information services institutions in Denmark. It presents some of the marketing strategies Danish public libraries and library authorities have employed during last few years and also presents the attitude of library managers concerning the relationship between the library and environment and its far reaching marketing implication.

Sissel Nilsen in her contribution *Marketing LIS in Norway - An Overview* gives an overview of the Norwegian librarians' efforts to market library and information services. It discusses education and training facilities available to students and working professionals for LIS marketing, syllabi, course content, thereof. Further finds marketing possibilities in public libraries through websites, lobbying politician by the associations, and campaign for school libraries and calls for ongoing marketing initiatives to become visible in the community they serve.

Àngels Massísimo and José-Antonio Gómez-Hernández in paper *Library Marketing in Spain: State-of-the-Art* describe development of library marketing in Spain since 1970 and discuss present day marketing related activities.

Rajesh Singh through his contribution *Understanding Marketing Culture in Finnish Libraries* gives details of the marketing culture in Finnish libraries based on a research being continually carried out in a university which seeks to understand the awareness of the knowledge base of library management about modern marketing theories and practices.

Chen Chao and J Pan contributed the paper *From Mind Shift to Paradigm Shift: Marketing Management in China Libraries*, experience a sea change in practices and research outputs on the basis of growth of literature on marketing in libraries in China during the last two decades.

Florence Muet in her paper *Marketing of Libraries and Documentation Services in France: A Difficult Integration?* finds that the integration between marketing and libraries and documentation services in France is about 20 years old, but this integration is developing at a slow pace. She seeks to find out the reasons for this slowness in regard to professional publications, training facilities and marketing practices.

Julita Nawe's paper *Marketing Library Services in Africa* discusses library marketing in Africa where brochures, websites, exhibitions are used to spread marketing avenues.

T Anup Tanui in his paper *Marketing Library and Information Services in Kenya* shares his Kenyan experience where marketing in different category of libraries is analyzed. Also finds stages of marketing practices in academic, pubic and special libraries.

Kanwal Ameen in her paper *Marketing of Library and Information Services in Pakistan: A Profile* gives a perspective of Pakistan libraries and evaluates the impact of marketing, gives a profile of marketing practices, literature, and coverage in syllabi of various universities and discusses in detail the developments in regard to marketing taught in LIS School at the University of Punjab, Lahore.

Janine Schmidt's paper *Marketing Library and Information Services in Australian Academic Libraries* gives a detailed account of the marketing approaches being used in Australian academic libraries. Analyses the environment thereof, identification of users and assessment of their needs, offerings, branding techniques, strategical issues, and evaluation mechanism.

Melinda Bükkei and István Király V. in their paper *Metaphors on Marketing: Symbolic and Effective Attempts in the "Lucian Blaga" Central University Library* share experiences of the symbolic marketing as adopted in the Central University Library of Romania, and underline such efforts to popularize marketing.

Verena Tibljas in her paper entitled *Finally Somebody Wants to Hear what Teenagers Have to Say: Marketing in a Croatia's Public Library* expresses concern for serving teenagers and children in Rijeka City Library of Croatia based on a project called "Teen for Teens", discusses about its outcome and recognition within the country and outside.

Kathy Kunneke in her paper *Branding as a Process: A Viewpoint from South Africa* puts a viewpoint on Branding and considers branding as a process for academic libraries in Africa, mentions importance of branding, various phases of branding, and steps for developing a logo as a part of brand for such libraries.

Lastly, John Ganly and Pam Rollo in their paper *Marketing of Library and Information Services: The View from Knowledge Management within the Financial Services Sector* discuss marketing of library and information services from the knowledge management perspectives in financial services sector.

MARKETING PUBLIC LIBRARIES IN DENMARK

Niels Ole Pors

Abstract *The paper deals with marketing issues in relation to Danish public libraries. The newest development of the public libraries are discussed and the conclusion seems to be that the newest development for the public libraries is due to a strong political and administrative support. The libraries are popular and at the forefront of the technological development and they are heavily used. The employment of marketing strategies is discussed. Through an analysis of surveys conducted among library managers the paper seeks to give profile of their attitudes towards marketing and environmental issues. The conclusion is that the library managers have very strong commitments in relation to contact with different stakeholders.*

INTRODUCTION

This paper deals with marketing of library and information service centers in Denmark. Despite the fact of the existence of numerous textbooks on marketing, it is evident that the concept of marketing is diffused and diversified. Marketing is often considered as a part of the strategic planning of an organisation directed toward increasing the customer's knowledge of its products and services. Marketing is about more than the awareness of customers. It is also about the customers' attitudes and feelings towards the organisation, its products and services. It is about the emotional and intellectual identification with the organisation. Therefore, in this context marketing is defined as "an activity of a strategic nature with the objective to increase market shares and launching of new products and as an activity intended to shape positive images of an organisation among stakeholders" [1].

The aims of this paper are twofold. The first objective is to present some of the marketing strategies Danish public libraries and library authorities have employed during the last few years. The public libraries have changed very much during the last couple of year especially due to a radical new library act that passed the parliament in 2000. The new act made it mandatory for all public libraries to give citizens free access to the Internet. It also made it mandatory for all libraries to build music collections and it encouraged acquisitions of other media like DVD, film and the like. The most radical consequence of the new act was the establishment of the service www.bibliotek.dk. It is a service that gives every citizen on-line access to the holdings of all libraries in the country and the right to order every document from whichever library they want totally free of charge. This has of course changed the relationship between the local public library and the environment very much. The question is not just how the new services are marketed but also how the public libraries are integrated into the local community through the means of web – pages and other forms of net based services. The first objective will be met through an analysis of the development of the public libraries. The argument focuses on the changes following the rather radical library act from 2000. The data are from the national library statistics and from selected web pages.

The second objective is to present some of the attitudes library managers express concerning the relationship between the library and environment. The second objective is met utilising the data from a comprehensive survey conducted among managers in the public libraries [2]. This leadership survey was first conducted in 2001 [3]. It was replicated in the United Kingdom in 2003 [4]. It was revised in 2004 and conducted again in 2004 through an online survey instrument. It consisted of 270 questions and statements, which in the revised questionnaire from 2004 were reduced to 180 questions, and statements.

MARKETING AND LEGITIMACY

Marketing is a part of strategic planning and it employs the same kind of tools and approaches. It means that marketing has to do with various analyses of users and potential users and it also has to do with market penetration and evaluation of the need and benefits of new information services and products. Strategic marketing then involves the employment of many different tools and approaches like customer satisfaction analyses, image analyses, evaluation of the relation between information services' perceived importance and their quality, assessment of competing products and the like. Newer concepts related to marketing are branding and corporate identity. Strategic marketing is a kind of focus that is part of the whole planning process of the single institution [5].

Public institutions such as libraries operate in an environment characterised by conflicting, competing and ill-defined forces, which can be characterised as the state, the civil society and the market [6]. Each of these forces puts pressure on the individual public institution and defines its freedom of action. The individual library has to accept and respond to pressures from each of these three factors.

Basic in the concept of the state is the notion of a social contract between public institutions and the citizens that emphasises democracy, control, efficiency and equal treatment of all citizens. The notion of the civil society has more to do with attitudes, feelings, values and symbols. The concept of belonging is central in defining civil society in the same way, as it is central in defining the culture of an institution. The institutionalised kit keeps a society together. The market is a quid pro quo relation with money as a mediator [7].

The individual institution is a mix of the pushes and pulls of the three factors or vectors. This mix differentiates between private companies and public institutions and, at the same time, tries to solve the conflict between the generic approach and the situational approach in organisational theory.

The cross-pressure that emerges from the interaction between the three factors has consequences for the organisational structure, for the strategy and for the leadership. A key issue in the theory is the concept of legitimacy.

Political legitimacy is a concept that is concerned with politicians' and other stakeholders' perceptions of the public institution. The degree to which a public library can maintain legitimacy is closely related to funding. What constitutes political legitimacy is not static: it changes over time. Thus services, which gave legitimacy in the 1970s or 1980s, do no longer automatically do so today [8]. When working with organisational development and change in libraries, an institutional approach is relevant because the link between the means and the end is often vague. If one wants to make a "better", more legitimate or valuable library there is no predefined or given way to success. However, it could be said that, in this day and age, organisational development is viewed upon as a reasonable and, therefore, appropriate choice.

According to Audunson [9] institutionalised norms, values and standards derive from two different places - the profession and the surrounding environment (i.e. users, politicians, etc). In time periods characterized by turbulence or change there is a probability that these norms and values will differ from each perspective.

CHANGES IN THE DANISH PUBLIC LIBRARIES

It is also of importance to note that there is a long and very strong tradition for cooperation among the libraries and the Danish National Library Authority plays a very active role in the development of the public library system. Denmark has probably the best-financed public library system one can find in any country. All municipalities are by law required to run a library service with free access for citizen to the Internet. All public libraries have media collections including books, journals, music, videos and multimedia. The average expenditure per citizen on public libraries is around £50 per year. It is necessary here to give some of the basic information on the Danish public libraries as a frame of reference. The Danish Library Authority publishes every year a very comprehensive book on public library statistics[10]. In the following, we will take a glance at some of the more pertinent figures in relation to how well the market is penetrated and how successful the different information services appear to be.

The public library system in Denmark consists of 16 county libraries and of approx. 270 libraries in a municipality system. Some of these cooperate about the library service. In total there are 227 main libraries, 484 branches and 50 mobile libraries. As such total nearly 800 service points. These libraries serve a population amounting to 5.4 millions people. The public library system has employed approx. 2300 librarians, 2200 library assistants and 500 employees with another background. The total holdings amount to 30 million documents of which 80 % is books and the rest are music, multimedia and films. The total annual acquisitions are over 2 millions. In total, there are 74 million issues per year of which 50 millions are books. This equals near 14 issues per citizen per year. The interlending amounts to 1,6 millions issues per year. The public libraries had 32 millions physical visits in 2003 and nearly 2 million people had a loan transaction. Nearly all the public libraries have their own web pages and the number of workstations with Internet access for the public amount to 3500. Overall, it is estimated that over 50% of the population use the public library services every year. The penetration of the market is very high compared to many other public library systems around the world. The above-mentioned figures are all from the 2003 statistics. Some trends ought to be emphasised. The acquisitions and holdings of books have gone down a bit during recent years because of investments in other types of media. The number of issues have been rather stable during recent years but the composition of the issues have changed because new media like music and films take up a bigger part of the issues. The number of renewals has also increased. The interlending activity has doubled during just a couple of years.

There has for many years been a very strong tradition for formal cooperation in the whole library system especially in relation to interlending and citizens' free access to loan from every library in the country. In many ways, this cooperation is reinforced by the introduction of services like the digital libraries.

The tradition for cooperation among all types of libraries in Denmark has brought forward two very interesting digital projects and solutions. It is the so-called bibliotek.dk (library.dk) and the deff.dk (The Electronic Research Library) projects. Both projects are unique. Bibliotek.dk is in essence a database covering the holdings of all public and academic libraries in Denmark. All citizens' can access it from a computer and order documents. They can decide at which library they want to pick up the materials. In other words, people from a small village on the west coast of Denmark can from their home order documents from the Royal Library in Copenhagen and get the documents delivered at their local library. This has of course meant a very huge increase in the ILL - system. It is also an example of the technology the drives the development of the libraries. The boundaries between different types of libraries tend to be more indistinct in the future. More important, it has changed the behaviour of the users very much.

The deff.dk project is in some ways a similar project but it is oriented towards research materials and one of its achievements has been to give researchers, teachers and students at Universities and Higher Educational Institutions access to distributed information resources independent of their institutional affiliation. Other objectives are the establishment of joint digitalisation projects, a common interface, joint cataloguing, cooperation concerning portals, e – learning and e-publishing and the formation of consortia and a joint administration of licenses for electronic resources.

The author believes that both bibliotek.dk and deff.dk are outstanding and unique examples of cooperation between libraries and visions of a state concerning access to information.

It is also important to emphasise that the public library system has a central place in the Danish national information policy. From the middle of the 1990s and onwards the public libraries were officially recognised as key players of the emerging information or knowledge oriented society. The government report called "The Information society 2000"[11] published by the Ministry of research contained a whole section on the role of the public libraries in shaping the knowledge society. It meant for example that the library system was seen as very important facilitators of computer and information literacy. This report was probably the direct background for the pervasive free access to Internet resources and computer facilities characterising the Danish public library system.

MARKET PENETRATION AND THE SUCCESS OF INFORMATION SERVICES

From time to time the public library system has conducted a formal marketing. A couple of years ago there were an investment in posters placed at buses and other public places with colourful statements like "The public library is a jungle of entertainment and knowledge" or "the library has the answer". After the introduction of www.bibliotek.dk, the Danish National Library Authority sent out a postcard to all households in the country with information about the new service. Another new way to market the whole public library sector has been the establishment of the Internet guide named www.fng.dk. It is an abbreviation of Folkebibliotekernes net guide (The Public Libraries Guide to Internet Resources). This guide is a product of cooperation activities between a number of public libraries and it markets itself using terms like a guide to quality-controlled resources. In this context, it is also worth to mention the digital service with the name www.biblioteksvagten.dk (the information counsellor). This is a digital reference service, operated by a consortium of public libraries and research libraries.

Selected public libraries play an important role in relation to the national consumer information. The libraries function as access points to information and counselling in this area.

Apart from examples like these most of the marketing takes place at the local or institutional level. First and foremost, nearly all public libraries have their own web – pages containing a wealth of information and different access points to both local and national information services and resources.

It is probably true to say that most of the municipalities regard the local public library as a main focus of the local cultural and educational activities. Many of the chief librarians have extended responsibilities running and integrating other services in the municipalities. The libraries play an active role in relation to integration activities related to refugees, immigrants and other people with a different ethnic background than Danish.

Most of the public library systems have set up popular outreach programmes serving different organisations and institutions in the local area. It can be high schools, kindergartens, homes for elderly people and so on.

Overall, the local public library has a very high degree of political legitimacy and the objectives of the services are very seldom questioned in the public sphere.

THE PUBLIC LIBRARY MANAGERS' PERCEPTION OF MARKETING ISSUES

This paragraph uses data from a leadership survey (2 & 3). The content of the survey was not directed towards marketing issues but aspects of marketing were incorporated in the survey. There follows a presentation of some of the relevant data.

It is obvious from table 1 that the managers in the public libraries have a strong sense of the necessity to integrate the library in local political system. Especially, it is noteworthy that nearly all the managers express a sentiment that it becomes more and more important to make the library visible in relation to the political system. The answers to the statements in table 1 clearly demonstrate that library managers have a clear understanding of the need to establish the public library firmly in the local political system as part of the marketing directed towards one of the important stakeholders.

Table-1: The library managers' answers to the following statements : 2004 - survey

	Strongly agree	Agree	Disagree
To an increasing degree the manager must make the library visible in the political system	79%	20%	1%
The political legitimacy of the manager will become more important	57%	36%	8%
The manager must establish political contacts	57%	37%	6%

N: Number of respondents varies between 252 to 271

From table 2 it is evident that a majority of library managers perceive that the library has a high degree of legitimacy and that the library is an institution well respected. It is also obvious that library managers feel that the contact with the local powers and authorities are well established. These perceptions are supported by activities. Nearly all the libraries have succeeded in penetrating the local media on a regular basis and networking is common in the same way as different kinds of outreach programmes seems to be.

Table-2: The library managers' answers to the following statements: 2004 - survey

	To a high degree	To a certain degree	No
The politicians and decision makers respect the library	70%	27%	3%
The library has a close contact with the local political and administrative system	46%	42%	11%
The library is profiled in the local media	48%	47%	6%
To an increasing degree, the library teach citizens	28%	47%	25%
The library solves it tasks networking with other institutions	31%	52%	18%

N: Number of respondents varies between 252 to 271

The next table shows other aspects of the relationship with the customers. It is evident that the number of libraries that have conducted different forms of user surveys during the last three years have increased very much. In this context, it is worth mentioning that user surveys is a form of communicating with customers signalling that the organisation cares about the customers and the perceptions they have and their level of satisfaction (12). We can also see a growing interest in investigating the processes in the library and benchmarking with other libraries.

Table-3: The proportion of managers that answered YES to the following statements: The library has during the last 3 years...Data from the 2001 and 2004 investigation.

	2001	2004
Conducted a systematic user survey	35%	38%
Conducted quality investigations of services and processes	17%	42%
Conducted benchmarking processes	12%	37%
Established service level agreements	47%	53%
Established ethical guidelines	27%	38%

These kinds of analyses are of paramount importance in the legitimising process because comparing with others and evaluating quality are considered as necessary tools in the public sphere. The increase in libraries that have made service level agreements and different kinds of ethical guidelines are also interesting in this context. Service level agreements are marketing tools directed towards the establishment of realistic expectations among customers and ethical guidelines can also be seen as a marketing tool, especially in a digital environment. The ethical guidelines are often established in relation to admissible behaviour using Internet resources signalling caring in relation to especially children and young people.

PERSPECTIVES AND CONCLUSION

Marketing is a part of strategic planning and management and it is obvious that Danish library managers in the public library system as a whole perceive that they succeed in profiling the library in the local community. The library managers state, that the activity or task they spend most of their time on is strategic management and change management. There are of course differences between the directors and managers. Detailed analyses of the surveys indicate that library managers in the small municipalities find it much harder to penetrate the market and accommodate the stakeholders than managers from bigger library systems.

The public library system in Denmark has a very strong support among politicians and at the same time it is a service that reaches a very high proportion of the population. It does not mean that marketing is unnecessary. It simply means that marketing must focus on informing citizen of the more advanced services and the access people have to the cooperating library system.

In the coming years, strategic thinking will be more and more important due to huge changes in the structure of the public sector. One of the challenges library directors will meet in the coming years is the fact, that the Danish parliament has decided to reduce the number of counties to just 6 regions and they intend to reduce the number of municipalities to less than 100, probably as few as 70 – 90. This will create demands for huge changes in the public sector in Denmark and it will affect every library system very much. The competitive mix will be different and requirements for strategic thinking will be much tougher.

REFERENCES

1. Kotler (P) and Andreasen (A). Strategic marketing for nonprofit organizations. New Jersey: Prentice Hall. 1991.
2. Pors (N O). Ledere og ledelse I danske folkebiblioteker: Bibliotekarforbundets lederundersøgels. Frederiksberg: Bibliotekarforbundet. 2004.
3. Johannsen (C G) and Pors (N O). Ledere og ledelse I danske biblioteker: Bibliotekarforbundets lederundersøgelse 2001. Frederiksberg: Bibliotekarforbundet. 2001.

4. Pors (N O), Dixon (P) and Robson (H). The employment of quality measures in libraries: Cultural differences, institutional imperatives and managerial profiles. *Performance Measurement and Metrics*. 5 (1). 2004: 20 – 28.
5. Bryson (J). Effective library and information centre management. Aldershot: Gower. 1999.
6. Klaudi Klausen (K). Skulle det være noget særligt? Kbh. Børsen. 2001.
7. Ibid
8. Brunsson. The organization of hypocrisy: Talks, decisions and actions in organizations. Copenhagen: Copenhagen Business School Press. 2002.
9. Audunson (R). Folkebibliotekenes rolle i en digital framtid: Publikums, politikernes og bibliotekarernes bilder. *In,* Audunson (I R) and Lund (N W), Ed. Det siviliserte informationssamfunn: Folkebibliotekernes rolle ved inngangen til en digital tid. Bergen: Fakbokforlaget. 2001: 206-224
10. Cranfield (V), Ed. Folkebiblioteksstatistik 2003. Copenhagen: Biblioteksstyrelsen. 2004.
11. Forskningsministeriet – Info-samfundet 2000. Rapport fra udvalget om informationssamfundet år 2000. Copenhagen: Forskningsministeriet. 1995.
12. Hernon (P) and Altman (E). Service quality in academic libraries. Norwood: Ablex Publishing Corporation. 1996.

MARKETING LIS IN NORWAY - AN OVERVIEW

Sissel Nilsen

Abstract *Libraries are important agencies for social development but their visibility is not enough in Norway. Marketing possibilities through web, lobbying politicians, and campaign for decision makers are important. Marketing education in library schools is also needed to be vitalised. There is further need to put concerted efforts to be visible in the community they serve.*

INTRODUCTION

The libraries are not on the agenda; they are not visible enough in the society. We have heard it before and this message will probably be repeated over and over again. Even if the library plays an important role in many parts of society, other institutions and professionals might be closer to the different usergroups than the library, be it children, immigrants, elderly, unemployed. The library will often be a secondary institution and as such does not get the attention it deserves. In the present age we also have more competitors than before, and the role of the librarian as a professional navigator into cyberspace and modern knowledge society is still not appreciated.

If we are going to survive, the libraries need to be more visible and promote their services and qualifications more aggressively. One single campaign one year or an occasional article in a national newspaper is not enough – this task needs continuous work. Locally many public libraries do a good job in telling their users as well as the non-users in different ways about the services, and they are also visible in the local press, but sometimes they want and need help from the national authorities and the library associations to convince both the users and the local politicians that it is a wise investment to finance a good and professional library system.

Norway has a Public Library Act of 1985 that imposes all municipalities to have a public library and a chief librarian with a librarian's qualifications. There is no law comprising all types of libraries, although this has been discussed politically for some years now to propose one. In the school-law, however, it is mentioned that each school has to have a school library.

USE OF LIBRARIES

Every year the National Archive, Library and Museum Authority (ABM-utvikling) collects statistical data from both public, school, university-, research-

and special libraries. These statistics are published as part of the Norwegian statistics from Statistics Norway, our national statistical bureau.

Norway is a long, densely populated country. From the capital Oslo to the Russian border in the North it is about 2500 kilometres. Total population is only 4.6 million.

Even if we have had no organised marketing campaigns lately, the figures from 2002 and 2003 show that the use of all types of libraries increases. This might be connected with the fact that the library services in many libraries have improved in recent years and in addition Internet is used actively to show what services the libraries offer and what material they have. This is certainly in itself method of promoting the library.

In 2003 the public libraries lent 24.8 millions items, which was an increase of 3.5% from the previous year. 74% of the items lent are books. The book and staff budgets for public libraries, however, have not at all increased. The figures show that the budgets do not compensate the raise in salaries and the prices of books and other media.

The national statistics on cultural activities in the municipalities also show that the libraries are the most frequently used institution. The statistics for 2003 for visiting the public libraries show that the average figure was 5 visits per citizen. 99% of the public libraries now give free internet-access to the public.

The figures for the university-, research and special libraries show a similar development. The use of the libraries has increased by more than 20% in the last two years, while the figures for lending are the same as in the previous years.

WHAT DOES THE STUDENT LEARN ABOUT MARKETING?

Compared with the other Nordic countries that have much in common with Norway and with whom we co-operate a lot, the Norwegian library world does not initiate many national library campaigns. Why is that? Does it have anything to do with the way we educate our library staff or do we simply not prioritise or believe in these types of actions?

At the library school in Oslo - at that time the only one in Norway - there was until 1991 a separate course on communication and marketing in public libraries for one semester in the final year. Today the education in LIS is merged with the education for journalists and forms one department of the Oslo University College. There is also librarian education at the University of Tromsø and the Bergen University College. However you have to look very thoroughly indeed at the curriculum to find the subjects communication, public relations or marketing mentioned.

To become a qualified librarian you have to attend studies for three years to get your BA, at least two of them being LIS-studies. During the third year of the studies in Oslo marketing is part of the lectures in Libraries and Society and the list of set reading is 1000 pages. This year communication and marketing has been taught together with strategy, library development, leadership, innovation and change etc. that altogether is taught for half a semester. However, it seems to be completely up to the lecturer how much stress is put on communication and marketing. The same is the case in Tromsø. You can get a BA in Documentation science at that university, but there are no separate lectures dedicated to marketing. Some guest lectures, giving case studies, might include it though. In both study programmes the students have periods of practise in different types of libraries, and hopefully they learn something about both communication, how to handle users and marketing in these periods.

Those students who choose literature in their curriculum might also have lectures in how the librarian can be an intermediary in dissemination of books and literature and also make various arrangements. Of course communication is also included in other lectures during the three years of studying. I would, however, have preferred a separate course in communication and marketing, because I think it is basic for most librarians to have certain knowledge in these subjects.

TOO INVISIBLE

Two years ago the Ministry of Culture in Norway established the Archive, Library and Museum Authority (ABM-utvikling) by merging the Directorate for Public Libraries, The Norwegian Museum Authority and the National Office for Research Documentation, Academic and Special Libraries.

I think the Norwegian library sector had great expectations that this new authority should make the libraries more visible nationally by marketing libraries as a vital source for education, reset information-dissemination and reading. At their web-page the authority concludes that in order to reach their main objectives, they among other things, aim at supporting and inspiring new developments and adoption of new perspectives across the sectors, by initiating and stimulating development and joint projects within and across the individual sectors, by acting in a consultative capacity and being a driving force vice-à-vice the public authorities at various administrative levels.

However – so far – they have not been very visible in the national debate in the newspapers, on the radio or television as a driving force for archives, libraries and museums. One might be allowed to raise the question whether a national authority like this is more the ministry's extended arm into the professional arenas than an independent force and spokesman for the areas they are supposed to support.

They might do lots of good work within the sectors - as for instance running a Norwegian digital library project that aims to facilitate access for all to complete electronic information resources, but externally this has not made any headlines as it should have done, and the content of such a digital library is not defined in order for users to know what to find there.

USE OF THE WEB AS A PROMOTIONAL TOOL

ABM-utvikling is also responsible for Culture Net Norway, which is supposed to be the public gateway to Norwegian culture on the Internet. As far as I know, at the moment comparatively few use this way as a portal. Most people prefer to go directly to their library's or archive's own web page. This might change, but then the Cultural Net Norway web-page has to get a much better design and be promoted in a more active way nationally. Curiously enough the word library is absent at the home page.

Many libraries in Norway – University-, research- and special libraries as well as public libraries quite early used the Internet very consciously to reach the users and non-users. Most public libraries were far ahead of the municipal authorities for instance. To day we can find lots of very good and informative home pages for all types of libraries in Norway.

Let me mention some examples of what some libraries have done locally as one way of promoting their library: collected information and made a gateway to local information and local home-pages (http://barum.folkebibl.no - Bærum public library), overview of literature and annotated reading proposals (http://nettbiblioteket.no - Bergen public library and http://www.tfb.no - Trondheim public library), collected information on music with lots of links to bibliographic- and reference databases (http://www.deichmanske-bibliotek.oslo.kommune.no - Oslo public library, a special database on the composer Grieg http://nettbiblioteket.no). Many libraries have different web pages specially made for children. 16 libraries have gone together running a web virtual reference service http://www.bibliotekvakten.no. The National library has multimedia databases on Norwegian emigration to the US and on literature on 1905 – the year Norway became independent (http://www.nb.no).

Library journals are also a way of promoting the libraries internally as well as externally – if these are well edited, will raise important debates. ABM-utvikling publishes the oldest and most professional library journal in Norway, Bok og Bibliotek, whose articles occasionally are picked up by the press and lead to debate. They now want to "outsource" the journal, and a discussion about this is running on the librarians list-serve (Bibliotek-Norge) at the moment. The Norwegian Library Association also publish a similar journal "Bibliotekforum" and the trade union for librarians, Bibliotekarforbundet publish "Bibliotekaren". One might be allowed to ask whether it is necessary with three library journals in this small country instead of collecting all the efforts into creating a powerful one.

PUBLIC LIBRARIES MOST PROFESSIONAL

In my opinion the public libraries are promoting their libraries in the most professional way.

One look at the country as a whole will almost daily provide you with news or information in a local paper about activities or services in the library. Many libraries have good contacts with the local press and bring the good news to the papers. Often the local journalists also turn up and write about what is happening in the library. I think this positive way of promoting the library locally is good and also reaches those in the community that are not regular users of the library services.

This is also important towards the local politicians who like to know that the resources they give to the library is used in a positive way for the citizens. To have a dedicated chieflibrarian and a staff that interact with other organisations on the local level is very important to make the public library visible.

The university, research and special libraries are all parts of an institution or organisation and much of their activity promoting the library service are directed towards special target groups and users within the organisation as students, staff, parliament members ... My assumption is that the institutions and organisations in recent years have become much more conscious offering regular courses for learning how to use the library directly targeted towards the special groups. These libraries do very seldom make any headlines in the main papers or in other media, but now and again when prices on periodicals and databases increase, like they have done lately, the papers do write about it. The copyright question and how this can influence the way libraries disseminate information has also been a topic for debate lately.

Children are an important target group for public and school libraries. Many public libraries in Norway work in close collaboration with the nursery schools and local Public Health Service to inform the parents that reading for the children and talking with them at an early stage is vital for them to develop a language. Co-operations with the school libraries are also common in most places. And the figures in the national statistics show that the children are the most active users of the public library services.

The last two years the government in Norway has launched a strategy to encourage school children's interest in reading and thus improving their ability to read. In connection to that there are different campaigns that also include libraries in one way or another; for instance "The cultural Rucksack", "READ!", "Into the Text", "Free choice". The Minister of Education has done a good promotional job for these reading campaigns and stressed the importance of school libraries, but the public libraries' role has not been mentioned much in the media on a national level, neither from the ABM-authority nor from the Norwegian Library Association.

LOBBYING POLITICIANS

The Norwegian Library Association (NLA) has for years seen it as a challenge to lobby the politicians in the Parliament and the Ministry of Culture and the Ministry of Education and Research, and the county branches of the association have done the same towards local politicians on municipal and county levels. The NLA also often receive papers from the ministries for consultation before they are finalised and sent to Parliament. In that way the NLA has been a vital force for instance, to keep up the principal that borrowing books, videos and music as well as ordinary information dissemination on Internet in public libraries, shall be free of charge. The Library Association every autumn, when the State budget is proposed to Parliament also follows up by having appointments with the relevant committees to present their view on current topics to the proposals from the Government.

When it comes to writing articles, however, or taking part in a debate on the same topics in the national press, having opinions on current topics that may affect the libraries, the association does very little. Now and again you can hear a voice on the cultural channel of the radio, but it is a common view that the libraries and librarians are more or less invisible.

At the moment the NLA has no special committee for marketing, so it is the Governing Board and the biannual General Assembly that, when accepting the Action plan decides what is going to happen for the next two years. The current plan for 2004-06 has a lot of general statements on improving most aspects of the library services and co-operating with others, but no special campaigns are mentioned and there is no priority among the seven chapters and 27 bull-points mentioned in the action-plan.

CAMPAIGN FOR SCHOOL LIBRARIES

In 1994, the board at that time engaged a well-known communication and marketing firm to form an information strategy for the NLA. The firm concludes that the libraries in Norway neither had the tradition or the knowledge of how to market their services. They also pointed out that the professionals were eager and idealistic, but lacked the ability to have clear priorities. We were also too inwards looking instead of having the focus externally.

This is true even to day when we read the internal list-serve every day. There are lots of well-written contributions, but they only reach our own congregation - and we are already redeemed.

The report from the communication and marketing firm in 1995 made the board at that time form clear priority. A comprehensive campaign for improving the school libraries was launched. All the county branches of the NLA co-operated and posters and brochures were sent to all schools and local politicians. There were full-page advertisements in national and regional papers, a feature article in the biggest national paper by the president that year of the NLA, reports and debates in the main news on the radio etc. The president was invited to speak in many counties for teachers about the school library. This is the most professional, biggest and most expensive campaign the NLA has had in recent years, and it was made possible mainly thanks to the Norwegian Library Bureau and the Confederation of

Norwegian Business and Industry sponsoring the campaign. The authors and publishers associations also contributed. The timing was essential, and by using the different media in the whole country continuously for a fortnight we achieved to get the attention we wanted. We know that the school libraries in some municipalities and counties received more resources after this campaign, but still they have to fight to prove their existence.

The marketing committee of the NLA at the time of their existence made a small brochure called "Killing the myths"(1996). This was distributed extensively throughout the country.

The last six years the marketing committee seems to have gone to sleep. The present Governing Board of NLA does not prioritise this sort of marketing and promotional work. They have, however, had occasional targeted campaigns mainly directed towards national politicians.

The local (county) branches of the Norwegian Library Association have also directed information towards the local politicians in front of the local elections every fourth year.

Often they confront the different parties with their achievements for the public and school libraries in the last period - or lack of achievements - and ask what they intend to do for the next election period. In some cases this has actually made the politicians more attentive of the role that the municipal and school libraries have in the community. Many chief librarians also write a letter to the newly elected members of the municipal board, tell about the public library and offer the library services that the politicians might need in their new capacity as a politician. Some local libraries have also invited the mayors to meet the community at the library regularly.

The association has also, mainly in co-operation with the then Directorate for Public Libraries, translated and printed posters and brochures of important IFLA statements like the UNESCO/IFLA Public Library Manifesto and School Library Manifesto and IFLA-guidelines. NLA has recently printed and distributed widely a poster and brochure based on the IFLA Glasgow Declaration on Libraries, Information Services and Intellectual Freedom as well as the Internet Manifesto. A working group together with the authors associations was established a couple of years ago to watch the development of the library-budgets and action for more resources if necessary, but this group does not exist any more.

However, a Nordic committee with a Norwegian representative still exist, and every year they encourage all the Nordic countries to celebrate a library week proposing a special theme each time, usually with different programmes and activities in the public and school libraries.

This spring one of the student at the LIS-studies in Oslo in her final thesis wrote about the library position in the knowledge society. She interviewed both politicians, staff at the ABM-utvikling, the president of the NLA and others and concluded that libraries are not on the current agenda. The media are more concerned about other aspects of the cultural field. Libraries are not controversial enough to attract national attention. The national politicians however, are willing to listen to the professionals. They look upon those as important suppliers of information. We must be aware that the libraries compete with other forceful sectors, and the NLA really has a job to do to make the libraries more visible in the public opinion.

CONCLUSION

Above discussion clearly reveals that there has been many incidents of marketing libraries and information services in Norway. But, still effective marketing in all libraries does not exist. Therefore, there is a need to consolidate efforts of marketing in a way that all good marketing practices are used in other libraries where it is lacking. More marketing oriented activities need to be undertaken in order to become more visible in the community.

LIBRARY MARKETING IN SPAIN : STATE-OF-THE-ART

Àngels Massísimo
José-Antonio Gómez-Hernández

Abstract *This work describes library marketing in Spain, beginning with the first theoretical works on the subject until the present situation, with the daily practices of libraries and related organisations. The current practices include principally the application of empirical knowledge to design tailored services for target groups, as well as promoting specific services and centres, such as reading and libraries in general, and studying the public, especially with user satisfaction studies carried out for the purpose of evaluating services, but which are still underdeveloped in terms of market segmentation studies.*

INTRODUCTION: THE THEORETICAL BASE

The initial studies on library marketing in Spain appeared during the 1940s, with the works of Lasso de la Vega [1] and certain articles and digests that appeared in the Revista de archivos, bibliotecasy museos, such as Bostwick's well-known work: The public library in the United States[2] Librarians would have to wait until 1970 in order to find an article[3] and, slightly later, an original book introducing the topic specifically to them[4].

These works – although separated by almost three decades – can be considered as isolated precedents since, unfortunately, neither one succeeded in awakening much interest on the part of the library community in this topic in subsequent years, other than some occasional isolated contribution.

In spite of the scant theoretical background, the reality of the times pushed Spanish librarians in two directions. On the one hand, they organised promotional and recreational activities, promoting reading, etc. (that clearly can be considered a form of attracting readers to the library—especially to the public library), together with the related publicity. On the other hand, and considerably later, librarians in both university and public libraries have undertaken users studies –generally, as satisfaction studies—that provide a means of learning about the public, although still not about potential users.

The design of appropriate products for specific user segments

During the past 10 years in different parts of the country, we have seen the development of services clearly directed to user segments identified by the library, although not studied systematically. These groups include housewives of between 45 – 65 years of age and dedicated exclusively to home and family (for whom "bibliomarkets"[5] have been created: Barcelona, Salamanca); people on holiday with spare reading time while pursuing leisure activities for whom "bibliopools", "bibliobeaches" and other variants have been created) [6] ; workers and students who commute by public transportation to work or school, without having time to get to the library ("bibliometro": [7] Mislata (Valencia), Madrid); or grandparents, etc. responsible for taking care of their grandchildren (parents corner at the "babyteca"[8] Barcelona). Curiously, these very successful services were not based on formal studies, but rather on empirical knowledge of specific market segments. This in no way invalidates the decision to carry them out: on the contrary, though, these cases constitute an example of how librarians with too few resources, nor support, to carry out systematic studies can frequently achieve success through applying empirical knowledge and through their involvement with user communities. Further, along we will see the scope of user studies that have been undertaken in recent years.

PROMOTION AS PART OF THE MARKETING-MIX

Promoting reading: The role of different stakeholders

The first promotional activities on a national level in Spain were the campaigns carried out by the Ministry of Education in the 1970s. (These had a precedent in the campaigns held within book fairs and book days by book dealers during the 1950s and 1960s). The aim behind these was to promote reading as an individual activity, rather than promoting the libraries themselves or any other cultural infrastructure. Gómez Hernández and Saorín[9] noted the great difference between the resources provided by the government for promoting certain habits (eating, health and recently social attitudes towards women, minorities, etc.) and those aimed at cultural activities such as reading, etc. Even so, when the government has decided to carry out such campaigns, it has always opted to address the citizen's personal responsibility. While similar to the book sellers' promotions, this type of campaign also seemed more in keeping with the small investment made for promoting reading in libraries, and even less, for other types of uses of these public services[10]. This approach continues to the present-day, as can be seen in the slogan of the 2004 campaign: "If you read, they will read" (referring to the example that parents can give to their children).

In one of the oldest campaigns promoting reading was the slogan: "A book helps one to triumph" (1969), identifying reading with utilitarian information. As such, better learning will lead to economic improvement and social advancement. A very partial view of reading, indeed, bringing to mind the "training" and utilitarian intentions of the first public libraries in Great Britain and North America ... but a full century later.

It was not for another decade that the second national campaign came out, also with a message aimed at the individual: "Live reading". This campaign focused on reading as a daily practice, necessary for all aspects of life. The slogan was, perhaps, more appropriate than the previous one, in spite of the tone of its underlying command. The Ministry of Culture contributed substantial funds to this campaign that produced numerous posters designed by well know illustrators, etc. But the results were uneven and, in some cases, frankly unfortunate[11].

Somewhat later was the institutional campaign run by the Generalitat de Catalunya, the first to air on television and in the press: "Feed your mind." The slogan was accompanied by images of people reading and the text "It contains vitamins a, b, c....", in reference to the book being read. In spite of the message of usefulness (linking reading to advantages, not pleasure) and the obvious word play, the campaign did not have a significant effect among the public. The subsequent Spanish broad campaign, at the beginning of the 1990s, had a greater effect although not altogether positive. This campaign had the slogan: "Those of you that can do it, don't waste it,"; in the poster a chimpanzee places a book on its head as a hat, not knowing what else to do with it. A similar campaign took place in Catalonia with the well-known image of the evolutionary phases between apes and [reading] men, with the slogan of "You who can, ... evolve." This obvious pejorative allusion to non-readers was paralleled in the late 1990s in a poster referring to the abstention of youth in the elections. It contained a cow that looked out from the poster with this text: "She is 18 years old and doesn't vote either." None of the aforementioned campaigns had yet made reference to the use of libraries, but solely limited themselves to promoting reading as an individual activity.

Despite the very different social-political contexts, up to this point the basic attitude of the persons designing and carrying out these promotional campaigns for reading was much the same as Lasso de la Vega's, in 1946, when he called on his colleagues to make an individual effort to reach out to users, but with no sign of resources from government agencies that could contribute to their initiatives.

The type of aggressive, ironic campaign that attempted to link those not following the posters' advice to negative images have not been repeated – at least for the time being. On the contrary, the preference has recently been to associate the experience of reading with positive, desirable qualities such as –finally— pleasure ("The pleasure of reading", with a photo of people reading, in Salamanca, or the older "The book: your adventure"[12] , of the Germán Sánchez Ruipérez Foundation at the beginning of the 1980s); personal growth ("Grow reading", also of the same Foundation, with a lovely image of a large child who no longer fit on the poster, for having read and grown so); opening up of unsuspected possibilities ("Get close to books ... and you'll see"[13] or the not very original, "You can't imagine it"); and even expectations over and above the purely rational ("A book is something magical", from the Basque land at the end of the 1980s).

Along these same lines, and based on collaboration between the private sector and the public administration, the campaign of Madrid publishers and book dealers entitled "Books to the street" has been held annually, with the novelty of distributing and posting promotional materials in the public transport system of Madrid and surrounding areas[14]. We find their slogan a little off the mark, since it does not make it clear if it is about reading in the street – although no such activities are known of in Madrid's public space – or rather, about tossing the books out the window!

The latest examples of government campaigns were those carried out by the Ministry of Culture in 2003 and 2004. The first one had the slogan of "Reading gives you more" (turning again to the utilitarian message), which was promoted through posters and bookmarks, and also television ads, etc. In 2004 the Ministry ran the campaign "If you read, they read", with TV ads and billboards, large signs at bus stops, as well as small format items such as fliers and bookmarks. It is worth pointing out that, for the first time, this campaign ran together with another one on the use and promotion of public libraries. The same dissemination methods were used, this time with the slogan of "Public libraries: come, look, listen, navigate, read". We will discuss it later.

Also in Barcelona, the City Hall has dedicated the year 2005 to the reading and the book, taking advantage of the celebration of 400 years from the publication of "El Quijote". The slogan is "More books, more free", which is a word play in Catalan, also in Spanish. More of 500 activities are scheduled through 2005, most of them at the city's public libraries[15].

Promoting the use of libraries

The search for cases directly related to the promotion of library service, in its broadest sense, takes us to the end of the 1970s. Though there had been precedents such as posters announcing activities and bookmarks with edifying messages, it was not until the 1970s that librarians felt a more intense need to broadcast the library's potential. And, following the death of the dictator, Francisco Franco, in 1975, it finally became possible - socially and politically - to do so. Nevertheless, those years of high hopes also coincided with an economic crisis marked by an annual inflation rate of 15%, large budget cuts, political uncertainty, and a lack of clear directives. All of that held back the possibility of promoting an image that was long overdue for a change, in a process parallel to the improvement of services.

Promotional librarian activities in Spain begin with the clear intention of informing potential users of the available resources. Librarians had long been concerned about how to let the public know about the existence and content of libraries, their hours and services, etc. Initially, promotional activities were limited to providing information about their services, considered the best possible, given the circumstances and the shortage of funding. In this phase, the aim was to increase the visibility of library services available to the public, and the most appropriate tool for doing so was the informational flier. This traditional folded flier containing basic facts about the library, hours and services, address, requirements for acquiring a library card, etc., is one of the oldest methods for dissemination - followed by reading lists - for attracting attention to the collection and thus achieving higher use. At the same time, posters announcing activities were being used more frequently: initially they advertised traditional activities that had proved effective, and later went on to promote activities addressed to new segments of the public and their needs.

The paucity of both human and material resources, as well as a certain aversion towards using "commercial" techniques, kept Spanish librarians away from marketing, but not from publicity. Similar to what had happened in the United States during the first half of the 20th century, in Spain from the 1950s and 60s on, promotional techniques began to be used. These included posters announcing activities, promotional exhibitions of the collection, or the participation of librarians in local radio programmes, etc.[16].

Nevertheless, these attempts were nothing more than isolated initiatives that at times had no continuity beyond the individual that carried them out. Other activities frequently came about as promotional initiatives of single libraries (Castellvell i El Vilar, Barcelona). Also important was the involvement of the public that requested—and achieved—library programmes. Public relations were present in the daily activities of library directors, even if the political climate did not permit much improvement in the services. On the other hand, marketing activities that librarians would have willingly set up –such as use studies or studies of users needs, or market segmentation— were not possible due to the lack of personnel, infrastructure and also —it may as well be said— of ongoing training that marked those years.

One of the first library campaigns was the aforementioned "We have a million books", by the Network of Public Libraries of the province of Barcelona. Highly criticised at the time for not being quite true – since many of the books included in this number were already obsolete – this campaign had one fundamental accomplishment: the messages about the libraries put them in the public eye. The public began to become accustomed to hearing libraries mentioned, as happens with many other public services.

During those years the province of Barcelona's Network of Public Libraries published posters and stickers that were distributed through the libraries, without slogans or other messages. The only text was a mention of the institution or, on occasion, the then novel phrase, "Networked libraries". There was a certain tradition of creating graphic products of this type, which subsequently included bookmarks and other items, for which well-known illustrators provided their services for enhancing the image of public libraries. In addition to the text and slogans were drawings evoking childhood fantasies or tranquillity of reading (Carme Solé Vendrell, Joma)[17] , or the diversity of users that could use the library. However, these materials rarely left the libraries or other professional forums and, therefore, did not reach the public at large.

Older yet is the only campaign that we are aware of in Catalonia of the private network of public libraries of La Caixa (a savings bank). This institution had for many years devoted large amounts of resources toward its institutional image, as was apparent in its reading lists, guides to services, and promotional posters.

During this initial period institutional efforts were devoted to "changing individual behaviour" and transferring cultural competencies to the different autonomous administrations. Following this phase, both the autonomous administrations and the Ministry of Culture began campaigns for promoting the use of public libraries, for disseminating their image, etc. These campaigns were frequently based on the fact that the public at large was unfamiliar with what the library could offer them. This public was the new target of library services that until then had been very limited, serving mainly school children. Therefore, campaigns such as "Come ... you can get [sacar] a lot of things" (Network of Public Municipal Libraries of the city of Murcia) plays with the double meaning of the word "get" in Spanish, representing obtaining something of value and at the same time taking items out temporarily on loan. Several years later, "Come prepared ... you'll leave loaded [carregat]" of the Libraries of Barcelona. Here there is also a double meaning, with loaded referring to the amount of material that can be taken from the library, as well as the second meaning of being a little drunk, which intended to attract the attention of the youthful user. "Grow with us" (Public Libraries of Burgos) stresses personal growth, as had the earlier campaign of the German Sanchez Ruiperez Foundation —but without mentioning reading although, being a library poster, this was implicit. This slogan also implies the permanence and fidelity of users through their entire life as clients of the library, as well as the change and evolution of the library itself.

New concepts – barely touched upon in the past—included the use of information and communication technologies (ICT) in libraries and of political messages to transmit values that, it was thought, could be promoted together with equal access to information. "To think with freedom" (Network of Libraries of Castilla-La Mancha in 1997) used the technique of comics to show different activities that take place in the library, from the more traditional up to those involving ICT, all framed within strictly classical columns and front, similar to the "Carnegie" style. "Different, equal" (Network of Public Libraries of Castilla-La Mancha, 2000) uses the image of different types of people –by sex, race—with an accompanying text that referred to the basic contents of the library and the statement itself occupying 50% of the surface. "Let's connect [Conect@mos]. Libraries of Extremadura. Not one village without a library" was of a mixed character, where the long slogan was accompanied by the modern image of ICT together with graphic images of traditional and rare books and globes. At the same time, the style of the textual message was similar to those of political or social protests.

A specific case is that of regional libraries that, given their position within each region, also have the responsibility for promoting each one's specific culture and identity. This activity, especially prominent in historic regions such as Catalonia or the Basque land, is nevertheless present in all of Spain's regional libraries, through the publication of books, bibliographies, etc., as well as promotional material that frequently transmits an advertising-type slogan ("Our knowledge now takes its place", announcing the new Library of Castilla-La Mancha)[18].

Toward the end of the 1990s we begin to find attempts to differentiate between general campaigns and others addressed to a specific type of public – generally, to young people. Many general campaigns are based on the availability of resources ("70 public libraries at your disposition" Region of Murcia) ("We have a million books" Province of Barcelona). Among those aimed at specific groups, there are campaigns such as the "bibliomarkets", "bibliopools", etc. that hope to attract new types of readers: housewives, leisure readers during their summer holidays, etc. Accordingly, the fliers published in 2000 in Barcelona had this same intention when they referred to the variety of documents available for "the price of 0". The aim was to emphasise that the service was free and, as such, the campaign was aimed primarily at those segments of the population for whom paying for services is a more critical issue, such as the young, retired, etc. An important example of initiatives directed to young people is the Public Library System of Catalonia's annual "Come to the libraries" campaign. They feature, for the first time in Spain, pictures of famous persons that presumably are library users, such as the actors of soap operas or movies (Montserrat Carulla, Ferran Rañé, Ariadna Gil); theatre actors (Pepe Rubianes); or soccer players (Pep Guardiola), combined with slogans in youthful slang. The latest example of this type of campaign, mounted much more elaborately with ads on TV and in the press, is "Libraries are cool [guai]" of the Barcelona Library Consortium. Here for the first time two levels of language are used: that of the slogan, in a youthful slang, and that of the underlying theme where it is clearly obvious that those who use the libraries are richer culturally, have a greater capacity for using language, etc. A third level can also be discerned, concerning gender (one of the current myths of the sociology of reading) and physical appearance of actors in the TV ad. In it, there is an intelligent girl using the library and a boy whose attitude leads the viewer to assume that he is not a library user. Are we returning to the aggressive campaigns of the past? Initially it might appear so, but—with a difference from the campaigns of the 1980s. Here the immediate focus is placed on the qualities of the libraries rather than those of the individuals.

Last year, in more limited settings, the government of the Communities of Castilla-La Mancha set up an exhibition to transmit the current concept of library, in an attempt to combat the existing unawareness about them: "The public library, door to the information and knowledge society" is its appealing title. As a part of their strategic plan,[19] a book has been also published, with the title "Palabras por la biblioteca pública" (Words for the public library), where a number of writers and experts offer their vision about the social function of the public library. In addition to these specific initiatives, it is worth highlighting the activities for promoting reading and public libraries that the German Sanchez Ruiperez Foundation has carried out over the years. In Catalonia, the most recent campaign in the province of Barcelona has the title "Now we have one million members", and is disseminated through posters, bookmarks, and stickers.

Since the middle of the 1980s, promotional campaigns are frequently transmitted using various types of material. Without diminishing its importance, the poster is often accompanied by more transportable objects, such as bookmarks, calendars, stickers, or other printed material (post cards, fliers). As we will see below, the Network of Public Libraries of the province of Barcelona was a pioneer in many of these designs.

Well into the 1990s, the printed material – without disappearing— gave way to objects that are more typical of merchandising: folders, pens, pencils or erasers; containers or cases for pens, bags, and key chains; T-shirts, caps, pins, cut-outs or fans are the most typical examples in recent years. Frequently libraries do not charge for much of this material, but rather give it away. Although in many cases the users can take the items with them directly, in others the library delivers them personally, thereby increasing its visibility on the street. In this sense, the latest campaign of the Ministry of Culture on reading was linked to one that encouraged the use of libraries, with the slogan, "Public libraries: come, see, listen, navigate, read". This campaign runs through radio and television spots –especially in high audience items, like sports, etc.-, as well as in posters distributed in the bus stops, etc. Its aim is to "enhance the social image of public libraries and to enlarge their utilization through promoting a change of level."[20] The ads are based on the phrase "How much is it?", and their aim is underlying the free service. The slogan and the images point to five main activities you can perform in the public library, with the objective to inform the non-user about all he or she can do in the library.

Another recent development has been the use of logos: an image applied extensively on many of the materials mentioned earlier, incorporated onto all documents issued by the library or network, onto letterhead, the web page, etc., as a quick, visual identifier of the institution. One of the first manuals for graphic identity was that of the government of the Communities of Castillay Leon. Meanwhile, there has been a certain evolution of the designs themselves, and consequently of the messages and images libraries want to transmit about themselves. The first libraries used images of books or other documents, in a more or less stylised manner (Network of Public Libraries of Castilla-La Mancha, Public Municipal Libraries of Zaragoza, Library of Aragon, Libraries of the Maresme); with a more or less schematic typography (Municipal Public Library of Zamora, Central Library of La Rioja, National Library of Catalonia, Municipal Library Network of Murcia, Terrassa.... at times, with connotations of images suggesting books: Libraries of Barcelona); with old typography, especially in libraries performing patrimonial functions (National Library, Library of Andalucia). Others used the images of the building housing the library (Library of Castillay Leon, Library of Castilla-La Mancha, Public Library of Vila-Seca) or of another distinguishing feature of the zone, such as the wave used in Cambrils. Recently, Public Libraries of the

State have created their own logo, with a lower case "b" framed within a square – representative of schematic typography for which the usage manual has just been issued[21]. The interest that this topic has awakened has been translated into the creation of a database of logos from around the world, prepared by the Library Network of Murcia[22] that contains more than 300 images to date.

Although addressed to another kind of public, the videos in the collection "Biblioimatges", co-published by the District of Barcelona administration and the Faculty of Library and Information Sciences of the University of Barcelona, serve both as teaching materials and as a tool for explaining what public libraries are – and are not—through the use of images of recent activities, etc. They are quite appropriate for use as a promotional item at trade fairs, exhibitions, etc.

A NEW RELATIONSHIP WITH THE PUBLICS

But not all are purely promotional objects containing solely the publicity and image. Since the mid-1990s especially, libraries have continued to create a number of documents stemming from the need to provide user satisfaction and to establish a rapport with them. Among the more classic documents, there are those that are merely informative, such as fliers on the library or its services and book lists. Later came information pamphlets, charters of user rights, and other products that attempt to communicate with the end user through the most convenient manner available.

In the middle of the 1990s many libraries also began to issue informative bulletins. These form a part of the local press, the reach of which is directly related to the number of distribution points.

USER STUDIES: A PART OF MARKET RESEARCH

Much more recent is the development of user studies—generally satisfaction studies tending more toward the library evaluation rather than to the segmentation of users or studies of their needs. One of the first was the Programme of Library Analysis (PAB), of the private Bertelsmann Foundation in collaboration with local Spanish administrations that run public libraries. This programme, set up in 1994, approaches users through an evaluation, since it attempts to assist libraries in evaluating themselves and to undertake an analysis of indicators. Furthermore, it is contributing to the redesign of procedures for collecting data in order to adapt them more to the evaluation's needs[23]. Currently it is in a new phase (2002-) that is attempting to work towards a comparison among libraries of the same network and also among networks, known as "PAB Programme-Networks"[24]. Twenty key indicators have been designed, many of them related to the use of, and impact on, end users. The use of focal groups for studying user satisfaction in public libraries has been introduced.

In 2003, the Studies Group of the province of Barcelona undertook a general study of active users, over 14 years of age, of municipal public libraries. The data of this study are still being explored. This study, based on 400 structured telephone interviews, collected data from citizens of towns with population of over 30.000 and in all ten districts of Barcelona. It was based on another, from January 2001, in which the same population were analysed. The objective, as stated earlier, was for evaluation[25].

Another interesting experience was a telephone survey on user habits and satisfaction that the Public Library of Tarragona carried out in 2002.

Experiences with evaluations involving user studies have also been undertaken in recent years in many university libraries, always within the framework of general university evaluations: noteworthy are those of the Universitat Politècnica de Catalunya,[26] Universidad Carlos III de Madrid, Universitat Pompeu Fabra de Barcelona,[27] etc. All these studies have in common an analysis of use and, especially, the satisfaction of different user segments: teachers, students of varying levels, etc. This tendency can be explained by the pressure – and in some cases, the legal obligation—on institutions to evaluate their libraries. On the other hand, we are unaware of the existence of needs studies or of general studies (demographic, psychographic, etc.) in Spanish libraries.

REFERENCES AND NOTES

1. Lasso de la Vega (J). La propaganda y el servicio público de bibliotecas en los Estados Unidos. Madrid: Revista de bibliografía nacional. 1946. (In fact, this work is, above all, a report on a trip to the US and the situation of libraries there).
2. Bostwick (A E).. The public library in the United States. Chicago, Ill.: ALA. 1941. (The translation, unsigned, entitled: "Las bibliotecas públicas en los Estados Unidos," was published in Revista de archivos, bibliotecas y museos, LIII: 2 (1947), p. 411-429).
3. Escolar Sobrino (H). El planeamiento bibliotecario. Una experiencia aprovechable: el márquetin. *Boletín de la ANABA*. 56. abril - jun. 1970: 3-15.
4. Escolar Sobrino (H). Márquetin para bibliotecarios. Madrid: ANABA. 1970.
5. "Bibliomarkets" are stands, installed by public libraries in city markets, with books, records, etc. available for loan, where persons that are shopping can see, and borrow, recent works on given subjects.
6. Basically, these are service points set up by the public library in centres of leisure, such as public pools, beaches, etc. Space is provided for reading in the open air at the stand, and people are also allowed to take the material to be read at their convenience while stretched out on a towel.
7. Some public libraries have installed stands with books and other materials available on loan in metro stations.

8. The "babyteca" is a space in the public libraries where adults can look at stories with babies or read them to pre-literate children who are accompanied by their parents, care-givers, or grandparents. Taking advantage of the presence of these adults, collections of materials are installed of interest to educators and other persons responsible for child care within the family.
9. Gomez-Hernández (A J) and Saorín Pérez (T). La imagen actual de las bibliotecas públicas en la cultura de masas. *In*, La biblioteca pública: portal de la sociedad de la información. Madrid: Ministerio de Educación, Cultura y Deporte, 2002. http://travesia.mcu.es/documentos/actas/sumario.pdf . P. 6 of 19. [Consulted: 28.08.04].
10. Ibid.
11. When compared with posters that were well designed graphically, the message transmitted by some other drawings was, frankly, discouraging. For example, one was a drawing of a man who had cut off his tie to use it as a bookmark – an image that would not stand up well under a Freudian analysis!
12. A similar idea can be found in the slogan, "The adventure of reading", that identified a whole series of cultural and recreational activities provided by the libraries of Barcelona; but this is an activities programme on a more complex level.
13. According to Gomez-Hernández (A J) and Saorín Pérez (T), this campaign "...was not effective in calling attention to reading" (Gómez and Saorín, La información y las bibliotecas en la cultura de masas.València: Biblioteca Valenciana, 2001, p. 62). In addition to the lack of originality of the slogan, the expression of "...and you'll see" often has, in Spanish, a negative, even threatening, connotation.
14. Text and images used in that campaign since 1977 are available at http://www.librosalacalle.com/textos.htm.
15. Information about this campaign is available at http://www.anyllibre2005.bcn.es/.
16. Pérez-Rioja and Antonio (J). La prensa y la radio como elementos de difusión bibliotecaria: una experiencia provincial. Boletín de la Dirección General de Archivosy Bibliotecas, II: 15 (nov. 1953), p. 5-8, and in Penetración social del concepto "biblioteca." Madrid: Dirección General de Archivoy Bibliotecas, 1954. (There are reports and reflections on this type of participation)
17. Both artists are well-known in the international field, escpecially because of their participation in events like Bologna Fair (Italy), where Carme Solé-Vendrell was awarded with the Price "Critici in Erba" (1992). their activities reach also the animation and the press.
18. Gómez-Hernández (JA) and Saorín Perez (T). *La información y las bibliotecas en la cultura de masas.* Valencia : Biblioteca Valenciana. 2001:

63. There is an obvious reference to the Spanish saying "El saber no ocupa lugar" (Knowledge doesn't take place).

19. The strategic plan and the foresseing marketing activities are available at http://www.jccm.es/cultura/liarbi/planbibliotecas/index.html.
20. Correo bibliotecario (Oct. 2004), http://www.bcl.jcyl.es/correo/.
21. Ministerio de Educación, Cultura y Deporte. Secretaría de Estado de Cultura. El nuevo identificador de las bibliotecas públicas: manual de uso. Madrid: MECD, 2004.
22. Red Municipal de Bibliotecas de Murcia. MAGICO: logoteca. Murcia, RMBM, 2001- . http://www.rmbm.org/magico/logoteca.php.
23. Ref. Carmen Artal, La Biblioteca pública vista pels ciutadans: informe de l'estudi realitzat a tres ciutats: 1998/99 (Barcelona: Fundació Bertelsmann; Diputació de Barcelona, Àrea de Cultura, 1999) and La Biblioteca pública vista pels ciutadans: informe estadístic: municipis província de Barcelona: juliol 2000 (Barcelona: Fundació Bertelsmann; Diputació de Barcelona, Àrea de Cultura; Metra Seis, 2000).
24. Available at http://www.fundacionbertelsmann.org/pab/.
25. Ref. Feliu, Toni; Jordi Permanyer, "Avaluació de la satisfacció dels usuaris de les biblioteques públiques." BiD: textos universitaris de Biblioteconomia i Documentació, núm. 9 (desembre 2002). http://www.ub.es/biblio/bid/09feliu.htm. [Consulted: 12 agost 2004].
26. The latest version of this study can be consulted at: http://www.bibliotecnica.upc.es/Enquesta_satisfaccio/informe2003-PDI.pdf.
27. Ref. http://www.upf.edu/bib/coneixer/coneixer.htm?opcio=0.

UNDERSTANDING MARKETING CULTURE IN FINNISH LIBRARIES

Rajesh Singh

Abstract *This article stresses the importance of marketing culture in the context of library and information centers which has yet not got its due consideration. A brief overview of the marketing scene of Finnish libraries is presented. It also explains the research that aims to investigate the marketing culture of Finnish libraries and seeks to understand the awareness of the knowledge base of library management about modern marketing theories and practices. Some preliminary findings are discussed to show the extent to which the libraries' culture can be marketing oriented. Further, this paper calls for library and information managers to develop and nurture an appropriate marketing culture as a means to achieve consumer satisfaction by developing lasting relationship with them by providing customer-oriented services and products in their organizations.*

INTRODUCTION

Adopting a customer oriented approach is a fundamental concept that is central to marketing, total quality and service quality. The customer is at the center of the organization, is the reason for its existence. It focuses on an organization's commitment to design and develop products and services that meet its customer needs and expectations. Therefore, identifying users, segmenting them, prioritizing them, knowing their main expectations and needs and understanding, prioritizing and turning them into service characteristics are all key marketing activities. Thus, the purpose is to adapt the library or information center to its demands and, consequently, to try and fulfill them [1].

Due to the unique characteristics of services (i.e. intangibility, inseparability of production and consumption, perishability, and variability), the nature of the culture of a service organization is particularly important and worthy of attention. The concept of marketing culture is nebulous and has yet to be defined precisely [2]. So far library market research has concentrated largely on users of the service. But, the importance of marketing culture has yet not got its due consideration in library and information services organizations and so far no attempt has been made earlier to explore the marketing culture in the context of library and information service organizations. And, most of the studies conducted earlier explain theoretical application of marketing concepts in libraries (not "marketing culture") more and thus lack empirical evidences. Marketing is basically an attitude towards consumer satisfaction. To market information services successfully, librarians must be sensitive to the needs of both staff and users and provide services, which really meet the patron's needs. Sensitivity does not come if one is not positive about it. The marketing concept will fail to work, if the environment in which it is applied is not conducive, and the librarian is not positive and enthusiastic about it. A positive change in the attitude of librarians towards marketing is a pre-requisite for making it successful in the library. The library, as a non-profit making entity, can and must apply marketing as a philosophy, marketing techniques and tools as a function, both in its strategic approach and its day-to-day operation. To make it happen, it is, therefore, necessary to infuse a marketing culture in the environment of library so that customer satisfaction may become a way of life of all employees from top to bottom.

Marketing culture refers to the unwritten policies and guidelines, which provide employees with behavioral norms, to the importance the library as a whole places on the marketing function, and to the manner in which marketing activities are executed. Since service quality is one dimension of marketing culture, it follows that the kind of marketing culture an organization would be particularly important for a service organization like library, since the simultaneous delivery and receipt of services brings the provider and customer physically and psychologically close.

Therefore, it is important to understand the marketing orientation that initiates at the top management and flows through the whole organization and is thus, responsible for creating a particular kind of library culture. Hence, in this paper, the key issues to be tackled are those relating to the individual psychology, attitudes and knowledge of the library directors on the usefulness, utility and relevance of employing marketing concept in the library environment. It also explains a brief overview of the marketing scenario in the context of Finnish library and information services organizations. Some preliminary findings have been explained to show the extent to which the libraries' culture can be marketing oriented. Further, this paper calls for library and information managers to develop and nurture marketing culture as a means to achieve customer satisfaction by developing lasting relationship with them by providing customer-oriented services and products in their libraries.

WHAT IS MARKETING CULTURE?

Every organization has some features, which makes its culture different from others. Day [3], mentions in this respect the capabilities of market-driven organizations: market sensing, market relating and strategic thinking as fundamental and very operational issues in defining and implementing market orientation. These capabilities and conditions are linked to the underlying "values" of the company: its culture. Webster, defines marketing culture as that component of a firm's overall culture that refers to the pattern of shared values and beliefs that help employees understand and "feel" the marketing and thereby provides them with norms for behavior in the firm. It refers to the importance the firm as a whole places on marketing and to the way in which marketing activities are executed in the firm [4].

Thus, by synthesizing the above definitions, it can be said that marketing culture is a thinking that permeates in the whole environment of a library or information service organization which develops and uses its understanding of customer requirements to shape its marketing activities and strategies to fulfill the same on continual basis by sensitizing everyone in the system to 'feel' the marketing values from top to bottom. It refers to the key function of library managers for articulating a compelling 'marketing' vision and making it 'shared' throughout the entire activities of library and information services. Moreover, this is a philosophy that places customers and their needs at the heart of everything what the library does [5]. Hence, marketing culture is nothing more than the recognizable core of the modern concept of marketing, whose basic elements are: "product" (observed through elements of "classic marketing", and these are product policy, price policy, promotion policy and place policy), people who create the processes, which they manage, supervise and constantly upgrade (progress). This modern approach to marketing implies that marketing culture is something, which can be managed. This is one of the basic "values" of a company which, just with any other basic value, must be actively managed [6]. Leadership seems to be very important to formulate those values and "translate them into daily practices". It is only very recently that leadership issue has come up in research in marketing [7]. Thus as observed, the task of the director of a customer-oriented library is to help employees offer value to the customer by creating corresponding processes (including creating corresponding procedures and marketing policies-4P), by a corresponding distribution of resources (human and financial) in order to be successful, i.e. as possible over a period of time.

MARKETING SCENE IN FINNISH LIBRARIES : A BRIEF OVERVIEW

The concept of customer service is succinctly embedded in the Finnish libraries, around which revolves the marketing principles and theories. Several initiatives have been taken in Finland to adopt the concept of marketing in the field of library and information services. Many libraries and information centers of national importance have been established with specific missions and objectives. It was Finnish Library Association (established 1910) which had started some campaigns and reach-out activities for the public and mass media already in the 1960s. But, more active public relations and communication/information activities were developed 1970 onwards.

Finland has a very lively contact with its Nordic neighbor Sweden. Therefore, in library matters too, many ideas have been exchanged. "Public Relations (PR) in libraries" was an issue where Finland was influenced by the experience of Swedish libraries. In Sweden, PR-librarian Greta Renborg (who later worked within library training at the Uppsala University in Sweden) wrote several books on this theme in 1970s. These books were also studied in Finland and the author was also lecturing in Finland that helped in creating awareness towards developing the PR activities in libraries. It was in seventies, when the first full time PR-librarian was appointed in Espoo City Library. Shortly after that Helsinki City Library, the National Central Library for public libraries, appointed also a full-time PR librarian which was followed by other county libraries in different cities such as Tampere, Turku, Lahti and Jyväskylä during 1970-80. But, the economical depression decade 1990 forced the libraries to cut their costs as a result of which now only few libraries have a full-time staff for marketing and communication activities. Different aspects related to the PR-work of Finnish libraries have been:

i) information about library services to the public;
ii) information about the collections to the public;
iii) information about the use of library and reading to the public;
iv) information about the library celebrations to the public;
v) information to the political/community decision makers; and
vi) information to the press.

Libraries have traditionally given more or less information on the first four aspects mentioned above however there has been less focus on the last two issues.

Finnish Library Association has been offering following activities and support to the libraries:

- campaigns, Library Day (8.2., "Lainan päivä"-in Finnish)
- press connections
- posters, brochures, information leaflets
- training courses/ seminars and workshops on PR
- publications; a book, a magazine.

Since 1984, Finnish Library Association has arranged every second year a National Library Day or Week called "Lainan päivä". There have been various themes and ways to celebrate the day. Sometimes a library political issue has been taken to the members of parliament, and sometimes a special library service, e.g., the music libraries have been the topic of the discussion of library day/week, and so on. There has also been a campaign of library themes before municipal elections (1994) and there will be one this year (2004) too.

In Finland, the libraries have high quality web sites of their own. They inform about their events and customers have access to the library collections via Internet. Libraries are developing approaches to make their web sites more informative and attractive so that visibility of the libraries could be more enhanced in customers' eyes even though libraries already enjoy a very high reputation in general.

Since its existence, Finnish Library Association has also been arranging training for the library staff. There has also been education on PR and marketing, but not very much. This year, 2004, the association arranged two times a 3-days seminar on marketing and also "Kirjastolehti" (The Library Journal, a monthly magazine which the Association publishes) made a special issue on the theme of marketing. And, it is very recently when Finnish-Swedish Library Association organized its annual conference on marketing during 19-20 August, 2004 in Jakobstad.

The trends available from the Finnish scenario indicate that some of the libraries of national repute are doing quite well as regards to the marketing concepts in their day-to day work. The National Library of Finland has developed marketing strategies to take care of the customers in the more sophisticated and professional manner. Some other libraries have made their marketing strategies too and are quite familiar with the contacts to the press. Libraries of Business Schools and some other special and university libraries have been marketing their services and making serious efforts to improve upon them. In this regard, it would be worthwhile to mention the "Helecon" database of the Helsinki School of Economics and Business Administration library that doesn't need any introduction because of its global presence like a brand in the management academia. However, in most of the other libraries, the awareness about marketing concepts is still in its infancy stage even though they are very highly service oriented. But, there is evidence that different library associations and spirited professionals in Finland are making serious efforts to create awareness and trigger interest among the library professionals about the need for adopting marketing approaches in their libraries.

THE PRESENT STUDY

This study is based on the notion that a leader in an organization can have large impact on its culture, which has been suggested in many earlier findings [8]. Therefore, it is important to learn about the marketing orientation that initiates at the top management and flows through the whole organization thus resulting in a particular kind of library culture. Research was started in Autumn 2001 that aims to investigate the marketing culture of libraries and seeks to understand the awareness of the knowledge base of library management about modern marketing theories and practices.

The specific research questions are:

- What attitudes do librarians have about marketing of information products/ services in different kind of libraries?
- How much knowledge do librarians possess about new marketing theories and practices?
- What are the commitments of the staff and management in libraries towards customers' needs and demands?

- To what extent is the construction of a service philosophy practised in Finnish libraries?
- What are the implications of marketing for the libraries?

SOME PRELIMINARY FINDINGS

The research data has been collected in 33 different research libraries of south Finland during September 2002 through April 2003. The interviews have been conducted with the library directors on various issues of marketing such as its meaning, need, planning, quality, and philosophy, etc. Customers' feedback (3-10 per library) was also sought as marketing is basically an attitude towards consumer satisfaction. The processing of data is under way. The quantitative data has been coded in SPSS, and interviews are being analyzed. Hence, the purpose is more to create awareness and apprised with my limited experiences than to report any exhaustive findings. I must mention that at different places I got different type of responses, which range from negative (few) to very positive and talking with chief librarians on various facets of marketing has been a fascinating experience. The cursory survey of research data seems to reveal some interesting findings, which have yet to be analyzed deeply. The libraries have been divided into three categories: *more marketing oriented, medium marketing oriented, and less marketing oriented*. This categorization is based on the factor analysis of the marketing orientation activities of the libraries (behavior).

There are few cases where respondents have positive attitudes but express the opinion that marketing is not necessary for libraries. The factor of years of experience (younger versus older generation) also doesn't seem to have much impact over their awareness about marketing. The respondents, who have had exposure to marketing education, seminars, etc., were very positive except few. At the same time, it was also interesting to find out some persons who strongly supported the marketing idea for the libraries without having any formal marketing education and exposure to seminar, workshops, etc. and thus very positive. The knowledge measuring questions reveal that respondents have strong inclination towards promotional aspects especially developing public relations. There are also few exceptions wherein some respondents keep quite good marketing knowledge individually (in the category of 'less marketing oriented') that does not reflect in the marketing behavior of their libraries but it still needs to be analyzed more deeply to find the rationale for it.

The most peculiar feature of the Finnish library system is that all the libraries are open to everyone and anybody can use its resources, facilities and services without any restriction and discrimination due to which libraries enjoy a high profile in their customers' mind. Although customers are very happy with their respective libraries, but to become truly customer oriented, libraries need to go much more beyond this. To obtain customer feedback is not a regular activity in libraries except few. Majority of the libraries perform it some time. It has also been revealed that some of the library directors have some reservations on the concept of market segmentation techniques, which may be attributed to the fact that they know their customer base well as they think. They favored the personal contact as the most suitable way to promote its services and products. But, there seems to be less evidence of systematic and planned use of marketing approaches. Team spirit is highly valued in Finnish library system and all the library administrators are of the firm opinion that it is very important for ensuring the success of libraries. Most of the library directors held weekly meeting with their staff to discuss library problems. It assumes a great significance in the competitive global environment, as the attitude of the employee is a crucial factor in the performance of the customer-oriented library, not only in offering the basic product but also in offering all extra services, in other words, in offering the total product. Most of the library directors were not agreed with the issue of 'charging' the fees from average users. They were only in favor of charging the 'private companies' and 'industries'

The libraries are quite successful in developing a deeper relationship with their customer base via e-mail and mobile phone services although some of the library directors are not happy with the home pages of their libraries and they aim to make it more informative, attractive and customer friendly so that libraries' visibility could be enhanced in their clients' minds. In most of the libraries (except few), no construction of a service philosophy exists on paper, but in some, it's under construction. *Cooperation but not competition, and let all the flowers blossom seems to be the philosophy of Finnish library system.* Discussion with library directors has given the impression that they realize the need, importance and high utility of marketing concept, but lack of necessary training and skills on marketing and time constraint on their parts besides some other factors (lack of willingness, priority and resources, etc.) appear to be stumbling blocks to put it in practice as expressed by some of them. It was also interesting to find that the respondents attached a great importance to marketing despite of the fact that some of them had an erroneous perception of the concept at the same time. But, all of them strongly feel that the societal and technological changes, the "information explosion", dwindling resources, and ever-increasing customers' expectations for information and quality service together forcefully impose the need to understand and to make use of marketing thinking upon library managers and information scientists.

DISCUSSION

On the one hand, the research project concerns with the investigation of the perception and knowledge of libraries on the usefulness, utility and relevance of modern marketing theories/practices, and on the other hand it attempts to see the extent to which the working culture of libraries is marketing oriented. At the moment, it is hard to predict the extent to which Finnish libraries are following their customer-oriented activities. It would be interesting to see the relation among different variables into three categories of libraries (more, medium, and less marketing oriented); what are the characteristics of these libraries and how their marketing attitudes, perceptions, knowledge, service quality, marketing activities, philosophies and cultures vary in defining consumer satisfaction. Is there any relation between the marketing attitudes, knowledge and behavior of libraries??? But, one thing is quite sure that the customer base of the Finnish libraries is very happy irrespective of the libraries being in more, medium or less marketing oriented category. What does all this indicate? On the one hand, it gives the impression that the concept of customer relationship management is being practiced in a well-organized manner. But, this is not the whole truth as there are some libraries which do not possess enough exposure to marketing concept and practices but yet very customer oriented even though to obtain an organized customer feedback is not their regular activities. So, what can be the reason for this state of affairs? Monitoring customer value is such a cultural deviation that the introduction process must begin at the highest managerial level. It is only with their dedication that it is possible to start with the process of monitoring satisfaction, which is also the first step in creating marketing orientation as the library culture. Their dedication must be recognizable to all. But then, there seems to be another interesting explanation especially in the Finnish context. The entire Finnish system is itself very service oriented which has strong bearing on every organization irrespective of being public or private sector. So, it is not surprising when we find the highly service-oriented customer friendly libraries. Besides, Finnish libraries are opened for everyone without any discrimination that maximizes the use of libraries as the marketing approach suggests but it is not because of the fact that they are following marketing concept in practice. It is more because of the Nordic tradition that favors the right to information for everyone. Similarly, it is necessary to keep in mind the Finnish culture, where 'price' does not necessarily mean 'selling' a service for a 'fee' in the context of libraries. Although it does mean that there is a cost to the provision of the service, but this does not necessarily translate as a fee to the library's clients. The fundamental approach of the Finnish libraries resides in the fact that they are in the 'information business' from the point of view of being a 'service' as well as a 'nonprofit' organization and the 'price' of their core services lies in the fact of making ease of access to information as a mediator and thereby providing the solution of the information needs of their clients [8]. Therefore, it may be concluded that the entire culture of country also carries a special significance on service organizations which is clearly evident in the Finnish context.

CONCLUSION

To develop a customer-oriented marketing culture is a great challenge for today's library managers as customers are asking more challenging questions of the professional librarians on the staff, and they are not usually seeking "easy answer" information that they can find for themselves. Therefore, it calls for libraries to move away from traditional collection development methodologies to prefer to work with customers in a concept of "proactive anticipation." In summary, this paper attempts to define the marketing culture in the context of libraries and information providing organizations and calls for information practitioners to develop and nurture an appropriate marketing culture in their libraries. However, it does need emphasis that in adopting this commercial approach, the objectives and ideal of libraries and information centers should not be forgotten.

REFERENCES

1. Lozano (A R P). A customer orientation checklist: a model. *Library Review*. 49(4). 2000: 173-178.
2. Luk (S T K). An Examination of the role of marketing culture in service quality. *International Journal of Contemporary Hospitality Management*. 9 (1). 1997: 13-20.
3. Day (G S). The capabilities of market-driven organizations. *Journal of Marketing*. 58. October 1994: 37-52.
4. Webster (C). Marketing culture and marketing effectiveness in service firms. *Journal of Services Marketing*. 9 (2). 1995: 6-21.
5. Singh (R). Branding in library and information context: The role of marketing culture. *Information Services & Use*. 24(2). 2004: 93-98.
6. Vranesevic (T), Vignali (C) and Vignali (D). Culture in defining consumer satisfaction in marketing. *European Business Review*. 14(5) 2002: 364-374.
7. Kasper (H). Culture and leadership in market-oriented service organizations. *European Journal of Marketing*. 36 (1/2). 2002: 1047-1057.
8. Singh (R) and Ginman (M). Challenges and issues in the application of marketing principles in LIS environment: An experience. *Tidskrift För Dokumentation, The Nordic Journal of Documentation*. 57(4). 2002: 131-139.

FROM MIND SHIFT TO PARADIGM SHIFT: MARKETING MANAGEMENT IN CHINA LIBRARIES

Chen Chao
J. Pan

Abstract *Marketing management in the Mainland of China libraries is analyzed in this article. Primary documentation statistics and content analysis show that although the marketing management in Chinese business enterprises is very popular after more than twenty years' reform and opening-door policy, the concept in Chinese libraries is still not well understood. For many libraries in mainland of China marketing management is still in the stage of concept introduction and mind shift. Although there has been a prolonged arguments discussion on library marketing management, the theory and practice have been far from going to be a part of organization strategy, saying nothing of acme phase of "Marketing Reshape Management". To the mainland librarians, there is still a long way from establishment and shift of marketing concepts to transformation of management paradigm.*

INTRODUCTION

Marketing is a concept under market economy. Twenty years ago, marketing was a strange thing to most Chinese people as a planned economy does not need marketing. How to translate the word into Chinese was once a topic of the conference paper. At the beginning of 1990's, the bible of marketing discipline, *Marketing Management: Analysis, Planning, Implementation and Control (5th edition by PHILIP KOTLER)* was for the first time translated into Chinese in the Mainland, which interested just a small circle of readers and only several thousand copies were sold. However in middle 1990's and afterwards, updated editions of this book were translated and published continuously and timely. Chinese edition of 9th, 10th and 11th has more than 100 thousand printings respectively, and total circulation amounts to tremendous.

In 2002, a new record was made during the visit of Mr. Kotler to China. The most expensive ticket to lecture of the master priced RMB 9,880 (about USD1200). Nowadays, apparently all the managers and the managed know the word "Marketing", not only in business world full of fierce competition but in other organizations as well.

There has been a kind of organizations in China, namely, *Shiye Danwei* (undertakings unit, literally), which is close to the concept of non-profit organization

(NPO, has not yet defined officially in China, but the term has been used in some cases and may be called as NPO too in this paper). They are sponsored by the government budget to fulfill some tasks that the society requires but business is normally not willing to take. Library is one of these organizations.

Nevertheless, in China, a country in the process of transformation from a planned economy to market economy, business companies are pioneering the reform with a clear-cut goal while the NPOs, not at the high priority of reform, have been to a large extent just at the experimental stage. As a result, currently there is a huge gap between the understanding and practice of the business corporations and the NPOs in China. The former has gone beyond the concept shift and into a stage of application. Companies learned to apply western theories creatively to their daily marketing action. Marketing management has been the organic part, even the core part of management practice in the most top corporations, among which emerges successful world class marketing strategy cases, such as Haier, a home appliance manufacturer. Meanwhile, for the latter, most Chinese libraries and information services are yet busy in seeking the way for survival. Their understanding of marketing management is superficial and their corresponding practices are still partial, sporadic and separate. Marketing has not affected fully and profoundly the concepts and models of these organizations in- deed.

A LONG PROCESS OF MIND SHIFT

Bibliometrics and content analysis are the most traditional documentation study methods, and they could reflect the results of a certain action to some extent. I carried out a retrospective study of bibliometrics, and the data are from leading bibliographical *Database for China Newspaper and Journal Indexes (philosophy & social science)on CD-ROM* published by Shanghai library. The result shows that only 73 papers in domestic media have both "library" and "marketing" in their titles from 1980 to 2003 (see table 1). The earliest one presented in 1986, and articles released in 2003 are more than those in any other year. According to further analysis, during the period from 1980 to 1999, there were only 21 articles published in 20 years, in which 3 articles appeared twice with minor modification) and 1 article was serialized into 2 parts. That means actually only 17 papers were published during the 20 years, and the average is less than 1 paper per year. Moreover, 2 out of the 17 papers are edited translation of international publications, only 15 left are substantially probing into domestic library marketing issues, but most of all were just engaging in idle theorizing.

Table-1 : Statistics on papers published in 1980-2003 with topic of library and marketing

1986	1993	1994	1995	1997	1998	1999	2000	2001	2002	2003
1	3	2	2	2	3	8	6	9	12	25

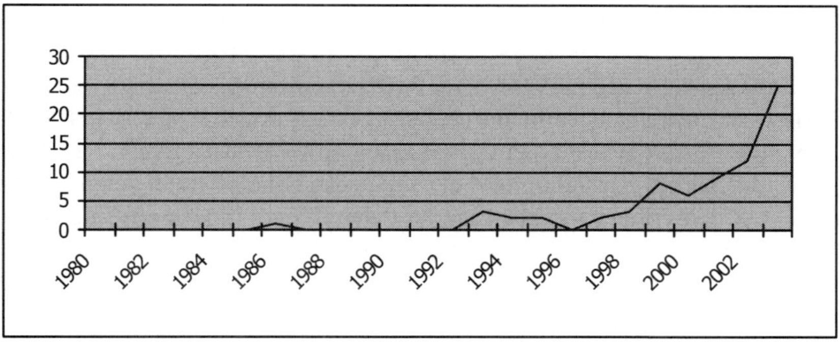

Data source: *Database for China Newspaper and Journal Indexes, Philosophy & Social science on CD-ROM* Shanghai library

This is to say, marketing theory has been "mentioned, discussed and studied" for more than 20 years. But the content analysis on these documents shows, very little progress was made on library marketing practice. Overall marketing practices in mainland libraries are superficial, even distorted, with only a few exceptions. For example, very few leading libraries introduced Corporation Identity System in the middle of 1990's, some began to establish public relation department or post, and another few started regular or semi-regular survey on readers' satisfaction. Quite a number of articles confined the concept of marketing within the value-added information provision, or other controversial fee-based services. Although above research has its limitation in terms of literature coverage and the time lag of published articles and the real world practice, its finding that the marketing management in Chinese libraries is generally in the preliminary status is convincing and confirmed by the agreement of librarians' feelings and impression as well.

In the last few years marketing as a topic becomes more and more heated among China librarians while the library management is still groping around. Statistics in Table 1 shows, entering into 21st century, discussion on marketing suddenly flourished in China library community. In 2003, the number of papers published in this single year exceeds the total of those in 20 years from 1980 to 1999. The more interesting is that the published study on library marketing is very responsive to new development of marketing theories, a number of articles have touched most updated marketing theories. For instance, network marketing, experience marketing, green marketing, brand marketing, relation marketing, knowledge marketing and service marketing, etc. have been tapped or covered by these articles. Thus, a prime judgment is China libraries has eventually come to a basic consensus that "library needs marketing" during more than 20 years' economic transformation and introduction of marketing concept has been completed. All these indicate the stage of marketing mind shift and concept establishment has been accomplished.

A STATUS WITH ABSENCE OF STRATEGY IN MARKETING

Against the benchmarks of either successful business enterprises or leading libraries in the rest of the world, the crucial weakness of public library in China is the absence of strategy in marketing management. With the continuous evolution towards the market orientation in the overall social and economic environment, and the trial-and-error process by libraries themselves, it is not surprising that the word *marketing* has been known to librarians extensively. This comes natural and reasonable. With marketing theories extending to non-profit enterprises, with branches of marketing such as service marketing, social marketing and etc., becoming more and more popular, the need for marketing management is more urgent than ever in library especially in public library. In 1970-80s' the international library community has experimented traditional marketing theory, creative service marketing and social marketing theory, in turn, beyond the basic theoretic core.

With a long history of ignorance of modern management ideas including marketing, and to some extent because of the ambiguity of the organizational nature of Chinese *Shiye Danwei*, obvious limitations exist in the understanding of the significance and role of marketing in library development, which have following characteristics:

Non-strategic: Marketing should have been a part of corporate strategy, however in most cases marketing is not yet strategic endeavor but just an operation focusing on for-profit information services, such as news-clipping, document delivery and other fee-based services. Few marketing study is carried out from the macroscopical angle under socialistic economic condition.

Non-systematic: Marketing concepts do not apply comprehensively and systematically to the whole library business process, thus the essence of modern marketing theory is absent.

Misunderstanding: There is still misunderstanding around the concept marketing. As the word itself implies, it seems conflicting with the noble mission library assumes to pursue. For someone marketing is often reduced to a tool helping to make a little money, thus, has to be an inevitable evil in the situation that the funding is always not enough.

Unstructured: In the Chinese libraries, marketing management has hardly been embedded into the organizational framework, thus there are seldom dedicated units or senior managers to coordinate marketing strategy and campaigns.

In lack of professional knowledge: Unlike some leading libraries of the world, it seems exceptional that any professionals with business background are employed in either public or academic libraries in China. Meanwhile in the traditional library and information science education, very little, if any, marketing management courses have been taught. The shortage of local practice and relevant case studies makes it even worse.

FINDINGS FROM CASE STUDY: REPORTS ON ACTIVITIES OF CHINA LIBRARIES

Documentation study is very helpful but limited, so we try to find more evidence to help us in forming the conclusion or judgment.

China libraries are playing a more and more important role in knowledge delivery and information service. Marketing consciousness emerged in library circle, but is not in balance. Some local pioneers may have more systematic planning and implementation, while most libraries haven't turned the idea into action. Although national program such as knowledge project puts public libraries on the stage, they are not urged to adopt strategic marketing management. Because rich libraries need not worry too much on the finance issue which is usually guaranteed every year. They will always have adequate funds to support activities to satisfy the government and decision maker on fiscal budgets. As a result, the drive for social marketing to general public is not very strong. While poor libraries, which do not have enough resources to provide quality services to public find it difficult to fulfill marketing obligations.

Marketing and marketing management has evolved in China libraries, although they did not happen under the word marketing. The evolution path of strategic level marketing is not straight forward, it depends on various influence factors and forces of all stakeholders. With the system reform advancing onto NPOs, pressure would be exerted on some libraries in competition for public resources. And strategic marketing management could be developed gradually in China libraries for better public services and better public supports.

Following are selected cases which could be helpful for understanding the status quo of marketing in China library community.

A Nation-wide yearly library event – Propaganda/publicity week on library services

In year 1989, propaganda/publicity week on library service ("the Library Week") was initiated by Bureau of Library of the Ministry of Culture, and the week across May and June was chosen as the event time. Through the propaganda, it aims to emphasizing on the significance of reading and learning, the significance of libraries as life-long schools in civil reading campaign. It appeals to more involvement in life-long learning and more utilization of public libraries.

Every year, national cultural department determines a specific theme for the week. And local public libraries carry out various activities under same slogan, including lectures, exhibitions, spot counselling and books lending to countryside and factories. These serial events may be disclosed on media and more public attention might be attracted by these reports.

Unified topic, consecutive occurrence and specific timing are basic features of social marketing activities. Judging from these facts, we could label this yearly program a marketing activity. However, it is spontaneous marketing, and the program itself has never been taken as a marketing activity from the beginning of launch, and such a good marketing opportunity is eventually wasted to some extent because of the lack in marketing management. Currently, neither brand effect nor far-reaching influence has been achieved by more than one decade's efforts. Even some librarians can not mark key elements of this program, let alone the general public . Should we have had marketing planning in strategy at first, the goal of "the Library Week" could have been fully and better approached. For example, CI design, market segmentation and target market should have been integrated into overall process.

A yearly civil reading campaign using libraries as main vehicles - Reading for all people (*Quan Min Yue Du*) Month

In December 2000, this campaign was first launched and embraced as one part of Knowledge Project, which is jointly conducted by nine national departments and committees. First civil reading month saw a name list of the elected readers' favorite libraries. Public libraries were chosen as the main places for people to read and learn, and were required to provide more information accesses and guide readers to better books.

China library association was trusted to co-ordinate this program in 2003 due to the important role of library in this kind of activities. For instance, both improving information literacy and facilitating civil reading are basic functions of a library. Also this is another perfect chance for public libraries to market themselves, and to promote public concern. Fortunately this time library circle did something closer to conscious marketing. During preparation, China Library Association brainstormed with experts from Peking University and people from all circles were invited as well to formulate a framework for the program. A committee was established for the campaign, a detail activities plan was figured out and a guidance document was distributed to local libraries.

Among these activities carried out for the reading month, logo design was one of marketing activity. The organizer called for a campaign of visual design. More than 2000 brochures were handed out, information was released on related websites and common people were encouraged to take part through extensive publicity. Design copies from nation-wide and even America were received and finally a logo was determined. On 23rd April 2004, the world reading day, following (see figure 1) image was declared campaign logo to stand for the words of "reading for all people (*Quan Min Yue Du*)". Wonderful events brought more media exposure, about 30 newspapers and TV stations reported the campaign and its events and the public involvements. A special TV program was made on this topic, discussion with scholars and Internet was taken as an alternative channel to the young. Besides, seeking sponsorship from business, it sets out a trend on market operation attracting financing from different parties other than government - another main point in NPO marketing. But all these efforts are not enough and there a lots still to be done to perform well in continuous library marketing.

CIS IN CHINA LIBRARIES

Strategic marketing management needs Corporation Identification System (CIS), which includes three levels, namely visual identification (VI), behavior identification (BI) and mind identification (MI).

CIS in Shanghai Library

Shanghai library is a leading China public library in CIS introduction. Early in 1996, visual identification design was completed and widely used in daily operation. Logo and color appeared congruously on buildings, uniforms, name cards, envelopes and other office supplies. At that time, only VI was considered in CIS.

Fig. 1 : Logo of Reading for all people (*Quan Min Yue Du*)

In Year 2002, a famous local consulting firm was employed to identify its organizational culture concepts to enhance its CIS. After questionnaire investigation, employee interviews and some paper work, Shanghai library defined its organizational culture concepts. The organizational mission is to accumulate cultural material and devote itself to excellent knowledge service. World-class city library is its organizational goal. And the core values are *serve elegantly, cooperate sincerely, guide learning, and stimulate wisdom.* Its focuses are cultural inheriting, knowledge navigation, information delivery and LIS study. Code of conduct for library staff was given to everybody in booklets together with the history and stories of the organization. This time, not only VI is taken into account, both BI and MI are on the agenda. In order to realize the blue print, Shanghai library set year 2003 as year of behavior and year 2004 as year of system.

Logos of China Libraries

Most of China libraries have no real CIS, but have their logos. Unlike English words, Chinese is hieroglyph. The characters themselves may originate from a picture or a scenario and can inflame one's imagination. Thus some China libraries keep the calligraphy of the names as their logos or part of logos, especially the handwriting of distinguished figures. Follows are some logos of China libraries.

Fig. 2 : Logo of China National Library

Fig. 3: Logo of Shenzhen Library (a famous city library in Guangdong Province)

Fig. 4: Logo of Shanghai Library

Fig. 5: Logo of Anhui Provincial Library

Fig. 6: Logo of Hunan Provincial Library

Fig. 7: Logo of Sun Yat-sen Library of Guangdong Province

Insufficient financial support is main constraint of CIS in China libraries. Although statistics shows from 1991 to 2001, public finance in libraries increased by 85%. There are altogether 2000 public libraries in this nation, among which 600 did not have budget for book purchase in year 2001. Without basic functions fulfilled, hardly can small libraries have money-consuming CIS and ultimately only big public libraries can take action.

CONCLUSION : A more arduous mission-from mind shift to paradigm shift

"Whatever is, is right"(′or What is real is reasonable. Taken from Hegel's famous dictum, "What is reasonable is real, and what is real is reasonable".in German original: "Das Wirkliche sei vernuenftig und das Vernuenfitige wirklich"). The living condition of China libraries decides that it took more than 20 years to complete elementary alteration of marketing concepts. But neither the front line librarians, nor the middle and high level management have understood marketing idea indeed. A strategic agreement on the significance of marketing of library has been reached. Marketing management should be consolidated into organizational strategic management, and there is no exception to library. This far-ranging consensus needs "internal marketing" to form and organization culture to maintain and solidify. Library must have strategy management first, and marketing management must serve to library development strategy. Then the marketing management becomes strategic marketing. With consideration of strategic marketing, the detail marketing strategies and tactics would be solved readily. With consideration of strategic marketing, marketing could reshape library management, and library management (including marketing management) could achieve paradigm shift. So, marketing management of China library community is facing great challenge from mind shift to paradigm shift.

BIBLIOGRAPHY

1. Andreasen (A R) and Kotler (P). Strategic marketing for nonprofit organizations. Ed.6. Prentice Hall. 2003.
2. Baldock (C). Marketing libraries: A survival course? *Library Management*. 14(1). 1993: 4-8
3. Booth (J). Marketing public library services: The gap between theory and reality in Britain. *Library Management*. 14(1). 1993: 9-23
4. Cao (S) and Zhuang (Y F). On library information service marketing. *Library Theory and Practice*. 2. 1999: 17-19
5. Chen (C). The Strategic marketing management of public library. *Library Tribune*. 22(5). 2002:113-115
6. Chen (L Q). A Discussion of online marketing and service for libraries.*Journal of Information*. 10. 2003:28-30
7. Chen (X K). Reader's loyalty and marketing research of digital library. *Researches in Library Science*. 11. 2002:51-52
8. Jiang (X Y). On the marketing policy of the information service in libraries of colleges and universities. *Journal of Fuqing Branch of Fujian Normal University*. 3. 2003: 94-96.
9. Kotler (P). Marketing management: Analysis, planning, implementation and control. Ed.9. (Chinese Translation). Ruhe (M), Qinhao (M) and Heng (Z), Trs. Shanghai People Press. 1999

10. Joseph Pine II (B) and Gilmore (J H). The experience economy. Boston: Harvard Business School Press. 1999
11. Li (J). On marketing LIS. Library Journal. 18(4). 1999: 1-4
12. Li (X H). The Network Marketing of the College and University Library in China. *Information Science.* 18(9). 2000: 858-860
13. Lin (H Q). Introducing marketing to develop the LIS. *Journal of Information.* 19(1). 2000:48-49,51
14. Liu (G) and Chang (A). On network marketing of libraries. *Library and Information Service.* (7). 2000:69-71
15. Lovelock (C H). Service marketing. Ed.3. (Chinese translation). Xiongwen (L), Li (Z), Trs. Chinese People University Press. 2001.
16. Miao (Q H). To be or not to be: Public libraries and the global knowledge revolution. Papers of 64th IFLA General Conference, http://www.ifla.org/IV/ifla64/082-78e.htm
17. Qin (S W). A trial discussion of strategy of library service and system of service sale promotion. *Journal of Guangzhou University (Social Science Edition).* 2(3). 2003:75 -77
18. Ren (Y F). On the marketing library information service. *Researches in Library Science.* (1). 2003: 81-82,90
19. Shen (L). How to implement internal marketing in library. *Yunnan Library.* (2). 2002:12 -14
20. Tan (S F). Online marketing of library information service. *Journal of Information.* (9). 2003:13-14
21. Tu (X B), Ren (Z Q) and Liu (B). Academic library and new marketing conception. *Library.* (2). 20 03:69-70
22. Wei (W H) and Tang (X J). Knowledge marketing: The important means to improve library users' satisfaction. *Modern Information.* 8. 2003:177-179,181
23. Xiang (Y J). On Cs marketing strategy and library management. *The Library Journal of Henan.* 21(5). 2001:83-84
24. Xiao (Q). On marketing management of digital library. *Information Service (Qing Bao Zi Liao Gong Zuo).* 6. 2002:25-27
25. Xie (C Z). The marketing strategy and fashion of digital library. *Modern Library Information Technology.* 1. 2003:7-9
26. Xie (C Z). The application of e-marketing to digital libraries. *Library and Information Service.* 9. 2002:97-100
27. Yang (L). On the selling tactics of library knowledge services. *Library.* 1. 2003:40-42,46
28. Yin (A L) and Li (S G). On network marketing of digital libraries information service. *Shanxi Library Journal.* 4. 2003:22-25
29. Zhai (H L). Establishment and application of library marketing strategy. *Journal of Information.* 9. 2003:6-7,10
30. Zhang (H M). Experience marketing: New thought of promotion for library service. *Library Journal.* 22(6). 2003:54-56

31. Zhao (M) and Wang (Z). A study on the management of value marketing in the libraries of colleges and universities. *The Theory and Practice of Finance and Economics*. 24(122). 2003:111-114
32. Zhong (W Z). The user's needs and marketing strategies in the university library. *Information Science*. 19(9). 2001:922-924
33. Zhou bo. Developing the added value of information products: A new tendency of information marketing in the library. *Library and Information Service*. 12. 2003:41-44
34. Zhu (Y W). How to extend library service by marketing. *Library Development*. 4.2001:61-63
35. China library association [http://www.csls.org.cn/reading.htm]
36. Activities guidance on "Reading for all people" month [www.booktide.com/news/20031121/200311210025.html]
37. www.chinainfobank.com
38. Current situation of the public libraries' development in China. *China culture daily* 2001-02-21: 2
39. China National Library http://www.nlc.gov.cn/
40. Shenzhen Library http://szlib.szptt.net.cn/
41. Shanghai Library http://library.sh.cn/
42. Anhui Provincial Library http://www.ahlib.com/index.php
43. Hunan Provincial Library http://www.library.hn.cn/
44. Sun Yat-sen Library of Guangdong Province http://www.zslib.com.cn/cn/index.asp

MARKETING OF LIBRARIES AND DOCUMENTATION SERVICES IN FRANCE : A DIFFICULT INTEGRATION?

Florence Muet

Abstract *In France, the integration of methods and techniques of marketing in libraries and documentation services is recent and slow: few professional publications, background presence in vocational training, marginal implementation in ordinary documentary structures illustrate the problem as it exits. Several elements, essentially linked with the culture of professionals of information, explain this situation. Professionals give traditionally more importance to a technical approach of their function. The latter has a tendency of placing on a secondary level, rendered service and the relationship with the user. Marketing is more and more considered in a restricted way, in its commercial dimension. So it is distanced from the concerns of many information professionals. More fundamentally, many professionals are in a culture of public service and have the tendency to reject methods stemming from the competitive sector. Lastly, marketing perceived as a whole of techniques used for attracting public and creating demand, is to be used only in last recourse.*

INTRODUCTION

Setting an assessment of the actual state of marketing of libraries and documentation services in France, on the academic level as well as on the practical level, brings to note the slowness of the integration of the discipline and of its approach in the eyes of the professionals of information. The aim of this contribution is to try an analysis of the reasons of this situation. Three evolutions in the perception of professionals of information of documentation seem necessary: a specific approach of documentary marketing, the integration of the strategic dimension of marketing, the development of adapted tools, in particular through the approach service.

A RECENT AND SLOW INTEGRATION

In France, the integration of marketing in libraries and documentation services is relatively recent. One can date it to around the last 20 years. The strictly French bibliography (which is not entirely quoted here) on documentary marketing is, to this day, relatively poor. One can evaluate it, today, to 3 published works, around 20 articles in specialized reviews and a few reports. The first French written works appear at the end of the 80's and essentially develop themselves in the beginning of the 90's. We are then, in a phase of sensitization and of justification of the use of marketing in the information services. The first two French works which explicitly deal with the subject, are published in an interval of two years. The first , is that of Jean-Michel Salaiin, lecturer-researcher at the ENSSIB (Ecole Nationale Supérieure des Sciences de l' Information et des Bibliothèques), published in 1992, following two articles published in Bulletin des Bibliothèques de France in 1990[1]. It's subject is explicitly to sensitize one to the marketing approach : << to provide to professionals of libraries and documentation ... a first critical approach of marketing>>. The second is that Eric Sutter, consultant at the Bureau Van Dijk, published in 1994[2]; the work is a more practical workbook, more centered on the concerns of the documentation services.

At that time, two reasons seemed to explain this more massive development of thoughts on the subject of marketing, applied to libraries and documentation services :

- The acknowledgement of a need to introduce management methods judged more modern, in the information services. Libraries and especially documentation services, more so than others, have difficultly survived the bad economic conjecture prevailing since the few decades. The rationalization of their management, in particular, by the definition of clearer objectives and the control of activity becomes a must. Besides financial management, (the same period, for example, sees the publication of a work on the costs in documentation), techniques of control of the activity, tools for management of teams and organization of work, etc. Marketing is presented as one of the methods which can contribute to a better management of information services.
- The observation of a weak use of mechanism to access information. This use which should thus be stimulated. It is, in a way, the promotional aspect of techniques of marketing which is then put forward. The work of Eric Sutter, as a matter of fact, follows an order from the French Ministry of research, on the observation of an insufficient use of the on-line documentary database. It is, on one hand, to take into better consideration, the needs of users in the conception of mechanism of information and on the other hand, to attract the public towards these mechanisms, in particular, by a better communication.

One then needs to wait till 2001 to see the publication in France of a new work on marketing, applied to libraries and documentation services, co-written by the author of this contribution and Jean-Michel Salaün [3]. This work is resolutely turned towards a strategic approach of marketing and wants to propose original and adapted tools, at the same time for the marketing diagnosis of a service, as well as, for the definition of strategic devices in the field of public, offer and positioning.

In ten years, we have thus passed from sensitization to the suggestion of methodologies of analysis and of marketing decisions which are more accomplished and especially more suited to the characteristics of the information services. But, at the same time, the weak diffusion of this more recent work is still the witness of a luke warm interest of professionals for the field of marketing.

We also note a weak development of marketing in the field of initial and continuous training of professionals of information. Of course, the theme is present in the syllabus of most of the institutions of training since 10 to 15 years. But, it still occupies a secondary position. Even if it is considered as important, it doesn't form part, in the mind of the designers of the teaching syllabus, of the "heart core of competences" taught to future professionals. For example, in the department of Information – Communication of the IUT (Institute of Technology) of Grenoble, which coaches students for a level of technician in documentation, marketing is integrated in the management of documentary course (training of 26 hours for the specialization "documentation in enterprise"; course of 24 hours for the specialization "library"), of which it represents about 40% of the content. The trainings are globally more developed in the superior levels. Marketing is a discipline of management, particularly aimed for the heads of the documentary structures. INTD (Institut National des Techniques Documentaires), which forms engineers of documentation, offers a module of only ten hours specifically on the subject, beside other courses on different aspects of management and business. Concerning the training of conservators of public libraries, undertaken by ENSSIB, a strategic angle in the course of project's methodology. We also note that in various institutions, the course of marketing method is integrated as a transversal approach in a more strategic angle is given by lecturers of management and not by those from the field of information. In other institutions training documentation-officers, the teaching of marketing is integrated more as a transversal approach in a general course on economy and business administration, fields considered as a must in the "general professional culture" of the students. It is the case, for example, for the Master in Business Management of Information, given by the Institute of Political Studies in Paris. Marketing is approached in an introductory course to the system of the enterprise and to the tools of management, given by lecturers of economy.

Lastly, the same observation of a weak integration of documentary marketing can be made on the field. There certainly doesn't exist a nation-wide survey which can give specific elements on this point. The results of a recent study done by a small panel of professionals (working in specialized libraries or documentation services) are nevertheless revealing [4]: if half of the questioned professionals say that they, more or less, know what is marketing, only 10% indicate knowing the measures and methods of marketing applied to information services and 14% considered that marketing is essential to the functioning of their service. We can also take as an indicator, the slow progress of marketing on the professional field, the low number of training courses and trainee. The theme of marketing is almost never offered in continuous training given to professionals of libraries or documentation. But, we can also note the investment made by ENSSIB in the realization of on-line training on marketing strategy, aimed for heads of libraries and documentation services, (see www.enssib.fr). It is equally important to note that marketing as well as other approaches are largely represented in Euroreferentiel des competences, whose new edition appeared in May 2004 especially under the direction of Adbs (Association des professionals de l' information-documentation, see www.adbs.fr)[5]. Besides sales and communication, marketing is recognized as a specific competence: " to analyses and situate the position of information of one's enterprise in one's culture, one's strategic and competitive environment; to be at the service of this strategy by adjusting the adapted tools."

So, a certain number of documentary structures, be it of public libraries (the municipal library of Port-Dieu in Lyon, has thus recently recruited a marketing and development director) or of documentation services, actively practice documentary marketing. We will note that the experience is more systematic when the information service is found in an explicitly competitive context. It is the case of important actors of the Information industry (l'INIST, Institute National de l' Information Scientifiue et Technique, important French centre of documentation, has since long a marketing management.) or even more bigger organizations which offer services on payment (one could quote, for example, the French Petroleum Institute, which has also developed a marketing and commercial management) But the reality is that, for most of the "ordinary" information services, we stay a classic management structure with at best, a real concern to adapt to the needs of the user and a few communication actions.

HESITATIONS RELATED TO PREJUDICES AND ASSUMPTIONS

To this hour, the observation is more or less mitigated. Little editorial production, no research work undertaken which would specifically deal with themes related to documentary marketing, a poor initiative in the trainings of librarians and archivists, and a still marginal development on the field. Several factors can bring to explain this relative indifference to documentary marketing, even this reluctance, that we find not only in France, but also, it seems, in other countries found in the South of Europe. These factors are to be put into relation with a strong professional culture, which leads to a number of prejudices and the application of marketing to the documentary function.

A first explanatory element holds most certainly to a very <<technician>> culture. This is largely spread among the French information professionals, be they be librarians or information specialists. The essence of the profession is implicitly, defined around the management of documentary resources (yesterday, the book's circuit, today, the management of electronic systems of contents). The relation with the user, services to be offered to him, are of course important. In all the cases, they are at least stipulated as thus in speeches, but they are only situated around the core of this profession and are not always experienced as vital in the activity. To be brief, we still have in the French professional milieu of documentation, more of the culture of document than that of the user. We could still argue to the action and engagement of some important documentary structures of national scope in the research of efficient modalities of the integration of the user in the documentary system (we, for e.g., think about the whole of works undertaken, particularly, in the sociology of reading, by the Bibliothique Publique d'Information, Paris). But the investment of the professionals and of their structures, have always been placed more on the level of techniques and technologies of treatment and management of information (and this investment renews itself today with the internet and numerisation technologies) than on the modes of the management of the relation with the public and on the service rendered to the user, which are of the marketing domain. Things, are of course, changing, but slowly. Some officials of public libraries or of internal documentary structures are today seeking to recenter their activities on the rendered service, the relationship with the users', through users oriented approaches, like marketing or quality. But, beyond operational evolutions in the activity or the organization, it really is about approaches of change aiming to develop the postures and the teams' culture.

A second element holds to the hesitation of many professionals towards marketing, because of an exacerbated vision of this discipline. This hesitation is sometime even expressed with vehemence, as some professionals identify themselves with an opposite world to that perceived through marketing; in such a way that they can feel it, undergo it as consumers. Marketing is, in fact very much associated with a highly commercial aspect. But, public libraries and many documentation services, internal to organizations or intervening in the non-trade sector (research, teaching, associative sector...) have nothing "to sell". As a result, many of them don't feel concerned by the techniques used to increase market shares and thus guarantee the profiles of the enterprise or, in all cases, that they perceive as only dedicated to this type of objectives. In a way, they decode the methods of marketing as tools of profitability and not as possible means to better the performance and efficiency of their structures.

More deeply, professionals are still highly in a culture of information-knowledge, as a collective property, whose access should not be prevented. As a result, there is, among some professionals, a real concern for the user and a preoccupation to felicitate the access to information. But this commitment is lived in logic of individual professional ethics. This is deeply rooted in public libraries but is also found in many documentation services. In this context, and on it's institutional side, marketing can easily be seen as an <<ideology>>, related to the consumer society, and not like a technique contributing to the good management of information services. There is for e.g., some professionals who are strongly reticent to segment and target some user profiles, which would come to favor these categories of user at the cost of others. This positioning is particularly strong in public services, to which are affiliated many documentary structures (the network of public reading, university libraries, but also specialized libraries and documentation services of teaching organizations and public research).

The notion of public services is still understood as the fact of providing the same service to each and everyone; the modernization of public services around the quest of individual satisfaction, so important with services or levels of specified services is not yet accomplished, far from it.

Globally, there is a hesitation from professionals of public sector, or working in structures targeting a large public, even the general public, towards any approach of management coming from the private sector. It can be noted that this situation is bound to change: the evaluation and management techniques are more and more investing in the public sectors. The situation is perhaps slightly more evolved in documentation services of the private or competitive sector. On a hand, these documentation services are integrated in a culture and more managerial operating modes. On the other part, this context generates a high pressure in term of results, of <<the return on the investment>>, from management. The officials of documentation services are in fact implied in an approach, which favors a targeting of actions, the satisfaction of needs, and thoughts about the contribution of the enterprise, etc…

A last characteristic trait of the French information documentation milieu (which is perhaps, as a matter of fact not specific to our country) is a strong deficit of image and notoriety of the functions and professions. This is especially true for the archivists. Librarians are perhaps more integrated: the municipal library is usually implemented in the center of the town, and a university necessary has a university library for the archivists, the term of <<discontent>> about the profession comes in a frequent regularity in speeches and this, since quite long. And added to this, the threats of eviction of professionals by more and more efficient information and communication technologies (documentary data-processing and then today numerisation and internet technologies).

In this context, many professionals , librarians and archivists, are tempted to consider marketing as a tool for extreme situations, or to be used in last rescourse.When everything goes wrong (fall of the public, non-acknowledged information service, distant and even supervision, etc…)- the marketing of the service is done. We justify it's existence, we take maximum initiatives regarding users, we promote the services, etc. But, when everything goes well, it is not really interesting. Many professionals can hence think that marketing should essentially be used to facilitate the justification of the service, and also to attract a public, which doesn't spontaneously sollicitate the documentary structure. In brief, marketing could permit to create demand.

Are there some issues for a development of documentary marketing in France?

To conclude this quick state of things of the French documentary marketing, some research ideas can be evoked. Yet, they evoke a renewal of the pedagogy aimed to actual and to-be information professionals, as far as the methods of management and especially marketing are concerned. They would also certainly necessitate a more strong investment in the matter of research.

A SPECIFIC APPROACH OF LIBRARY AND DOCUMENTATION SERVICES MARKETING

A too direct transposition of the methods and techniques of marketing, as they are applied to enterprises, libraries and documentation services, seem obviously harmful. And this direct transposition certainly explains the actual hesitations. On the one hand, like already indicated, it sends the professionals of information to a world of reference which is not globally theirs. On the other hand, more fundamentally, it could lead to a misinterpretation, and this has been well understood by the information professionals: a library or a documentation service doesn't completely function like an enterprise. Contrary to an enterprise, which is financed by it's market, the whole majority of information services is financed by the related structure of each service (a local community for a municipal library; university for the university library; the enterprise, the center of research or even the association for an internal documentation service). So, one should hold a specific pedagogy of marketing applied to our activities, one that puts emphasis on the satisfaction of public needs, on the adaptation to their characteristics, as well as on the respect and implementation of missions entrusted to the documentary structure of the related organism. This necessary taking into account of the public and of the institution related to the information service, in a logic documentary marketing, helps to clear uncertainties. It can, for e.g., allow public reading libraries to conciliate the specific and individual requirements of the users, the needs of the social body, translated in terms of cultural development, and the social role of libraries among others. It can allow an internal documentation service, an enterprise to contribute to the stakes of functioning and the development of the enterprise without forgetting the specific needs of such and such category of users.

Integrate the strategic dimension of marketing

On the training of the professionals of information, generally it's the operational aspect of marketing, which is forwarded. Particularly, it's the marketing conception of products and services proposed by the documentary structures, and of course, communication. Besides, one notes the development in France, of trainings or workshops on the theme of marketing communication on the last past years. In a way, documentary marketing is presented as a backing tool intervening to accompany the activities of the information service. But, at the same time, we note the deficit in decision-making tools for the professionals who, more and more, must offer choices of orientation, established priorities, manage projects, implement action plans, etc… Putting forward the strategic dimensions of marketing, as a method of decision-making, because it can help in professionals in future, is perhaps more likely to favor a user-oriented culture among the professionals of information.

Develop tools and methods which are really adapted to information services

The first French works on documentary marketing have largely been inspired by the mass marketing approaches, which have dominated for a long time (today we have a business-to- consumer marketing). The first book of Jean-Michel Salaün, in 1992, proposed for example, a long development on the adaptation of the marketing-mix model to the "production" of information services. The work published in 1994 by Eric Sutter as well as an author one published in 1997, more about public libraries, used the same logic [6]. This approach is widely used across the Atlantic establishing, what seen from France, one could call the "Anglo-Saxon model" of documentary marketing. But one can quickly feel the interest, even the necessity, to question about the model of reference, in other words, of the type of marketing approach with which one feels closer and from which one will borrow tools and methods. France has been one of the countries to develop the approach service, with repercussions in terms of service marketing in particular, since the founder work of two lecturers and researchers of the University of Aix-Marseille : Pierre Eiglier and Eric Langeard[7]. The service approach has also seen prolongations in the field close to the quality approach, with the notion of quality of service. New offers can be found for an another apprehension of marketing of libraries and documentation services.

CONCLUSION

We can consider that the situation is progressive and that the initiatives of sensitization are showing their results on the integration of marketing in the information services, be it about public libraries or documentation services or internal documentation services of an organization. Yet, it seems to us that an important work of modeling still has to be done so as to give to the officials of these information services, scales of analysis or decision making moulds, which take into consideration the distinctive features of their context and allow them to at last find interest in implementing a specifically documentary marketing. We, in particular, think about development, which are still to be done on the structuration of the proposal of documentary services or even on the strategic choices of the positioning of the information services. These development, evidently, have to take into consideration the changes, in progress, generated by the technologies of information and communication on the status of the document, information, mass production and diffusion of knowledge, etc.

REFERENCES

1. Salaün (JM). Marketing desbibliothèques et des centres de documentation. Paris : Cercle de la Librairie. 1992 : 133.
2. Sutter (E). Le marketing des services d'information: Pour un usage de l'information documentarie. Paris: ESF. 1994: 207.
3. Muet(F) and Salaün(JM). Stategie marketing des services d'information, bibliothèques et centres de documentation. Paris: Cercle de la Librairie. 2001: 221.
4. Torres (I). Representation et perception du marketing par les professionels de l'information et de la documentation. *Documentaliste-Sciences de l'information*.41 (1). 2004: 26-33.
5. European Council of Information Association. Euro referential I&D Volume 1. Competences et aptitudes des professionels. Europeans de l'information-documentation. Paris: Abds. 2004: 107.
6. Gioppiconi(T). Ajuster l'offre.Les outils du marketing au service des objectifs des bibliothèques publiques et de la qualitè de leurs services. Foundation Bertelsman. 1997: 71 .
7. Eiglier (P) and Langeard (E). Servuction. Le marketing des services. Paris: Ediscience, neediction. 2000: 222

MARKETING LIBRARY SERVICES IN AFRICA

Julita Nawe

Abstract *The objectives of this study were to find out if librarians/ information officers in Africa market their services, to explore avenues used by libraries in Africa for marketing their services, and to find out if marketing activities were systematized. Marketing of services is discussed in the traditional and the emerging electronic information environment with special reference to the experiences of Tanzania and the University of Dar es Salaam Library in particular. Data was gathered through informal discussions with some librarians while attending the Standing Conference of Eastern, Central and Southern African Library and Information Associations (SCECSAL) conference held in July 2004, responses from questionnaires circulated to various librarians and the inferences made from information gathered from various library websites. The study noted that marketing of library services in Africa still leans more to publicity than to the operational marketing term. It recommends librarians to be more proactive and systematic in marketing library services in order to consistently win the hearts of their clients in totality.*

INTRODUCTION

It was not until 1970s when libraries and information centers started grappling seriously with marketing of their services, gradually moving from predominance of promotion to other processes of marketing. As observed by Koontz [1], application of systematic marketing activities is a phenomenon of the past 20 years. In the developing countries, and Africa in particular, it is yet to take roots widely because of a number of factors, including infrastructural and financial constraints to support even the basic tools such as assessment of user needs, production of promotion materials, as well as the necessary marketing skills. However, marketing of library services raises a number of issues. Information economy and new developments in information and communication technologies have impacted libraries and library operations tremendously and have forced libraries to revisit their missions and strategies for the accomplishment of their missions, with marketing of services being one of the key areas raising a number of issues from what, how, where and who should be involved. This study addressed some of these issues.

STATEMENT OF THE PROBLEM

Marketing of library services raises a number of issues, bearing in mind new developments in information and communication technologies and the mixed views regarding charging fee for access to information, a commodity considered as one of the basic human right [2] the newness of the concept of marketing in the profession. As observed by Koontz [3], marketing was first introduced to the library field in the late '70s" and was surrounded by "much confusion between marketing and publicity". Marketing for library raises so many questions: what are libraries doing? - are they marketing or publicizing their services? Is there a difference between the two? If so, what is the difference between them? Is/are there appropriate marketing strategy/strategies? What should it/they cover? If so who should be responsible for setting such strategies? What avenues are used for marketing library services? What indicators would be used to assess the quality of marketing and products marketed? Why did libraries start marketing/publicizing their services as late as late 1970s?

OBJECTIVES OF THE STUDY

The main objectives of this study were:

- To find out if librarians/information officers in Africa market their services,
- To explore avenues used by libraries in Africa for marketing their services, and
- To find out if marketing activities were systematized.

Libraries, over the years, have concentrated on the promotion aspect of the marketing process. Traditionally, marketing in library circles paid more attention on publicity in the form of current awareness and selective dissemination of information for the purpose of reaching specific customers. The main purpose was to provide the clientele with the information they needed. The earlier tools used for publicity were accession lists, brochures, leaflets, circulars, display of book jackets on notice boards and book display racks for new arrivals.

According to Leisner [4] marketing is a necessary component of any organization, be it public or private, when drawing its business plan for three basic reasons:

- Each institution wishes to achieve high levels of customer satisfaction
- Each wants to enhance the perceived value of their services
- Both want to insure the survival of their respective institutions

Thus, libraries like other organizations need to market their services in order to create a link between them and their clients. This bond is necessary for mutual benefit. Libraries need support of their clients in order to survive. This need is more apparent now than ever before because libraries are no longer the only source of information.

However, marketing in its strict sense in library circles started very late, as late as 1970s. Marketing in libraries became necessary because of the economic climate and new developments in information and communication technologies. Resources can now be accessed from various places. The availability of resources on the web has a strong influence on the way the information is accessed by various users. Networks once used by libraries for exchanging information needed by their clients are being marginalized by the presence of information in the form of international databases that can be accessed by individuals directly, thus rendering librarian's presence unnecessary in the process of connecting an individual to the source of information. This means that libraries have to have something that will make people opt for libraries rather than other places by not only providing something that is missing from other sources but also by marketing the value added services that libraries provide and can provide. For instance, while marketing of tangible goods can effectively be done through good advertisements, the quality of marketing is heavily dependent on personal experiences passed on to actual and potential clients. The willingness of clients to support libraries depends on registered customer satisfaction derived from human touch of experienced and knowledgeable staff keen in sustaining the interests of clients through provision of value added services based on continuous clients' needs assessment.

In current economic climate, where costs are increasing tremendously and profits are dwindling significantly, organizations are increasingly concerned with every bit of expenditure. Cutbacks in funding generally, and for libraries in particular (as heavy investors of invisible products), accompanied by inflation and staff freezes on one hand and raised user expectations on the other have made libraries' working environment very volatile.

In this age of information economy competition in the marketplace is increasing the demand for information. One would expect an increase in demand for information to have a positive impact on library budgets. To the contrary the budgets for libraries and information centers are increasingly decreasing. As a result libraries are compelled to justify their survival/existence. In response to these developments libraries started adopting marketing in its strictest sense in the 1970s. The profession is increasingly systematizing marketing. According to Koontz, "over the past 20 years the field has focused on understanding and applying systematic marketing activities that embody four main steps" [5] namely:

- Identifying customer wants and needs,
- Grouping customers with similar wants and needs,
- Developing a product with the right price, distribution place, and promotional message for those customer groups, and
- Evaluating the marketing program.

However, because of historical development and economic disparities it might take longer for most of the libraries in Africa to catch up with various marketing strategies due to infrastructural and other constraints[6]. For instance, some libraries still do not have access to the Internet while websites are increasingly used for marketing. Even for those libraries with websites it takes a long time to access some of them because of the bandwidth problems. In addition, the necessary skills are also lacking.

Libraries in Africa had the same trend of laxity. Development of libraries in Africa is an extension of services introduced as part of the colonization process during the colonial period and thereafter as part of basic services in the post independence era. As observed by Kiondo "the history of library development in most African countries can be divided into three distinct phases. Phase one was characterized by rapid development with assistance from donors in the 1960s and 1970s, while the second one was characterized by "a sharp decline in investment services in the 1980s" and the third one by "revival in the 1990s characterized by modern innovative information technology (IT) projects, new approaches in management and planning, and a new organizational dispensation" [7] which included marketing of services and competencies albeit at a limited degree in order to cope with current developments requiring organizations to fight for their survival in these competitive environments characterized by rising costs and dwindling profits.

MARKETING CYCLE

Successful marketing cycle needs a careful and strategic participative planning process involving all interested parties. According to Weber [8] the cycle revolves around 9 distinct stages:

- Formulating a mission;
- Reviewing situational analysis;
- Formulating marketing objectives;
- Undertaking market research;
- Modifying marketing objectives;
- Formulating marketing strategies;
- Implementing marketing strategies;
- Monitoring success; and
- Reviewing strategies.

In a nutshell the process involves continuous clients' needs assessment, understanding of the working environment and how it impacts clients and services offered in order to remain on a track leading to the vision.

METHODOLOGY

This study used a case study approach because of three reasons: Because of the historical developments of libraries in Africa, the findings of this study can be fairly generalized to Africa South of the Sahara except South Africa. They are all grappling with challenges posed by globalization to avoid exclusion and exploit opportunities offered by developments in information and communication technologies, thus a case study would be fairly representative. Secondly, a combination of survey (which is relatively cheap to conduct) and an opportunity of interviewing librarians from various libraries at the SCECSAL conference helped to enrich and validate the quality of the data.

Primary data were collected through interviews, focus group discussions, involving information rich cases, and personal observations. A quick survey through questionnaires distributed to forty professionals was made in order to crosscheck information gathered through interviews conducted with some of the SCECSAL conference participants and information obtained through focus group discussion and personal experience and observation. Thirty five responded to the questionnaires.

Various secondary sources, including library websites, were consulted for secondary data. Several websites were visited, with the search beginning with websites of eight universities from the Eastern, Central and Southern African region involved in a study on income generation, edited by Diana Rosenberg [9]. It was assumed that these libraries would be more aggressive than others because of their initial involvement in a study involving funding, an item that is of interest in marketing.

FINDINGS

Introduction

It was generally noted that libraries lacked concrete dynamic marketing strategies and plans commensurate with the current marketing practices and was dominated by the promotion mix aspect of the marketing processes. Multiple avenues were used. These included: brochures, newsletters, publications, posters, leaflets accession lists, displays, and websites for those libraries which had the relevant facilities. Other avenues used were meetings, workshops/conferences, training and exhibitions at various occasions, outreach services in the form of mobile libraries, reading tents, reading competitions, writing essays, and library day/week.

Publicity/marketing avenues used

The most popular avenue used was library notice boards (100%), followed by circulars and current awareness services (91.2%) and brochures (85.7%). The least used avenues were mass media (2.7%) and others (14.3%), which included workshops, conferences and training. For details see the table below.

Avenues used for publicity/marketing of services

Item	Frequency of use	Percentage
Brochures	30	85.7
Circulars	32	91.4
Library notice boards	35	100.0
Other notice boards	20	57.2
Mass media	1	2.9
Websites	7	20.0
Exhibitions	23	65.7
Newsletters	3	8.6
Current awareness services	32	91.4
Other	5	14.3

N=35

Brochures and websites

Brochures are widely used to briefly highlight basic information on the library and conditions for access to services provided, and at times names of key personnel and contact information. Websites provided more information than the brochures. Information provided include: library rules and regulations, materials available and conditions of use, organization of the library/collection, facilities and collections, link to the open public access catalogue (OPAC) and various other links of interest to respective institutions and staff lists, including contact information.

The website search began with four of the eight university libraries from the Eastern, Central and Southern African region involved in a study on income generation, edited by Diana Rosenberg [9]. It was assumed that these libraries would be more aggressive than others because of their initial involvement in a study involving funding, an item that is of interest in marketing. However, involvement in that study did not seem to have observable impacts on strategies of marketing of services. Various other websites visited displayed similar features – both had strong and weak features depending on available facilities, including ease and speed of accessibility.

Exhibitions

Public libraries exhibitions are either part of the library day function or other functions where libraries are invited to participate. University libraries participate in university wide exhibitions on site or other venues.

A library staff welcoming Hon. Dr Juma Ngasongwa, Minister, Trade & Industry, United Republic of Tanzania, to the University of Dar es Salaam Library pavilion, at the 28th Dar es Salaam International Trade Fair, July 2004.

Marketing/publicity avenues considered as most effective

Focus group discussion and interviews revealed that the effectiveness of an avenue is strongly influenced by an environment and the kind of information/ product publicized and method used for publicity. For instance, in a more sophisticated environment websites or information circulated electronically would be an appropriate method, while in less sophisticated environments more traditional avenues would work better. Each case may be accompanied by either sensitization or training. For example Manda [10] in his study on the impact and usage of electronic resources in academic and research institutions in Tanzania noted that "training in the use of electronic resources is an important factor in the eventual use of electronic resources." Other factors such as skills of staff, resources etc also influence the choice of appropriate means.

Strategic plans

All the nine respondents, except one (from a special library) who responded to this question had strategic plans. Marketing of library services is not included in the strategic plans of two of these and is vaguely included in one of these. Three cases had budgets for marketing and one used some of the funds allocated for stationery for production of marketing materials.

Strategies for marketing services

Strategies used for marketing libraries seem to be more informal than formal. Marketing also seems to be confused with publicity and at times is unconsciously carried out. For instance, while at the SCECSAL conference I asked a colleague to find out what else is done at the relevant institution, and what is the general practice in the country. The response I got indicates that marketing is not formalized and is being adopted as part of coping strategies as a result of financial constraints and demand for accountability.

> *"... The week after we came back I put the question to librarians in a meeting we had. They promised to give me some feedback but to date none has responded. The reason really is that none of us has any such programme. University libraries however take part in university exhibitions. The problem we are facing due to inadequate funding which in some is not even available is making do some thinking and I have heard us now beginning to talk about marketing and advocacy. ..."*

Satisfaction with how services offered are publicized/marketed

None of the respondents except two (from a research library and the other from a university library) was satisfied with the way marketing was done. When asked what could be done and by who, one respondent said:

> *"I would like to see more collaboration between the library staff and its users in areas of marketing. There is need more for sensitization rather than relying on websites or e-mails which are never fully utilized. There is a need to move out of the library to meet the users out there so that your services are made known. It should be a continuous relationship."*

While another one said he "would like senior library staff to be more aggressive in producing brochures and website announcements of services."

Most (85.7%) respondents had similar sentiments. Other suggestions included training of library staff in library services marketing strategies and techniques, and library staff spearheading the initiative.

Skills in marketing

Out of the 35 respondents only two respondents had marketing skills. One had attended a short course while the other one was involved in teaching a marketing course.

Recommendations

Recommended strategies for improving marketing of services at individual library levels

- Imparting skills and techniques to the staff
- Marketing to be community based where visits are made to the clients

instead of waiting for them to come to the library
- Being more aggressive with the current strategies
- Keep on marketing library services and products
- Setting aside budget for marketing library services (including training in marketing)
- Including promotional materials on websites
- Recruiting a specific person for marketing library services

Recommended strategies for improving marketing of services offered by libraries in Africa

- Putting marketing as a priority issue
- Setting standards for marketing
- Always following a marketing plan and marketing strategies
- Imparting skills and techniques to the staff
- Marketing to be community based (market segmentation) where visits are made to the clients instead of waiting for them to come to the library
- Being more aggressive with the current strategies
- Posting on websites strategies used for marketing for the purposes of sharing information
- Creating a listserv of staff dealing with marketing for the purpose of sharing information
- Library schools to strengthen modules on marketing in line with current demands
- Library Associations to look into the modalities of co-organising training programmes on marketing

CONCLUSIONS AND RECOMMENDATIONS

The findings of the study indicated that publicity/marketing of library services in Africa leaves a lot to be desired. Although various avenues are used for the purpose, marketing activities generally are not systematized and are heavily dependent on traditional tools. Reasons could be sought in lack of skills for drawing appropriate strategies and lack of funds. Thus, in order to survive the library and information sectors have to market their products systematically and aggressively through acquisition of appropriate skills and making it an integral part of their operations. This is necessary for at least justifying their existence and at most proving their worth like any other department of any organization, be it a service or profit making organization. They have to institute strategies for planning programs, making money/creating value, and increasing business like any other unit of an organization.

REFERENCES

1. Koontz (C M). First IFLA/3M International Marketing Award , presented in Glassgow, Scotland in August, 2002 http://www.infotoday.com/mls/sep03/koontz.shtml (accessed 10.8.04).
2. Lwoga (E T) and Chilimo (W L). Resource mobilization in public university libraries: A Paper Presented at the East African University Public Librarians Conference. Bagamoyo, Tanzania, 17-19th October, 2002.
3. Ibid,1.
4. Leisner (T). Should libraries engage in marketing? http://www.ifla.org/IV/ifla61/61-leit.htm (Accessed 30.7.2004).
5. Ibid,1.
6. Nawe (J). Management and marketing of information services in Africa. *Information Development*. 9 (1/2). 1993: 52-57.
7. Kiondo (E). Resource mobilization for library and information services development in Africa. *African J. Lib. Arch. & Inf. Sc.* 12 (1). 2002: 15-26.
8. Webber (S). The Marketing Cycle. http://dis.shef.ac.uk/sheila/marketing/cycle.htm(accessed 25.8.04)
9. Rosenberg (D), Ed. Income generation: experiences from university libraries in Eastern, Central and Southern Africa, Bristol: The International Network for Availability of Scientific Publications. 2001.
10. Manda (P A). The impact and usage of electronic resources in academic and research institutions in Tanzania. Research Report Submitted to the International Network for Availability of Scientific Publications, August 2004.

MARKETING LIBRARY AND INFORMATION SERVICES IN KENYA

Tirong Arap Tanui

Abstract *Marketing library and information services (LIS), which include university, public, college, school, special and government libraries in Kenya is at initial stage of development and is more prevalent in those organisations which are efficiently and professionally managed. The qualitative research done revealed that all LIS bears similar marketing activities, awareness creation, ways of informing and communicating with users, dealing with marketing strategies and handling marketing limitations. Adaptation and use of marketing for LIS in Kenya is therefore dependent on extent and level of development of individual LIS; level of professional education and training of staff, especially those is leadership position; competition among LIS; and changing and increasing user demands.*

INTRODUCTION

LIS in Kenya are at initial stage of implementing and developing marketing as an effective strategy for quality information service provision and delivery.

A qualitative research was conducted in three public and two private universities, at least one of each public, college and school and three special libraries on extent of use of marketing in service provision. The research established that marketing is more prevalent in university and special libraries than in the public, college and school libraries. Library managers in general perceive marketing as creating awareness in users on LIS information materials stocked and not the services being provided. Although marketing is perceived as an important strategy for effective service provision and delivery, the LIS have not initiated any formal practical activities to implement the notional ideas held about marketing.

The literature reviewed highlights the development of marketing concept and its implication to LIS service provision in general and with specific reference to Kenya. The general literature on marketing practices in LIS in developing countries, Kenya included, are reviewed. The best practices identified are relationship marketing, internal marketing, interactive marketing, technological marketing, emotional marketing and experiential marketing, so as to give a comparative view of existing new marketing paradigms in the developed world and Kenya.

Different LIS in Kenya have more commonalties than differences, with regard to marketing awareness, communication, strategies and limitations. Most LIS staff in Kenya understands marketing as synonymous with advertising. However, special libraries go beyond advertising and implement in limited capacity other aspects of marketing such as promotion, distribution and public relations. Generally, staff appreciates the importance and role of marketing LIS in Kenya but the identified marketing limitations have yet to be overcome so as to permit full implementation of marketing. However, marketing LIS in Kenya is rapidly developing owing to LIS managers' appreciation of the role of marketing in information service provision and delivery.

Qualitative research methodology was used to conduct the research and grounded theory procedure was used to collect and analyse the data[1-3]. Triangulation data methods of interview, observation and document analysis were employed for data collection. A structured interview schedule was used to collect the qualitative interview data. Field notes were taken on observation of ongoing activities at the time of library visits. Purposive sampling was used to sample study population of libraries selected, users and staff interviewed.

DEVELOPMENT OF LIS IN KENYA

There are different types of LIS in Kenya ranging from university, public, college, school, special and government. They all are at different stages of development - some are still operating within traditional LIS set up in terms of types of information resources stocked such as print materials and manual routine operations, others including university and special LIS are as good as any other in developed countries, being fully computerised and have integrated multimedia resources. With an exception of the few university and special libraries, which are modernised, the rest remain traditional.

Access to financial resources and viable policies are the two key dimensions, which dictate and determine LIS development agenda. Most public funded LIS operate with limited funding and face lengthy bureaucratic procedures without adequate capacity to establish, develop and sustain quality information systems and services. Most special libraries comparatively have sustainable annual budget for use. However, owing to rapid user awareness, change of government policy and professional advocacy on the importance and role of information for national development, most sponsors of LIS in Kenya have now accepted a gradual paradigm shift towards maintenance and sustainability of effective and efficient information services.

The level of LIS management in the parent organisation determines the capacity on whether or not to adopt modern management trends such as use of marketing. The higher the level of management in terms of availability of professional and technical skills among the staff especially the leadership, the higher the chances of adoption of marketing concept and strategy. In this respect some university and special libraries are among those that have expert professional staff with capacity to implement aspects of marketing. A LIS, which has adopted marketing fully, is rare to find in Kenya. Given the rapid utilisation of ICT in all sectors of social and economic development in Kenya, LIS are, however, among the leading service organisations to try and change their approach and adopt viable modern systems of information management including marketing.

LITERATURE REVIEW

More recently, theoretical studies on marketing libraries in Africa emerged in the professional literature, which present local experiences and justifications for the need to use marketing in managing libraries[4-7], also emphasise identification and meeting the users' information needs rather than the library's needs in the process of marketing library services. More recently, Martey[8] discusses the marketing principles that are amenable for managing an academic library, citing the Ghanaian experience stating the reasons why there is need for Ghanaian libraries to embrace marketing.

The literature reviewed reveals that libraries in developing countries do not develop their own library marketing views or concepts. They share what is published in the marketing literature of the developed world. There is little comparison on the extent to which marketing has been practised in Kenya[9] with those of the developed countries. For example, because of the different social, economic and political environmental factors that influence library management, it suffices to say that both extremes of extent of marketing in libraries exist in all countries.

MARKETING LIS IN KENYA

Marketing Definitions

Marketing definitions vary in all the LIS whereby it is perceived, defined and expressed differently. There is therefore no common definition and standard way of perceiving marketing. Most definitions given, define marketing in the light of one of its aspects, especially advertising, which is taken to be marketing per se. However, all LIS bear almost similar marketing activities, awareness creation, ways of informing and communicating with users, marketing strategies and marketing limitations.

Research and Evaluation

In the academic arena, several qualitative research theses and dissertations on marketing LIS have been published. These include investigating customer satisfaction among part-time students of Heriot-Watt University [10]; studying the marketing of public libraries for a profit[11]; a comparative study of marketing management of British and German university libraries [12].

Core Marketing Categories of LIS in Kenya

UNIVERSITY LIBRARIES

Service Marketing Awareness	Marketing Communication	Marketing Strategies	Marketing Limitations
Users not aware of all services	Through brochures, leaflets, handbooks and pamphlets	No formal marketing strategies	Inadequate collection management policy
Users seek help from library staff only when in difficulty	Advertising, sales promotion, personal selling and product publicity	Users want reference, archive & technical services to be marketed	Staff incompetence
Library staff unhelpful	Signage, noticeboards, feedback, procedures & rules and regulations	Users want value added services	Inadequate infrastructure
Awareness done through memos, and leaflets			Lack of financial

SPECIAL LIBRARIES

Advertising	Printed notices and brochures	Group talks to visitors and potential users	Staff shortage
	Electronic mail		Being bogged down with routine work
	Displays of new materials		
	Spoken word		

GOVERNMENT LIBRARIES

Brochures	Circulars on notice boards	Providing a good service	"Captive" users
Spoken word	Accessions list		Lack of local area network
	Spoken word		Lack of competitiveness

COLLEGE LIBRARIES

Orientation	Memos Spoken word	Orientation for new users	Lack of trained staff Lack of adequate funds

PUBLIC LIBRARIES

Service Marketing Awareness	Marketing Communication	Marketing Strategies	Marketing Limitations
National Book Week event	Memos	Brochures	Lack of adequate space
Exhibitions Children	Letters	Questionnaires for customer service feedback	
Reading Tent event	Spoken word		
Media	Email		
Website	Signage		
Brochures			

SCHOOL LIBRARIES

Display of new books	Notices	Stocking relevant books	Users ignorance of the importance of library
	Spoken word		Lack of adequate funds
			Lack of adequate space

These studies in general aim at discovering relevant management techniques for providing efficient library services, in addition to identifying other significant areas for further research in the use of marketing for managing libraries.

The cited literature points to emergence of several scenarios regarding the extent of use of marketing in LIS. Firstly, that library managers are convinced and see the need to use marketing in libraries, and gradually developing relevant marketing concepts for today's and future libraries. Secondly, there is relevance also in the use of marketing for LIS in Kenya regardless of stage of development of the LIS. And thirdly, there is a growing number of empirical qualitative researches being done on use of marketing in LIS, which is an indication of increasing interest in the topic relevance among the library and information science professionals and scholars.

So far, there are few academic researches done on extent of marketing LIS in Kenya. Apart from the ongoing academic study by the author[13] on use of marketing for management of university libraries in Kenya and that of Tuitoek [14], there are no other known advanced researches being done specifically on marketing LIS in Kenya. However, there have been several individual journal articles, which have been written on the topic including those by Tanui [15] and Kavulya [16]. Marketing is yet to emerge as a priority academic and research phenomena among LIS professionals in Kenya.

Best Practices

The best practises identified are relationship marketing [17-18], internal marketing [19], interactive marketing [20], technologicalship marketing [21-23], emotional marketing [24-25] and experiential marketing [26-27]. Although LIS managers in Kenya perform these best practices to some limited extent, they hardly recognise and identify them as such. It is only a professional marketer who can identify these activities in their normal context. Again, it is the university and special libraries that tend to implement these best practices in marketing.

CONCLUSION

Marketing LIS in Kenya is at its initial stage of development as compared to those of developed countries. LIS directors including university librarians and heads of public, government, special, college and school libraries are responsible for initiating marketing LIS in their individual organisations. Those LIS, which have implemented at least an aspect of marketing, are those managed by professionals with stronger belief in marketing as a viable service provision and delivery strategy.

LIS managers do not perceive marketing in the broader sense as including advertising, promotion, public relations, selling and distribution but think of it as advertising. Marketing as a philosophy and concept therefore is yet to be understood properly. The term 'marketing' has therefore been used loosely in this research paper as perceived by interview respondents, and not in its strictest sense of the word. Marketing awareness, communication, strategy and limitations were identified as core marketing categories especially in university libraries. Other types of popular methods used to market LIS are displays, exhibitions, advertising, direct marketing, publications, talks, open days and social parties.

REFERENCES

1. Silverman (D). Doing qualitative research: A practical handbook. London: Sage Publications. 2000.
2. Patton (M Q). Qualitative research and evaluation methods. Ed.3. London: Sage. 2002.
3. Strauss (A) and Juliet (C). Basics of qualitative research: Techniques and procedures for developing grounded theory. Ed.2. Thousand Oaks: Sage Publications. 1998.
4. Kavulya (J M). Marketing of library services: A case study of selected university libraries in Kenya. *Library Management.* 25(3). 2004: 118-126.
5. Tanui (T) and Andrew (S K). Why marketing? The experience of Moi University Library, Kenya. *Library Management.* 14(4). 1993: 43-47.

6. Ojiambo (J B). Application of marketing principles and techniques to libraries and information centres. *Library Review.* 43(2). 1994: 46-51.
7. Otike (J). Marketing an information service in a research organization with reference to developing countries. *Information Management Report* .1994: 13-15.
8. Martey (A K). Marketing products and services of academic Libraries in Ghana. *Libri* 50(4). 2000: 261-268.
9. Ibid,4
10. McDonald (G A). Applying the marketing concept to university libraries: An investigation of customer satisfaction among part-time students of Heriot-Watt University. MBA thesis. Heriot-Watt University. 1991.
11 Jones-Evans (A). The marketing of public library services for a profit. PhD thesis. University of Sheffield. 1995.
12. Cockrill (A). A comparative analysis of marketing management in British and German University Libraries. PhD thesis. University of Wales Aberystwyth. 1996.
13. Tanui (T). Use of marketing for managing university library services in Kenya. 2003 (On-going Ph. D. research, at University of Wales, Aberystwyth
14. Tuitoek (R M). Developing marketing strategies for the school of environmental studies documentation centre. M. phil. study. Moi University, 1999.
15. Ibid, 13
16. Ibid, 4
17. Parvatiyar (A) and Seth (J N). The domain and conceptual foundations of relationship marketing. *In,* Seth (J N) and Parvatiyar A), Eds. Handbook of relationship marketing. Thousand Oaks: Sage Publications. 2000. 3-38.
18. Singh (R). Developing relationship marketing with Customers: A Scandinavian perspective. *Library Management* 24 (1/2). 2003: 34-43.
19. Palmer (A) . Principles of services marketing. Ed.3. London: McGraw-Hill. 2001.
20. Gronroos (C). Service management and marketing. Ed.2. Chichester: Wiley. 2000.
21. Sowards (S W).Libraries and imagination at the dawn of the world wide web." *Libri* 30. 2000: 137-156.
22. Zineldin (M). Beyond relationship marketing: Technologicalship marketing. *Marketing Intelligence & Planning* 18 (1). 2000: 9-23.
23. Stern (J). World wide web marketing: Integrating the web into your marketing strategy. Ed.2. New York: John Wiley. 1999.
24. Feig (B). Marketing straight to the heart. New York: American Management Association. 1997.

25. Williams (T). Emotional response marketing : The key to producing results! *BankersOnline.* Online. Available: http:// www.bankersonline.com/marketing/produce.html. 6 Nov.2003.

26. Schmit (B H) Experiential marketing: How to get customers to sense, feel, think, act, and relate to your company and brands. New York: The Free Press. 1999.

27. Fiore (AM). Effects of experiential pleasure from a catalogue environment on approach responses toward fashion aparrel. *Journal of Fashion Marketing and Management* 6(2). 2002: 122-133.

MARKETING OF LIBRARY AND INFORMATION SERVICES IN PAKISTAN : A PROFILE

Kanwal Ameen

Abstract *The prospect of marketing of LIS is growing globally in the present state of kaleidoscopic changes. It is affecting various aspects of library and information services. This paper presents an overview of its status in Pakistan with an emphasis on the academic aspect. It specifically mentions the marketing course being taught at the Department of Library and Information Science, University of the Punjab in Lahore. It also describes the status of library practices regarding marketing. At present marketing of LIS is in its infancy in the country. It is neither taught at all LIS departments nor practiced commonly in the libraries.*

INTRODUCTION

The modern concept of marketing emerged in the second half of the 20th century in the business world and got introduced in the non-profit organizations in the 1969 with the publishing of Kotler & Levy's classic article in the *Journal of Marketing* [1]. Though, libraries have been using various marketing tactics, such as publicity and public relations in the developed world but, the need to introduce and extend the marketing thought in libraries was felt in the early 1970s in the North America. Since then its application in libraries has mounted considerably in the developed world, and there appeared a plenty of literature on the subject too. Specifically, the issue of *Library Trends* on Marketing of LIS [2] and the section of IFLA on 'Management and Marketing' supported significantly the correlation of marketing philosophy to the philosophy of libraries. However, a review of the literature demonstrates that the use of marketing in LIS is either in its infancy or nonexistent in the developing countries. Most of the literature on marketing and its application in libraries has originated in North America followed by other developed countries.

MARKETING AND ITS CONNOTATION WITH THE LIS

There are number of definitions of marketing by various experts with its implication on the business world, services sector and non-profit organizations. These definitions discuss marketing as a managerial and social process, as a philosophy and as an attitude. They elaborate that marketing philosophy enforces to pursue *client-centered approach* and *management style* in order to create valuable exchanges between the organization and its clients.

Kotler profoundly discusses the social and managerial aspects of marketing and states that it is a *societal process* by which individuals and groups obtain what they need and want through creating, offering, freely exchanging products and services of value with others; and *marketing management* is a process of planning and executing the conception, pricing, promotion and distribution of ideas, goods, and services to create exchanges that satisfy individual and organizational goals [3].

In nutshell, marketing is to manage an organization and deliver its ultimate *output/product* to provide the clients/consumers/customers with the maximum satisfaction and value for their needs and wants: It is to consider the whole functioning of any organization from consumers' point of view.

According to Kotler the marketing concept rests on four main pillars, namely target market, customer needs, coordinated marketing, and profitability. Considering the goals of library and information services, the element of *profitability* [in terms of money] appears controversial. Nevertheless, the profitability may be referred as the *acknowledgement and appreciation* of the library services by its target community. Though, the *profit* appears abstract here but, this *recognition* becomes instrumental in establishing the status of a library as well as in getting needed resources by the authorities.

Weingand, a big advocate of the role of marketing in LIS, states that marketing is an exchange relationship: a process providing mutual benefit to both parties in the transaction [4]. Much has been written on the need and ways of using marketing process in LIS. Smith concludes his articles in the following words:

Marketing is a stance and attitude that focuses on meeting the needs of users. Marketing is a means of ensuring that libraries, librarians and librarianship are integrated into both today's and tomorrow's emerging culture. Marketing is not separate from good practice. It is good practice [5].

Presently, a look at the courses of LIS at various schools, the published literature and the functioning of libraries indicate that the scope of marketing has been amplified in the library and information world, however, the pace of its adoption varies between the developed and developing countries.

LIBRARIANSHIP IN PAKISTAN

Pre-independence

The city of Lahore (now in Pakistan) was the centre of library movement under British rule, and was called the cradle of library movement in the subcontinent. James, C. R. Ewing, the then vice-chancellor of the University of the Punjab (UOP) in Lahore, played an important part in creating that panorama by selecting Asa Don Dickinson (1876-1960) as the university librarian to reorganize the Library of the UOP and to teach modern library methods. Dickinson was a student of Melvil Dewey at Albany (1902-1903).

He introduced *Dewey Decimal Classification* scheme in the Library. It was widely followed by other libraries in India. During his stay, he also wrote a textbook, *Punjab Library Primer*, which was published by the UOP in 1916. Anwar declares it the world's first textbook on the subject [6]. It may be safely claimed that the UOP got the honor to publish the first professional textbook. As Kaser testifies:

The preparation of true textbooks in the field of librarianship was in its infancy when Dickinson wrote his *Punjab Library Primer*.... Although books had been written about libraries ... [they] were seldom intended to be used for the purposes of instruction at all [7].

Dickinson established Punjab Library Association (PLA) in 1915 in Lahore. First All India Conference of Librarians, sponsored by the Government of India, was also held in Lahore from 4 to 8 January, 1918 [8]. PLA produced its official journal *Modern Librarian* in 1930 from this city, and played fundamental role in the establishment of *Indian Library Association* in 1933. In 1945, the journal *Indian Librarian* started publishing from Lahore too.

The above overview portray that this city enjoyed the honor of serving as the hub of professional librarianship under the British rule. The city is still the cultural and historical centre of the Pakistan. Unfortunately the library school and libraries suffered a lot after 1947 due to the ethnic riots and migration of population to and from the country.

Post-independence

Pakistan inherited two important libraries; the Punjab Public Library in Lahore (founded 1884) and Punjab University Library (founded 1882 and opened in 1906). The current directory of the libraries in Pakistan is not available. Yet, the following statistics about educational institutions may help in estimating the number of academic libraries. As in order to get accreditation from relevant government bodies any university or institution or colleges need to establish a library with certain number of books and professional library staff. Therefore, the academic libraries constitute more significant and large group of libraries in Pakistan. However, the condition of school libraries in the country is very alarming. Only a few schools have libraries of varying sizes from only a cupboard of books to a room with a few cupboards and audiovisual aids.

According to the *Economic Survey of Pakistan* in 2002-2003 there were 925 Arts & Sciences colleges and 374 professional colleges [9]. According to the Higher Education Commission (HEC) of Pakistan, there were 105 universities and institution of all types in the country up till August 2004 [10].

In addition, there are public and special libraries. The *Directory of Libraries in Pakistan* (1996) enlists 302 public libraries in the country [11]. This is an old directory yet the figure regarding public libraries may not be considered redundant because there have not been significant rise in their number since the publication of this directory. These libraries are maintained by the local government bodies.

LIS EDUCATION IN PAKISTAN

As mentioned earlier, it was started in 1915 by Asa Don Dickinson at UOP; the first university to start professional courses at the university level outside America in the British Empire at that time [12]. This program laid down the foundation for the formal library education and professional librarianship in the subcontinent. However, its continuity suffered after 1947 regrettably and was resumed again in 1950. Karachi University started its library education program in 1956. Later, other universities also established departments of library education to overcome the severe shortage of qualified professionals in the country.

At present 6 universities (viz., UOP, Karachi University, University of Sindh, University of Baluchistan, Islamia University of Bahawalpur and University of Peshawar) have been offering the degree of Master's in LIS on the successful completion of two-year/four-semester residency in the Department of LIS. Another university (viz., Bahaudin Zikriya University in Multan) is at the verge of commencement of this program in 2004. In addition, a long distant university (viz., Allama Iqbal Open University in Islamabad) has started Masters Program for the residents of Islamabad and its twin city Rawalpindi. To get admission at any university in MLIS program, the candidate must have successfully completed four years of college education, i.e. the degree in Bachelor of Arts or Sciences.

Curriculum Development and Marketing

Departments of LIS in all universities have their own indigenous courses, teaching and assessment methods. The faculty proposes revision in the curriculum to present to the Board of Studies for approval. The approved curriculum is then presented to the Board of Advanced Studies of the University for the final endorsement. Once approved by these bodies the department may start offering the new or revised curriculum. The whole procedure may take a year or more.

On the other hand, University Grants Commission (UGC) of Pakistan also made efforts to develop a curriculum with the help of library educationists and professionals. The aim of the Commission was to propose *one* course for all universities in order to standardize the professional education throughout the country. The commission formulated its first Curriculum Revision Committee (CRC) in 1987 to review the curriculum for post-graduate and undergraduate library education but, the Departments of Library Science (now LIS) did not adopt this curriculum.

Soon after, the Commission got the curriculum revised in 1991. The CRC suggested more emphasis on teaching information technology (IT) [13]. Again, to implement this curriculum was not feasible for the departments due to their state of affairs regarding the availability of the required faculty, IT infrastructure and other needed resources.

Course on LIS Marketing

It was introduced in the curriculum revised in 1995 by the new CRC. However, due to the non-availability of the printed and electronic resources on 'marketing of LIS' the list of "Books recommended" included books on *business marketing* only [14]. The marketing course was expanded in 2002 and included the books on marketing in non-profit and service organizations[15].

Islamia University of Bahawalpur implemented the 1995 curriculum recommended by UGC in 1999 [16]. The Department of LIS at UOP also introduced the curriculum after the necessary modifications in the year 2000 and introduced an *elective* course on Marketing of LIS to be studied in the final year. Interestingly, more than two-thirds of the total students opted for this course. When the department switched over from annual system of assessment to the semester system in 2002, the status of the subject was changed into the only *core course* out of six to be offered in the final semester. The step was taken due to the recognition of the importance of marketing thought in the current professional scenario. Sindh University in Hyderabad also started, in 2001, teaching marketing of LIS as a core course in the final year [17].

At present, the course on marketing is being offered at these 3 universities of Pakistan. Another university (viz., Bahaudin Zikriya University in Multan) has adopted the curriculum of the UOP and will be the fourth university offering the subject in 2004.

Despite all these developments, there exists no sharing of knowledge at official or personal level among the faculty of various departments. This writer contacted the other instructors over phone to collect the information, and urged to stay in touch in future to share experience and knowledge. (At present there was no personal email contact of the relevant faculty members available; both of them stated that they would have it soon). Professor at Sindh University told that she often invites faculty members from *Business Administration* to deliver lectures on marketing, and she gets relevant literature mostly from the Internet. She stated that students are required to relate the theory of marketing to libraries [18]. At Islamia University of Bahawalpur the teaching and assessment is all theoretical since its beginning [19].

TEACHING OF MARKETING AT UOP

Aims of the Course

Keeping in view the local professional scenario, the aims of marketing education were devised to prepare the students to:

(i) Look at the institution of library and its services from user's end for sound understanding of their *needs* and *wants.*

(ii) Consider themselves *the product* of the department to be able to meet the needs of modern library users in a satisfactory manner.

(iii) Capable of making strategies to review and reshape the functioning of library to stay in tune with the ongoing advancements, and

(iv) Render their services in an *active* manner instead of following old-fashioned *passive* routine.

Teaching Methods

At present, the course is of 3 credit hours offered in the final semester of 4 months duration. The author has been teaching the course at UOP since it started. The readings are based mostly on a couple of textbook on marketing of LIS for the understanding of basic concepts plus articles from *Encyclopedia of LIS,* the issue of *Library Trends* (Winter 1995) and articles from the Internet.

It appears appropriate here to mention that there is much time lag (a few years) between the publishing of a foreign title and its availability in the local book market. So, getting books on marketing of LIS have been a problem in Pakistan. To discuss this problem is going beyond the scope of this paper but, the following incidents are just to present a glimpse of the situation: (i) the book by Weingand [20] got in our departmental library in 2004 (ii) a book importer was ordered 5 months ago to acquire the titles on marketing published in India but still there was no response. The author makes extensive use of the literature available on the Internet.

The students get the *selected readings' package* and are *encouraged to go through the next topic before coming into the class* which is an innovative practice for them as compare to their previous learning experience, that was 'listening to the lectures during their college education'. To adjust to the *participative method* is difficult for them because of the language barrier too. So, they have to be persuaded and motivated to read by themselves and come up with questions for classroom discussion. In the classroom their doubts are cleared while making them understand the lesson.

Assessment Method

In the present assessment system, students are encouraged to make a marketing plan in lieu of their term paper, focusing on any specific service/product of the library that they go for their internship. The aim is to force them to learn *to apply* the theory and *write down* their plan. Then, they also have to give a classroom presentation on a topic. Most of the students come through a traditional education system which is based upon rote learning and does not contribute to developing good oral and written communication skills. These exercises contribute in the improvement of desired skills and help build their confidence. Students also need to take their mid-term and final written exams. The 100 marks distribution for this subject is as under:

Written tests: 30 (mid-term) + 50 (final) = 80		
Term paper/project	:	15
Oral presentation	:	5
Total	:	**100**

THE IMPACT OF STUDYING MARKETING

The notion of applying marketing concept and process in libraries appears quite strange to students. In the beginning they would ask "why do we have to study marketing. It is related to business" or "it seems that we are going to sell books, etc., etc. However, after some lessons and readings, their comments become positive such as, "it is enlightening to study marketing" and "we feel good when other students on campus ask us why we study marketing", etc. The education of LIS generally carries a low profile as compared to other disciplines such as Business management, IT, Computer Sciences, Medicine, Engineering and so on. To some extent, the study of management and marketing helps in building the morale of newcomers regarding the profession of LIS.

The author conducted a survey from the students of current session (2002-2004) asking them the following question : "Has the study of marketing enabled you to look at the library and its services from users' end? All of them (N = 45) supplied affirmative response [21].

The study of marketing should contribute significantly towards learning to face the challenges ahead and turn them into opportunities. To get acquaintance with the current marketing thought is very much needed in Pakistan where, on one the hand libraries have meagre financial and material resources at their disposal and on the other the functioning of libraries is very old-fashioned. Furthermore, digital paradigm is on its way along with certain misconceptions among the minds of users regarding the need for libraries: Users are usually shy, coming from different educational, social and economic backgrounds and information literacy programs for users hardly exist in the libraries.

The course on *library management* is a part of library education in all university programs but, there is a dire need to introduce the course on marketing of LIS in all universities and short courses/workshops must be arranged as part of continuing education programs for working professionals.

CONCLUSION

The phrase 'information centers' in the above heading has not been added because in Pakistan the term 'library' is still commonly used. This author's experiences as a library user, as an instructor of LIS and as university librarian reveal that, by and large, the libraries in the country function in a traditional passive manner. Both, perception and practice regarding the role of libraries and librarians suggest that 'knowledge is sacred and information is a need'. So, the *needy* should be coming to the library instead of library services and librarian reaching to them. The mindset is still very much like as Weingand states, "Libraries and information agencies have come from a tradition of being a 'public good'. Staff have historically been confident that their products had such intrinsic merit that customers would automatically be attracted; they believed that people 'should' use the library" [22]. She declares it as "yesterday's thinking".

But, this is not the case in Pakistan. Only a few large libraries in public, special and university sector make use of some *public relation* tactics like *content alert* service to selected clients, conducting seminars and exhibitions. However, the notion of applying marketing concept and process in libraries is quite alien among the working professionals. Partly it is because of the non-availability of formal education on marketing of library services. Besides, continuous professional development programs have been mostly geared towards IT literacy. Nonetheless, it is hoped that in order to survive in a competitive global environment, educationists and professionals will recognize the dire need to redesign library services in a "client-oriented" manner following marketing thought. They need to learn current information & communication technologies as means towards accomplishment of this aim and not an aim in itself.

REFERENCES AND NOTES

1. Norman (G). Information marketing in libraries. *In,* Kent (A), Ed. Encyclopedia of library and information science. vol.50. 1992. New York: Marcel Dekker: 256-272.
2. Weingand (D E). Editorial. Marketing of library and information services: Editorial. *Library Trends.* 43 (3). 1995.
3. Kotler (P). Marketing management. Upper Sadle River, NJ: Prentice-Hall, 2000: 8.
4. Weingand (D E). Marketing/planning library and information services. Ed.2. Englewood, Colorado: Libraries Unlimited. 1999: 2.
5. Smith (D). Practice as a marketing tool: Four case studies. *Library Trends.* 43 (3). 1995: 450-462
6. Anwar (M). Asa Don Dickenson: The founding father of modern librarianship in British India. In, Dickenson (A D). Punjab Library Primer . Lahore: Asia Book Centre [reprinted]. 1990: 1-19.
7. Kaser (D). Asa Don Dickenson: A librarian of his time. *In,* Rehman(S), Chaudhry (A S) and Qarshi(A H), Eds. Library Education in Pakistan. Lahore: Punjab University Library Science Alumni Association. 1992: 3-10.
8. Khurshid (A). Library education in Pakistan: Concerns, issues and practices. *In,* Rehman(S), Chaudhry (A S) and Qarshi(A H), Eds. Library Education in Pakistan. Lahore: Punjab University Library Science Alumni Association. 1992: 11-30.
9. Economic Survey 2002-2003. Islamabad: GOP. 2003.

10. Pakistan. Higher Education Commission. Available at: http://www.hec.gov.pk/new2/
11. Directory of Libraries in Pakistan. H.K.A and A.L. Damani, Eds. Islamabad: Pakistan Library Association, 1966.
12. Ibid. 9.
13. University Grants Commission (UGC), National Academy of Higher Education, Curriculum Revision Committee (CRC). Curriculum in Library and Information Science for B.A. B.Sc. & B.Com. and Master of Library and Information Science. Islamabad: the Commission, 1991.
14. UGC, Curriculum Division. CRC. Revised Curriculum of Library and Information Science for MLIS. Islamabad: the Commission, 1995.
15. UGC, Curriculum Development Project. Curriculum of Library Science for B.A./BLIS/MLIS. The Commission, 2002.
16. Fazil (B) (ex-Chairman, Department of LIS, Islamia University Bahawalpur). Telephonic communication on August 10, 2004.
17. Rafia (S). Professor of LIS and Dean Social Sciences, Sindh University, Hyderabad. Telephonic communication on August 2, 2004.
18. Ibid.
19. Bukhari (AR). Present instructor of Marketing of LIS at Department of LIS Islamia University Bahawalpur. Telephonic communication on August 22, 2004.
20. Ibid. 2.
21. Kanwal (A). Survey conducted during the class on June 15, 2004.
22. Ibid. 4.

MARKETING LIBRARY AND INFORMATION SERVICES IN AUSTRALIAN ACADEMIC LIBRARIES

Janine Schmidt

Abstract *Australian academic libraries have been considered essential to educational and research endeavours and have relied on institutional financial support for their continuing operations. However, change is in the air. Students are paying increasing percentages of the costs of their education and direct public funding from government is shrinking as a percentage of income. The value of the library is also being called into question with increasing "googleisation" and new generations of students are making new demands on library service provision. Directors of libraries are competing with multiple demands for funding on their campuses. They must understand client needs, plan service provision, promote the services available, deliver them efficiently and effectively and fight for financial and other support. Marketing has become an essential tool in ensuring required funds are secured and that services provided meet the needs identified. Using various market research techniques including surveys, focus groups and analysis of suggestions, libraries can understand the needs and design appropriate services and facilities.*

INTRODUCTION

In the last few years, the products and services provided by libraries have changed considerably. The challenges to library services from changes in educational approaches, the impact of technology, new methods for information provision and declining budgets have meant that marketing is now so basic that it cannot be considered a separate function. It is the whole business seen from its final results; that is, from the client's perspective.

In determining new approaches, many libraries have come to appreciate the contribution of the application that marketing concepts can make. In designing the marketing mix and developing the marketing plan, the so-called 4Ps have become central to libraries – product, price, place, promotion. Any library using marketing techniques to develop its operations focuses on its products (including services); the price paid, which may be in money, time or energy; the promotional strategies by which library collections and services are made known to potential clients, including publications, displays and participation in events; and the physical facilities or place from which services are made available and distribution strategies which increasingly use the internet and virtual as well as real approaches. Positioning and politics can also be considered in the mix and incorporate positioning the product in the mind of the client and public policy and politics [1].

Relationship marketing, in particular, reflecting the mutual interests of libraries and the clients they serve, is being seen as a concept for libraries to embrace. Libraries, after all, are built on relationships [2]. Marketing is directly linked to the clients perceptions of the services the library offers and the library's interpretation of the clients needs [3]. In developing and maintaining relationships, it is essential that all clients are identified and their needs understood. Market research is a useful tool for discovering and understanding client needs and identifying better ways to meet those needs. In the change process involved, it is always easier to change oneself than it is to change others.

THE AUSTRALIAN UNIVERSITY ENVIRONMENT

Australia is a large country whose population is located primarily in the large capital cities but also in smaller regional cities. There are 36 publicly funded universities in Australia and several privately funded ones. The universities can be grouped according to size, location and emphasis. The Group of 8, also known as the sandstone universities, comprises the older universities. They are located in capital cities of each state, are comprehensive in their discipline spread and research intensive in their approach. The regional universities, of which there are about 12, are located in smaller cities like Townsville, Cairns, Wollongong and Wagga Wagga. Another significant group of universities is the Australian Technology Network, with five members and disciplinary strengths in business and technology. A fourth group is the Innovation and Research Universities (sometimes known as the Gumtrees). These universities are smaller and focused in their disciplinary coverage, both in teaching and learning and research. A fifth group is the New Generation Universities. As the name indicates, they are the more recently established universities and are generally located in suburban areas of large capital cities. Their emphasis is on teaching and learning, rather than research. Almost all Australian universities maintain more than one campus, given the highly distributed nature of the Australian population, with a few operating overseas campuses and several operating twinning programs with overseas institutions.

Australian students customarily complete secondary education at the age of 18 and proceed to a university to complete a three or four year degree program. Student numbers at each university range from a few thousand to almost forty thousand at the largest. Over half of all higher degree research students are taught within the Group of 8 universities. Increasing numbers of students are completing multiple degrees. International full fee-paying students comprise an increasing percentage of the student body at each university.

Government funding is primarily from the central federal government with some funding from state and local governments. The federal government sets student numbers (supposedly negotiated with each institution) and allocates funds to each university according to a formula which is disciplinary in its basis. The funding includes a capital component for new buildings. Research funds are also allocated according to numbers of higher degree student numbers and a variety of indicators which include publication rates and the ability to attract research funds from various sources. The primary research funding authorities are also government-related, the Australian Research Council (ARC) and the National Health and Medical Research Council (NHMRC). Most of the research funds go to the Group of 8 universities.

Students pay a contribution towards their education, known as HECS (Higher Education Contribution Scheme). A package of reforms was presented to the higher education sector in Australia, in 2003, to offer new assistance to both universities and students [4]. It included increases to the student contribution (HECS) and a five-year learning entitlement to each Australian citizen for a federal government-supported higher education place. Individual institutions are increasingly offering full fee-based programs to students unable to access a federal government supported place, particularly in those programs like law and medicine, where demand for places exceeds the supply. Loan schemes from the government are available to students paying fees, both HECS and full fees. Various reforms proposed include amended conditions of employment for staff and changes to governance models for universities. Some additional government funding to be introduced over the next ten years supports these reforms.

The higher education sector in Australia is under increasing pressure. At least nine reviews of aspects ranging from information and communications technology provision to the basis of research funding are currently in train or have been completed in recent years. All universities are seeking to enhance income from non-government sources. Universities have become more market-driven and have adopted various strategies to increase income in a challenging environment.

Directors of academic libraries in Australia meet several times a year and exchange information through a group called CAUL (Council of Australian University Librarians). This group has become important in sharing strategies for effective operations. A sub-committee known as CEIRC (CAUL Electronic Information Resources Committee) has also negotiated consortium prices for various database and fulltext electronic services.

WHO ARE THE CLIENTS?

In an academic library, the primary clients are the staff and students. There are general or administrative staff, including library staff, who have a wide range of needs, as well as university management. Other educational institutions and their students or staff are also significant clients and libraries who require document delivery services. The wider community also uses academic libraries. In most Australian academic libraries, external users can use the libraries freely without special identification cards. However, they are not usually able to borrow or use online services remotely without authorisation. Some academic libraries have developed community service arrangements in these circumstances. Less obvious as clients of academic libraries are potential employees of the university or library, potential future students and suppliers with whom libraries deal. An analysis of website use can establish that the client base service is very wide.

Academic library clients are varied. They can be segmented using market research strategies by age, discipline of study, origin, ability (or special need) and differential services have been developed by libraries to meet the various needs identified. Clients range from school-leavers skilled in playing computer games and communicating via e-mail to those returning to study after several years' absence from education who have had little contact with computers. Both the total numbers and the percentages of postgraduate, mature aged and international students are much higher then in the past. In developing services to meet the needs, the Library has identified categories of students by discipline, program, course, as well as level of study and learning approach. Many students are remote, located some distance from any physical facility. Postgraduate students are represented in the user community in greater numbers than their statistical composition would indicate. They are heavy library users. All students want quality services – they are paying for their education.

The HECS fee that students pay constitutes only part of the costs, but students do believe they are "paying for their education". The University of Queensland engaged a market research firm to explore the student attitudes, with the Library targeted as part of the various services provided by the University [5]. Students were seen to be self-centred, regarding themselves as important and deserving of a university education as a right. They also consider themselves "poor", although socio-economic analysis of the student population would deny this. They were passive in their approach to issues, unlike their activist colleagues of some years ago, but nevertheless there is an underlying anger. Inherent in their expectations is a belief that the University should somehow make everything come out right for the student. The students relate primarily to their teaching faculties or disciplinary schools and have little understanding of the other types of University services available. The Library is seen as the only essential service outside of teaching, because of its direct link to academic progress.

In focusing design on the client, a restaurant analogy of library use has been used. How do clients use the library? Some like the "take-away" method. They look up, locate, borrow, photocopy, print or return an item. Some are looking for a leisurely "eat in" experience, borrowing, studying and working in-depth, individually or in groups. Some clients use libraries to "self serve", others want detailed help and guidance with "menu" choice. Many others now remain at home or in their offices and "order in" the information they require.

Many academic staff use the branch libraries less frequently than in the past. They use the services delivered to their desktops. They are busy people. They use large datasets in the sciences. Print remains important to users in the humanities and social sciences. The growing numbers of staff who are researchers have put additional demands on information supply. The provision of services to spin-off companies and commercial research arms of the University has presented difficulties in relation to license and other agreements.

HOW DO WE KNOW WHAT THEY WANT?

The simple way is to ask them. Surveys can be done, in both print and electronic formats. Through CAUL, Australian university libraries have chosen several survey tools to use. Individual institutions can gain knowledge about their own users but also benchmark their results against others. One survey tool used has been the Rodski survey (http://www.rodski.com.au/). This survey determines what services are important to clients as well as measuring the performance of those services. Focus group interviews can be used to develop solutions to problem situations and investigate further the results of simple questionnaires and surveys. For example, at the University of Queensland Library, focus groups have been found invaluable in determining the appropriate design of the website to ensure students find the information they seek. Complaints and suggestions can be analysed. Key visits are also made to significant clients, including Deans and Departmental/Faculty/School Heads to determine needs. The library's numerous advisory committees should be consulted.

Visits to key clients can explore new research directions, developing curriculum areas and new methods both of teaching and research. Librarians can adopt strategies adopted from their commercial colleagues and explain new services available, leaving documentation about them and following up with letters or presentations to staff of the School or Faculty.

All services and products provided to clients should be regularly evaluated. After service delivery, immediate feedback can be sought. Without any sort of evaluation, librarians and library managers may wrongly assume that they know what the client wants. Many organizations have discovered they can find a great deal about their clients from asking their staff. They, after all, are in constant contact with clients. Having asked, it is important to listen to what is said. Another approach is to watch what clients do. One can conduct door counts of entry to libraries and count the number of clients in the library at particular times to assist in determining appropriate opening hours. Libraries collect many statistics and these can be analysed to understand changing client needs. CAUL has also played a role in Australia in ensuring statistics are collected annually. They are available centrally on a website (http://www.caul.edu.au/stats/). Flowcharting the movement of clients through the Library has been carried out to determine the areas most heavily used and the sequences to assist in library design. There are also many tools available to analyse the use of the website. At the University of Queensland Library, a logfile analyser called Analog (http://www.analog.cx/) is used for usage patterns of the web server, including the most heavily used pages of the website, the domain location of the host server, monthly, daily and weekly reports. In 2003, at the University of Queensland Library, we have learned that over 30 million pages of the website were used, that the catalogue was the most heavily used component, that it has increased by 76% from 2000 to 2003.

AND WHAT DO THEY WANT?

Overall, our library clients want basic services. They want competence, reliability, responsiveness, timeliness, honesty and a caring approach. They want everything to work properly and they want assistance with use both of the library and of the resources. They want promises made to them to be kept and they want what they need, when they need it. Students want information content for assignments, research or knowledge acquisition. They want assistance with assignments and research support. They want e-books and e-journals and real books and real journal articles. They want training and motivation in resource discovery, IT skills and equitable service delivery. They want instant gratification. Australian students are in a hurry and they want everything now.

Students in general see the Library as an icon, a haven within an alien world. Students tend to be crisis-driven in their approach to the Library, are task-oriented, lack information seeking skills and frequently find the Library a source of frustration. Few will ever acquire in-depth knowledge of services available, but they are interested in learning how to search more effectively. Classes in information skills are valued by those who attend, but classes only attain credibility when recommended by teaching staff. A customer survey [6] is now conducted every two years, seeking information regarding the Library's communication, service quality, facilities and equipment, service delivery and library staff and much of what we learn from about students needs is taken from this as well as feedback from information skills classes and other in-house surveys.

Academic staff are also in a hurry and operating under significant pressure with increased class sizes and greater research loads. Surveys [7, 8] have shown that researchers are reading more articles although they have less time. While surveys of this kind are still to be carried out in Australia, there is no indication that Australian figures would not replicate the results of surveys done elsewhere.

WHAT PRODUCTS AND SERVICES IS THE LIBRARY MARKETING?

The library has many products and services that it can market. Each library needs to identify what it wishes to market and how. Marketing is not just about developing and promoting new services and products but about bringing awareness to clients of existing services and products and determining their appropriateness. A marketing plan needs to be developed and implemented with ongoing enhancement of the services and products should follow.

The Library is marketing its collections. In particular, the availability of new acquisitions like a new online patent database or a set of medical electronic journals, must be communicated to clients who need them. Donations of large research collections of potential use to particular disciplinary areas must be publicised.

There is an enormous responsibility to ensure that value is received for the significant resource expenditure being made on many of these areas. New services like online versions of examination papers, the development of an e-print archive of institutional research papers, the use of plagiarism detection software and online thesis submission must all be publicised to potential users. For new products or services, part of the planning must involve the creation of a marketing and promotional strategy and the allocation of responsibility to library staff to ensure that the plan is carried through.

Marketing is directly linked to the planning process. Having a formalised plan and direction of where the library is going as opposed to being reactive to change and problems that arise [9] enables managers to successfully develop marketing strategies and successfully identify new services and products. Part of the planning is developing a suitable mission statement for both internal and external use. The statement should be clear and descriptive of what the library is doing and where it is going. Few Australian libraries would not have a statement [10]. The mission statement is a motto that all library staff can adopt and believe in.

ADOPTING BRANDING TECHNIQUES

Commercial techniques like branding and badging have been adopted by libraries, particularly in promotional strategies and in ensuring the "place" meets needs. Branding encompasses "the tangible and intangible aspects of a product, service or entity" [11]. Classical library design focused on the collection, on its projected growth and on its protection. The library was a serious building for the storage of materials, the seating of readers and the provision of workspaces for library staff. Scholars, or users, went to such a building, an "edifice", to obtain access to recorded knowledge, while librarians sat behind desks and assisted users find their way. This traditional library paradigm was matched by traditional library design.

In the light of these differing uses and needs, the physical layout and facilities in academic libraries can gain much from visits to service organizations like airports, banks, shops, supermarkets, restaurants and internet cafes. Express workstations for quick searches, auto-loan machines, specialist study spaces with lock-up desks for graduate students, coffee facilities and computer laboratories for information skills training should all be featured. The look and feel should be friendly and fashionable and the internal attributes should be aligned with the external [11]. There should be different kinds of spaces to appeal to different individuals and to different groups. Flexibility is the keynote. The appropriate flow of people using the university libraries is the cornerstone of any design. The physical place is still important to encourage clients to stay and return. Australian academic libraries have gone a long way in delivering the "new look."

The term "badging" is frequently used in marketing parlance. Badging on the physical level can be carried through to each branch library, so that each has the same look and feel, with the same facilities. Certain colours can be used to theme areas that are identical in each library like loans or circulation areas, inquiry desks and photocopying and printing areas. Badging is successful in multi-library universities as many students no longer use one library to complete their academic studies. Having the same look and feel from one library to the next will make it easier for clients to use the new library that they have visited.

Badging need not stop at the physical facilities. Carrying a common design theme on the web page and through print publications is just as important. Adopting a clear layout and professional design for print publications should flow through from the promotional handouts as well as print help and subject guides and any other library handout including those given to students during information skills sessions. Powerpoint presentations should also reflect the university or library logo.

Branding is not just about ensuring uniformity in colour, design and layout but a "share of the mind" [12]. Successful branding should create a feeling about the organisation and impact the community that use the products and services. It is not just about the products and services but the attitudes, ethics and presentation of the staff and organisation. Having a catch-cry or logo that is easily recognisable and the quality product and service to support it, is what branding and marketing is all about. The American Library Association (ALA) and the Association of College and Research Libraries (ACRL) have developed and implemented the '@ your library' campaign, a toolkit and logo to help "heighten awareness and support of academic and research libraries and attract quality candidates to the profession" [13]. Many Australian academic libraries have adopted strategies similar to these. For example, the University of South Australia Library (http://www.library.unisa.edu.au/) use a logo and phrase 'Your library @ your place' to promote flexible delivery and *Ask*IT (http://askit.uq.edu.au/index.php) at the University of Queensland Library is synonymous with quality help and advice (both in-person and online) on a range of information and communication technologies issues university-wide.

MARKETING STRATEGIES AT WORK

Communicating what libraries do has always been a challenge. It has become even more difficult now with online information resources and services, with many users not coming to the library physically as frequently or at all. Marketing today is also challenging because library clients are "more sophisticated and knowledgeable, maybe even cynical about marketing activities"[10]. Communicating to the University's key players, academic staff, and senior university management is vital. After all, it is academic staff that encourage student use of the library and senior university management who allocate budgets.

Selling and communication strategies involve all library staff. All library staff are involved at all levels in dealing with clients. Simple strategies like name badges and uniforms clearly identify service staff. Part of any service strategy is to reduce the number of people with whom each client is involved, as being directed from one to another can be frustrating. Recruiting staff who are highly service-oriented is paramount. Librarians have all too frequently been characterised as fearsome gorgons and guardians who occasionally and begrudgingly assist users – rigid enforcers of rules, more interested in themselves than the clients. What is needed are bright, cheerful, intelligent, friendly professionals providing quality services to all.

To ensure that all staff are able to promote the library and communicate effectively with their clients, there must be appropriate induction programs, which should include customer service techniques. Ongoing training can be used to continue to update staff and provide new techniques. Many Australian academic libraries have allocated library staff to each Faculty/School and this liaison role has always been an important marketing strategy [14]. The liaison librarian provides an ongoing link from the library to the faculty, school or research centre promoting new services and information resources, providing staff and students with information assistance and integrating information skills session into the curriculum.

The marketing literature tells us that every person who receives poor services mentions it to at least seven other people. Unfortunately, good service frequently goes unremarked. Library staff do make mistakes and an apology never goes astray. Good ideas from commercial companies can be adopted. A supermarket chain in Australia, Woolworths, employs a very useful staff development and training program for its staff. Several elements of this have been used, in particular, the *Sorry, Glad, Sure* regime. It helps defuse a situation to say, "I am *sorry* you have had a problem with our service today, I am *glad* you have talked to me, and I am *sure* we can do something about it." The customer adage *The customer does not care how much you know, until he/she knows how much you care* has also been taken to heart – and action.

Many Australian academic libraries provide students with incentives to undertake surveys. Book vouchers are a simple and effective reward mechanism to encourage students to provide feedback to the library. RMIT (Royal Melbourne

Institute of Technology, http://mams.rmit.edu.au/0sq8rkkuhbr2.pdf) and the University of South Australian (http://www.library.unisa.edu.au/spotlight.asp#voucher) have successful implemented this incentive.

A range of written promotional strategies can be used. Different ones will appeal in different situations. It can be difficult to obtain coverage within newsletters produced by one's own organisation. Good copy written by professionals is more likely to be used by news sources. The inclusion of photographic content and illustrations will ensure a more interesting presentation and the preparation of "press releases" for various uses will guarantee that the content is more likely to be accurate.

Borrowing the business model of use of *unique selling propositions* is effective. These are usually simple statements which convey meaning in relation to service provision, but become firmly associated with specific products. Representation at university functions is another simple but successful mechanism for promoting the library. Alumni events, parents' activities, open days, orientation sessions or expos within the university are good starting points for marketing of the library and its services. Adopting techniques and communication strategies that appeal to all students is important. For example, at Curtin University Library (http://library.curtin.edu.au/) students can SMS the library at any time with any query or to respond to requested feedback.

WHAT IS RIGHT MEDIUM FOR MARKETING?

Using the appropriate medium to market libraries services and products is extremely important and challenging. With an increasing number of users not physically entering a library, getting the message across is harder. Flexibility is essential and on occasion using all media to communicate to the clients is the best technique. Print and online means are all important.

A good website is an effective marketing tool in itself. Promoting new services and resources in a prominent position on a website is important but is frequently not as effective as one would like to believe. Many clients bookmark specific pages on the website, rather than entering via the homepage. Ensuring that new services are discovered by clients is frequently difficult. This is not to say that communication online is a waste of time. As use of the internet and electronic resources becomes commonplace [15] the web becomes an essential medium for marketing and promoting services and resources. Interpersonal means will remain important communication means.

To reach all users it is important to adopt several different, new and old, marketing techniques. Print and online, broadcast e-mails, direct e-mails and personal letters. Word of mouth is just as effective for spreading the word about good service as it is for bad. Influential members of the University community and others speaking for the library can achieve more for the library than any self-promotion. An effective advertising technique that will reach the largest proportion of the population is on the back of toilet doors [16].

CONCLUSION

Marketing approaches are proving to be effective in assisting Australian academic libraries to adjust to changes in its client base and will ensure that services delivered continue to fit the needs. The products and services provided by libraries range from knowledge access and research support to printing services and the provision of information skills, supported by one on one assistance and advice. Strategies examining the distribution and delivery of services and their successful promotion will ensure that those who need information obtain it.

REFERENCES

1. Walters (S). Library marketing that works! New York: Neal-Schuman Publishers Inc. 2004.
2. Besant (L X) and Sharp (D). Libraries need relationship marketing. *Information Outlook*. 4 (3). 2000: 17-22.
3. Weingand (D E). Managing outside the box: Marketing and quality management as key to library effectiveness. *In,* Savard (R), Ed. Education and research for marketing and quality management in libraries (IFLA Publications. 99). Munich: KG Saur. 2001: 8-17.
4. Department of Education, Science and Training. Our Universities: Backing Australia's future. Canberra: DEST. 2003. http://www.backingaustraliasfuture.gov.au/policy_paper/policy_paper.pdf.
5. Olsen (M). Customer service: Client attitudes and perceptions. Brisbane: University of Queensland. 1996.
6. The University of Queensland Library. *Library* Client Survey. 2003. http://www.cybrary.uq.edu.au/about/rodski2003.pdf.
7. Tenopir (C) et al. Patterns of journal use by scientists through three evolutionary phases. *D-Lib*. 9 (5). 2002.
8. Tenopir (C), King (D W) and Bush (A). Medical faculty's use of print and electronic journals: Changes over time and comparison with other scientists. *Journal of the Medical Library Association*. 92 (2). 2004: 233-41.
9. Weingand (D E). Marketing/planning library and information services. Englewood, Colorado: Libraries Unlimited. 1999.
10. de Saez (E E). Marketing concepts for libraries and information services. London: Facet Publishing. 2002.
11. Shaffer (R I). Using branding to make your mark (et): What lessons leaders can learn for library and information science. *In,* Owens (I), Ed. Strategic marketing in library and information science. 2002: 81-91
12. Emberton (F). Brand awareness - more then a logo, viewed 12 August, 2004, <http://www.johnstanley.cc/news_and_articles/articles.phtml>.

13. American Library Association & Association of College and Research Libraries. @ *Your library TM toolkit for Academic and Research Libraries: messages, ideas, and strategies for promoting the value of our libraries and librarians in the 21st century*. Chicago, Ill.: ALA and ACRL. 2003.
14. Burgess (Y) and Newton-Smith (C). Resources to help lecturers develop their teaching skills: A collaborative effort from a lecturer and a librarian. In *The Proceedings of the 4th Annual Teaching Learning Forum*, Edith Cowan University. 1995.
15. Coombs (M). Website design for public libraries: A marketing tool for the new millennium. *Australian Library Journal*. 48 (2). 1999: 117-27.
16. Stanley (J). Marketing libraries is about using unique opportunities. *InCite*. 23 (10). 2002: 33.

METAPHORS ON MARKETING : SYMBOLIC AND EFFECTIVE ATTEMPTS IN THE "LUCIAN BLAGA" CENTRAL UNIVERSITY LIBRARY CLUJ-NAPOCA, ROMANIA

Melinda Bükkei
István Király V.

Motto: "Concentrate on the results, not on the activities"
- Sergio Zyman

Abstract *The paper grasps and outlines the concepts and practices of library marketing as well as generally the marketing of non-profit institutions or organizations, conceptually defined as symbolic marketing. However, what is termed here as symbolic should not be understood as a "weaker" version of marketing, but as the proper way in which marketing perspectives can be actually implemented in such institutions; that is, as a practice which concerns and mobilizes all services and activities of such institutions. The paper also presents the factual initiatives which have been going on for years – quite successfully – in the "Lucian Blaga" Central University Library, Cluj-Napoca, Romania, especially around the library's periodical, the review Philobiblon, and on the basis of which recent "projects" can also be conceived more consistently.*

INTRODUCTION

Before being a simple, mechanical need, or more than that, a fashion, *marketing* is and remains, in its essence a *challenge and a fundamental possibility* for the libraries. That is, a possibility and a challenge which focuses and touches upon the institution's structure, internal dynamics, the ensemble of institutional relations, but also the whole range of its mission and means of achieving and developing it. Any possibility is, in its turn, the outline of a *horizon.* A horizon which - even if it is mainly oriented towards the future -, touches and embraces in fact all temporal dimensions of the institution: its future, its present, and also its past.

These aspects are valid – obviously, with due particularities – in the case of those libraries, perhaps even the majority of them, which are non-profit organizations or institutions and therefore their products and services are not *merchandise* meant to be *sold*. Consequently, the products and services of these institutions have a different view of *market*, which we here call *symbolic*.

SYMBOLIC MARKETING

Symbolic marketing though, in our understanding, is by no means a *weaker* form of *real* marketing, nothing of the "as if..." kind! We are not talking about shaping the services and products in such a way "as if" they were goods meant for the "market". That is, *pseudo-goods,* the presence and acceptance of which would only be validated on a merely *imaginary* market.

On the contrary: symbolic marketing is the most suitable and authentic way for non profit institutions to conceive and fulfill their traditional, actual or prospective efforts and attempts in order to meet the challenges of the contemporary world. Thus, the horizon of symbolic marketing fundamentally implies and concerns library institutions as a whole, as well as in their complex relations.

What is new then in this concept of marketing for libraries as compared to the previous, and already traditional, concepts of "public relations"? The answer to this question has to consider, first of all, a certain effect of *explication* and *indication*. No matter how intensely PR actions keep in mind the dynamics of meanings of an institution in its relationship with a real or virtual public, they are not automatically able to mirror and focus the challenges of the society towards the interior of the organization. No matter how efficient PR departments seem to be in institutions of public administration, they can still leave many of the bureaucratic structures untouched, which are mostly convenient, inert and inflexible as to their functionality. Marketing concepts, and especially marketing practices have as a first result, precisely the revelation, the explanation and indication of insufficiencies unidentified before. In the same time, marketing also offers a new and efficient possibility for a dynamic reconsideration and outlining of the institutions, establishing itself as a change-management "engine". Beyond these aspects, marketing concept and mentality offer the possibility of *current institutional opening*, receiving not only the needs and demands from the "outside", but conceiving its own shapes and offers. This last aspect becomes more obvious, especially through the theories and practices promoted by Sergio Zyman.

As it is shown, we think that marketing is no mystery and no fashion, but, in the words of Sergio Zyman[1] , it's an extremely serious discipline, not only and exclusively in business, but generally in taking our institutional and organizational efforts seriously. That is why we have to make it clear, also in the case of "symbolic" marketing, that all its costs turn to a good account, always and invariably. First of all these are "symbolic" benefits, as a result of prestige and positive institutional image, which normally influence fundraising activities, and on a different level help us achieve some *experience*, *competence* and *self-reliance*, which can guarantee the success of the *real products* on the market and direct incomes. Or, this means not a "symbolical marketing", but a real one.

Most services offered or created by libraries are in fact *produced* by them. The core of these products is *information.* It is nowadays unanimously accepted that the libraries not only administrate and mediate information, but they also create it on a daily basis, making it specific and specialized. We have to admit, though, that in the process of orienting users, clients, beneficiaries, these pieces of information get in touch, at least contextually, with the *information market.* Or, during that dynamic and lively daily contact, it is often the gaps of offers which may show, related to some unidentified and unshaped needs or possibilities. We can identify and shape these needs, by using specific products from the libraries.

Of course, we realize every day that contemporary marketing is not limited to the identification of existing needs for different clients, customers, buyers, etc., but involves itself in the "birth", shaping and articulating the effectiveness of needs, in an active and creative way.

LIS MARKETING IN ROMANIA: SOME OBSTACLES

In spite of all these, there still are a lot of various obstacles against the implementation of marketing techniques and practices in libraries, and not only in Romania. The first obstacle, which is a quite complex one, is that of mentality, with multidirectional ramifications. Although most librarians are aware of the necessity of marketing in libraries, at least on a "verbal" level, there are very few who can actually "make time" for it. The argumentation "lack of time" however proves to be totally ridiculous and compensatory if we acknowledge the fact that marketing activities open up, gain and complete the meaning of any library activity. "To have no time" in this case means, strangely and intriguingly enough, to have no time to analyze and shape everything else that one does *during the time of having no time*!

The mental "time barrier" is associated with one of the most frequent problems: "lack of money", money which could be allocated for the marketing activities and efforts. In reality, the outlining of the problem is exactly the opposite. That is: instead of asking ourselves if we have enough money to conceive, to support, develop and implement marketing activities in the libraries, we have to ask if we have enough money to give up the direct or indirect incomes, profits and benefits gained by their help.

We can also mention as a mental barrier the fact that for a traditional type librarian, the connection between his daily activity and a modern economical discipline as marketing can be only obscure. So, we have to admit, there is still a serious lack of understanding, competence and opening towards the importance of marketing in the field of library science. However, if we try to imagine and reflect upon the relations between library services and the (possible) entirety of its beneficiaries as a *global confrontation,* also involving the costs and requests, then marketing will become totally justified.

Generally speaking, we can ask ourselves, if it is not inappropriate to leave the implementation of marketing techniques in the care of librarians? Shouldn't this task belong to the policy of total management? And librarians to be chosen and shaped only afterwards? All this for the simple reason that marketing today, and especially in this perspective, is not an optional matter at all!

Beyond mentality obstacles, there certainly is another category of obstacles in implementing contemporary marketing. If we refer to the Romanian situation, especially regarding the budgetary university libraries, we can talk about administrative barriers. The major university libraries are all budgetary institutions maintained by the government, but the allocated sum of money doesn't only depend on the libraries' marketing performances, but also on some quantitative and administrative indicators, applicable invariably and undifferentiatedly to all libraries in the "network". This means that, although it allows, the system does not encourage, support or *reward* marketing performances in libraries. Even if successful activities can improve a library's financial situation, they will not bring supplementary money from the budget, and this fact has a negative influence upon the interest of the libraries to deploy such efforts. And all this in spite of the fact, as we shall later see, that there are real possibilities to use money from the budget in a profitable way, by even doubling or tripling their utility value.

We also have to talk about another barrier in the way of marketing implementation: the institutional one. The habits, the institutional structure and the traditional managerial attitude of most major budgetary Romanian university libraries very rarely represent a favorable factor for changes, essentially led by the idea and motto of our study: to concentrate not on activities, but on *real and consistent results*.

From the year 1998, the Romanian Governmental Ordinance No. 84, par. 3 allows Romanian university libraries not only to obtain incomes from individual activities, but also to use these for self-benefit. This represents an excellent opportunity to complete the incomes of the libraries. In spite of all these, Romanian library legislation requires, encourages or recompenses neither marketing efforts, nor the implementation of marketing-concerned approaches.

Nevertheless, library marketing is a well known notion discussed in Romanian specialized literature, dealing, more *in abstracto,* and unfortunately rather as an unapplied *desideratum*, with the necessity of introducing marketing concepts and practices in the daily activities of Romanian libraries. Thus, without realizing the fact that "marketing strategy" represents on one hand to re-think, re-analyze, re-articulate and communicate what already exists, on the other hand, with all its efficiency and consistence, to show what is about to be done. Although it is true that generally every interaction with a client/reader is a possible moment of marketing, every interaction and every service also represents a possibility for marketing actions. We have to be aware of the fact that these possibilities cannot be "achieved" and actualized effectively or automatically unless they are planned, prefigured and outlined from the beginning, in virtue of certain approaches, concepts and practices, themselves also of an inner marketing-substance[2] . The close connections with economic and social life influence library activities, imposing the implementation of marketing procedures as a necessity in Romanian libraries.

Marketing strategy is usually based upon the acquaintance of the "customer", who in our case is the active or passive, real or potential reader. But in order to acquaint the customer, we need to do market research with result to reflect information about the necessities, expectations and opinions of present services, in order to be able to re-think them trough marketing actions. To re-think the services with maximum efficiency, we have to direct our attention towards library staff, who not only contributes to the improvement of services, but also represents a special user stratum, whose positive or negative opinion influences the image of the library. In the same time we should not forget about our partners, financing and cooperative institutions, which represent the most structured and important segment of public opinion which also decisively influences a wider public opinion.

The success of marketing actions is ensured precisely by obtaining exact and necessary data. It can be obtained not only by testing the public opinion , but also by direct interaction with readers and institutions, these having a direct feed-back. Market research and public opinion are very important elements for libraries to find out useful information about their users needs and as an effect of the information to satisfy their needs. Without these actions no library would be functional. Every library elaborates their own marketing concept, which has to correspond with necessities, requests and local conditions.

MARKETING AT THE UNIVERSITY LIBRARY

The Central University Library of Cluj, which some years ago adopted the name of a Romanian poet and philosopher, Lucian Blaga, is one of the largest libraries in Transylvania, Romania, and at the same time one of the largest from Central Europe, having an encyclopedic, scientific and didactic profile. Due to its Special Collections and Legal Deposit, the library also has a museum character. After the 1989 changes, the necessity of information intensity imposed the re-sizing of library activities. This required in the first place, the introduction of new professional techniques and solutions, but also more or less outlined efforts towards institutional evolution.

So far, our particular, significant and relevant experiences in the marketing field show very clearly the possibilities, abilities and reserves in elaborating some works which are really selling, that is, can be put to account on the real market, but also numerous obscure and un-functional aspects not only from the marketing point of view, but also regarding the administrative and institutional ones. These are aspects and problems which influence the development of potentials and chances in a negative way.

First of all we have to mention the publishing of the library's Bulletin *Philobiblon* beginning with the year 1996, a product meant to be sold from the very beginning. It is also very important that the publication was conceived for international library exchange[3]. Of course, it is very clear that "exchange" is a market operation, a transaction. A publication produced, *ab initio* for exchange, is a real marketing action, attested and verified by the exchange market and its challenges. The review had outlined a quality and professional level to satisfy a direct and effective marketing vision.

The review, as an international exchange product, was published in English. Studies and analyses were made in order to situate it within the framework of other publications of major libraries – e.g., Bodleian Library Record, Harvard Library Bulletin, Knygotira, etc. – and to establish its specificity. For a better knowledge of the different levels of international partners we used the experiences of the International Library Exchange Department from our library, questioning new possible partners. To promote the publication and to confirm its solidity, we required some speciality analysis by international reviews as: Bulletin des Bibliothèques de France, Libraries & Culture etc. Beyond this we succeeded to intercept the attention of Romanian intellectuals and specialists, who work or study in the USA, and who have launched a signal about the review on the Internet as well. Simultaneously with the international promotion, there were some internal promoting actions too. On the one hand with the purpose to obtain intellectual, culture and professional support for its program, on the other hand to obtain extra-institutional financial support. The publication was analyzed and appreciated in several prestigious cultural and scientific (library science) reviews, signed by prestigious Romanian personalities. As a result, the review could now compete with success for extra-institutional financing, its appearance being provided until then by the Soros Foundation for an Open Society, supported by the American millionaire of Hungarian origin, George Soros.

If we regard its economical efficiency on the international exchange market, we can assert that the review brings a 200% profit to our library. This profit means valuable and indispensable publications: books and periodicals, which in the lack of financial resources could not have been bought. Beside all this, there is also a symbolic profit, for our image.

We have to underline the fact that the first volume and volumes from 1999 to 2002 had to be financed by the library, meaning from its budget which is distributed in a centralized way. This challenge, this need and attempt offered us and still offers the possibility for meditation and attempts to use budgetary resources in concordance with marketing criteria.

The regularly ensured, anticipated and calculated budgetary resources offer not only certainty, stability and comfort, but also opportunity to deploy horizons. The use of these resources to produce quality "objects" which not only cover their own costs, but also bring some profit, means in fact the doubling of that particular segment of the budget. For example, the same quantity of paper – allocated from budgetary resources – used for editing the review Philobiblon and/or other publications linked to it, when sold on marketing basis, becomes "useful" for the second, the third time. But the same quantity of paper used for purposes not analyzed on a marketing basis (even in a symbolical way) regarding their efficiency and utility, represent a loss for the institution, for the budget and for the tax payer. Symbolic or not, marketing has to be a responsibility for every library, even for the budgetary ones.

These attempts materialized in a relatively short time in the year 1998, with the publication – in Romanian – of a *Philobiblon Anthology*: *Hermeneutica Bibliothecaria (I),[4]* supported by the Soros Foundation for an Open Society. However, despite of the volume's solid conception, it was not sold, because of moral obstacles and lack of internal market knowledge. Anyway, the volume was published with external (extra-budgetary) and central budgetary resources, its symbolical benefits having a redundant effect. That experience pointed out the necessity of special efforts towards marketing.

Since this volume contained an innovating analysis on Romanian bibliological literature from the periodicals of the field, and regarding the importance of newly used methods, data and results, outlined the intention to a more detailed analysis. But this time through a *Bibliographic Database*, which uses not only new bibliometric techniques, but also content analysis. The database was actually sold in the year 2000, making a profit of 120 million leis.

In the same year, 2000, the *Philobiblon's* editors published a new volume: *Management for the Future – Libraries and Archives[5]* , which was also meant to be sold, obtaining in a relatively short time orders for all copies, making a 25% profit (7 million leis) beside its costs[6]. This year, 2004, at the end of October, we are about to publish the second volume of the Philobiblon Anthology: *Hermeneutica Bibliothecaria (II)*. Obviously we are going to take it out to the market and sell it, the marketing efforts concerning this action developing at the moment. After an ample promoting and advertising action, *Hermeneutica Bibliothecaria (II)* gathered the necessary orders in order to bring profit.

We are convinced that our experiences show and argue for the fact that even in libraries, while being non-profit organizations, there are challenges for the implementation of real marketing actions. It is also important to realize the fact that using these possibilities in a narrow manner, it reduces our general, actual and future possibilities, weakening the "background" of potentiality, necessary for future development.

CONCLUSION

Generally, "Lucian Blaga" Central University Library should increase the transparency of its services, so that users may appreciate their complexity and use them for their educational experience. It is important to think first of all about new users, fresh-mates, who confront with problems of orientation, use of our databases, information search, not being aware of all the free or fee-based services they can make use of. It is necessary to improve the library's offers and to attract more students by this.

Our library shows some lacks, disfunctionalities and needs offering a high standard of quality services, indispensable for an institution with different categories of users, to provide quality information as a support for teaching, learning and research. We have to consider first of all the need to have an information desk, very important for new users, visitors, partners and everyone who needs information about our services or library. Near the entrance, as a first orientation point, we should have a legend tag containing every location in our library.

As a marketing point of view and not only, it is very important for the users, the potential users, the partners, the financial supporters and the public opinion to be acquainted with the institution, the services and even the personnel involved in offering the necessary information, but also the possibility to explore new horizons. It is highly important for the library's partners and financial supporters to get in touch with the functioning system, through efficiency. So, it would be necessary, at the beginning of the university year, to initiate some library presentation, not only for our library, but also for other similar institutions; this way, these actions become not just some simple presentations, but real experience exchange. The publicity and advertising also contribute to outlining the library's image, through the distribution of informational "flyers", posters, mass-media (press media, radio, television) and the Internet.

As long as the readers are the main segment of users, it is necessary for us to find out their own opinions about the services we provide, as well as their needs, upon which we should reorganize some of the services.

One of the information strategies concerning this matter is represented by the "suggestion boxes" placed in accessible locations, nearby reading rooms and even on the library's web-site, where users can express their opinions and suggestions without indicating their names. Many of these practices are extremely simple and traditional. That's why it is crucial to understand: they do not automatically become marketing techniques just by re-naming them with a marketing terminology, but also by including them in well-structured and determined conceptions. In the same time these conceptions have to be sufficiently opened, "lively" and dynamic to once again re-open the horizons for creative metaphors[7].

REFERENCES

1. Sergio (Z). Sfârsitul marketingului. Editura Nemira: Bucuresti. 2001: *Introduction.*
2. Association of Research Libraries, Marketing and Public Relations in ARL Libraries, SPEC Flyer no. 240. Online: http://www.arl.org/spec/240fly.html.

3. Philobiblon, Bulletin of the "Lucian Blaga"Central University Library, Vol.I.,Issues 1-2/1996, pp. 134; Vol.II., Issue 1/1997, pp. 136; Vol. II., Issue 2/ 1997, pp. 237; Vol. III., Issues 1-2/1997, pp. 319; Vol. IV-V-VI-VII., 1999-2002, pp. 538; Vol. VIII-IX., 2003-2004, pp. 573.
4. Iliº (F) and Costea (I). Biblioteca Bibliologica, Editura Presa Universitarã Clujeanã. 1998: 283.
5. Anghelescu (H G B) and Király (I V), Eds. Biblioteca Bibliologica. Editura Presa Universitarã Clujeanã,. 1998: 216.
6. István Kiraly (V) and Florentina (P M) *Proiect pentru implementarea viziunii si a practicilor de marketing în biblioteca,* under way of appearance. 2004
7. Ricoeur (P). La métaphore vive, Études. Éditions du Seuil. Paris. 1975.

FINALLY SOMEBODY WANTS TO HEAR WHAT TEENAGERS HAVE TO SAY : MARKETING IN A CROTIA'S PUBLIC LIBRARY

Verena Tibljas

Abstract *Teenagers, is the most important segment of users of a public library. But, meeting their needs is a challenge for information and library professionals. Library study trip is new and innovative strategy of the project and critical for understanding each other. Personal involvement in craft, design, painting, creative writings, and surfing are important strides to bring intimacy, which ultimately lead to developing trust for the services of the library. This mutual understanding, intimacy and trust will lead developing relationships between the library and users. More so, the habits and interest developed during this age goes through life. The present paper shares such experiences in a public library in Croatia.*

INTRODUCTION

Rijeka City Library is a public library of the city of Rijeka, the largest Croatian harbour located on the west-north Adriatic coast. The library tends to be cultural, educational, social and information centre of the City (as much as the circumstances allow it). It is open to everybody. As a public library, it promotes democratic values and acts as the heart of the community. Founded on the principle of openness, it is a local access point to knowledge, information, culture and quality leisure time. Library is one of the places where people can be introduced to new technologies and new media. Social inclusion is an important part of library policy.

The Library founder is the City of Rijeka. Library depends on the finances of The City of Rijeka, Ministry of Culture of the Republic of Croatia, Primorsko-Goranska County and Library's own income.

It is situated in nine different locations, with 4 suburb branches + bibliobus and the Central Library which consists of: Adults' Department, Children's Department, Periodicals Department, Newspaper Reading Department and Self-educational department.

Rijeka City Library doesn't have a Youth Department. This project explains how a group of young people started a fight for what they're entitled to and how shaken hormones can become effective.

ABOUT TEEN FOR TEENS PROJECT

The *Teens for Teens* project presents a special kind of library service which is being felt as a need in raising new generations of readers and which has been offered by Rijeka City Library to its members. It shows an actual example how to organize a library lobby out of a group of library users, starting from their teenage years.

An educated and non-typical librarian chooses out of a big group of teenage users those who are potential associates. The librarian initiates their involvement, gets their approval and willingness to cooperate, helps in creating their involvement and is responsible for unusual innovations that the young bring to library programmes with their easy-going and creative attitude. Training (user education) makes young volunteers cross the bridge from passive users to active designers of library atmosphere. Trained teenage moderators of library programmes become active participants in the process of their own social inclusion. They also become a role model for their peers who enter the process and spread the network.

At the same time, by organizing socially aware teenage volunteer community, the library gains a strong lobby. The lobby strengthens the role of the library in the local community. It is expected that the lobby should be involved in various social and political issues, even in authority agencies that eventually decide on finances and the role of the library in the community.

Teenagers, defined as young persons aged 13 to 19, are a hypersensitive age group caught somewhere in between childhood and adulthood, demanding special care and attention. Therefore, it is surprising that in many countries there are no special library services for the young. In Croatia they have only started.

In addition to Guidelines for Library Services for Young Adults issued by IFLA Section of Libraries for Children and Young Adults, libraries have real and special opportunity to participate actively and in good faith in the process of growing up. This is the opportunity that shouldn't be missed.

How do teenage workshops in Rijeka City Library differ from the other library activities? They have been created, prepared and hosted by teenagers themselves. Library's program coordinator, as the project manager, coordinates the workshops. Contents and structure of the workshops are very diverse, as a result of different personal preferences of young people creating and moderating the workshops. Workshops take place regularly, at predefined times, once a week, every two weeks or once a month. They are open to public. Workshops are moderated by teenagers-volunteers. Their voluntary work is the result of years and years of living with(in) the Library.

In the context of the city where free time activities are defined by spare time market, organized and realized with a commercial purpose, Rijeka City Library with *Teens for Teens* project offered much more humanistic approach and became the true centre of the community, imposing itself in public as a place popular even to those people who would otherwise never have visited it.

Teens for Teens project of Rijeka City Library started in autumn 1998, culminated in autumn 2001, and, with certain changes and improvements, still goes on.

Since 1998, approximately 4000 kids and young people participated in project activities, with 35 teen–workshop-moderators. Training-the-trainers-method made the Library cultural centre of the teen-community. Teens are happy to join activities presented by their peers, and often new workshops hosts are recruited among participants.

The project met with appropriate response on national level, because it is innovative and because it introduces children and teenagers to reading activities, volunteering, teamwork and living in the community. Group of Rijeka City Library's volunteers have a special way of presenting their work and spreading the network: as library ambassadors, they're visiting other libraries in the country and abroad, training other young library users to reveal their own creativity for each other.

The idea of teenage-workshops started as a teenage-brain-storming. Striving to offer new contents to the young of Rijeka, away from smoke and alcohol, they decided to take advantage of their own sources of creativity and start workshops for their peers.

WHAT IS OFFERED?

Different contents depending on teenage-interests: a creative writing workshop, readers' club, a relaxation workshop, arts & craft creative workshop, the Internet workshop, a debating society, discussion and socializing workshop, a communication workshop, Teen Tea Time - an informal way of socializing, a small talk in English among teenagers who regularly meet in the library, an ecological workshop, a chat workshop, (dead) poet's society, loud readings, a friendship workshop based on psychological games etc.

Teen-workshops contain…

Magic pen: a creative writing workshop intended for those who like writing and discovering depths of one's creativity. Helped by the book Creative Writing by Dianne Doubtfire and upon the example of Toby Litt's creative writing workshop, two 18-year-olds teach workshop attendants different forms of writing. Among topics of the workshop you can find: What is a novel and how to write one? Is writing poetry as simple as it seems? How to compose an interesting interview? Has a letter died out?

Bookworm café: readers' club, for teenagers of 14 and older who love reading and are willing to share their impressions and thoughts with others. Two 16-year-olds guide their peers through teenage literature introducing various games: introduction, relaxation, charade, game of knowledge, quick wit, word association, book recommendations and so on, all named after popular drinks available in every café. Besides good will and love for literature, the only thing you need for this workshop is your own mug!

Book Quiz – a yearly entertaining and educational quiz competition. Through games of knowledge and quick wit competitors show how well-read they are. There are some popular guests and valuable prizes both for competitors and the audience.

Dead Poets Society – informal poetry readings inspired by the movie of the same title, by candle-lights and flashlights, on special occasions with special guests – young poets and musicians from Rijeka.

Popular citizens of Rijeka & their favourite childhood books – a programme in which famous citizens recommend favourite books from their childhood. Among guests, comprising musicians, actors, fashion designers, athletes, journalists and so on, there was the mayor of Rijeka at the time.

Literary round tables on subjects from teenage literature, with guests professionals on certain topics – drug addiction, family violence, violence against animals and so on.

String: a relaxation workshop, including stretching, guitar music, releasing weekly negative energy, accumulating positive energy, laughter therapy. Stressed by numerous demands at school, teenagers eagerly look forward to Thursday evenings – after the Library has closed its doors to clients, an hour of complete relaxation begins. Moderated by two girls (17&18-year-old).

Patchwork: an art-creative workshop which produces, over small talk, unusual original artefacts made by imaginative hands. It is the workshop that shows, in a most obvious way, a special connection among participants. Hosted by two 17-year-old creative girls.

Surf: the Internet workshop, teaches participants the possibilities of the Internet, browsing useful and interesting web sites, specific searches on the web (information for school papers, homeworks, personal interest and so on), how to use e-mail, how to search CD-ROMs (the poll showed that Croatian teenagers are not familiar with this activity). Moderators of the workshop are two 18-year-olds who took their "job" very seriously. They wrote a set of rules to protect the Library, themselves, technology equipment and participants from possible difficulties and misunderstandings.

Let's go, naked!: a debating society, discussion and socializing workshop, intended for high school students only. It discusses topics of interest to the young, for example: Can an individual change the world?; Do you believe in fate?; Should society accept an individual or should an individual adjust to the society?; Legal limitations for the young; Can students change the educational system?; Are the football players over-payed?; Is reading in or out?. The latter topic proved to be very appropriate for an intense discussion; it showed that there are young people who like reading and that they can fight for their right to read. Moderated by two 18-year-old girls and one 19-year-old boy.

Special programme: Teen Tea Time, with a motto "To act as an Englishman from time to time isn't bad at all", takes place on Wednesdays at five o 'clock. Teen

Tea Time, as the title shows, is a workshop for teenagers at the time when the English traditionally have their tea. This workshop presents an informal way of socializing, a small talk in English among teenagers who regularly meet there. The purpose of this workshop is to inform teenagers of rich library stock in the English language in Children's department, as well as to make them aware of the importance of conversation in English as a way of applying contents learned in classrooms. The British Embassy in Croatia has supported this programme. The British Ambassador in Croatia, Mr. Nicholas Jarrold, during his visit to Teen Tea Time donated Rijeka City Library a valuable teenage book collection.

Twins, interlibrary teen chatting...there are teenage teams like ours elsewhere in the world as well, so we want to find them and play with them...An 18-year-old-boy have the leading role...

Face, young & successful...Yes, they are all around us, they just need to be brought to Corner and they will share the secret how to become successful (and still stay young). A girl (17) and a boy (19) act as main actors. This is their workshop.

Open globe II, traveling stories...For years we have been traveling around the world, searching for...? Who searches for what, a matter of his/her own, but we all like to here it! With photos, souvenirs, films and music we are travelling to a memory of...A 17-year-old-girl is responsible for the itinerary...

Story Super Short, festival of loud reading...Marko Luka Zubèiæ (18), young celebrated author of two novels (*Open sea dream, IN-Ri)* is a host. And everyone is welcome to Little festival of the alternative literature and feast of loud reading.

"Let's be friends": a friendship workshop based on psychological games represents a motto of all the workshops mentioned earlier. Friendships that will arise as a result of all these workshops are invaluable. They will become a source of new ideas and new workshops that will develop through time. Although this year's workshops are a result of the process of their moderators' growing up in earlier Library programmes, this is just a beginning. A beginning of new growing-ups.

The same group of young people decided to start together another project, the "Bookmarker": a magazine for young people that promotes reading.

The workshops mentioned above exclude all who are not teenagers, but there are some workshops that welcome younger children as well:

Checkmate: a chess workshop for those who like stretching their brains, for those who don't have a clue about chess but are willing to learn, and for those who can play chess but don't have a partner. The workshop is open for children of 7 and above, and hosted by a 15-year-old girl who is very successful at chess tournaments (state junior champion).

Eko-koe: an ecology workshop offering various outdoor and indoor activities to children of 9 and older, in order to encourage their environmental awareness. Hosted by two 16-year-olds.

Help: the English language workshop moderated by a 14-year-old girl who has been learning English since she was 6. To 11-year-olds she offers help in learning, creative exercises, conversation exercises, establishing contacts with pen-pals from all over the world.

All the workshops:

- take place regularly (once a week, ones or twice a month)
- are open to the public
- are free of charge

offer a new, richer kind of growing up, with a dimension of friendship and sharing, something that is missing in the modern race for unknown values.

Volunteer community organized within the library became an exemplary focus-group of national network of programmes to include teenagers into life and work of the library and to include the library in the life of the community.

TRAVELLING LIBRARY

Travelling library – visiting library works as a part of *Teens for Teens* project (presented in poster session at 2002 IFLA Conference in Glasgow).

Project presentations are organized live outside the home library:

- in primary and secondary schools in Rijeka
- in public libraries all over Croatia (Zagreb, Zadar, Osijek, Koprivnica, Bjelovar)
- in public libraries outside Croatia (Ljubljana, Slovenia) – international cooperation
- at national book fair in Zagreb (in cooperation with Medvešèak Library, Zagreb)
- at science festival in Rijeka

Presentations were organized for visiting groups:

- participants of Croatian Readers' Association conference (2002)
- school librarians from two of Croatian counties (2003)
- young volunteers from Koprivnica City Library (2004)
- young library patrons from four Croatian towns: Bjelovar, Koprivnica, Zadar and Zagreb (2004)

By direct presentation of results outside the home library we try to disseminate the mission of open doors, cooperation and experience-sharing, and to motivate broader community to start activities and cooperation with teenagers. It is a special educational pyramid - everybody gains something, both the participants and the community.

In accordance with mission of public libraries stated in IFLA Manifesto for Public Libraries, workshops contents correspond to key guidelines:

- encouraging reading habits and literacy
- encouraging participants' personal creative progress
- promoting democracy, social skills and rhetoric
- adding a dimension of global awareness, promoting the English language as the most useful foreign language, absolutely indispensable in computer literacy today
- offering easier information exchange, developing computer literacy and teaching about the Internet as a compelling source of information
- developing environmental awareness, important in times when we realize what each individual can and must do in preserving our planet.

Project results:

- more than 1000 teenagers, 3000 younger kids and about 100 grown-ups involved in the project
- raising citizen awareness about library existence in the city centre, about necessity of stimulating reading habits
- adding Youth Department in the project of future, new Rijeka City Library building
- changing and enriching young volunteers with experience of giving, taking and sharing abstract and non-material values
- preparing them for the real life

Project is supported by different sponsors: a local cinema, video stores, theatre society, youth club, book publishers provide awards for winners of prize contents (tickets for shows and rock concerts, DVD films, books and similar).

Local and national media come to the *Teen Library Corner* on their own initiative to report on library programmes and interview participants. Finally somebody wants to hear what teenagers have to say.

More and more talented young people want to volunteer in our library programmes, even the age average is getting higher – university students also want space to express their need for culture.

Teens – library volunteers participate in creating project plans for a new library building, where they will finally get the Youth Department. They have worked very hard to get it and they have definitely deserved it.

RECOGNITION

The project was nominated for the Astrid Lindgren Award (2004), and it's got the City Award for the best project for teenagers' healthy growing up (2004). The Project manager won the Young Librarian's National Award (2002) and Annual City Award (2003) for the same purpose. At the 70th IFLA Conference in Buenos

Aires (2004) the poster presenting the way of developing young library volunteers from passive users to active designers won the 1 st prize among 80 posters from all over the world.

There are obvious improvements in collective awareness within the community: the Library attracted public attention.

Besides regular marketing actions such as publishing library programs in media and public places in the community, one of the strongest marketing tools are presentations of programs for aimed users groups, particularly travelling presentations beyond the library borders (schools, public manifestations, other cities in the country and abroad), exchange and training of young volunteers from other city libraries in Croatia.

Wise (planned) marketing reflects in media covering library programs, in sponsors interested for involving, in reactions by city government which award the project and bring decisions in Library benefit (one of the most important: priority of building the new City library), more financial means for library programs, in growing youth interest but also in all other users of library contents and services, in stronger awareness community where the Library works.

RESPONSE FROM THE COMMUNITY

The best marketing for a library are satisfied users. Praise spread by word of mouth. These teenagers' main motto is: "If you want to change the world, start with yourself". Teen-volunteers...about...*Rijeka City Library*, *Teen Corner*, themselves and growing up...

"Socializing and attending workshops in *Rijeka City Library* are among my favourite activities. I met a respectable number of interesting people there, found some new friends, hosted some of the workshops and together we all started to change our part of the universe, our city of Rijeka." (Petra Mrsa, 18)

"I think of my library as a sort of a home. We often go there to lose ten minutes or so, and sometimes we go there just because we feel like it. Librarians have created a really pleasant air there, and it is great to lie back in *Teen Corner* for half an hour, browse through magazines, play a game, listen to a new CD of some cool band, or simply join the workshop." (Zoran Uzar, 17)

"The essential reason why our city library is so great is that we, teenagers, now have the alternative to hanging out in bars. And we can learn something along the way, do something creative, meet new people and whole new worlds, we can find our own dreams (mine is a journey to Brugge, Belgium) and goals, we can listen to music and discover a new great band." (Eliza Bertone, 17)

"Besides, librarians at *Teen Corner* are not just ordinary librarians. They are very supportive, starting with those moments in life when you need a nice word or hug, to offering advice and support about writing. I often ask myself: What would I be like if I hadn't discovered my library?" (Una Rebic, 16)

CONCLUSION

Organizing diverse pedagogical animating programmes for kids and teens, especially working with young people, with final aims – promoting reading, socialization of children and teenagers, raising public awareness of public libraries as central points in connecting interdisciplinary domains in education, upbringing and creating free time for children and teenagers, gives a purpose of Teens for teens project. Eventually, through programmes with children and teenagers and through stronger cooperation with local media, sponsors and a number of experts, the Library becomes more visible, with stronger position in the community.

The special advantage of this project is that it doesn't depend on substantial financial resources. It's equally relevant all over the world and can easily be applied any place, in places where there is no money for expensive projects, as well as where the digital world separates young people from one another. All that such a project requires is a good will, skilful organization and young people needing to prove their abilities. In the long run, this project helps librarians to dispense more time for other activities, because in this way they get trained assistants and independent team-leaders.

It is all very simple: *teenagers are all around, they only need to be picked.*

BRANDING AS A PROCESS: A VIEWPOINT FROM SOUTH AFRICA

Kathy Kunneke

Abstract *Many questions arise about the necessity for branding a library. Branding is identified as an essential process in the service delivery of the academic library in a scenario of constant change, in the technological and publishing environment. The academic library has to remain synonymous with visionary information sourcing and delivery. Libraries have to use marketing tools such as branding and the development of an appropriate logo, which encapsulates an image of what the service offering of the library, is, and which keeps its brand top-of-the-mind as an information sourcing organization. The quality of the service delivery of an academic library will determine its worthiness as a brand. The phases of brand recognition are briefly discussed as well as the steps in developing a logo. The necessity for staff to accept the logo is highlighted as well as the costly exercise of brand rollout.*

INTRODUCTION

Many questions arise about the necessity for branding a library. Are libraries a force in the market? Why? Why do customers acknowledge the value of a brand? Will the brand promise of the library be reflected in the actual "shopping" experience of the library customer and prove to be trustworthy? Why does an academic library need its own brand? Are libraries brand-worthy?. These questions are addresses in the paper.

MEANING OF BRANDING

A brand is the "corporations promise to deliver specific attributes, its credibility based on reputation and the visitor's possible previous experience[1]. Frankel [2], the most widely read on (and off) line branding expert, on the other hand feels that "branding is not about getting your prospects to choose you over your competition: its about getting your prospects to see you as the only solution to their problem".

Branding gives the organization personality. The organization's brand gives it a distinguishing character and is enhanced by a name, symbol, icon or logo and or catch phrase or jingle which distinguishes it or enhances the recall about the character of the organization and its products or services.

To the organization the brand forms the cornerstone of marketing decisions. The brand enhances the ability of the organization to demonstrate its value in the marketplace. Once it has established the value of its services or products in the marketplace, it uses its brand recognition as leverage for future marketing campaigns.

PROCESS AND PROCESS IMPROVEMENT

"A business process is a set of related activities that produces specific end products"[3]. A business activity includes marketing, and branding as a process within the marketing cluster of processes. Processes very seldom exist in isolation. Processes must continuously be improved or adapted to new demands to continually add value to the customers' information seeking experience.

A brand requires extensive organizational commitment. Brands come from within the organization. What the organization does is therefore its processes. These processes reflect on the organization's image. When you improve a process you attempt to make it better. When improving marketing processes one is attempting to improve processes by means of which the customer is made aware of the personality and qualities of the organization and its products or services. The customer is one of the critical participants involved in marketing, and has a diverse set of interests and preferences. One desires to improve a process in the long term and in the short term and thereby improves the supply chain of the organization. The specific goal therefore of improving marketing processes in the library is improving the process by which the library assists the customer in acquiring knowledge about the services the library offers. Processes must provide exemplary services to customers and therefore it is not only the marketing processes that must be improved, but also the processes that back up the library's service delivery. This, therefore, includes processes involving customer facing services as well as support services, which all lead to improvement of the quality of services, reduced time of delivery and greater efficiency. This does not just involve reducing costs since this can lead to poorer services, when the resulting processes are so lean that they are no longer effective. To remain a top-of-the mind brand the organization must constantly work at improving what is good.

To implement and improve the branding process, an in-depth understanding of what the business offers is essential. The brand should reflect the reality, not a blue-sky scenario. Are libraries giving branding the necessary attention? Are their operations fine-tuned to exploit the power of their brand as engines of growth and success? There are many critical success factors involved in ensuring that all employees of the organization accept the brand. Are academic libraries giving their brand the investment, care and feeding it needs to grow and develop its greatest possible value to the organization?

ACADEMIC LIBRARY CUSTOMERS DEPEND ON HAVING TRUST IN THE BRAND OF THE LIBRARY

Academic libraries in the 21st century need to vigorously market their services since the traditional library consisting only of books does not exist any more. The immense changes that technology and the Internet have brought about and will continue to be instrumental in library service delivery have to be communicated to the library customer. The library has to remain synonymous with visionary information sourcing and delivery. Libraries have to continue making their brand, top-of-the-mind information sourcing organizations. Many processes exist to actually deliver the service of the library. As commented before branding is a specific process that enhances the customers' knowledge and recall of the quality and kind of services being offered by the organization. Out of between eight to ten marketing processes that can be identified to market the services of an academic library "branding the services of the library" is one of the processes.

The quality of the service delivery of an academic library will determine its worthiness as a brand. Just like any customer, library customers "buy" benefits. They seek information for a purpose e.g. enhancing their knowledge; for a research project in order to complete a research project; or perhaps completing an assignment or obtain a degree. The library creates a service with features that enable the customer to find appropriate information in the most efficient way. The customer, by means of finding appropriate information, is seeking a benefit. The library must therefore understand the benefits that its different customer segments are seeking and create the most appropriate route for the customer to be satisfied that they have benefited by using the library.

Academic libraries form part of the overall brand of the university to which they are a support system. The university owns the brand and the library must comply with the university brand; however the library has its own sub-brand. The university therefore requires of the library to display the 'mother' brand together with its sub-brand. The library needs its own brand, since it offers other unique aspects of the learning experience to the student and researcher than the various faculties or colleges within the university offer. The library's brand however is enhanced by the mother brand's legacy. The university can also use an excellent library service as a unique selling point when marketing the university itself.

A service organization runs on the perceived quality and value-add of the service offered to its customers. This happens in the processes followed by the staff of the library in offering the information gathering service to the customer and they either enhance or break down the customer's experience. The library customer should depart with a piece of the library's 'soul' when they feel that they have benefited from using the library. Innovative processes, which supply timeous and efficient service delivery, add to the library customer's shopping experience. The strong "flavour" of quality of the library services should shine through in any contact that the library customer has with the library.

THE PHASES OF BRAND RECOGNITION

The following phases can be distinguished in the customer's attitude toward and knowledge of a specific brand [4].

- **Brand unawareness**: At this stage customers view a product or service as the same as any other similar product. They therefore do not have knowledge of or recognize its distinguishing characteristics
- **Brand recognition**: At this stage the customer has heard about and/or seen the brand and remembers it. The customer can therefore distinguish it from other similar products or services. Brand recognition increases the chances of repeat use of the product or service.
- **Brand rejection**: In this phase the customer finds the brand unacceptable and even though there is brand recognition they will not buy or use the product or service. Brand rejection hardly ever changes to brand acceptance unless something extraordinary happens. It is immensely difficult to change the perception of the customer from rejection to acceptance since it is based on certain experiences or perceptions.
- **Brand acceptance**: A brand is accepted as soon as the customer considers a specific brand as one of the alternatives of similar products or services and considers it acceptable to buy or use.
- **Brand preference**: This step follows brand acceptance. Based on previous experience the customer may prefer this product or service to those of competitive product or service. Here the product or service starts occupying a favourable competitive position in the market.
- **Brand insistence**: At this final stage in brand acceptance the consumer refuses to buy or use another brand or service. In the eyes of the consumer this product or service has become special. This is the point where the customer in a service organization such as a library insists on only using this service.

The excellent marketing and branding processes of an organization result in the customer having an extensive knowledge and experience of the products or services that an organization has on offer or can deliver. If the experience has been good brand insistence most often is the result.

IMPORTANCE OF ACADEMIC LIBRARY BRAND

Brands depend on people to deliver them, especially in a service organization, where the customer's contact with the brand and impression of what it delivers can be reduced to a telephone conversation with, or e-mail to, a customer service representative. The people delivering the brand image have to understand it, spontaneously embrace it and be fully committed to convey it in the best interest of the brand. This often results in people and process-related change. An organization's culture ,therefore, needs to be changed to become more positive, focused and productive. A branding campaign has to be launched which weaves the brand into the fabric of the organization into every decision that both the customer faces and support staff makes. This involves introducing key brand messages into service delivery and acting on inappropriate actions by staff, which failed to keep the promise of the brand. This does not involve little branded give-always to customers, like glass coasters, bookmarks, pens, etc. This actually involves looking at where the process to deliver the service and the brand promise has gone wrong. This is the responsibility of the marketing cluster of processes of a library.

Staff have to be assisted in identifying with the fact that they are key in satisfying the customer's need for ideal service delivery. They have to want to please the customer. This takes a special kind of person. Managing the brand, especially where the human element is involved remains a difficult process for the brand manager to keep under close control since the staff member brings his/her whole set of life experiences and views of his/her fellow man to the workplace. Since this involves the human element, staff have to have an emotional investment in the organization. If the brand is not saleable and do-able, on a day-to-day basis, within the organization by members of staff, how will customers be convinced?

"One key aspect of establishing trust with consumers is the reputation of a brand, together in many cases, with personal experience" [5].

THE CREATION OF A LOGO AS PART OF THE BRAND

A logo is the encapsulation of the personality and quality services or products an organization offers. It assists in instant brand recognition and is a powerful tool in marketing and branding processes. It is important to test the perceptions of staff before choosing a proposed logo. Staff should be proud of the logo of the organization that they work for.

In one of the biggest academic libraries in South Africa a branding exercise was entered into as part of the University's corporate branding campaign. It was important to be part of the branding exercise for both the library and the university, since the library was seen as a unique selling point for the university as a hole. Branding therefore has to have a similar look, feel, colours and format to the corporate brand. An outside branding company was used to do the creative interpretation of suggestions offered to them by representatives of staff who had identified the organizational properties of the library in consultation with various members of staff. With a staff component of over 200 it was essential to get maximum acceptability of a proposed logo.

A marketing representative presented an explanation of the purpose of branding and the branding exercise to staff. The process of arriving at several possible logos was explained. A polling exercise was open to all staff to vote on their choice of logo.

Staff did not like the first set of proposed logos, with various colour combinations, which were rather avante guard (similar to Example 1) for the library world and gave reasons and ideas. These ideas and suggestions were again shared with the designers who created a new logo in various colour combinations based on the recommendations of staff.

THE NECESSITY FOR STAFF TO ACCEPT THE LOGO

The following logos are given as examples and do not apply to any academic library. A logo with more traditional elements (similar to Example 2) was more acceptable as a second polling proved. This clearly showed that it was not simply the appeal of various colour combinations that were the catalyst in the choice by staff but the inherent, meaning the symbols in the logo conjured up in the minds of staff. This deduction is based on many comments received by staff concerning the meaning of a proposed logo (similar to Example 1) presented to them. Some of the comments were:

"That logo does not say anything about our Library. It does not say anything about all the various sources of information that we offer access to".

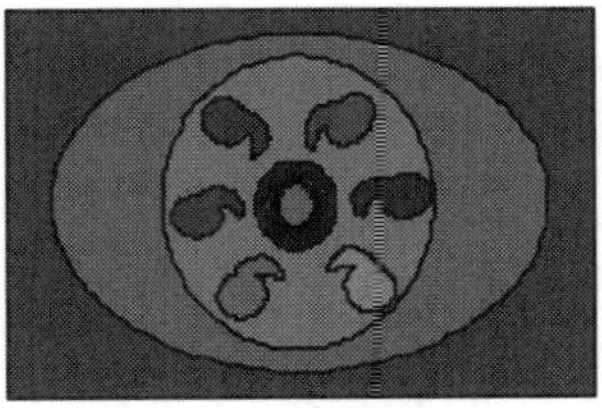

Example 1

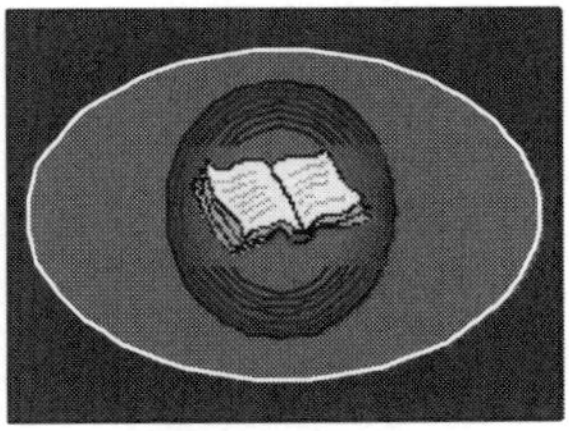

Example 2

"We are not in the communication business. Speech bubbles depicting our information delivery to our various colleges (Example 1) do not incorporate anything which we really stand for not.

Which logo in your opinion would be more acceptable? Which would you as librarian be able to identify more with?

Entrenched emotional associations with the characteristics of an organization such as a library that has a long history, which then suddenly starts changing its nature through the influence of information technology and communication often does not find immediate acceptance in the minds of staff. From a personal point of view for libraries a more conventional content of a logo (as in Example 1) finds more acceptance. A logo should have a universal meaning and endeavour to convey the same message to a variety of audiences from various backgrounds. The designer of a logo must be aware of this and not design a logo too abstract a form.

THE BRAND ROLL-OUT: A COSTLY EXERCISE

A branding process should not be entered into lightly. The success of the brand depends on the multiple applications of the logo to heighten brand recognition and establish knowledge of the set of assets linked to a brand's name and symbol. The heightened brand recognition eventually establishes the brand equity that an organization is striving to obtain. This is an expensive exercise, yet if performed in the correct way and applied optimally by the library in all the various marketing formats, it is worth the money and time spent. Branding must touch the entire organization and has to be managed well. Here are a couple of examples covering most areas where the brand of the organization can be applied or reinforced.

- People – awareness of the brand qualities and training in customer care
- Freebees – give-aways like mouse pads, glasses, notebooks, caps, pens, pencils etc.
- Any communication – bookmarks, brochures, booklets
- Interior decorating – Colour is a very important feature which can either make customers or staff agitated or calm.
- Web pages – web access must reflect the power of branding. An important window for communicating what the brand can offer
- Posters
- Staff cards
- Clothing
- Stationery – letterheads, envelops, memos etc.
- Conference presentations or any other presentations by members of staff.

This is quite a handful for a brand manager to regulate as far as adherence to brand requirements is concerned. If adherence is not consistent throughout the organization great damage can be done to the brand.

CONCLUSION

As referred previously to the "flavour" of the services that the customer of the academic library experiences when interacting with our academic libraries a concluding analogy can be shared concerning the services of libraries. The "flavour" should never be watered down or only be "vanilla flavour". It must always be the best you can offer, the richest most beneficial service available to your customer. Is the service your library offers rich, sweet, creamy and fruity like a marvellous pavlova, or is it watery, with a touch of sweetness and fruitiness, like an ice lollypop? If it is like a pavlova, you have a good brand, which tells customers a lot about your service. Yes, your library is brand-worthy and your brand is a good asset, an asset that should be treasured and nurtured. Do not neglect it. Be sure that the customer experiences this "flavour" of your service every time he or she visits your library, be it physically or online.

REFERENCES

1. Marcella (A J). Establishing trust in virtual markets. Altamonte, Springs, Florida: Institute of Internal Auditors. 1999: 9.
2. Frankel (R). Revenge of the brand [Online] http://www.revengeofbrandx.com/brandx/index.html Viewed 7 September 2004.
3. Lientz (B P) and Rea (K P). Achieve lasting process improvemen: Reach six sigma goals without the pain. Amsterdam: Academic Press. 2002: 3.
4. University of South Africa. Only study guide for MNM202-6: Product management. Pretoria: University of South Africa.
5. Ibid, 1. p.5

MARKETING OF LIBRARY AND INFORMATION SERVICES : THE VIEW FROM KNOWLEDGE MANAGEMENT WITHIN THE FINANCIAL SERVICES SECTOR

John Ganly
Pam Rollo

Abstract *The right information delivered to the right person in the right format at the right time is the mantra for both marketing and knowledge management (KM) in a financial institution. Achievement of these goals requires an understanding of the factors involved in financial transactions and the role played by staff at varying levels. Issues confronting the financial KM librarian include scarcity of analytical information, dynamic nature of information, global impact of information, confidentiality requirements and administrative competitiveness and a reluctance to share information. This paper will describe the environment in which the financial KM librarian works and the steps which are taken to meet the requirements outlined above. Information storage, information choice and distribution models effective in these settings will be identified and described.*

CONCEPT

No general agreement exists on a universal definition of knowledge management. The closest we can come to defining the concept is to say that it includes "delivering the right information, in the right format, to the right person at the right time." Financial information in a knowledge management environment carries with it a specific set of problems.

Classic KM looks to the selection, classification, storage and distribution of information once it has been acted upon or changed by that institution. The interesting thing with KM is that the organization renders the value, so one organization may value a body of knowledge that another organization finds unsophisticated or impossible to share or manage.

In financial institutions there are two levels of information gatherers - an unsophisticated user and a very sophisticated user. One might suggest that knowledge deployment is also operating at two levels, that knowledge which supports transactions and that knowledge which supports strategy.

The junior user is looking at the information which in current jargon is commoditized information which is repetitive, changeable but still important due to due diligence and regulatory constraints or responsibilities. The KM effort here is to prevent mindless repetition and the ever increasing budget of finding and distributing the exact same information to the same or different junior customers.

The sophisticated user or the rain maker is interested in the organization's relationship to clients and its position among competitors. Mere marketing information isn't applicable. This is the user group which is looking for, trend analysis, some very basic benchmark information (through which they interpret much) and the advisory insight that they can take from one another.

Within the investment banking silo of financial services, most of the knowledge management efforts have been in support of the junior professional. The junior professional is engaged by the firm to collect, distribute and present information, much as the participants in an MBA case study program are used. These young people create three kinds of documents, one called the "public information book" which is created to initiate a base line of information bringing all the participants in a deal up to the same level of knowledge, a presentation for "the beauty contest" which is a marketing document and a presentation document which is a strategy document prepared for clients

The senior professional is looking to create a sophisticated CRM system which documents: who is known by members of the Firm within current or potential clients, what is the quality of the business relationship between the Firm and the client, and are their any current or impending market issues which could influence an opportunity for business with the client base.

While firms within the United States must follow the new regulatory standards stipulated in its "Patriot Act" for demonstrating "knowledge of their customer", this pervasive recommendation is influencing other banks outside of the United States as well. Most of the European members of the financial services sector are also collecting and checking customer identity data to ensure that proscribed classes of consumers may not assume names, open accounts or buy securities illegally. This activity also creates a demand for clean customer databases.

The insurance silo also operates at two levels: the strategist is examining those issues which influence risk and the opportunities for investing the firm's wealth acquired from premiums contributed by those insured and those who are interacting with clients, solving business problems and underwriting policies. While insurance companies have been more successful in making knowledge management techniques successful, it would seem that they are most successful in selecting and calling for knowledge development at the strategy end and initiating communities of practice and technical business solutions at the transactional level of the business.

SETTING

No single entity describes the current universe of financial institutions. As early as 1918 the world of finance began to move away from the individual controlled model established by J.P. Morgan and the 19th century financial barons to a more widespread universe which provided a variety of services including banking, insurance, credit management, and underwriting among others. Until fairly recently in the United States these services were provided by discrete organizations each focusing on its particular service; however, starting in the 1980's an accelerating trend to absorb a variety of services into one organization can be observed, although these behemoth firms still functions most commonly as a series of businesses or fiefdoms, with technology platforms most often their only shared device. It is common today for what began as investment bank to be perceived now as an insurance company, a credit management operation, and a retail securities operation.

The traditional underwriting role of the organization has become only one of the operations which the KM librarian must serve. Despite the information center's desire to serve all members of these huge organizations it seldom is financially supported by all the lines of business. The information center in the financial sector, while still reporting as a cost center must be led and managed as if it were a money making enterprise, booking all of its expenses to the subsidiaries and lines of business which use it and linking all of its work to successfully completed deals. This constant emphasis on ROI influences the acquisition and distribution model.

In a multi service organization the idea of viewing the operation from a resource-based perspective would appear to be the appropriate KM plan; however, in many cases although nominally one company each of the separate service units operates independently of the others with the resulting lack of shared knowledge. Unwillingness to adopt a resource based information model is one major reason why KM has not be widely adopted in the financial sector Lacking strong senior management support due to the reporting structure, both IT and information centers report away from the front office and usually to back office or administration lines, and due to a culture of IT dominance, the success of the KM librarian in these organizations will be difficult to achieve.

The learning organization concept in which a strong will to acquire information and under which a positive attitude toward knowledge sharing are basic preconditions for acceptance of resource-based KM is the primary responsibility of the KM executive in a financial institution. The development of the learning organization brings with it a list of issues that the KM librarian must deal with. Perhaps primary among these is the need to prevent the creation of a knowledge repository which becomes filled with dated, inaccurate and surplus information.

A financial institution can be identified as a Community of Practice (CoP) defined as "knowledge networks, referred to as institutionalized informal networks of professionals managing domains of knowledge" by Gongla, P and Rizutto, C.R. in their paper "Evolving communities of practice: IBM global services experience".(IBM systems journal (40) 4:842-862.2001) or more accurately as a series of such CoPs. In the financial organization these professionals will include portfolio managers, investment analysts, brokers, client managers and accountants among others. The firms clients constitute a separate CoP. Establishing a COP within many financial organizations is challenging due to the fact that research is often seen as a delegated activity and CoPs do not benefit from experienced voices. Most members are junior in experience except in the problem solving arenas within insurance.

The available information resources within the organization include raw data sources such as streaming financial information real –time information, (such as Bloomberg or Reuters) , corporate financial statements, full text electronic journals, newspapers and press releases (Nexis, Factiva) and completed internal reports and studies. This information is stored on the web portal and the intranet. In their paper "Measuring knowledge management effectiveness in communities of practice" (37th Hawaii International Conference on System Sciences Proceedings 2004) Martin Smits and Aldo de Moor evaluate the utilization of the available information resources in a hedge fund operation from the point of view of communication between CoP members, the externalization of this communication in meetings and reports, the addition to the KM information base from the CoP process and the operational value of the KM information base. While portals are superb in providing the single desk-top access to information, the actual gathering of information is often perceived as a time consuming and a type of drudgery due to the heavy emphasis on due diligence in the strictly regulated world of financial services.

The insurance industry in comparison, is an environment eminently suited to the basic concepts of KM. Numerous clients, a wide variety of separate business activities, extensive regulatory requirements and vast amounts of data generated within the organization and available on a flow basis from outside the organization. Faced with the need to retain, analyze, organize and deliver from the storehouse of knowledge available in real terms and combine it with the virtual knowledge available from key employees insurance companies such as AIG and Skandia Insurance have been in the forefront of the KM movement.

Intellectual capital in the insurance industry is recognized as a prime asset and utilizing a wide variety of customized and off- the-shelf software products, this asset is shared within individual companies via traditional channels such as newsletters and specialized encrypted channels on an as needed basis. Skandia Insurance has taken the approach of documenting its intellectual capital in an annual report. Directories of company expertise, divisional report files, competitive intelligence studies and Community of Practice meeting summaries are among the knowledge related modules available in companies in the insurance sector.

In addition to the obvious value of effective KM for internal use, insurers are utilizing their intellectual capital to better inform clients and improve customer relations as well as to meet shareholder reporting requirements. Web page explanations of changes in insurance company policies and rate increases with related Q and A sections and interactivity have in many cases replaced the traditional mailings formerly used for these sensitive client communiqués. Many firms have provided access to information for their clients as well, purchasing, and distributing information through client extranets; AIG provides sophisticated resources for Risk Managers, Legal Professionals and CFOs.

In a company such as CAN, which underwent a major reorganization resulting in the need to consolidate customer information available from over 30 separate operating divisions, Gordon Larson, knowledge officer corporate development, expressed the problem when he stated "We had experts all over the company. We had to make it easy for the employees to tap into the organization." The implication in Larson's statement was the need to enable representatives to effectively provide customers with a wide range of product information. Ask Me Enterprise was the software product employed by CNA in its knowledge centers to facilitate the KM operation within the organization.

All of the factors listed depict the general climate of the insurance company and the specific situations help to crystallize the reality within individual companies. The problems with KM implementation are no different within the insurance setting than in other financial services areas. Resistance on the part of knowledge workers to sharing information, limitations of existing technology to meet the demands for evaluation of knowledge, necessity for full senior management support and start up and ongoing costs are the chief barriers encountered.

PLAYERS

The financial services industry is vast, now more than ever. The investment banking community which is led by the "bulge bracket" Firms, (those five firms at the top of the performance league tables), and their many close competitors are joined by asset managers, private equity firms, venture capitalists, wealth managers, brokerages and hedge funds. Each of these firms is further defined by the instruments they specialize within to fulfil its business, so we have the above firms specializing in public or corporate finance, the debt or fixed income market or the advisory (mergers & acquisitions business), the research business or the trading of securities both institutional and individual.

As commercial banks join this market, we look to the acquisition of information centered on mortgages and credit cards in addition to the normal targets of retail banking whipped into a recipe of marketing and client segmentation (special demographic marketing) for both individuals and businesses (small business to global corporations). Lastly, insurance companies offer several lines of insurance support for specific industries, lines of protection and the lives and possessions of individual clients. Insurance particularly is challenged by the current threats of terrorism and its own protection, that of reinsurance.

Financial services organizations can roughly be segmented internally into two main components, the operating units or CoPs and the executive managers. The external players can be thought of as input factors which would include colleagues, government agencies, clients, shareholders and published information sources.

Investment Banking has experimented with Knowledge Management and a leading bulge bracket firm, Goldman Sachs has recruited and retains a Chief Learning Officer. Morgan Stanley has begun investigating the frame work for a project within investment banking. The majority of these Firms use KM as a way to make the transaction process (the due diligence process) less burdensome and uses the process not as a way to build strategic creativity but to cut costs and save time. Due to the intense pressure on the return on investment, this silo makes no leap of faith into the potential benefit of shared knowledge. Interestingly enough, the champion of the program is rarely the CEO or the Head of a Business Line, but an administrative officer. This means that the application is relegated predominantly to building a thesaurus, creating an indexing system and recycling information from previous proposals. In their own experience, executive professionals have not yet benefited from a KM function as they connect informally finding the formal platform not yet containing the quality of information necessary to their success.

Most of the potential knowledge users or contributors see the process as one that must take place without their integral participation. As the pace within investment banking can be daunting, no individual player wants to be burdened by an activity which does not generate immediate and calculable revenue. Since the revenue value can not be reliably projected if not guaranteed, persuading the actual professionals to participate is usually unsuccessful. This again contributes to the process being an IT driven program as software is relied upon to select and index materials transparently as they are created by the author/user.

While investment banking enjoys some of the most advanced technological platforms, design often concentrates on freeing the user from interaction with others within the organization rather than enhancing communication. The organizations have devised intranets and information access portals, but because of the organization of task assignment, groups function separately and not cohesively.

The KM function within the insurance industry can be used as a model to examine the needs and interaction of the key components of the knowledge network. Skandia which has already been introduced as a best practices model for KM in the insurance industry during the late 90s and views the players as structural elements in its Value Creation Process. In its effort to maximize the value of the intellectual capital within Skandia the KM unit established a matrix of players which includes staff, shareholders, clients and external information providers. Each of the identified groups and individuals in the Skandia model is then assigned a role as a user and contributor. Navigator Approach is utilized by Skandia as an internal tool to deliver the right information to the right player at the right time. The technology structure at Skandia combined with human resources capabilities is directed to providing the players with the highest value level of available knowledge.

Skandia has developed an evaluation scheme which purports to provide an understanding of the value of the intellectual capital players to the company and to report on the level of success the company is achieving in meeting the needs and utilizing the strengths of these components. The success level reporting scheme at Skandia is a matter of interpretation and discussion; however, it is clear that a KM model to be successful must learn the knowledge capacities of the players and implement a plan to develop these competencies on an ongoing basis. The strong support of senior management and the cooperation of the human resources function and the IT group within the organization are necessary for internal player capacity enhancement.

Communication between the nodes in the established KM matrix is a critical factor in the ultimate success of the deployment in a financial services operation. The IT structure within the organization is the major channel for the exchange of knowledge; however, the KM plan in successful implementations includes human interaction in the overall concept. Portal development which encompasses an understanding of the available knowledge resources within the company and which provides for the continual enhancement of the competencies of the players and facilitates effective communication is the ultimate goal for KM within financial institutions.

At Wells Fargo, the commercial bank, the Search and Taxonomy Enterprise Portal was developed in accordance with an understanding of the function, service responsibility, and security level of each player in the matrix. The resulting CoP structure at Wells Fargo is organization wide rather than based on organization chart structure.

Training is the key factor in maintaining the maximum capacity level of each component in the KM structure. In financial services institutions this necessitates the continual input of learning with regard to financial operations as well as to the external regulatory and industry framework surrounding the company. At present the training plans for a majority of financial service organizations consist of separate unit based programs; however, in some instances an effort has been made to centralize and formalize the training and education activities into "corporate universities" which include online classes and less formal training opportunities directed to the common objective of increasing the profitability of the organization by keeping the knowledge structure current and informed. The technology structure of the intranet within the organizations adopting the "corporate university" model must accommodate the training needs established by the KM unit.

NEEDS

The Financial Services industry demands information immediately, hence the demand for real-time information. It relies heavily on the transmittal of tacit knowledge and the margins rely on re-tooling very little and using comparable solutions for consistent transactions. The key is finding the business solution which solves the most problems in the most efficient way; efficiency defined as time and investment saving.

We have seen that the information gathering is segmented as is the quality of information provided. What we have failed to review is a prominent purpose that the due diligence process provides, which is instructional or the transmission of tacit knowledge. During the 1970s and the 1980s, the commercial banks were renowned for their credit training. Junior executives who entered these programs had their careers made and fortune by the tail; the training was excellent and they were provided with all the financial and cultural insight that they might need throughout their long careers. Increasingly financial services professionals do not enjoy long careers with a single employer, forcing acculturation to take place in record time.

Currently in investment banking, the entering banking professional is not formally trained beyond a few weeks. Interim training throughout their career is seldom available. For the maturing professional, the MBA earned many years ago suffices and provides all the professional learning that the executive might need. The vast frontier of knowledge needed to function within the organization is learned on the job. The due diligence or the knowledge transaction experience which is spent in the support of "live" deals is the experience which educates the professional and provides him or her with all the insight necessary to serving the client, learning the ways of the profession and living successfully inside of the organization's culture. Increasingly, this "just-in-time" or "on-demand" style of learning characterizes the demand for knowledge. Many take pride that the demands of this business is so varied and unique that it would be impossible to prepare resources in advance. This is negated by the fact that the financial institutions develop industry and instrument specialities and tout their experience throughout their marketing presentations.

Any knowledge management program in the venue would have to fit a "learn-by-doing" platform which would be interactive in nature and immediately evaluate results for relevance and applicability. Most KM programs are imagined as an art and when imagined as "scientific" fall far short of the scientific performance standards necessary for reliance in this industry. Most of the successful "smart systems" used in this industry rely on financial modelling, enabling software to make trades on behalf of institutions and rate corporate or country debt against a financial standard. This is not an industry looking to access "raw information" through a portal or information selected through alerts triggered by XML tagging. A system which provides several resources which "may" be valuable or "may" be relevant is not going to be relied upon. What this industry is looking for is a sophisticated search engine which can "weigh" the retrieval based on parameters described. This industry is looking for a decision making or business intelligence tool which can evaluate stored materials based on their previous deployment, whether or not the previous deal succeeded and the success of the instrument subsequent to release.

In clearer terms, the tool would find information used in comparable deals which the firm won away from its competitors and then performed according to a success matrix which could be adjusted for market performance during the aftermarket, or let's do a deal just like the one we did for the "tip-top company" which them tripled its stock prices within 24 hours of going public on the exchanges.

This industry also needs scenario building software which is probably more frequently used in war games which would allow the professionals to load assumptions and information from past deals enabling it to run scenarios in today's markets. This would vastly improve an opportunity for new products. Presently, this industry can only run innovation in a live market which is akin to ammunition manufacturers firing a bullet to determine if it's a live round.

Insurance also demands timely information but at the transaction level and has begun to act on those needs. Assessors and customer service personnel have immediate and timely updates to client information. Those professionals who must work on site evaluating claims can not rely on hand-held devices and formless content packing which can immediately upload information to the centrally managed repository.

As insurance is a long term investment and relies on performance both immediate and over time, users have time to evaluate past white papers and research and can predict with some templating the components of future intellectual contribution. This falls between the purely efficient transactional and the scenario building and looks similar to traditionally supported research with which the information professional is most familiar and comfortable.

PROCESS

Currently the content available to users in financial services is their own proprietary content to which they have assigned value, and the commercialized content either real-time, financial, industry specific or news for which they have agreed to pay. With the exception of market research, most of the commercialized content is not providing these users with the analysis that the industry is demanding. The industry is looking for content which is analytical and presents recommendations or at very least instructs. Desirable content might be that which defines targeted industry trends or provides instruction on how targeted industries are constructed- or how do industries work. This industry is looking for the work of the specialist.

Financial services does provide itself with insight but only insurance has the lead time to actually prepare analysis which has long term or strategic value for the average user and is not a snapshot of today's thinking. In financial services, five years is a long historical study and most information has little value if it's older than six months. This industry is also confronted with the heavy use of financial data.

We have said that there are two levels of research going on in financial services, that done by junior people entering the professions and that done by those in strategic planning or product design. The former is a highly rule driven process which lends itself to automation and can be provided by a variety of staff. Much of the desire with transaction support is to delegate it to an ever inexperienced level of staff who can go through the motions of information collection, hoping that the bundle of information will transmit knowledge. The process itself transmits the tacit knowledge necessary to getting the job done. All of the staff involved at this level, whether they are junior bankers, information professionals, electronic publishing specialists find it hard to rouse themselves from the somewhat desensitizing experience. The greatest stimulation here is from stress incurred in the short turn-around time that the players have to complete the projects and the personal challenge of learning the basics of a new industry. The greatest challenge is in selecting the "pearls" from a vast expanse of information which is generated in this process. While there have been some improvements made to this process due to technology, these challenges and the reliance on "rules" have encouraged several organizations to outsource this work in addition to IT infrastructure maintenance and code development. Since the KM process can not seem to improve it, then the only solution is to export it.

Currently our IT colleagues are the most successful in providing support for the KM experience as they do not take responsibility nor provide any evaluation of the data to be distributed; they leave this to the audience served. The audience supplies its own value. This is why KM and its technical capabilities has been successful in those financial services industries which are looking to solve specific problems and not generate new products. It seems to be weakest when the audience insists on treating the necessity of creative idea generation as something that can be made in a routine, the factory of creative ideas is an idea which is difficult to make a reality.

Financial services is at the mercy of its mission, its history and its culture. During the internet bubble, the industry did a huge number of transactions and that demand for deal management fueled innovation but not necessarily new products. The competitive field called for IPO factories in investment banking, refinancing machines and the elasticity of credit from commercial banks, and a retrenchment for insurance including a reduction in premiums. Financial services responded in learning to write prospectuses faster and compete at break-neck speed for firms desiring to go public, expanded standards for credit and tried to penetrate new markets to sell the same type of products, This innovative time (1998-2001) did not provide continued knowledge management innovation for this sector. The information collected within these segments, with the exception of insurance, so far does not lend itself to classic knowledge management as we interpret it today.

Technically, these industries expanded into creating proprietary desktops which had more in common with intranet sites feeding information into work-flow solutions. The classic portal designers did not penetrate investment and commercial banking because they didn't manage the intense financial modelling that these industries demanded. Other software designers managed those meddling and trading paradigms and folded selected textual streams to create hybrid products which emphasized uploading information into proprietary models and sophisticated trading platforms. The final format or the formal cause completely drives the platform, and information selection at its best is done transparent to the user. Even the expansion into extranet development for client use did not use classic portal platforms but proprietary platforms which enabled custom driven work solutions specifically relevant to the client. The client received a proprietary model and commercially available date.

The most interesting issue in the conception and deployment of knowledge management within the financial services industry is the matter of finding the champion and administering the system. Insurance companies still recruit and retain a professional staff who work in support of the entire Firm's objectives. While no firm keeps expensive staff out of charity, insurance provides a level of professional staff which works on firm wide initiatives. Within investment banking and increasingly within commercial banking, firm wide initiatives are not supported as each activity is booked against the revenue generated by each line of business. With each line of business or subsidiary managing its budget as its own "p and l", business units have the opportunity to "opt out" of firm wide initiatives; they choose not to pay, not to hire professional staff to support the initiative. IT development is supported and paid for on a business line basis . The CEO has yet to act as the Firm wide champion for the KM initiative within investment banking and the normal commitment for commercial banking is to hire a knowledge officer.

PROBLEMS

Most players within financial services would not say that they experienced problems with knowledge management. They would suggest that KM capabilities have yet to match their culture, including the need for rapidly identifiable information available within systems which take little administrative burden to manage.

Realistically, the reporting structure with information evaluation and distribution reporting to administrative functions or operations management will not encourage the creation or experimentation with knowledge management. These functions emphasize cost cutting and time management; they seldom interact with clients and do not market on behalf of the firm's revenue generating business. Those that manage the information (including IT professionals) are not aligned with the revenue generating aspect of the business. The multiple businesses within global financial institutions also cloud the ability of the information professional to get his or her hands around the competing and interlocking businesses within the firm and lastly the politics of fiefdom management, reporting and revenue recognition make the efforts Herculean.

The approach to information is also challenging. This market looks to provide instant success to clients. The competitive atmosphere even between client and advisor creates tension. Clients do not share information with those they hire to advise them as advisory fees in this industry are high and clients want advisors to earn their fees. Much time is spent in acquiring information usually only available to the client segment in an effort to demonstrate intellectual omnipotence which is a task set before the advisor by the client.

Insurance companies circumvent this by charging fees which link to risk and not specifically to professional or consultative advice. Insurance is also not seen as a gate-keeper to clients. In both the investment banking world and commercial banking world, these businesses can keep client firms from taking on the roles or entering the markets which they most desire.

Financial services, with some exceptions, does not routinely educate its employees with the same fervor as technology, law or classic manufacturing firms. There is definitely a competitive tension inside of the Firm with team members competing against each other as often as they compete against the other players . There is little time to allow employees to participate in conferences, educational classes and even on-line internet mounted training is difficult to complete.

This sector is looking for solutions that fit its current culture and its current way of life; it isn't open to adapt to and adopt new models, just to find others to whom it can delegate what it sees as time consuming chores.

The role of research and its ability to generate revenue is really the issue here and not the management of information. The sector would welcome a new entry into the commercially available field of information, particularly one that answers its demands for analysis and recommendations and it would welcome a search and evaluative engine which delivered information in a cleaner and more specific manner.

CONCLUSION

Successful KM in a finance organization will have included recognition of the human intellectual capital available as well as the internal and external information resources necessary to the continued profitability of the company. The knowledge base established within the financial organization in successful implementation of KM will be structured on a clear understanding of the need to insure its availability and reliability at the right time.

For this purpose, the demand of both investment banking and commercial banking as well as insurance sector must be well understood. Training and retraining of employees must be reinforced. Evaluation of KM processes, outcomes need to be evaluated on continuous basis so that difficulties are overcome and KM becomes the hallmark of the entire system.

BIBLIOGRAPHY

Books

1. Brian (L)et al. Beyond knowledge management. Hershey, PA: Idea Group Publishing. 2004.
2. Bounfour (A). The management of intangibles: The organizations most valuable assets. New York: Routledge. 2003.
3. Collins (H). Enterprise knowledge portals: Next generation portal solutions. New York: American Management Association. 2003
4. Detlor (B). Towards knowledge portal: From human issue to intelligent agents. Boston: Kluwer Academic Publishers. 2004
5. Firestone (J M). Enterprise information portals and knowledge management. Amsterdam: KMCI/Butterworth-Heinemann. 2003
6. Fuller (S). Knowledge management foundations. Boston: Butterworth-Heinemann/ KMCI. 2002
7. Harvard business review on organizational learning. Boston: Harvard Business School Press. 2001
8. Harryson (S). Managing know-who based companies. Northampton: MA Edward Elgar. 2000.
9. Karloff (B). Benchmarking: Good examples as a lever for development. Chichester: Wiley. 2001.

10. Knowledge flows, governance and the multinational enterprise. New York: Palgrave Macmillan. 2004.
11. McKenzie (J). Understanding the knowledgeable organization; nurturing knowledge competence. London: Thomson. 2004
12. Mezoorganizations and the creation of knowledge: Yoshiya Teramoto and his work on organization and industry collaborations. Westport, CT: Praeger. 2004
13. Nemati (H). Organizational data mining...Hershey, PA: Idea Group Publishing. 2004.
14. Organizing knowledge Methods and case studies. New York: Palgrave McMillan. 2004
15. Pfeffer, (J). The knowledge gap: How smart companies turn knowledge into action. Boston: Harvard Business School Press. 2000
16. Towards the semantic web: Ontology driven knowledge management. Hoboken, NJ: Wiley. 2003
17. Wiig (K M). People focused knowledge management...Boston: Elsevier Butterworth Heinemann. 2004
18. United States. General Accounting Office. Maximizing the success of chief information officers Washington, DC, The Office (GPO Internet GA 1.13:GAO-01-01-376 G)
19. Vollnhals (O). Multilingual dictionary of knowledge management. Munchen: Saur. 2001.

Articles

20. Alvi (M) and Leidner (D E). Review. Knowledge management and knowledge management systems: Conceptual foundations and research issues. *MIS Quarterly.* 25(1). March 200: 107-36.
21. Bock (G W) and Kim (Y G). Breaking the myths of rewards Lan exploratory study of attitudes about knowledge sharing. *Information Resource management Journal.* 15(2). April-June, 2002: 14-21.
22. Crossan (M M) Lane (H W). and White (R E). An organizational learning framework: From initiation to institution. *Academy of Management Review.* 24(3). July 1999: 1522-537.
23. Firestone (J M). Portal Progress and knowledge management.(Power Point presentation). www.kmci.org. 2002
24. Graham (R). Benchmarking Jackson State. *Knowledge Management.* 4 (5). May 2001: 11.
25. Hansen (M T), Nohria (N). and Tierney (T). What's your strategy for managing knowledge. *Harvard Business Review.* March-April 1999: 107-16
26. King (W R), Marks (Jr.P) and McCoy (S). The most important issues in knowledge management. *Communications of the ACM.* 45 (9). Sept.2002: 93-97

27. Leonard (D) Sensi (S). The role of tacit knowledge in group innovation.", *California Management Review*. 40(3).Spring 1998: 112-132
28. Management Review. Survey on knowledge management. *Management Review* 88(4). April 1999: 20-26
29. O'Dell (C) and Grayson (Jr. C). If only we know what we know: identification and transfer of internal best practices. *California Management Review*. 40(3). Spring 1998: 154-174.
30. Szulanski (G). Exploring internal stickiness: impediments to the transfer of best practice within the firm. *Strategic Management Journal*. 17(Special issue).Winter 1996: 27-44
31. Thomas (J B), Sussman (S W) and Henderson (J C). Understanding 'strategic learning': linking organizational learning, knowledge management and sense making. *Organization Science*. 12(3). May-June 2001:331-345.

Websites
1. AIG. http://www.aig.com
2. Ask Me. http://www.askmecorp.com
3. CNA. http://www.cna.com
4. Knowledge management forum.(KMForum) http://www.kmnews.com
5. Know-Net Consortium. http://www.know-net.org
6. Skandia. http://skandia.com
7. University of Texas at Austin. Knowledge management home page. http://www.mccombs.utexas.edu/kman.
8. Wells Fargo. http://www.wellsfargo.com

Section - III

ROLE OF LIBRARY ASSOCIATIONS

Section - III
Role of Library Associations

Library associations, both at national and international level have played a vital role in popularizing, promoting role of libraries, their present and potential services, resources and facilities for the benefit of the community at large. And also in developing their member's marketing skills, and providing them with support for the campaign.

The role played by different international and national level library associations in promoting marketing activities in libraries has been demonstrated briefly in the table on the next page.

The contributors in this section have dealt in detail about the role of some of the libraries and information associations that have played their part in developing their members' marketing skills, and providing them with support for campaigns.

Réjean Savard in his paper *Brief History of the IFLA Management and Marketing Section (1995-2003) and its Activities* mentions activities of IFLA Management & Marketing Section in historical context. It reviews its contribution and impact through annual conferences, satellite meetings, discussions, workshops, publications, newsletter, IFLA-3M International marketing Award, etc..

Barbara Clubb's paper *Marketing in Public Libraries: An International Perspective Based on the Public Library Service, IFLA/UNESCO Guidelines for Development* details marketing in public libraries based on the "Unesco Guidelines for the Development of Public Libraries" developed by the IFLA Section on Public Libraries, as applicable for libraries world over.

Michael Dowling in his paper entitled *The Role of the American Library Association in the Marketing Orientation of Libraries* clarifies the role of ALA and underlines its effort in marketing orientation of libraries.

Whereas, Linda Smith in her paper *We cannot Talk too Loud!: An Investigation into the Role of CILIP in LIS Marketing* underlines the efforts of PPRG of CILIP, the UK Library Association that has produced various publications and organizes an annual conference and training and other events.

John W Berry's contribution entitled *The 'Campaign For America's Libraries' and The 'Campaign for the World's Libraries'* gives an overview of "@ your library" the Campaign for America's Libraries and related activities within USA and worldwide.

Similarly, Audronë Glosienë in her paper entitled*National Library Week in Lithuania: Advocacy and Marketing Campaign* describes experiences of National Library Week-an advocacy and marketing campaign in Lithuania, discusses its communication strategy, about its publics, purpose and effect of Lithuanian libraries.

Name of the Association	Main Section(s) for Marketing activities	Main Publication dealing with Marketing	Trainings Workshops/ Conferences	Awards	Other Activities
IFLA	Management and Marketing (www.ifla.org/VII/s34)	Publication of conferences proceed-ings, project reports	Satellite meetings, discussion group/	IFLA-3M Inter-national Marketing Award	Glossary Database
FID		Nuts and bolts of marketing	Short term training programmes		
ASLIB (www.aslib.co.uk)		Marketing…by Cronin (1981 and 1992) Coote (1998 and 2002)	Short term training programmes	Conferences	Discussions at various forums
SLA	Advertising and Marketing Division (www. sla.org/ division/dam/index.htm)	Information Outlook (often brings out papers) Bibliographies	Conferences	Public relations awards	Int. Special Librarians day; Promotional Tools; Discussion list.
ALA	Public Relations and Marketing Section (www.ala.org/ala/lama/ lamacommunity/ lamacommittees/ publicrelationsb/ publicrelations.htm)	*Future Driven Library Marketing (1998); Libraries, Mission, and Marketing: Writing Mission Statements (2004); Visible Librarian (2003)*	Conferences	John Cotton Dana Library P R Awards Marketing; Academic and Research Libraries Award	National Library Weeks; Promotional material; Discussion list; Regional institute
CILIP	Publicity & Public Relations Group (www.cilip.org.uk/ groups/pprg/)	*Putting Marketing Ideas into Action; Marketing Concepts for Libraries and Information Services (1993 and 2002)*	Conferences, training programmes on publicity, public relations and marketing	CILIP/ Emerald Public Relations and Publicity Awards	National Library Weeks
The Swedish Library Association	Committee on Marketing and Information	Publications	Conferences		Campaign

BRIEF HISTORY OF THE IFLA MANAGEMENT AND MARKETING SECTION (1995-2003) AND REVIEW OF ITS ACTIVITIES

Réjean Savard

Abstract *The IFLA Management and Marketing Section is a forum for discussion of all aspects of management and marketing for all types of library and information agencies, the world over. It organizes various activities, conferences, undertakes projects and conducts meetings, and discussion groups. The paper gives a detail account of the achievements of the section.*

How was the Section born?

In 1995, I was invited to IFLA conference in Istanbul to give a speech on marketing. I was very busy at that time (as it is today…), working on a project with my African colleagues, and I hesitated to go there. My remembrance of previous IFLA conferences where I have been in the past was limited: I had the vague memory of a crowded gathering with impersonal relationships. However, Marielle de Miribel who initiated the invitation was very insistent and I decided to go and quickly return.

I did not know at that time that I was going to enter into the most interesting professional experience of my life, at least in terms of international cooperation. I did not know Marielle before and was immediately impressed. Together with Christina Tovote from Sweden, they were a very effective pair of advocates. As I met them I learned that they were both active in the Management Roundtable of IFLA and working to foster marketing ideas in that group. Their enthusiasm was contagious that it was not difficult for them to enlist me in their campaign to develop a marketing group.

Arriving in Istanbul I discovered that if IFLA was indeed big, it was also a very interesting place to work if we joined on the various active groups and sections. At last, I realized that IFLA is an amalgam of many small professional groups, more or less official, and for those interested in issues on the international scene, these groups can be a very interesting mechanism. Since that time I am involved with IFLA and for that I am grateful to Marielle and Christina for inviting me to Istanbul (which is also a very interesting place to visit of course !).

Going back to the history of the M&M section, the first task was to convince IFLA of the importance of marketing, which Marielle and Christina had already started to do. I attended my first meeting with IFLA officials in Beijing in 1996, one year after Istanbul. The meeting was organized by Ralph Manning - then Chair of the Professional Board - and I remember that he was receptive. At that time we were participating into the Management Roundtable. The question was to see if we should start a new Roundtable on Marketing within, or if we should develop a new Section dealing with both management and marketing.

Following this meeting which was rather positive, there was a discussion at the business meeting of the Roundtable on August 24, 1996. The various options were considered. It was decided to submit a proposal for the December meeting of the IFLA Professional Board proposing that the Round Table on Management become the Section on Management and Marketing. The proposal (*Proposal for an IFLA Section on management and Marketing*, 7 pages) was written in collaboration with the chair of the Roundtable Michael Koenig, Marielle, Christina and myself. On October 24, 1996, it was officially sent to IFLA, and then discussed at their meeting in December 1996. This document was determinant since the Professional Board approved the establishment of the new Section on Management and Marketing, the decision being effective at the 1997 conference in Copenhagen.

Michael Koenig, former chair of the Management Round Table was the first chair of the new Section, and Patricia Layzell Ward who was the former secretary-treasurer took the same position in the new M&M Section. As shown in Table 1, the interest in the Section was evident: while there were only 36 members at the dissolution of the Management Round Table, the figure increased up to 170 in 2003 for the new Section.

Table-1 : Membership in the M&M Section

Year	1998	1999	2000	2001	2002	2003
No. of Members	74	114	121	133	156	170

PROGRAMMES

In the following years, the M&M Section organized many activities (alone or in partnership with another Section):

- 5 programs in Bangkok (1999)
- 5 in Jerusalem (2000)
- 4 in Boston (2001)
- 3 in Glasgow (2002)
- 5 in Berlin (2003)
- 2 in Buenos Aires (2004)

These were all highly successful programs that built upon one another, enhancing and increasing knowledge of management and marketing for our colleagues around the world. Not many IFLA Sections have had such an excellent and productive performance.

Among those activities, a satellite meeting was offered every year by the M&M Section. These are difficult to organize, and must be approved by IFLA Board of Governors. Two satellite meetings were even organized in 2003, one before and one after the General Conference! The idea of having a satellite meeting is now an established tradition in the Section. Moreover, the Section has established a standard of excellence for such meetings. Satellite meetings are also important because fewer people are attending, which allows more opportunities for the participants to know each other better. And it is also a good place to recruit new members !

Table-2 : M&M Satellite meetings

1999	Bangkok, Srinakharinwirot University: "*Marketing your library*"
2000	Haïfa, in collaboration with Haïfa University Library (Hotel Shulamit): "*Marketing libraries with a focus on academic and large libraries*"
2001	Québec, in collaboration with École de bibliothéconomie et des sciences de l'information : "*Education and research for marketing and quality management in libraries*"
2002	Glasgow, in collaboration with University of Sheffield, at Ibrox Library: "*Using management and market research to improve customer satisfaction*"
2003	Geneva, in collaboration with Education and training section, École nationale supérieure des sciences de l'information et des bibliothèques and University of Geneva Library: "*E-learning for management and marketing in Libraries*" ; and Vienna, in collaboration with Statistics and evaluation Section and University of Vienna Library: "*Leadership and risk taking in library management; performance measurement and statistics in library management*"
2004	Sao Paulo, in collaboration with University of Sao Paulo: "*The virtual client: a new paradigm for improving client relations in libraries and information services*"
2005	Bergen, in collaboration with the Public Libraries Section and the Library Theory and research Section: "*Management, marketing, evaluation and promotion of library services, based on statistics, analyses and evaluation in your own library*"

PUBLICATIONS

Although a young Section, the members of M&M have been active in publishing. One of the first publications was the *Glossary of marketing definitions* proposed by Christie Koontz. Adapted from Peter Bennett's Dictionary of Marketing Terms, it proved to be a very useful tool since marketing is not always well understood by the librarians in different countries. The publication of the Glossary is still under way since it is considered as a work in progress.

Another useful tool is the *Newsletter* published normally twice a year by the Section. It contains reports of several activities put together by the Section. You can thus find there all the information concerning the programs as well as the publications of the Section. Other interesting articles have been published since the beginning, for example an analysis of the various IFLA conferences logos.

We should not forget also the publications in the IFLA/Saur series of the proceedings of two Sections programs:

- Adapting marketing to libraries in a changing and world-wide environment/ Le marketing des bibliothèques à l'heure du changement et de la mondialisation; Papers presented at the 63rd IFLA Conference, Copenhagen, September 1997, edited by Réjean Savard, and
- Education and research for marketing and quality management in libraries/ La formation et la recherché sur le marketing et la gestion de la qualité en bibliothèque. Satellite meeting, Québec, August 14-16 2001, edited by Réjean Savard

And recently, the Section gave access on its web site to *Matpromo*, a database of promotion material. Coordinated by Àngels Massisimo of Barcelona, this new project is intended to collect images of objects currently used by all types of libraries to promote their services and to raise their profile: posters, leaflets, badges, calendars, stationery and all kinds of objects from all over the world can be included. Graphic description, kind of object and the role it plays in the promotional task are described for each image. This will certainly become a popular web tool and will generate many hits in the future.

THE IFLA-3M MARKETING AWARD AND MID-YEAR MEETINGS

Another interesting innovation offered from the Section was the IFLA-3M marketing award. John Berry, member of the Standing committee and also president of the American Library Association, created the idea of organizing this award and convinced 3M to be the main partner.

Over the years the Section gained a lot of expertise in organizing the competition. The jury was formed with members from different areas of the world and also from the different linguistic communities to make sure the propositions could be evaluated in all the five IFLA official languages.

The members worked on this idea in 2001 and 2002, and after all approvals from IFLA, the first award was attributed in Glasgow 2002. The first winner was the Houston Public Library. The year after, the award went to the Barcelona Public Libraries, and in 2004, the Australian Islamic College won the award.

Thanks to 3M, the jury now meet to discuss the proposals during the Section's mid-year meeting which are held in winter every year. This is another successful tradition that was established soon after the creation of the Section. These were all interesting and productive meetings where the members of the standing committee discussed and finished to plan future activities.

Table-3 : M&M Mid-year meetings

2000	Paris, March 23-24
2001	Vienna, April 28-29
2002	Rome, February 14-17
2003	Barcelona, February 20-22
2004	Budapest, March 26-28
2005	London, March 11-13

IMPACT OF MANAGEMENT AND MARKETING SECTION

If we look at the Management and Marketing Section's goals:

1. To promote marketing principles and practices to ensure that the vital role of libraries is well understood and acted upon
2. To strengthen the abilities and knowledge of library and information science professionals in managing libraries.
3. To provide guidance on the effective management of libraries

Of course there is still a lot of work to do: these are general objectives which will not be attained in the short - and not even in the medium - term. But as we can see from the list of the Section's activities in the last years, what has been done is fantastic.

This success is the result of a lot of work by several pillars of the Section, many from the beginning: Christina Tovoté (Sweden) and Marielle de Miribel (France) of course, who started everything ! The first chair, Michael Koenig (USA). And Tom Wilding (USA), Christie Koontz (USA), Àngels Massisimo (Catalogna), John Berry (USA), Alice Calabrese (USA), Perry Moree (Netherlands), Sissel Nilsen (Norway), Sheila Webber (UK), Sergei Kazantsev (Russia), Sueli Ferreira (Brazil), Natalia Santucci (Italy), Dinesh Gupta (India), Peter Hegedüs (Hungary), Thierry Giappiconi (France), Yawo Assigbley (Togo), Claudia Lux (Germany), Tatiana Ershova (Russia), Maria Seissl (Austria), Patricia Layzell Ward (UK), Novella Castagnoli (Italy) and many others who have contributed to the Section in the formative years.

I have enjoyed working with such fantastic people who comprise the M&M Section. We have many new members and continue to grow. Even if our goal is for our work to profit libraries through increasing marketing and management expertise, we nonetheless profit personally from our involvement in the Section. The friendships we share are precious.

And since the job is not yet over, I challenge and hope the Section will continue to gather support from all of you, and that we will continue and remain the best IFLA Section !

MARKETING IN PUBLIC LIBRARIES : AN INTERNATIONAL PERSPECTIVE BASED ON THE PUBLIC LIBRARY SERVICE, IFLA / UNESCO GUIDELINES FOR DEVELOPMENT

Barbara Clubb

Abstract *Public libraries are social institutions to fulfil education, recreation, information and communication needs of the community. IFLA has developed guidelines for development of public libraries which gives much significance to marketing and promotion of libraries. The present paper developed on the basis of those guidelines. These guidelines shows the concerted efforts of a group of library enthusiasts to magnifying library activities in order to make libraries as effective service in the community.*

INTRODUCTION

The IFLA Section of Public Libraries is one of the largest IFLA sections with more than 300 members. One of the section's major on-going goals has been the development of the *Public Library Manifesto (1994*) in partnership with UNESCO and the accompanying guidelines called *The Public Library Service: IFLA/UNESCO Guidelines for Development* (IFLA Publications #97/G.D.Saur, Munich 2001). These are now available in their entirety in a constantly increasing number of languages on the Public Library section of the IFLA website: www.ifla.org/VII/s8/spl.htm

The *Public Library Manifesto*, first produced in 1940 and revised several times, most recently in 1994, is an important international statement of principle of public library services and is sufficiently broad to be applicable to almost every public library service in any country of the world. It has been translated into more than 20 languages. However, as with all statements of principle, no matter what the topic or area of discipline, there is an ever present need for more explicit guidelines, standards or a combination of both, to provide greater support and guidance to library practitioners, educators, trainers, associations, governments and funding bodies.

In 1973 IFLA published *Standards for Public Libraries*. In 1986 this was replaced with *Guidelines for Public Libraries.* Following the publication of the 1994 edition of the *Public Library Manifesto* there came a loud and persistent call for a new version of the guidelines/standards. After much study and consideration, an international team of public library drafter/practitioners, sponsored by the IFLA Public Libraries Section was established under the leadership of Philip Gill (UK).

The team realized that given the rapidly changing nature of the public library service, any new guidelines had to include some practical standards. However, the team members were also fully aware of the enormous variety of social and economic circumstances within which public libraries were operating throughout the world. At the forefront of the development of the new guidelines was the team's respect for the public library that must meet the needs of the local community and operate within the context of that community.

The drafters were also in full agreement that a section on marketing, communications and public relations was absolutely essential if the publication was to meet the modern, emerging needs of the target audiences. This is one of the features of the new *Guidelines* which distinguishes it from its predecessors.

WHY GUIDELINES ARE IMPORTANT FOR PUBLIC LIBRARIES?

There are many answers. Most important of all is that the *Guidelines* document is a short, and succinct but major communications and marketing tool for public library development throughout the world. The *Guidelines* is a practical working document with a variety guidelines and standards that are useful in developing local public library services. In particular, it provides targets for librarians working in libraries at an early stage of development to aim for. It can be (and is being) used to persuade politicians and other decision makers of the importance of well-funded public library services. It provides advice on developing priorities and policies for public library services. It includes examples of how public library services are provided in many countries. Finally, the recommendations, standards and guidelines contained in the Guidelines are supported by IFLA and UNESCO, the most important international organizations for public libraries world-wide. And perhaps best of all, the *Guidelines* save library practitioners and legislators time and money because they don't have to completely reinvent the wheel in developing local library service.

Public librarians are using the *Guidelines* in their organizations. Rashidah Begum of the Sarawak State Library in Malaysia, says "*Public libraries are the most important types of libraries in developing countries as they are accessible to every resident of that area. The IFLA/UNESCO Public Library Guidelines provide policy makers and librarians with a very authoritative and comprehensive document for the development of this crucial group of libraries in their countries."* And Jadranka Slobodanac of the National and University Library in Zagreb, Croatia states *"Croation translation of IFLA/UNESCO Public Library Guidelines gives a new direction for the development of public libraries in Croatia, particularly in recognizing their fundamental mission and improving their legal and financial framework. The Guidelines will help in introducing some new services to the end users and bring changes in management and marketing of Croation public libraries, because of their relevance for a large number of different libraries."*

The *Guidelines* were launched in 2001 at IFLA Boston. Since that time, the IFLA Public Library Section, with financial support from the IFLA project funds as well as library groups in Canada and the UK, has managed a project to market the publication to the world. The *Guidelines Marketing and Translation Strategy* project has an International Guidelines Liaison Team which, in conjunction with IFLA Headquarters has: promoted and encouraged the translation into many languages (to date 8 languages are up on the IFLA website and translations in another 20 languages are in preparation); developed a world-wide marketing strategy; organized speakers and displays at national and regional conferences in varied places such as Malaysia, Italy, Zimbabwe, Spain, Canada, Portugal; produced marketing materials including a multi-functional poster and accompanying brochure available on the IFLA website; and distributed copies of the Guidelines to targeted library schools.

CHAPTERISATION

At a very high level, the *Guidelines* offer guidance, information and examples on how to plan build and develop a public library services with a focus on:

1. The role and purpose of the public library
2. The legal and financial framework
3. Meeting the needs of users
4. Collection development
5. Human resources
6. The management and marketing of public libraries.

The *Guidelines* also contain recommendations on a range of important issues, for example the use of information technology in public libraries, equal access to services for all and taking the public library service into the community.

Chapters six, one and two relate directly to the theme of the role and practice of marketing and communications in a public library context. One must assume that before something can be marketed, its mission, role and purpose must be understood and defined clearly. Therefore chapter one of the *Guidelines* pays considerable attention to helping the reader find the right words for that most important definition of the public library service in a local context.

MARKETING IN PUBLIC LIBRARIES

The general focus is to describe the agency – the public library - as one that provides resources and services in a variety of media to meet the needs of individuals and groups for education, information and personal development including recreation and leisure. The chapter then touches on the key concepts underlying the development of the service: library as agency of social change; freedom of information; guaranteeing access for all; meeting local needs; respecting local culture; becoming both a library without walls while simultaneously recognizing the importance of library as physical space, and finally, developing a user-responsive collection.

How development is achieved depends so much on the local context and level of available resources. For example, in Singapore, which some visiting practitioners have called the "heaven of public libraries", the stated mission for the public library services is to "continuously expand this nation's capacity to learn through a national network of libraries and information resource centres providing services and learning opportunities to support the advancement of Singapore". In Bulawayo, Zimbabwe, a weekly mobile library service visits thirty-seven primary schools greatly increasing access to the library services for children in the city. Librarians working in Amazonas, Venezuela, are trained to act as intermediaries between different cultures as many people living in the rural communities speak only their native languages. As the colloquial saying goes "different strokes for different folks" but the underlying, enduring values as outlined in Ranganathan's Laws of Library Science remain:

1. Books are for use;
2. For every reader, his or her book;
3. For every book its reader;
4. Save the time of the reader
5. A library is a growing organism.

The past 30 years have seen more change in public library service delivery and thinking than in the previous 100 years. Much but not all change is being driven by enabling technology but even more change has been caused by the evolving concept of patron as customer. Therefore the third chapter of the *Guidelines* focuses on developing the concept of providing good public library service by identifying and meeting user needs – not by sitting back and assuming that the librarian or the library board or the mayor, knows best. Of course the *Guidelines* drafters did not invent or discover this approach but wisely borrowed from the literature and practice of marketing and communications in both the public and private sectors as well as what was emerging practice in many public libraries. That is - to serve your users, customers or patrons you must both know your patrons and their needs; you must gain this knowledge by systematic and continuous questioning of the community, and finally your service must be continually evaluated and respond to what you have discovered.

Chapter three of the *Guidelines* goes on to further delineate the key elements in delivering an effective public library service: identifying potential users; analysing needs within the community; focussing on service based on analysis; developing the concept of customer care or customer service; providing user education; exploiting electronic networks; providing access to service and finally the role of library buildings in supporting service. The *Guidelines* appendix also contains a sample charter on customer care.

The drafters paid particular attention to helping the users of the *Guidelines* segregate the library customers into more targeted groups such as people at all ages and stages of life (from cradle to grave or as some now put it from birth to earth!): children, young adults, adults; individuals and groups of people with varying needs such as those from different cultures and ethnic groups including indigenous peoples, people with disabilities or the homebound; institutions within the wider community such as educational, cultural and volunteer organizations, and the business community and last but certainly not least the governing or parent body of the library especially elected and appointed officials. In this chapter the goal was to develop a matrix approach to thinking and acting on the concept of effectively targeting the patron, customer and/or user.

Again to be as useful as possible, the drafters included many examples showing how the *Guidelines,* in this particular task of meeting identified user needs, can be implemented at the local level. For instance, in Bucharest, Rumania, the city library is offering summer programmes, run by volunteers aimed at children from 11 to 14 whose parents are at work; in Ottawa, Canada, the public library has partnered with the local health authorities and uses its excellent distribution system to loan out pedometers to citizens thus supporting a city-wide campaign to encourages the population to get walking and thereby improve health outcomes; in the Netherlands, groups of people over 50 are trained by the public library to read to children in schools, kindergarten and child care centres. Very different strategies but all supporting the underlying concept of meeting user needs as they are identified in the local context.

The *Guidelines* also stress that while the physical facility is important, public library service must market and meet the people where they live and work. For instance, library services are provided at metro stations in Santiago, Chile. Beach libraries are provided in Catalonia, Spain and in Portugal during the summer months. In Kenya camel trains carry boxes of books (and eyeglasses) to nomadic tribal users, while donkey-carts are used in Zimbabwe. In Thailand, a floating library, serves the needs of water dwellers. In some areas in Canada, public health nurses deliver the library's infant literacy kits to mothers and their newborns right in the home and talk about the importance of reading to the child while demonstrating how to give the baby a bath.

Because the drafters understood that formalizing the concept of customer care or customer service was unfamiliar to some practitioners, the *Guidelines* stress the importance of having a positive policy of customer care or customer service that goes well beyond "smile-training". The elements of such a policy are carefully delineated and include :

- creating a neutral and objective image for the library
- developing courteous, respectful, helpful and friendly staff
- continually training staff in customer service and working with special groups

- using plain language in written and verbal communications
- being friendly and informative on the telephone
- having a convenient and inviting physical layout
- opening up access to catalogues and resources
- creating equipment, procedures and systems that save the time of the reader
- involving customers in service development
- analysing and responding to user complaints
- providing user feedback
- monitoring and evaluating user response to new services and features

The final chapter of the *Guidelines* focuses most specifically on the management and marketing of public libraries. In devoting a complete section to support this topic, it was the drafters' intention to drive home the importance of marketing and communications as a specific professional skill and an important organizational underpinning for successful and modern public library service. The section emphasizes that library managers can use marketing strategies and techniques to help them understand the needs of their users and to plan to meet those needs. The Guidelines also emphasize the absolute necessity for library managers and staff to promote its services to the public and to have a written communications, marketing and promotional policy and program to support the *planned* promotion of its services. The key elements of the plan are identified (and I have added a few more in this article) including :

- library websites that are user-friendly, informative and tested for same
- positive and consistent use of print, electronic and communications media
- creative displays and exhibits
- effective interior and exterior way-finding schemes
- regular publications in both print and electronic form
- on-going reading and literacy campaigns
- friends and advocates of the library groups
- annual library week celebrations as well as library participation in other "weeks" such as Black History Month; Information Rights Weeks etc.
- fund-raising and friend-raising campaigns
- celebrating special years and prizes e.g. 100th anniversaries, innovative service awards with users, potential users, funders and decision makers
- effective library listings in local telephone books and directories
- public speaking training and programs for library staff
- staff members having a "30 second elevator speech" ready at all times to engage a politician, funders, user, non-user or neighbour in a discussion about the importance of the library in the community
- library participation in larger user satisfaction surveys e.g. a city services or country-wide satisfaction survey and strategic use of results

Patricia Cavill, a Canadian public library consultant, specializes in helping public libraries develop advocacy and marketing policies, programs and campaigns in Canada and the USA. She continually emphasizes that "everyone loves the library but libraries cannot live on love alone". She believes that developing public support for the library program and cause is best done through a targeted and evaluated communications and marketing program where the library board and administration studies the community, speaks to the users and non-users and responds with a respectful and dynamic marketing strategy. She also stresses the need for librarians and board members to "get inside the head" of the decision makers so we can appeal to and support their needs...not just push the library agenda in a vague library-loving context.

This approach to library marketing is reinforced in the *Guidelines* which emphasizes that library staff should be trained to use communication media to promote library service and respond to media enquiries. It stresses that increasing numbers of the staff should be able to write articles for local newspapers and prepare press releases; that they should be familiar with the techniques of speaking and being interviewed on radio and television; that they should be able to promote the library and its services via computer and telecommunications networks including the creation of dynamic library websites that will draw in both users and non-users alike. Many public libraries and public service organizations routinely provide staff with "at ease with the media" training that is also useful in working with community organizations.

The *Guidelines* also strongly emphasize that all library managers (not just the chief librarian) should have a policy and participate in a sustained, on-going program for the development of community support. Some examples of this type of program include: creating a Friends of the Library organization; working with community advocates in support of major initiatives such as new buildings and new services; forming liaisons with "communities of interest" to enhance parts of the collection or strengthening specific services; working with groups that wish to speak out on behalf of the library service and its development; supporting staff participation in activities aimed at increasing awareness of the variety and value of library service. All of these activities take time, deliberation and effort but the results are well worth the work and essential for success in an increasingly competitive world.

Nothing is more important in a marketing and communications campaign than good strong relations with governing and funding bodies. Therefore the *Guidelines* stress that library managers and in some cases library trustees should meet at least annually with the these groups to review the library's services, development plans, achievements and obstacles. Furthermore, the *Guidelines* recommend that librarians should look for as many opportunities as possible to involve its governing or funding body in its major activities such as the opening of a new library, the launching of a service, the installation or extension of public Internet access, the opening of a new collection, the winning of prizes and awards (to share the glory and build institutional and community pride), or the inauguration of a fundraising drive.

Finally the *Guidelines* place special importance on the participation of well-informed library staff and committee or board members in community activities such as: presenting book and activity reviews on radio and television; working with adults and children's literature and cultural groups; writing a column for print or electronic media; supporting literacy organizations and campaigns; assisting with school-based reading and literacy initiatives; being a member of a service organization such as the Rotary Club; visiting local organizations to promote the library.

Copies of *The Public Library Service: IFLA/UNESCO Guidelines for Development,* are available for free downloading in a variety of languages from the IFLA Public Library Section Website: www.ifla.org/VII/s8/spl.htm. It includes an extensive resource list. Published print copies in English can be ordered from the publisher K.G. Saur Verlag GmbH, München. Members of the IFLA Public Libraries Section are available (finances permitting) to work with and speak at national and regional conferences on the topic of using the *Public Library Manifesto* and the *Guidelines* as instruments for public library development. The 2004-2005 chair of the Section is Torny Kjekstad (Norway) and the secretary and co-lead on the *Guidelines* marketing strategy is John Lake (UK). Full contact information is available on the section website.

THE ROLE OF THE AMERICAN LIBRARY ASSOCIATION IN THE MARKETING ORIENTATION OF LIBRARIES

Michael Dowling

Abstract The mission of the American Library Association (ALA) "*is to provide leadership for the development, promotion, and improvement of library and information services and the profession of librarianship in order to enhance learning and ensure access to information for all.*". Among different role played by ALA, marketing , promotion and advocacy are important. The present paper entails such efforts.

INTRODUCTION

The mission of any library association provides the foundation of all the work of the association. Embedded in the ALA mission is- 'to provide *leadership* for the....*promotion*...of library and information services.'

Libraries in the United States rely primarily on local funding from their municipal government or parent institution. Public, school, academic and special libraries have always needed to show the value of their services to their funding agencies and to the community that they serve. The general public in the United States has a positive role with regard to libraries in the traditional role as the provider of books, information, and knowledge. In 2002, 84% of citizens said they were satisfied with their public libraries. [1]

Libraries in the techno age of the 21st century face challenges that they have never faced before, competition to their monopoly-from bookstores providing story-times, authors and lattes to the new knowledge universe of the Internet and Google. The need for libraries to promote themselves is more essential today than it has ever been.

Libraries need to promote themselves to showcase their move from a passive repository of information to a dynamic partner in the education and social process. They need to showcase how they are able to move beyond their physical boundaries by embracing new technologies to provide enhanced services. They also need to showcase their involvement, investment, and value in creating solutions for the community at-large.

ALA not only provides leadership in promoting libraries through the efforts of the association, but also in promoting the need for libraries to market themselves. To help libraries be successful ALA provides librarians and libraries with tools and resources to better market themselves.

There are six major components of ALA's efforts to help in the marketing orientation of libraries.

- national campaigns and annual events that focus on libraries
- marketing tools that libraries can use
- graphic materials that libraries can use to assist their marketing
- programs on marketing at conferences
- awards for marketing excellence
- books and articles assist in marketing

NATIONAL EFFORTS TO PROMOTE LIBRARIES

ALA as a national (international) organization has the ability to create and promote activities that provide attention on the important role that libraries play in society. Below are some of the ALA initiatives that highlight libraries throughout the year.

The Campaign for America's Libraries

In 2001 ALA created 'The Campaign for America's Libraries' @ your library, a public awareness campaign that all types of libraries to adopt and adapt to promote the value of their libraries and to reintroduce their communities to all the services they now offer. For further information on the 'Campaign for America's Libraries' and ALA's partnership with IFLA on the 'Campaign for the World's Libraries' see John W. Berry's paper in this volume.

National Library Week

ALA association-wide efforts to promote libraries include National Library Week, a national observance begun in 1958 and sponsored by the American Library Association (ALA) and libraries across the country each April. It is time to celebrate the contributions of our nation's libraries and librarians and to promote library use and support. All types of libraries – school, public, academic and special – participate.

In 2005, National Library Week is being promoted with the theme, "Something for everyone @ your library®", incorporating the @ your library® brand of "The Campaign for America's Libraries"

Many school library media programs celebrate the whole month of April as School Library Media Month in conjunction with, and sharing the same theme as, National Library Week.

Library Card Sign-Up Month

September in the U.S. is Library Card Sign-Up Month - a time when the American Library Association and libraries across the country remind parents that the most important school supply of all is @ your library® - it's your library card.

Banned Books Week

Banned Books Week, an annual celebration of the freedom to read, is observed the last week of September. Each year, librarians, booksellers, teachers and countless others take this opportunity to highlight the importance of intellectual freedom and remind us not to take this precious democratic freedom for granted.

Teen Read Week

Teen Read Week is a national literacy initiative through ALA's Young Adult Library Services Association (YALSA) that is aimed at teens, their parents, librarians, educators, booksellers and other concerned adults. The continuing message of the Teen Read Week initiative is to encourage 12-18 year olds to "Read For The Fun Of It". Each year an annual theme allows YALSA to focus on timely topics and teen interests. Teen Read Week is celebrated the third full week in October every year.

ALA MARKETING TOOLS

To help libraries participate in the initiatives above and their own marketing efforts the ALA Public Information Office takes the lead in creating tools that help the libraries to market during *National Library Week*, *Library Card Sign-up Week, The Campaign For America's Libraries, etc.*

The Office creates 1) lists of programming ideas for libraries 2) sample press releases libraries can use to send to media 3) public service announcements and sample letters to the editor that the libraries can send to the local media to get publicity for their efforts.

With the continued increase in Spanish-language speakers in the U.S. these materials are now also provided in Spanish for Spanish language media. Libraries can translate these into other languages as well to reach other portions of the community.

Communication Handbook

ALA has also just created a *'Communications Handbook for Libraries'* that is on the ALA website which outlines how libraries can create a communications plan to market the value and services of the library.

Toolkits

The Public Information Office with help from other units within ALA create toolkits for specific initiatives such as:

- *Campaign for America's Libraries Toolkit for Academic and Research Libraries*
- *Campaign for America's Libraries Toolkit for School Library Media Programs*
- *Advocating for Better Salaries and Pay Equity Toolkit.*

These toolkits and the *'Communications Handbook for Libraries'* provide background information on the initiative, data, resources, and clear guidance on how to get the word out.

ALA GRAPHIC MATERIALS HELP LIBRARIES MARKET

To help libraries market themselves the ALA Graphics Department provides posters, bookmarks, t-shirts, book bags, key chains, and other items for *'promoting libraries, literacy, and reading'*. The best-known ALA's graphic materials are the READ posters, in which national and international celebrities pose with a book of their choice to promote reading. The celebrities do not charge ALA to be on a poster, and it is considered an honor to be asked to pose for an ALA Read poster.

ALA has now created versions of the famous READ posters on CD-Rom so an individual library can create their own READ posters of local celebrities-teachers, high school basketball team, etc.

The READ CD is now only in English and Spanish but there are plans to add more languages to help expand the universal appeal of the posters.

With increased flexibility due to new technologies ALA has created a number of products like the READ poster CD and bookmark software that local libraries can customize.

Libraries, schools, and other groups purchase ALA graphic materials to promote libraries, literacy, and reading. The products help the libraries as well as produce revenue for ALA to carry on important activities of the association. In 2004 ALA Graphics total revenues were nearly two million dollars, with positive net revenue of $350,000.

'MARKETING' PROGRAMS FOR LIBRARIES AT ALA CONFERENCES

Every year at ALA at the Annual Conference, as well as at divisional conferences and institutes, there are a number of programs dedicated specifically to helping libraries market themselves.

For the 2005 ALA Midwinter Meeting the Library Administration and Marketing Association (LAMA) a division of ALA is offering a full-day workshop entitled *'Using Marketing to Enhance Library Performance'*

The workshop takes participants through a library marketing planning process to help them create a service plan to meet their customers wants and needs. Marketing is a social and managerial process whereby groups interact to create and exchange products and values with each other. Marketing planning involves anticipating future conditions and determining the course of action necessary to achieve long-range marketing objectives.

At the 2004 ALA Annual Conference programs included:

- *'What's In, What's Spin: Winning Strategies for Marketing Your Library'*
- *'What's next for your Library: Harnessing PR (Promotional) Magic'*
- *'Marketing Your Academic Research Library: The Good, the Bad, and the Useful'*

At each ALA Annual Conference there is also a *feature 'Swap and Shop'* where libraries bring in their creative marketing efforts to share with the rest of their colleagues in the library community. It is a chance for anyone looking to promote their libraries to pick up ideas.

JOHN COTTON DANA AWARD FOR PROMOTION

The John Cotton Dana Library Public Relations Award, sponsored by H.W. Wilson, honors outstanding library public relations, whether a summer reading program, a year-long centennial celebration, fundraising for a new college library, an awareness campaign, or an innovative partnership in the community. The award is named after John Cotton Dana, one of the first librarians to be a proponent of the need for libraries to promote.

Every year hundreds of libraries, public, school, academic, and special send in entries to be considered for selection of the award. Each winning library received $2,500.

Winners in 2004 were

Halifax Public Libraries (Dartmouth, Nova Scotia) for its complex and layered "Summer Reading Quest," featuring seven fantasy characters in an original, interactive adventure and a dynamic Web site designed to attract the reluctant reader.

Orange County Public Library (Santa Ana, California) for the imaginative Egyptology Lecture Series - a program of scholars and other luminaries that was developed from a unique partnership with the American Research Center in Egypt.

Edmon Low Library, Oklahoma State University (Stillwater, Oklahoma) for a stellar commemorative celebration entitled "That was Then ...This is Now," focusing on the successes and challenges marking 50 years of building pride.

Dr. Martin Luther King, Jr. Library (San Jose, California) for a building dedication campaign, highlighting a groundbreaking partnership between the San Jose State University and the city's public library.

The Pioneer Library System (Norman, Oklahoma) for an intriguing and visually appealing campaign that promoted libraries as prominent cultural agents. The Red Dirt Book Festival celebrated the Oklahoma literary experience.

Las Vegas, Clark County Library District (Las Vegas, Nevada) for Reading Las Vegas, Books: A Sure Bet!—a catchy public relations and branding campaign using casino imagery to promote the library's second annual adult reading program.

BOOKS AND ARTICLES TO ASSIST LIBRARIES IN MARKETING

As part of ALA's commitment to continuing education ALA provides resources for librarians through its Publishing Department, including a number of books to help libraries market. The titles currently available from ALA related to marketing are:

- *Future-Driven Library Marketing*
- *Powerful Public Relation: A How To-Guide for Libraries*
- *Community Networking Handbook*
- *Libraries, Mission, and Marketing*

In addition to books, ALA serials such as *American Libraries* the magazine of the American Library Association and journals from specific divisions include articles providing insight to librarians on a variety of aspects of marketing, from research to planning, to promotion.

CONCLUSION

As IFLA's awareness campaign for the World Summit on the Information Society (WSIS) highlights, libraries are the heart of the information society. But libraries around the world cannot afford to not market themselves today. If they don't they may not be around at the dawn of the 22nd century. Libraries are a service provider and we need to market our services, just as they do in the corporate world. ALA has provided a leadership role in instilling in libraries the need to market themselves and providing support and resources for libraries to become successful in their marketing efforts. This is a role that all library associations should consider as part of their mission.

NOTE

1. *Attitudes Toward Public Libraries National Survey Results'* KRC Research and Consulting for the American Library Association, March 2002 (a telephone survey of a random sample of 1,108 adults 18 and older in the United States).

WE CANNOT TALK TOO LOUD! : AN INVESTIGATION INTO THE ROLE OF CILIP IN LIS MARKETING

Linda Simth

Abstract *An overview of the development of PR and marketing as developed and practised in U.K. The paper describes how libraries have been forced to develop marketing strategies to survive against financial and technological threats. Library users (and non-users) have high expectations of marketing techniques fuelled by the huge resources of the commercial sector. These are highlighted and set against the constraints of library budgets and resources. It argues that as a profession, we need a standard of marketing that reflects the professionalism of the services and facilities that we offer. The way forward is through staff-training (to counteract the lack of specialist marketing personnel employed in libraries); co-operation and partnership and the use of technology as an effective marketing tool alongside the more traditional approach.*

INTRODUCTION

The concept of marketing libraries has evolved in the UK over the past twenty-five years. Prior to this, libraries were seen as an established part of the community, a pillar of society with little or no threat to their existence. Over the years their role and position in society has become less secure. The threat has been financial and more recently technological. There is pressure on financial resources from every direction; the Internet provides an opportunity for individuals to have direct access to information from their home or office without having to go anywhere near a library and there is a wide range of leisure options that compete for people's time. This situation has brought about a focus on marketing and promotion within libraries and information services. How do we justify our existence and what are the skills we need to effect this?

The evolution of marketing library services was initially piecemeal and introvert. Librarians were slow to learn the basics from the commercial world where strategic marketing is paramount to success of an organisation. We could have learned so much so quickly to our immediate benefit simply by observing the commercial world – how they communicate strategically and identify target groups; the importance of aesthetics and not least the use of unconventional means to catch the eye. Initially, we did not acknowledge the importance of the aesthetics and appearance of buildings or the importance of customer relations in marketing.

In other words, we did not see the value of first impressions. Set against this, was a real need to market ourselves to stake holders and suppliers. At this time, it was difficult to persuade authorities to allocate funding for marketing campaigns. There were more important calls on the budget and often the need for marketing was not identified. The image of the librarian was also poor and very much stereotyped by the press and media to the detriment of the profession. *The Visible Library'* [1] was probably the first book published in the UK to propound this theory. At this time there was no strong lead from the Library Association to develop marketing and PR. All these factors highlight the steep learning curve that librarians have undertaken.

CILIP's PUBLICITY AND PUBLIC RELATIONS GROUP

In the early 1980's there was an initiative from a few public and academic librarians working in the field who realised the importance of marketing and PR and the value to be gained from the sharing of experience and ideas. Out of this, The Publicity & Public Relations Group (PPRG) was established in 1983. The Group attracted considerable interest and although initially membership was largely from public library staff, it has grown to reflect all types of library and information service and all levels of seniority. This reflects our ethos that the PPRG is *every* librarian's group – every librarian has a responsibility to publicise and promote the service no matter what their level of seniority. Since its inception the Group has promoted standards of excellence and innovation in marketing and PR through national awards organised in partnership with The Library Association and recently CILIP; conferences; seminars and publications.

The Library Association appointed its first marketing officer in the 1980's. This was of course, a significant move (and very much welcomed by The PPRG). The post has evolved with the new organisation, the Chartered Institute of Library & Information Professionals (CILIP). It is now embraced within The Marketing Department and encourages the promotion of library and information services and it is also committed to marketing the organisation to its members. However, it does not, however, publish mass material for libraries to use, as do some library associations. Of course this type of generic material is difficult to scope but it is perhaps disappointing that CILIP does not undertake the design and publication of some material of this kind. CILIP has however developed a network of marketing professionals working within library and information services. This group is informal and is not part of The PPRG.

CILIP sees marketing as a key skill for library and information professionals. Marketing is vital in an increasingly competitive and performance managed world. LIS professionals need to develop and promote services that are customer focused and show measurable outcomes for their organisations. This is true for all sectors of library and information services from small information centres in commercial companies to large academic and public libraries.

Public relations and Publicity Award

The CILIP community is committed to sharing good practice through activities such as conferences, training and publications. The PPRG Public Relations and Publicity Awards are also a very important way of highlighting and rewarding excellence in marketing related projects. Details of the 2003 winning and commended entries can be found at http://www.cilip.org.uk/news/2003/211103b.html and http://www.cilip.org.uk/news/2003/211103a.html

Training and Development

CILIP Training and Development run popular workshops on marketing and promotion ranging from 'producing effective promotional literature' to 'evaluating the impact of your service'. Several branches and special interest groups of CILIP have also organised or are planning marketing related seminars.

The PPRG puts great emphasis on the quality of its courses which are separate to those organised by CILIP. It bases them on the training needs of members that have been ascertained from its biennial survey. The results of these surveys are reflected in the topics covered in their conference and course programmes. Wherever possible, speakers are engaged who are professionals in PR, marketing or related industries and professions. Topics range from design, managing print, copy writing, marketing, branding, evaluation, public relations, web design and signing and guiding. Emphasis has always been on practical and participative courses and seminars to maximise networking and the sharing of ideas.

The proof of the enthusiasm to improve the standards of marketing lies in the popularity of our courses. Invariably they are fully booked and waiting lists are common. Participants represent a wide range of library and information services and are normally middle or senior managers. They also attract the interest of some marketing officers who have responsibility for libraries.

Conferences

The fact that conference delegates leave our conferences with inspiration, enthusiasm and a range of practical skills means that in order to put these into practice they have to command the resources to develop PR and marketing activities. Some libraries have dedicated budgets; others may have to bid for funding; whilst others may have budget lines built into specific projects. The amount of funding is not always related to the size of the project. Many projects are financed on a shoestring. Constraints in funding inevitably mean that alternative resources must be sought. This may result in working in partnership with other departments, organisations, business or indeed a combination of all three. Support may be financial or in kind.

PR and Marketing Campaign

Compared with the commercial world, libraries in the main, have to finance PR and marketing campaigns with limited funding and staff expertise. (Some larger public library authorities do have significant resources). The number of professional marketing personnel employed in libraries is small. It is uncommon to find a member of staff with sole responsibility for this vital area of work. Usually staff will have a wider brief that includes marketing projects from other departments within the organisation. Within academic and special libraries the responsibility is usually shared amongst staff – specialism is rare. In general, marketing is a small part of any one person's job description and the level of available resources varies.

Publicity and Promotional Material

Brief reference has already been made about the effect that technology has had on libraries as information providers. It has also had another effect – PCs have facilitated easier production of publicity and promotional material. Unfortunately, this is a means to an end. Software provides the opportunity to use powerful design tools. However, few library staff have the appropriate design and layout skills to use it to professional effect in the production of posters and leaflets in-house. Inevitably there is a wide gap between material that is produced in house and that which is produced by professional designers. The quality of print media is in itself a marketing tool for libraries. It is back to the first impression again – something that is well designed and professionally produced reinforces the credibility of the service. It is vitally important that libraries produce material that makes a good impression. Users are subject to thousands of visual images and pieces of information each day – we have to ensure that they recognise and remember ours.

Branding

In an effort to create impact, the majority of libraries have adopted branding. If branding is to be successful it must be applied to all visual media – print, web design, exterior and interior signs, stationery and guiding. Therefore considerable care should be taken in drawing up a brief that will result in an appropriate design. This investment of time and resources is worthwhile as a good brand will give credibility to the organisation which it identifies.

Although essential; brand, layout, design and print quality are not the sole factors in the creation of effective marketing material. Effective, well-written copy is crucial and once again we can learn much of what to do and what not to do from the commercial world. The cliché *'it's not what you say but the way that you say it'* holds true. We have to sell the benefit of libraries clearly and distinctly. Different writing techniques have to be employed for print media to those required for the web. The PPRG holds this belief firm and therefore organised several courses lead by freelance copy writer Patrick Quinn, a master wordsmith. It soon became apparent that this information should be made known to a wider audience and the Group commissioned Patrick Quinn to write *Effective Copy Writing for Librarians* [2].

The PC is probably at the root of information overload either by the easy creation of the printed word, access to email or the Web. It is all too easy for people to disregard any marketing material if it lacks impact. Visual sophistication is evident in all aspects of promotion and advertising undertaken by business and commerce. It is designed to leave an impression and frequently does so by unconventional methods. People have now come to expect a more dynamic approach and anything less means that important messages may be lost. Libraries are usually more conservative and often reluctant to adopt the unconventional. In fairness, many libraries do not have the financial resources to take on large scale advertising. Large projects often rely on sponsorship or partnership as a way forward and indeed this has facilitated many successful campaigns. However, the economic climate is such that this type of support is becoming increasingly difficult to secure.

There is a common belief and acceptance that libraries must promote their worth and value, otherwise they may be lost. Financial constraints give weight to the argument that the lead on this should be taken at a national level, i.e., national television, radio and press campaigns with libraries sharing the cost. Perhaps driven by CILIP? If we value our libraries, our profession and our skills then this is the stand we should be taking.

THE IMPACT

The continued provision of quality courses, seminars and competition to improve the standards of excellence in PR & marketing by CILIP and The PPRG is paramount to the success of this government initiative.

The PPRG has done a considerable amount of work to promote and encourage standards of excellence in PR & marketing through its long association with the PR & Publicity Awards. (Indeed, as a marketing device to attract members, it ran its own publicity competition in its very first year. It then incorporated this with The Library Association & TC Farries PR & Publicity Awards). This year CILIP handed over the management of these awards to the Group. The significance of these Awards does not just lie in the presentation of a trophy. They provide a unique opportunity to share and celebrate success with readers, stake holders and governing bodies. They provide the opportunity to strengthen links with local press and media. And not least, they provide an immense and much needed boost to staff morale.

Over the years we have seen a significant rise in standard of entries. Initially, entries were submitted primarily by public libraries but now they represent all types of library or information service. The fact that these standards of excellence and innovative ideas have been attained makes a significant statement about the calibre of library staff. These awards present a time line of the evolution of trends in marketing and PR in libraries. The standard of entry in early 1980's was testimony to just how difficult it was for any library to produce quality publicity. They relied on staff with 'artistic skill', there was little or no allocation of time or appropriate resources. As we have already discussed, the late 1980's saw the advent of desk top publishing and PCs with powerful software. The temptation was to use this new technology without the necessary design skills. It was in the 1990's that we began to see the real benefit of technology both in local design and in the significant developments in the printing and allied industries. This had an immediate effect on standards and quality. Of course, entries did not just represent print media. Libraries began to explore the use of video and of course the Web as a means to promote and publicise their services. Once again, library staff needed to engage in a steep learning curve to adopt new skills. There is evidence that considerable work needs to be done in the area of marketing and promoting web sites. There is no point in having a web site if people are unaware of its existence or content.

We have argued that technology provides both threats and opportunities for libraries. But, as we know, if used to good effect it provides more opportunities than threats. It enables us to provide access to information 24/7 through the medium of the web; information skills tutorials on line; the possibility of searching across a wide range of resources and immediate contact with our users and much more. The traditional skills of librarianship are well positioned to enable us to exploit technology to full advantage.

It is also important that we adopt technology to support our marketing strategies. It goes without saying that a library website should be one of its best marketing tools. Well designed, straight forward to use, it should make a statement about the service. The web site may be a person's initial contact with his library service; we have a responsibility to ensure that it makes a good and lasting impression. Another highly visible use of technology are the thin film transistor (TFT) and plasma screens. These are widely used as a means of high impact client communication by business and commerce to and are supported frequently by advertising. We should be asking why libraries are slow to do the same. Why are we slow to adopt that which is clearly becoming accepted, commonplace and a communication standard?

Equally important is the use of technology to conduct e-business and e-marketing. Libraries are beginning to explore the potential but as yet, this is not commonplace. The PPRG is aware that there is a significant need for training in this area and therefore hopes to develop this as a conference theme for 2005.

FRAMEWORK FOR THE FUTURE

We must have confidence that The Frame work for the Future: http://www.culture.gov.uk/libraries communities/framework-for-the-future.htm launched on 10 February 2003 will serve to heighten the value and importance of marketing in libraries. This is the UK Government's first ever national public library strategy, setting out a long-term strategic vision for the public library service in England. Both CILIP and The PPRG welcome this long overdue initiative.

The product of extensive consultation within the public library community and with key library Stake holders, *Framework for the Future* aims to give the public library service network a shared sense of purpose, concentrating on libraries' roles in developing reading and learning, digital skills and services, community cohesion and civic values.

The Musuem, Libraries and Archieves Council (MLA) has developed a 3 year action plan aimed at taking forward the vision set out in Framework for the Future. The Action Plan outlines a range of projects and developments based upon the main themes identified in the original document.

It is good to see that in *Framework for the Future: Action Plan 2003–06, 'development and promotion of the role and contribution of public libraries through a clear vision supported by effective advocacy and communication'* is highlighted as Strategic Objective 1. It goes on to describe ways in which this will be taken forward:

- 'Complete review of public libraries to understand their role and value in relation to their markets and stakeholders and delivery of key national, regional and local priorities (September 2004)
- Define a clear vision, values and positioning for public libraries and complete advocacy and marketing strategies (December 2004)
- Use marketing strategy to focus impact evaluation, advocacy and promotional initiatives and to support delivery of key priorities (January 2005+)'

As I have already mentioned, libraries and librarians have suffered from a poor image. Largely, we are a self-effacing profession, reluctant to highlight the value of our contribution to education, business and society as a whole. This image has to be changed. We have essential skills for the twenty-first century and we need to make all sectors of the population aware of this. Recently, as a direct result of the *Framework for the Future*, the Museums Libraries and Arts Council investigated ways in which this serious problem could be addressed. DAVE/ Provokateur was appointed to develop a marketing strategy for public libraries in England. There has been wide consultation amongst stake holders, focus groups, staff and users. The first stage of this project is the development of a clear vision and mission for public libraries, leading in turn to the development of clear messages and positioning of the service.

CONCLUSION

So, let us be aware of the threat of technology but let us use the many opportunities to provide a way forward to the future of libraries. We have the skills to manage and structure information; source information that inspires and empowers people, saves their time and enriches their lives. This in marketing terms is our unique selling point. If libraries have a future then this is where it lies. We cannot talk too loud!

REFERENCES

1. Quinn (P). Effective copywriting for librarians. London: PPRG. 1992.
2. Usherwood (B). The visible library. London : Library Association. 1981.

THE 'CAMPAIGN FOR AMERICA'S LIBRARIES' AND THE 'CAMPAIGN FOR THE WORLD'S LIBRARIES'

John W. Berry

Abstract *@Your library campaign started in American libraries in 2001 and spread over in other countries with the IFLA conference in Boston (2002) as campaign for world's libraries. The paper discusses about the emergence, rationale, goals of the campaign and participation of libraries in the campaign in order to make it successful. Further, it deals with campaign for specific library type in detail and discusses the impact within the library community and the outside world.*

THE CAMPAIGN FOR AMERICA'S LIBRARIES

Libraries in the United States have long enjoyed a good reputation with the public, but with the public adoption of the Internet in the early-1990's there was talk amongst academic administrators and many legislators that 'everything would be on the Internet' and that there would no longer be much need for libraries.

Librarians were concerned that the public's view of libraries was based on their impression of the traditional library housing primarily print materials with card catalogues as the primary finding tool. The public did not fully understand that libraries have always embraced and adapted new technologies to improve service to users, and that libraries have much more to offer than a repository for books and magazines.

In response the concerns of many members, the American Library Association (ALA), as part of its five-year strategic plan in 2000, decided to invest in the creation of a sustained public awareness and education campaign to showcase the value of public, school, academic and special libraries and librarians in the 21st century.

Goals of the Campaign

ALA members and staff first worked to create External and Internal Goals and Objectives for what came to be known as the 'Campaign for America's Libraries.' The External Goals are:

- To increase awareness and support for libraries by increasing the visibility of libraries in a positive context and by communicating clearly and strongly why libraries are both unique and valuable;
- To update the image of libraries and librarians for the 21st century, sustaining and strengthening their relevance;

- To bring renewed energy to the promotion of libraries and librarians;
- To increase library usage - in schools, on college and university campuses, at work and in daily life;
- To advocate for an increase in funding for libraries;
- To bring librarians to the table at public policy discussions on key issues: intellectual freedom, equity of access and narrowing the digital divide; and
- To positively impact staff recruitment efforts for the profession.

The Internal Goals are:

- To bring the entire library community together to speak with a unified voice;
- To develop tools and materials to help libraries and librarians promote their value to their users and reach their unique and specific audiences;
- To extend the reach of the national campaign to local, state and regional levels, working with ALA chapters and sister library organizations as partners; and
- To ensure the campaign is useful to libraries of all types - school, public, academic and special - through close work with ALA's divisions.

The Campaign Brand

According to many marketing experts, it typically takes 5-10 years for a 'brand,' a 'tagline' or 'slogan' to become ingrained in the mind of the public, so ALA determined to create and commit to a brand for the campaign that would be flexible enough to be used by all types of libraries.

Working with ALA members and consultants the result was ***'@ your library'***, a tagline that accomplishes the goals of campaign. The '@' used in English for computers is synonymous with 'at' so the @ sign could be used as 'at' and represent that libraries have 'technology' and are a crucial part of the 21st century information landscape. 'Your' provides ownership for the public, it is their common 'library.'

Commitment of Resources

To ensure that the Campaign would be successful ALA realized that it needed to invest both dollars and staff resources in the Campaign. ALA created two staff positions to work on the promotion of the campaign. Over the 4-years of the campaign, ALA has invested $650,000, but has been able to get partners to provide an additional $1,000,000 to help finance the campaign. This make the campaign, the largest single public awareness effort in the history of the association.

Associations around the world will not be able to commit the amount of resources that ALA has been able to invest in its efforts, but associations and libraries will hopefully commit to a long-term use of the brand and commit resources and to this effort if they are to succeed in their goals.

It is hoped that through the creation of the 'Campaign for the World's Libraries' countries around the world will be able to share their ideas and initiatives to make it easier for individual campaigns to be successful even if they have very limited resources.

Unveiling the Campaign

The value of ALA and national associations around the world is that we can work to create national campaigns and provide materials that can be utilized and adapted by regional and local libraries. Libraries in the United States, just as those in other parts of the world compete for visibility.

Associations can create public awareness campaigns, but to be successful librarians and library trustees and supporters need to get excited about the campaign, embrace it as their own, and utilize it in their own promotion of their libraries. ALA now uses '@ your library' on all of its materials - letterhead, business cards, e-mail signatures, etc. Many libraries have begun to do the same.

To help ensure acceptance of the campaign, ALA has worked very closely with state libraries in the 50 states and the 50 state library associations that are affiliates of ALA to help them understand the purpose and value of being part of a national campaign in promoting libraries in their region. Before launching the campaign, ALA was able to get a commitment from at least one library in each state to participate.

To help get visibility, ALA was able to get U.S. First Lady Laura Bush, who is a librarian and teacher, to participate in the initial announcement of the campaign during *'National Library Week'* in April of 2001.

Beginning with ALA's Annual Conference in June 2001, and at every meeting since, ALA provides presentations on the campaign to provide updates on new programs within the campaign to assist libraries of all types.

ALA created a website that includes information on the campaign that libraries and library organizations can use to promote the campaign locally. The site is: http://www.ala.org/ala/pio/campaign/campaignamericas.htm

It includes campaign goals and key messages, free downloadable artwork and logos, sample press materials and information on specific sub-campaigns for different types of libraries.

PARTICIPATION IN THE CAMPAIGN BY LIBRARIES

Libraries of all types have participated in the campaign either individually, through library systems, state associations, state libraries or a combination of these. ALA does not have a specific number of how many libraries are participating in the Campaign but it is a large number based on participation in sponsored programs. To share success stories, the Campaign website includes a database in which libraries can input information on their use of '@ your library,' for others to search.

Many state libraries or state associations have created programs around '@ your library,' some even working together to increase resources and the reach of the campaign. ALA has found that libraries from smaller states have often taken more advantage of the program because of their limited resources. For example the Arkansas State Library and the Arkansas State Library Association teamed up the last three years to incorporate '@ your library' into their summer reading programs for children.

State libraries or state associations have also committed their own funds for the programs or have applied to state or federal grant programs to assist with funding their programs.

The Oklahoma Department of Libraries (ODL) used a federal grant to conduct a statewide public relations and television advertising campaign promoting its 210 public libraries using the '@ your library' theme. They produced and placed two of these types of television spots - one focused on a diverse audience and another focused exclusively on young adults.

The Maine State Library's Outreach Service created "You CAN get there from here..... @ your library" to get the message to blind, visually impaired, and geographically isolated citizens throughout the state to whom the library provides Books By Mail, Talking Books, and Large Print materials.

The Clearwater Public Library in Florida created posters and banners for local buses throughout the county with a photo of the library's teen volunteers. All of the library teen groups were represented on the poster. The caption was, "Got books? Find them @ your library." Twenty buses displayed exterior banners, 158 buses featured interior signage and approximately 32,000 riders saw the advertisements each day. Over 1000 people signed up for library cards that month and each received a free copy of the poster.

The University of Hawaii at Manoa Libraries highlighted the rich collections and services of the state's only public university system with the theme "Ideas flow @ your library" during National Library Week in 2002. The slogan's artwork included a volcano with an "@" sign rising above it. "Infoliteracy @ your library" is the name of a Web tutorial about the services that are available at the libraries.

EXPANDING TO CAMPAIGNS FOR SPECIFIC LIBRARY TYPES

The 'Campaign For America's Libraries' was designed to be used by all types of libraries, and the resources created by ALA at the start of the campaign in 2001 were intended to be generic. To expand the campaign and infuse momentum, ALA's divisions for academic, school and public created targeted campaigns to help address the particular needs and concerns of their libraries.

Information on these library type campaigns and their specific toolkits and resources can be found on the website. As with other materials produced by ALA for its campaign, ALA encourages other participants in the Campaign for the World's Libraries to adapt these resources to their specific needs.

School libraries

The American Association of School Librarians (AASL), a division of ALA created a campaign designed to help foster a greater collaboration with other types of libraries; to enhance the professional development of school library media specialists; and to provide customizable tools and resources that support the advocacy efforts of school library media specialists. The goals of the campaign are:

- To increase public awareness of the significant contributions made by school library media specialists through school library media programs to further the academic achievement and lifelong learning of students;
- To strengthen a belief in the value of school library media programs and school library media specialists;
- To position school librarianship as a desirable career opportunity.

Academic and Research Libraries

During 2003, academic and research libraries and librarians featured as part of a Academic and Research Library Campaign developed in collaboration with the Association of College and Research Libraries (ACRL), ALA's largest division. The goals of this new initiative are:

- To promote awareness of the unique role of academic and research libraries and their contributions to society;
- To increase visibility and support for academic and research libraries and librarians;
- To help librarians better market their services on-site and online;
- To position academic and research librarianship as a desirable career choice.

Undergraduate and graduate students, faculty, researchers, administrators, and staff are primary audiences for this campaign. Secondary audiences include alumni, donors and institutional funders, trustees, policymakers, parents, the general community, and media.

Public Libraries

In September 2004, ALA's Public Library Association (PLA) launched it's "Smartest Campaign-Get it Use it @ your library" The goals are:

- To make the library card the most valued and used card in every wallet.
- To ensure that funders/community leaders will value and support America's public libraries.
- To be sure all library staff understand the value of the campaign and be enthusiastic supporters.

ALA honors libraries with the best promotional effort with the '@ your library' slogan and has enlisted the Grolier Company, a library vendor, to sponsor the award to give funding to a winning.

UTILIZING PARTNERSHIPS TO EXPAND THE REACH OF THE CAMPAIGN

Even though ALA is a large organization with financial resources, the association does not have the resources to conduct a full-scale national campaign on its own. ALA needed to enlist 'partners' who had an interest in the value of libraries, information, and shared the campaign's approach. Associations should have criteria for the approval of partners, not only for the campaign, but for any cooperative venture. ALA has partnered with a variety of organizations and companies to get messages out to its diverse audiences.

ALA's partnerships provide an opportunity for libraries and library users to participate and benefit from programs.

3M, a very large global corporation, became the founding partner of the 'Campaign for America's' Libraries by providing in-kind support to promote the campaign by hundreds of thousands of dollars over five-years.

Major League Baseball

ALA also partnered with Major League Baseball to "Join the Major Leagues @ your library" which celebrates and promotes two of America's oldest institutions - the game of baseball and libraries - while heightening awareness of 21st Century literacy skills.

Walgreen's Pharmacies

The American Library Association and Walgreen's, a national pharmacy chain, teamed up on *"Be well informed @ your library,"* a national health information initiative that will address national health topics such as Medicare drug discount cards, how to manage rising healthcare costs, new medications and other topical health issues.

Working Assets Telecommunications Company and the League of Women Voters

'Register to Vote @ your library', is a voter registration and education initiative co-sponsored by ALA and Working Assets. Nearly 2,000 libraries have signed up to participate in 'Register to Vote @ your library.' ALA worked with the League of Women Voters (LWV) to distribute voter education materials to libraries for the November 2004 national election which had a very high voter participation level. Each participating library received 100 copies of materials created by LWV that feature tips about the "5 Things You Need to Know on Election Day" and "3 Ways to Make Voting a Breeze."

Dean Foods

'Get on Board and Read @ your library program', sponsored by Dean Foods and featured skateboard legend Tony Hawk, had a record-setting 3,500 libraries registering for the program and 1,500 contestants from teens nationwide.

Women's Day Magazine

"Put it in Writing @ your library" is designed to promote the wealth of opportunities that all types of libraries offer to spark writers' imaginations and creativity and help develop a community of writers. Fifteen community college and public libraries across the country hosted workshops for writers on April 20, 2004 during National Library Week. The workshops, which offered tips and suggestions on how to get published in a magazine, and were led by writers from *Woman's Day* magazine.

Media Coverage

Media coverage, television, radio, and print are crucial in helping to get the library message out. ALA has also worked to get ABC Television Network, one of four major US television networks to create public service announcements using ABC's primetime stars that air nationally and locally giving the library community tremendous exposure worth millions of dollars.

ALA creates sample radio announcements, press announcements, and letters to the editor that can be used by libraries to promote their own efforts with '@ your library'

EVALUATION OF THE CAMPAIGN

Part of the Campaign plan was a plan to evaluate the program every year to see what was working and what may need to be reconsidered. A strategic plan is essential but an association also needs to be flexible to adapt the plan as it moves forward.

The plan also needs to be evaluated to see how the campaign is being used. Is the message getting across to librarians, and finally is it getting across to those we want to influence most, the public, school, college and university administrators and state and federal legislators.

Before the Campaign began, ALA surveyed the general public through a survey firm in 2000 to 'benchmark' the public's attitude about libraries. At the end of 2005, ALA will again survey the public to gauge their attitudes toward libraries and to see if the '@ your library' brand has become generally known.

In 2003, ALA conducted a survey of a random sample of 1,000 ALA members (of 65,000) about the Campaign.

The @ your library' campaign has a clear base of support. The vast majority of survey respondents think the campaign is a good idea, two-thirds say their institutions are participating in some way, and a substantial number offer positive comments on the program - including many that are quite enthusiastic. The survey suggests that opposition to it is minimal. Only 2 percent of the respondents to the survey had negative attitudes.

The Campaign is seen as important to the degree it can promote the value of libraries and librarians, and give individual library institutions the tools to do the same. A majority of survey respondents also say the Campaign's importance lies in its ability to give libraries a unified 'voice' and 'brand.'

The most important thing the Campaign provides is material that libraries are adapting and using themselves. Secondarily, libraries are participating in state initiatives.

The implication of these findings is that the Campaign's success hinges primarily on tactics that are decentralized, giving libraries tools and materials they can adapt and use on their own, for their own purposes, to promote their value in their own ways. This is the aspect of the program that survey respondents say is most important, and they are indeed using materials locally in large numbers.

THE CAMPAIGN FOR THE WORLD'S LIBRARIES

A very important decision was made by ALA in 2001 to partner with IFLA to turn the 'Campaign for America's Libraries' into a global library advocacy initiative. John W. Berry was ALA president in 2001 when the 'Campaign for America's Libraries' made a debut. Since the IFLA conference was scheduled to be in Boston in August 2001, President Berry conceived the idea of expanding the campaign to the world with the assistance of ALA staff and the International Relations and Public Awareness committees.

During the creation of the 'Campaign for the World Libraries' it was soon discovered that the 'brand' would need modification to work in other languages, and have been glad to see the creativity of associations in their adaptations such as Italy's '@lla tua biblioteca.'

Since August 2001, twenty-five countries have signed up for the 'Campaign.' Though some have not actively pursued the campaign, many others have taken this opportunity to create a promotional campaign for the very first time and to tie it to a truly global campaign.

For those associations that do not have many resources, the World Campaign is something they can offer their members, use it to advocate for and secure support from government agencies, and become involved in influencing funding decisions.

ALA has coordinated a program at the last two IFLA conferences where participating countries provide presentations on their national or local Campaign activities and share ideas with other participants. ALA plans to continue this at upcoming IFLA conferences.

The IFLA website on the Campaign is very basic at present, but ALA and IFLA are working in the coming months to make it a resource site similar to 'ALA's Campaign site. The expanded site will include information on activities of the countries involved in the campaign, resource tools in several languages, campaign strategic plans, and links to individual national or regional association websites. ALA also created a discussion list to be used by participating countries to share ideas and ask for advice between IFLA conferences. IFLA has selected 'advocacy' as one of its four key action areas for the future and the 'Campaign for the World's Libraries' serves as a solid base for these advocacy efforts.

It is important for individual countries to use their campaigns to further the message that IFLA wants to convey to international organizations and events such as the United Nations' World Summit on the Information Society (WSIS).

OTHER COUNTRY CAMPAIGNS

Several countries have successfully incorporated and used the '@ your library' brand to achieve good results.

ALA has worked with the Association of Mexican Librarians (AMBAC) to develop their 'en tu biblioteca' campaign. Mexico also launched its campaign with the First Lady of Mexico as a sponsor of their efforts. Mexico adapted and translated ALA's *Library Advocates Handbook* to their needs and received funding from their Ministry of Culture to print and distribute 16,000 copies to libraries around Mexico.

A number of countries in South America have recently joined the Campaign (Venezuela, Uruguay, and Argentina) and it is hoped they will collaborate regionally to increase each other's effectiveness as well as encourage other countries to join the initiative.

The State Library of South Australia, part of the Council of Australian State Libraries, joined the Campaign in 2003 and created a monthly campaign using '@ your library' targeted at specific audiences. One month it was 'Treasures @ your library' for those interested in genealogy, 'Business @ your Library' for the business community.' The result was a 10% increase in the use of libraries around the state.

For the last two years, the Federation of Brazilian Librarians have used 'na sua biblioteca' in their national conference theme.

Singapore used '@ your library' to target commuter businessmen and worked with the transportation ministry to get posters placed on the subway cars around the country.

Small countries such as Armenia and Georgia have used '@ your library' to celebrate their 'national library week' and 'national library month,' and have been able to get well-known authors to pose for posters extolling the joy of libraries.

CONCLUSION

Libraries around the world need to promote themselves, their services, and their value to society and the 'Campaign for the World's Libraries' allows all of us to share in a global effort to speak in many different languages, but with one resonant voice.

NATIONAL LIBRARY WEEK IN LITHUANIA: ADVOCACY AND MARKETING CAMPAIGN

Audronė Glosienė

Abstract *The article summarizes the experience of Lithuanian libraries in organizing National Library Week (NLW) – an integrated campaign to promote libraries, to demonstrate their value and to prove their potential to innovate, to change and to make a difference in a knowledge-based society. Being a very successful tool for raising the library profile in the society, NLW is difficult to attribute to a single theoretical model. NLW combines many features of all of these activities and thus could be called an integrated public communication campaign. A classical formula of communication (source, message, aim, public, channel and tools and effect) is used in the article to analyze the four NLW in Lithuania. Impact of NLW for the professional community to articulate the potentials of libraries, to increase solidarity, to strengthen the sense of identity and pride is analysed.*

INTRODUCTION

The initiatives to demonstrate the value of library and information services (LIS) in practice and in literature are labelled differently: marketing, or publicity, promotion, public relations (PR), campaigning, advocacy, or lobbying. Rather often these names are used not precisely, or confused with one another. There is no common understanding in LIS what marketing, PR, publicity, advocacy and lobbying is and how important and useful for LIS they are. Some libraries and LIS schools are very firm in saying 'marketing is for business, PR and lobbying are for non-for-profit, thus also for LIS'. Others claim that 'nothing is easier to market than library services'[1], have powerful marketing plans and are successful in implementing them. As marketing is no longer understood as mere action taken to increase sales, but as 'a management process, not an afterthought'[2], as 'both a set of activities performed by organizations and a social process'[3], boundaries between marketing and PR are often blurred (e.g. 'Marketing is asking who you are, what do you want, how can I best deliver it to you, tell it to you and at what price?'; 'Public Relations is saying this is who we are, this is what we do, for whom and when. With this tool we sell our services to our target audiences'[4]. Advocacy, as defined by the American Library Association, is 'the process of turning passive support into educated action by stakeholders'[5] and lobbying – as 'any attempt by individuals or private interest groups to influence the decisions of governments'[6]. Neither advocacy nor lobbying are only political actions; as PR, publicity, marketing they are also *communication* activities having a common core. There also are initiatives that *integrate* many or even all types of communication activities; one of such integrated action is National Library Week.

The purpose of this article is to summarize a short but intensive and rewarding experience of four years of Lithuanian libraries in organizing National Library Week – an integrated campaign to promote libraries, to demonstrate their value and to prove their potential to innovate, to change and to make a difference in a knowledge-based society.

National Library Week in Lithuania: short history and communication model. The first National Library Week (NLW) in Lithuania was celebrated in April of 2001. The idea came from the students and staff of the Faculty of Communication, Vilnius University, which is the leading institution of higher education for a wide range of library, information and communication professions. The students of Public Relations for LIS course were given a task to explore library advocacy campaigns in foreign countries, and the examples of National Library Weeks they found in the USA[7], Australia[8], Nordic countries[9] and elsewhere were so exciting that the group suggested to initiate such an event in Lithuania. The Board of the Lithuanian Library Association (LLA) supported this idea, and the first NLW was organized in a very short time with huge success and enthusiasm in the whole library community. It began on April 24, World Book and Copyright Day as announced by UNESCO[10], and each year this day is a start of NWL.

A classical formula of communication.

1. Who says (source)
2. What (message)
3. With which purpose (aim)
4. To whom (recipient, public)
5. How (channel and tools)
6. With what effect?[11] is used to analyse the four National Library Weeks in Lithuania in order to map the critical success factors of this campaign.

Table 1 shows these elements in the course of the four National Library Weeks.

1. Source. NLW has many 'voices', but the main sources are a) LLA who announces the theme for this campaign, and b) libraries of all types and in every corner of Lithuania that use this topic creatively organizing various events under the common umbrella. The same framework is used each year: 'centralized' initiation, common message, underlying lobbistic action by LLA, and 'decentralized' implementation of the initiative by libraries.
2. Message. Each year the main *message* was different (*Lithuania without libraries – Lithuania without a future; Library is your bridge to the Information Society; Library as community centre; Library: Tradition*

and Modernity). Three underlying principles are considered while selecting a topic: it should be wide enough to be used as a common umbrella for all types of libraries; it should be well targeted at a specific problem that all libraries would recognize as their own and common; it should be easy to remember, easy to understand and serve as a slogan.

The first topic *Lithuania without libraries – Lithuania without a future* reflected a dangerous situation, called a *scissors effect*, when a demand for library and information services was growing much faster than libraries' potential to satisfy it (Chart 1). Since 1990 until 1994-1995, all the indicators of library network and their performance were decreasing, but after that the library usage began to increase rapidly, while the library network and especially the acquisitions were still decreasing. New electronic media and information channels based on ICT found their applications in libraries but too slowly taking into account the growing need of citizens for a free access to digital information as the economic capacity of the population was then hindering significantly such an access through commercial or private channels.

Chart 1: DYNAMICS OF STOCKS, LOANS AND READERS IN MUNICIPAL PUBLIC LIBRARIES IN 1990-2002

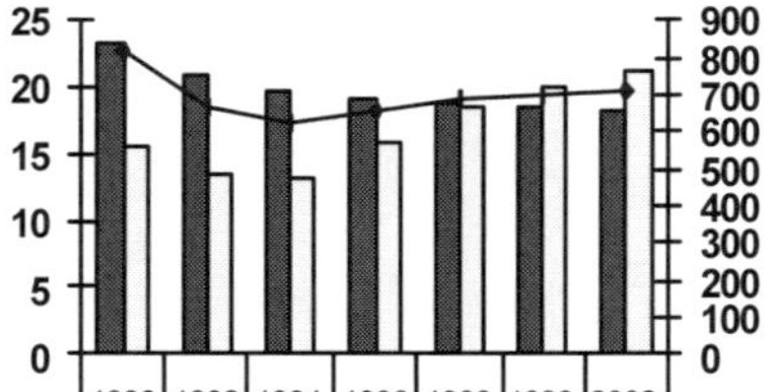

	1990	1992	1994	1996	1998	1999	2002
Stocks, mln	23.3	21	19.6	19.2	18.9	18.6	18.2
Loans, mln	15.5	13.6	13.1	15.7	18.4	20	21.1
Readers, th	816	663	620	658	684	704	706

The second National Library Week took place during April 24–30, 2002, and had a topic *Library is Your Bridge to the Information Society*. Information society is a buzzword with which many people in our countries and world-wide connect their future plans and hopes for a better life. It is a priority for the politicians, a symbol of and a metaphor for the new era. There are more than 17 million web sites with close to 3 billion web pages. Millions of web pages are introduced every day. Unlike a library, Internet does not have a catalogue. How do we live successfully in an Information Society? How can we distinguish fact from fiction, how do we find what is needed, relevant and reliable?

Table-1: Communication model of National Library Weeks in Lithuania, 2001-2004

	SOURCE	MESSAGE	AIM	PUBLICS	CHANNELS & TOOLS	EFFECTS
2001	LLA	Lithuania without libraries – Lithuania without a future	To prove the need for better funding of libraries To demonstrate the potential of libraries To consolidate professional community	Politicians, Media, Society, Foreign publics, Libraries, LIS students	Announcement; Press releases; Interviews on Radio and TV; Articles and interviews in newspapers	Professional community consolidated Visibility of libraries increased Positive attitude of the society gained
	Libraries			Local politicians, Users, Non-users, Community leaders, Community groups, Local institutions, NGOs, Schools, Local media	meetings, conferences, round tables, discussions, exhibitions, presentations, concerts, festivities, performances, carnivals, fairs, competitions, auctions, open doors, demonstrations, user education, “love-your-library” days, exemption of fees for overdue loans	
2002	LLA	Library is your bridge to the information society	To highlight the role of libraries as enablers of free, equal and qualitative access to digital information. To sensitize the role of libraries in fighting social exclusion and information inequality. To raise library profile, to demonstrate the usefulness and the attractiveness of the profession	Politicians, Media, Society, Foreign publics, Libraries, LIS students , Intellectuals, society leaders	Announcement; Press releases; Interviews on Radio and TV; Articles and interviews in newspapers, Congress and public discussion	Library and information related problems raised in a public debate Visibility of libraries increased Positive attitude of the society gained
	Libraries			Local politicians, Users, Non-users, Community leaders, Community groups, Local institutions, NGOs, Schools, Local media	meetings, conferences, round tables, discussions, exhibitions, presentations, concerts, festivities, performances, carnivals, fairs, competitions, auctions, open doors, demonstrations, user education, “love-your-library” days, exemption of fees for overdue loans	

	SOURCE	MESSAGE	AIM	PUBLICS	CHANNELS & TOOLS	EFFECTS
2003	LLA	Library as community centre	To raise library profile and visibility in society To demonstrate library value for politicians To consolidate the professional community To be better paid	Politicians, Media, Society, Foreign publics, Libraries, LIS students	Announcement; Press releases; Interviews on Radio and TV; Articles and interviews in newspapers; Gathering of librarians; Blue balloons	Media, social and political attention gained Visibility of libraries increased Positive attitude of the society gained
	Libraries			Local politicians, Users, Non-users, Community leaders, Community groups, Local institutions, NGOs, Schools, Local media	meetings, conferences, round tables, discussions, exhibitions, presentations, concerts, festivities, performances, carnivals, fairs, competitions, auctions, open doors, demonstrations, user education, "love-your-library" days, exemption of fees for overdue loans	
2004	LLA	Library: tradition and modernity	To bridge the tradition and modernity To increase library budgets by voluntary donations To increase public awareness about the role and importance of libraries	Politicians, Media, Society, Foreign publics, Libraries, LIS students	Announcement; Press releases; Interviews on Radio and TV; Articles and interviews in newspapers; Poster; Library congress	Much political attention gained Financial public support received
	Libraries			Local politicians, Users, Non-users, Community leaders, Community groups, Local institutions, NGOs, Schools, Local media	meetings, conferences, round tables, discussions, exhibitions, presentations, concerts, festivities, performances, carnivals, fairs, competitions, auctions, open doors, demonstrations, user education, "love-your-library" days, exemption of fees for overdue loans	

Luckily, the answer to these complicated questions is simple: Library is your bridge to the Information society. In Lithuania, there are almost 4 thousand libraries, who serve as information, education, culture, and recreation centres for their communities, universities, schools, firms, organizations and political bodies.

A key message of this campaign was that libraries and librarians are playing increasingly important role, particularly in managing electronic information and educating the end-users. Today libraries have exceptional mission not only to provide access to technologies and networked information but also to guide the users through the information jungles empowering them to get the best from the most. The aim of the campaign was to demonstrate and to prove the POTENTIAL of libraries to the politicians at all levels, to the society at large and to the media. Information society is not a society of computers; it is a society of well-informed and educated citizens; we can not create such a society without libraries.

The third library week in April 2003 focused on *Library as Community Centre*. Blue balloons with the inscription *Bibliotek@ - bendruomenes centras* were produced by the LLA, and libraries could acquire them to be used throughout the country. The main message of this campaign was stressing the library as an *opportunity* for everyone to seek, to find, to inquire, to find or get an answer, thus becoming more informed, educated and inspired. Librarians demonstrated their abilities and skills to navigate in a complex electronic information environment, to provide added value services to each member of the community, to heterogeneous community groups, and to community as a whole bridging the gap between the information rich and information poor.

Much attention was paid to the potential of libraries to stimulate the sense of locality in a globalised world, to foster national and cultural identity. Libraries were encouraged by the LLA to seek and make partnerships, networks, neigbourhoods as no community centre can be created by a single institution or group alone.

For the fourth time NLW was celebrated in April 23–30, 2004. and became a special event, indeed. We celebrated not just libraries, but the freedom to have them in the first place. The year 2004 was proclaimed by the Parliament of the Republic of Lithuania; the Year of Language and Book [12] to commemorate 100 years‘ anniversary of the lift of the ban on Lithuanian press. In 1864, the Russian Czarist authorities (Lithuania became a part of Russian empire in 1875) introduced in Lithuania a ban on printing, publication and dissemination of the books in Latin characters: Lithuanians were allowed to print and read only in Cyrillic script but that was firmly rejected by the population. Lithuanian schools and libraries were prohibited too. The ban lasted for 40 years and was taken away because of the tough national resistance. Lithuanian books in Latin characters were printed abroad and smuggled into the country illegally and disseminated under great risk. This resistance movement played an extremely important role in forming the national identity. The mutiny against the Russia's regime became not only wider and more popular, but it also accustomed Lithuanians to reading texts in their national language which is a primary symbol of the national and European identity.

Since then, for Lithuanians the book is deeply connected to the struggle for political and national independence. A book is sacred arms, a symbol of a silent resistance against the strangers and occupants. Along with such keywords as TRADITION and CULTURE, we must write NATIONAL IDENTITY to describe the historically formed role of a book and library in Lithuania's society. A key message of the NLW 2004 stressed the role of a library as a bridge between the tradition and modernity and its potential in communication, preservation and creative renewal of the cultural heritage and community memory.

PURPOSE

It was already mentioned that NLW as integrated LIS advocacy and marketing campaign has a general purpose to communicate the importance of libraries and librarians to our democratic society, to improve library funding and influence public policy about libraries and information-related issues, to increase public awareness about the role and importance of libraries and library workers in every community. Still, each year NLW has specifically targeted main aims as well as secondary ones.

In 2001, the aim was to draw attention of the politicians, media and society that library is a public good, that its funding has to be improved to meet the information and education needs of the society itself. Young democracy in Lithuania then was too much focused on economic objectives, forgetting that investments in education and knowledge, in information and libraries are the best investments for a better educated, more competent, better and richer society. That's why we said *Lithuania without libraries – Lithuania without a future*. In 2002, the main purpose of the NLW was to increase library visibility in society, to expose it in the public discussion sphere thus demonstrating its readiness and ability to be a viable player in the information society. Alongside with the already usual and "peaceful" message about the role and importance of libraries, the third NLW in 2003 also urged the professional community to prove their worth has higher value and to lobby for better wages. In 2004, reflecting on the historical meaning of the past and realizing that books and libraries were banned a century ago because *they were seen as powerful, influential and thus – dangerous for the ruling circles*, we asked if libraries seen as much powerful today. Aren't the budget cuts the signs of the fact that politicians see libraries as*not important* for contemporary society? Alongside with the aims to prove the importance of libraries, NLW'04 also aimed to encourage LIS professionals to reconsider if they conveyed, the "library message" strongly and convincingly enough to the world around to hear and take it.

NLW has also a purpose of uniting the professional community, building a sense of solidarity: only together we are strong.

PUBLICS

NLW as an integrated and multi-purposed campaign is targeted at different publics. Table 1 shows that the distinction of publics is made first of all on the level of 'source': LLA targets its messages and activities first of all at politicians on the national level, at ministries and government, media and society at large as well as at the whole professional community. A special public for LLA has been LIS students who are invited to attend and to monitor the NLW, to write diaries and analysis of the NLW. Thus students become not only familiar more closely with libraries' activities but also more engaged and better motivated to participate actively in building common professional space. Foreign libraries, library associations, international professional community and professional journals are also LLA's special public for whom a press release is issued in English and disseminated widely mainly via electronic channels.

Libraries have different publics; each of them plans and implements a unique NLW campaign. The analysis of libraries' actions shows that there are several principle target groups for them: local politicians, management of parent organization, users, potential users, communities, members of organization, community leaders, community groups, local institutions, NGOs, schools, local media.

Channels and tools are differentiated at the 'source' level, too. They also show both some stability and innovative features from year to year depending on message and purpose of the campaign. The basic 'kit' of tools and methods used to celebrate libraries is the same every year, but each NLW has it's special 'hit'.

As mentioned before, every year the NLW starts on April 23 World Book and Copyright Day, which is celebrated all over the world as well as World Intellectual Property Day[13] on April 26 is marked with NLW. What is special about *Lithuanian* NLW indeed, is the Award of the Librarian of the Year that is given each year to the most prominent Professional of the country. The award is given by the Ministry of Culture, and the ceremony not only attracts a lot of media attention but also has become real professional festivity. It also serves fund-raising purposes: several sponsors and firms have already introduced awards and prizes that are given on the same occasion to the outstanding representatives of the LLA community.

LLA takes special lobbistic and publicity actions during each NLW. In 2002 LLA organized a conference and public discussion*Libraries and societies: centres and peripheries* in a provincial town Anyksciai where intellectuals, social critics, academicians, famous authors, politicians and librarians shared their views and opinions about the new roles of libraries in a new society, about the right of citizen to have access to knowledge and information and the task of libraries to ensure the access even if politicians who make decisions of library funding are not fully aware of such new tasks.

In 2003, more than one thousand of librarians gathered at the National Library of Lithuania (which is situated next to the Parliament building) to petition for better salaries. As librarians on the whole are perceived as a passive professional group, their determination was met by huge resonance both in media and in political circles. As a result of this initiative, not only wages for all types of libraries (which was the most difficult thing to achieve as it implies the necessity for different ministries to coordinate their actions and decisions) were raised, but also a special library conference was *ad hoc* organized in the premises and by the initiative of Lithuanian Seimas (Parliament). ALA former President Maurice J. Freedman[14], who leads a remarkable advocating for better salaries and pay equity campaign in the USA, took part and delivered a speech in the conference.

After being so successful in lobbying for their wages in 2003, next year Lithuanian librarians decided to raise the budgets of libraries. A big fund-raising campaign *Donate 2% of your tax to the library*! initiated by LLA was held in a majority of Lithuanian libraries. A poster with a photo of Algis Petras Zurlys, the President of LLA, inviting everybody to donate for libraries was printed and widely used. The financial benefits of this fund-raising campaign will be clear in the end of 2004 but already now we are rich by the experience of this very proactive, often face-to-face marketing and fund-raising initiative. It certainly helped to raise not only money but also library profile in the contemporary society.

The, hit' of NLW-2004 as Library Congress held in Druskininkai, spa town in Southern Lithuania, April 22-23, 2004, with a participation of key political figures from the Parliament, Government and different agencies as well as wide representation of the professional community and foreign guests. The Congress focused on the library and information policy in a knowledge-based society and raised the strategic issues of library development.

Libraries use a whole range of tools and channels to reach their target publics and the aims of the NLW: they organize open doors days, invite politicians, community groups, readers and users, writers and publishers for round-table discussions and presentations; arrange "love-your-library" days for the readers; those whose loans are overdue, were "forgiven" and invited to come back to the library. Performances and happenings – some extremely unusual, e.g., "dog's tying festivity"(!) – are organized by creative librarians throughout the country during NLW.

EFFECTS

Usually it is rather difficult to estimate and evaluate the results and effect of a public communication campaign. Some results can be measured quantitative but to evaluate the effects one has to use a qualitative methodology. As mentioned before, the summing-up of the NLW is done by LIS students: they collect the date about all events in the whole country and produce diaries and analysis of the activities. In 2004 students produced a CD-ROM with video and photographs from the main events of the NLW: Library Congress, Librarian of the Year award ceremony, etc. Students' evaluation are discussed at LLA board meeting and kept in LLA archives.

Some effects of NLW are tangible: salaries increased, public financial support attracted. But there are also intangible effects that are no less important even if more difficult to grasp. NLW undoubtedly made libraries more visible in media, in society, in political circles, in government, in communities and organizations; their pro-active position recognized among other professions (museums and archives). A gap between the practitioners and academia has been lessened, and some international visibility gained. NLW definitely helps the professional community to articulate the potential of libraries, to increase solidarity, to strengthen the sense of identity and pride. Some changes of attitudes inside the profession can be noticed: demonstrating their value to the users and potential users, to all members of their communities, to politicians and the media, librarians are no longer passive representatives of conservative institutions but active and dynamic players in the emerging information society.

It is important to stress that NLW is an example of marketing and advocacy campaign with very modest budget and huge effect. The main resources are not the financial ones but the competence, professionalism, creativity, solidarity and enthusiasm of the professional community. LLA had even no promotional materials during the first two NLW, only announcement for the professional community and press releases were used to reach the target audiences. The third NLW had its blue balloons produced by the LLA, and the fourth NLW had a poster for a fund-raising campaign, i.e. centrally produced and used promotional tools were minimal but the success and response was huge. This experience is one more intangible effect of the NLW: it proves that there is no direct correlation between the budget of publicity campaign and its outcomes: a statement that many libraries do not trust assuming that it is not possible to be visible without money. It is...

Conclusions and critical success factors. If not money, what made all four NLW in Lithuania during 2001-2004 a real success? Two main success factors can be mentioned:

Clear distinction of tasks by the two main "sources": LLA (communicates powerful, inspiring, and convincing message; focuses on politicians on the national level; assumes one visible and influential action) and libraries (receive, support and implement creatively the message; defines target groups locally)

Constant, unchanging core (long-term objectives, same time, traditional emphasis on Librarian of the year award, World Book Day, etc.) and dynamic, changing emphasis each year (different topic, different aim, different main action).

CONCLUSION

To be visible and valued, libraries need many things. Good service, competent, friendly, and professional staff; up-to-date and relevant information resources first of all. But they also have to communicate their value. For that libraries need marketing, promotion, publicity, advocacy, lobbying, public relations, and other communication techniques. Library is complex, many-sided, has many 'faces'. One of them is turned to the clients; it may also look at the potential clients, and libraries mainly use marketing tools to attract them, to serve them better. But marketing techniques will not be enough for the libraries that turned to the politicians and the funding bodies to be acknowledge. In many cases such initiatives involve not a single library but their totality, and are represented in lobbying and advocacy initiatives of professional associations. Libraries also communicate their value to the society at large and try to get attention of the media as the most powerful channel in a contemporary world. This is publicity. To work within the professional community, with LIS staff members in order to help them realise their value, to raise the status of the profession, to ensure that "the moment of truth" (when the staff member meets a client, when he/she is sharing his/her views about the library informally) does not spoil the image that was built using all possible promotional tools, we need public relations.

REFERENCES

1. Orava (H). Marketing is an attitude of mind. 63rd IFLA General Conference - Conference Programme and Proceedings - August 31- September 5, 1997. http://www.ifla.org/IV/ifla63/63orah.htm
2. Ayres (P) and Jacobs (N). Marketing your service. *In,* Online information services in the social science. Oxford, New Hampshire: Chandos Publishing. 2004.
3. McCarthy (E J) and Perreault (W D). Essentials of marketing . Ed.5. Homewood, Il., Boston, MA: IRWIN. 1991: 8.
4. Siess (J A). The visible librarian: Asserting your value with marketing and advocacy. Chicago: American Library Association. 2003: XIV-XV.
5. http://www.ala.org/ala/pio/factsheets/nationallibrary.htm
6. Encyclopaedia Britannica online, http://www.britannica.com/eb/article?tocId=9048670
7. http://www.ala.org/ala/pio/factsheets/National_Library_Week.htm
8. Walsh (V). Lobby for libraries: Putting marketing principles to work! *In,* Savard (R), Ed. Adapting marketing to libraries in a changing world-wide environment (IFLA Publications, 89). Muenchen : K.G. Saur. 2000: 54-60.
9. http://www.nmr.lt/index.php?show_content_id=44&news_id=107
10. http://www.unesco.org/general/eng/events/book/book.html
11. Rice (R E) and Atkin (C K), Eds. Public communication campaigns. Ed. 3. Sage Publications. 2000: 45
12. www.spaudos.lt
13. http://www.wipo.int/about-ip/en/world_ip/2002/index.htm
14. Better salaries and pay equity for library workers addressed during ALA Annual Conference http://www.ala.org/ala/pressreleasesbucket/bettersalaries.htm.

Section - IV

EDUCATION, TRAINING AND RESEARCH

Section - IV
Education, Training and Research

When marketing is considered total solution for libraries, it is imperative that all information managers have to be marketers, may not be by title but by work they perform now a days in libraries and information centers. Studies show that marketing is an important skill needed for library staff no matter what their positions are in the library, some of the tasks of the marketer are an integral part of their jobs. Consequently, there have always been possibilities to include a full course on marketing in curriculum for information professionals. Rejean Savard has prepared useful *Guidelines for the Teaching of Marketing in the Training of Librarians, Documentalists and Archivists* , published by Unesco in 1988.

There are number of textbooks specifically on LIS marketing. One sign of growing interest in LIS marketing is growing number of books available in this area. A study in ARIST volume 25 identifies 13 books on marketing of electronic information as representative to more useful books of the decade during 1980-1990. Only, four of these fully dealt with LIS marketing that any serious student of information marketing should read. Similarly a website, www.lis.uiuc.edu/clips/2003_09.html identifies 10 key books on this area during 1998-2003. This development would appear to indicate a growing number of courses being taught in marketing in LIS Schools. There are also many continuing professional training programmes in the area of marketing for working librarians available both face to face and online.

There are number of academic outlets for LIS marketing research. Although there is no research journal, which exclusively covers LIS marketing theoretically and quantitatively, except that MLS Newsletter which offers popular articles on this area. But, a number of mainstream journals and magazines have brought out special issues on LIS marketing, which mainly include: Journal of library Administration, Library Trend, ASLIB Information, Computers in Libraries, Information Outlook, Desidoc Bulletin of Information Technology, FID Bulletin, etc. A large number of other professional journals also publish papers related to LIS marketing in regular issues.

This section makes a reference to those efforts by different nations to include marketing in their curricula and make it a full subject of study and research.

Mark Winston's paper *Marketing in the Curricula of Library and Information Science Education Programs* focuses on the importance of marketing and public relations in library and information services based on researches conducted in the US and the role and status of LIS education in preparing graduates in applying the principles and practices of effective marketing in libraries and information centers.

Sheila Webber's paper entitled *Education and Training for Marketing Information Services in the UK* describes the scope for continuing professional development of librarians in marketing and analyses the coverage of marketing courses in library and information science curriculum in the UK.

Diane Mittermeyer's contribution *Educating for Marketing of Information Services in Canada: An Elective Course in Five Graduate LIS Programs*[+1] makes detail study of the marketing courses offered by Canadian LIS schools in regard to objectives of the course, course content, reading list, assignment, etc.

G. Mahesh and Dinesh K. Gupta, in their paper *Education for LIS Marketing in India* examine the marketing component in LIS curriculum in India and discuss curricula of the marketing paper taught in three universities/ institutions.

Aira Lepik, in her paper *Education and Research for Library Marketing in Estonia* analyses the marketing practices in Estonia libraries, focuses on the training of library and information professionals in marketing and also presents an overview of the relevant researches conducted.

Roshan Raina's paper *Continuing Professional Development Programmes (CPDP) for LIS Professionals in Marketing Area: An Indian Experience* shares his experiences of providing CPDPs of library professionals (both the levels: top and middle) in the area of marketing at one of the top ranked business school in India.

Abhinandan K. Jain, T. P. Ramarao and (late) Ashok Jambhekar's paper *Research for Design and Testing of Library and Information Product* shares researches done for the design and development of new product called "Information Management Bulletin"- a value added product of the Library at the Indian Institute of Management, Ahmedabad.

Antonia Hermelbracht and Erik Senst in their paper *Application of the Conjoint Analysis as a Marketing Research Tool for the Development and Control of Future Academic Library Services: The ProSeBiCA-Project* discuss application of Conjoint Analysis for marketing research on the basis of going research in Germany.

MARKETING IN THE CURRICULA OF LIBRARY AND INFORMATION SCIENCE EDUCATION PROGRAMS

Mark Winston

Abstract *Marketing relates to the development and articulation of messages associated with an organization's products and services and the efforts made to encourage potential customers to select and develop loyalty for those specific products and services from the organization in question. The competitive environment of which library and information service organizations are a part requires that information professionals understand, embrace, and employ the principles and practices of effective marketing. This chapter addresses the nature of the educational preparation provided in the American Library Association accredited masters of library and information science (MLIS) programs, with a particular focus on curricular offerings and requirements related to marketing, public relations and the more broad area of management[1]. Thus, the research presented here addresses the extent to which LIS education provides the type of educational preparation needed by leaders in the area of marketing and provides a rationale for emphasizing the importance of marketing coursework.*

INTRODUCTION

The practical reality is that libraries and other information services organizations are operating in an era of increasing competitiveness, limited resources, the demand for increasing accountability, and a technologically astute and demanding user population. It is the case that for libraries to prosper in this environment, information professionals must define and articulate the value that they and their organizations offer to users who have information needs and who have choices. It is also the case that while those in the private sector, and to a certain extent, the non-profit sector more broadly, have embraced the concept of marketing their products and services in the competitive environment, the research indicates that librarians are, at best, apprehensive about, and, at worst, resistant to marketing information products and services to their target audiences. This is an important area of consideration in library and information science education, in terms of the development of educational opportunities associated with the development of products and services, which meet user needs and promote those products and services effectively, particularly in light of the fact that the research indicates that exposure to coursework in marketing is correlated with positive attitudes about marketing in organizational operations among information professionals. The research and discussion presented here address the importance of marketing and the related area of public relations in library and information services and addresses the role of library and information science education in preparing future graduates to apply the principles and practices of effective marketing in libraries and other information services organizations.

THE IMPORTANCE OF MARKETING IN LIBRARY AND INFORMATION SERVICES

Marketing involves defining an organization's target audiences, communication of messages intended to position the organization in a market or market segment, encouraging product recognition, promoting the organization's products or services, fostering patronage of and loyalty to the organization's products and services, and establishing venues for the delivery of those products or services[2]. The related area of public relations involves the development and maintenance of an organization's public image, using venues such as media outlets[3]. In today's information era, marketing is becoming crucial for librarians of all types, who are compelled to know their customers and potential customers. The current environment is characterized by increased competition from sources such as retail outlets, the Internet, and information vendors and brokers, as well as increased customer confidence in their own ability to retrieve and select the information they need, and the need for librarians to demonstrate continually their role in meeting organizational goals and fulfilling user needs.

A number of recent publications have indicated that marketing and the related areas of public relations and the promotion of library services are clearly valued in the library field[4-5]. For example, various professional associations have highlighted the importance of these issues and provided guidance for librarians in different types of settings, often in the statements of professional competencies. The Special Libraries Association's "Competencies for Information Professionals of the 21st Century," for example, includes marketing as a necessary skill [6]. *College & Research Libraries News* regularly publishes articles asserting the importance of marketing in college and university libraries[7].

While researchers such as Paul Wasserman and Gary T. Ford have addressed the importance of knowledge of marketing and marketing research techniques for library managers, it has not always been easy to convince librarians of the value and significance of marketing. Wasserman and Ford note the disdain many librarians have for marketing their services, asserting that many believe in the "idea of the essential nature and unquestioned usefulness of their stock in trade"[8]. In addition to disdain for marketing of libraries and their services, there is evidence that librarians often have misunderstandings about the nature of marketing and apprehension about its applicability outside of the private sector[9].

The ability to market and promote library services is a valuable one, as the literature clearly states. As Andrew Pace indicated that many librarians "think of themselves as above marketing" and wonder "why should such an altruistic endeavor [as library and information services would] have to be marketed" [10]. However, even in 1980 Wasserman and Ford noted that information specialists need to take advantage of marketing principles and techniques in order to be more competitive. In a study that provides a very limited discussion of the nature of librarian attitudes related to marketing, Shontz, Parker and Parker indicate that exposure to marketing coursework is positively correlated with positive attitudes about marketing in organizational operations. They found that "both those who had taken a marketing course or workshop in the past five years and those who took one more than five years ago had higher mean scores on positive attitudes toward marketing that were statistically significant as compared with those who hand never taken such a course or workshop" [11].

Thus, as marketing is integral to the longevity and relevance of libraries of all types, there appears to be the basis for considering the extent to which those completing graduate programs in library and information science receive adequate preparation with regard to marketing, as it relates to the fostering of organizational success. There is clear evidence that marketing is not being included in the curricula of LIS graduate programs to a great extent.

LIS CURRICULA

It is important to note that the curricular offerings in LIS programs must address a range of content areas, including information technology, including searching and retrieval, organization of information, classification and cataloguing, reference and information services, archives and manuscripts, among others. Addressing the range of content areas represents a particular "challenge because of the fact that the programs recruit and admit students from a range of undergraduate (and to a certain extent, prior graduate) educational backgrounds, including, most prominently, English and history, although that representation is changing somewhat.... Generally, there is no common theoretical base, which the students share" [12].

Certainly, graduate education provides a theoretical basis, as a part of what defines a true profession, in the context of practical, real-world examples. Thus, it is the case that LIS education, as is the case with graduate education, in general, "must address both the theoretical and the practical, fulfill accreditation standards, and do so with limited resources and within a limited number of course credit hours" [13].

The issue of the theoretical base is an important consideration. In a presentation at the Association for Library and Information Science Education conference in January 2003, this author was asked to address the nature of graduate education, in the context of the expectations of new professionals in the field. The presentation referred to the fact that a practitioner colleague had inquired as to whether the graduates of the LIS program of which the faculty member (the author) is a part are prepared for the first day of work in libraries when they graduate. The response related to the fact that a 'yes-no' answer to the question is not appropriate because the question itself, to a large extent, misses the point—in this case, the point of graduate education. Graduate education is intended to provide a theoretical and conceptual basis, representing a more sophisticated understanding to support the decision making that follows in one's professional or academic career. Clarity is particularly important in the case of graduate education that is tied to preparation for professional practice, as opposed to graduate education in the arts and sciences, for example[14].

Following the presentation, Robert Holley addressed this issue in the article "The Ivory Tower as Preparation for the Trenches," in *College and Research Libraries News*, indicating that [T]he fundamental purpose of library education is not to train students for their first jobs but to prepare them for a professional career in librarianship. In addition to practical skills, students must acquire the ability to integrate new knowledge and become socialized to the values of the profession, such as open access, service, objectivity, and intellectual freedom [15].

In the case of marketing or the more broad area of management, few of the students have studied management in general or marketing, in particular, prior to entering LIS educational programs. Although all of the ALA-accredited masters of library and information science programs offer at least one management course, a far smaller percentage require coursework in management for all students[16]. Thus, there is even less likelihood that the majority of LIS students will receive instruction in marketing.

MARKETING AS A COMPONENT OF LIS EDUCATION

There is not a substantial body of literature on marketing in library and information science degree program curricula. Marketing curricula is mentioned with regard to the discussion of research related to the educational preparation and competencies of at least two different types of special librarians. In 1998, Julie Hallmark published a study based on interviews with geoscience information specialists. Her goal was to study their perceptions of the ideal educational preparation for people in the field. Marketing was highlighted as an area that "should be taught more extensively in graduate school."[17].

Irene M. Lathrop of the Rhode Island Hospital surveyed hospital librarians to determine their continuing education needs[18]. Marketing was one of the top three areas in which they believed their education should be focused. The study focused on continuing education. However, if library programs offered marketing, integrated into the curricula, some of the needs of these hospital librarians would have been met sooner.

In a 1987 study of Australian library and information science programs, Mari Davis discovered that the majority of the institutions did not have courses focusing on the topic of marketing and few aspects of other courses were devoted to marketing. While she found that survey respondents rated marketing as important or integral to the library degree program, over a quarter did not offer marketing integrated into other courses in any part of the program [19].

An article by Pat Feehan and a number of her graduate students addressed public relations as a part of her *Programming for Children and Young Adults* course in the MLS program at the University of South Carolina. In the course, Feehan covers public relations and promotion, involving a personal learning experience for the students. In the article, the students describe the public relations lessons learned from hands-on library experience required as part of the coursework. All of the students noted positive experiences and saw great value in this aspect of the course [20].

Wasserman and Ford's research included the design of a detailed syllabus for a proposed marketing course, using resources from business schools and marketing consultants. While their focus was the continuing education of librarians, it is important to note that if marketing principles and techniques represent competencies that are necessary for librarians, MLIS coursework provides the opportunity to address these issues in the degree programs.

Generally, the literature associated with the changing nature of LIS education does not address the need for librarians to learn marketing skills in order to justify the value of their services in organizations[21]. The research results presented below address the extent to which marketing is included in the MLIS coursework of ALA-accredited programs in their preparation of information professionals.

THE STUDY

The results of a study of curricular and course content information for the American Library Association-accredited MLS (or MLIS) programs in the U.S. and Canada provide evidence of the extent to which there is coverage of marketing and the related area of public relations[22]. Course offerings, course content, and requirements, using the published program requirements, course descriptions, and syllabi, when available online, served as the basis for the data analysis for the programs accredited at the time of the study [23].

Management Coursework

Management courses (general management courses, in this instance), which represent the most likely exposure to marketing principles for the majority of students, are offered in all of the MLIS programs included in the study (See Table 1). Such coursework is required of all students in more than two-thirds (69.1%) of the programs, with the course being either an elective or required of those in certain areas of concentration in the remaining 30.9%. Of those programs that require core courses of all students, 75.0% include management among the required courses. And, of those that have required core courses, as well as other courses, which are required in certain tracks, management is required of all students in 62.5% of such programs. However, only 14.5% (or eight) of the programs offer a management track. Marketing is identified, specifically, as a component of the course content in 16.4% of the general management courses, although marketing may be addressed to one extent or another in the remaining 83.6%, as the available online course information served as the basis for analysis.

Specific management courses, relating to types of library settings, were considered, with regard to the inclusion of course content related to marketing. For example, a course in special library management or special libraries is offered in nearly two-thirds (63.6%) of the MLIS programs. However, marketing was identified specifically as a component of the course content in the special libraries courses in only 11.4% of the programs, which offer such a course. With regard to courses in academic library management, two-thirds (67.3%) of the MLIS programs offer such a course as part of the curriculum, with only 8.1% identifying marketing as a component of the course content. While a slightly higher percentage (70.9%) of institutions offer courses in public library management, only 20.5% include marketing as a component of those courses.

Table-1: Marketing as a Component of Management Courses

Course	Course Offered	Marketing as a Component of Course
General Management	100.0%	16.4%
Special Library Management	63.6%	11.4%
Academic Library Management	67.3%	8.1%
Public Library Management	70.9%	20.5%

Marketing Coursework

Separate marketing courses are included in the curricula of only 40.0% of the LIS degree programs (See Table 2). In addition, while 34.5% offer a marketing course that is either an elective or required of students in certain tracks or concentration in the MLIS programs, 5.5% offer a marketing course of fewer than three credits.

Table-2: Marketing Courses in LIS Programs

Marketing Courses	Percentage of Total
Marketing Coursework Offered	40.00%
Elective or Required in Certain Tracks	34.50%
Less Than 3 Credit Marketing Courses	5.50%

The course titles vary and include Marketing (29.1%), Public Relations (7.3%), and some combination of Marketing and Public Relations (3.6%) (See Table 3). Co-relational analyses, in the form of chi square analyses, revealed no significant differences in terms of course program offerings and requirements in management being correlated with a higher incidence of course offerings in marketing.

Table-3: Marketing Course Titles in LIS Programs

Course Title	Number of Programmes	Percent of Total
Marketing	16	29.1%
Public Relations	4	7.3%
Marketing and Public Relations	2	3.6%
No Marketing Course Offered	33	60.0%
Total	**55**	**100.0%**

The course content of the marketing classes includes various course topics, such as the following:

- Marketing principles and theory
- Market analysis
- User surveys
- Design of services, special populations
- Customer-oriented marketing, community analysis
- Advocacy
- Public relations, media relations
- Marketing research
- Planning, strategy
- Cost effectiveness
- Promotion
- Presentations
- Communication techniques

- E-marketing, web strategies, Internet advertising
- Market positioning
- Lobbying
- Fundraising

Coursework Offered Elsewhere

As a result of the fact that students might have a broader range of coursework options related to marketing and management outside of LIS departments, data was gathered with regard to the issue of whether students have the option of applying electives from other departments toward the MLIS degree. Slightly more than half (56.4%) of the programs indicate that such an option exists. While the remaining 43.6% do not specify that such an option is available, it is not necessarily the case that students are unable to pursue these types of courses in the other programs considered. Such an option was simply not identified explicitly.

CONCLUSIONS AND IMPLICATIONS

Marketing has been identified as one of the areas of competency that is important for professionals in library and information science. However, the research results presented here indicate that the study of marketing is not a major area of focus in graduate LIS education. It is certainly the case that library and information science programs must fulfill the role of graduate programs in general, with regard to presenting the theoretical and practical in a range of content areas.

The fact that such a large percentage of LIS programs offer courses in management, as well as specialized management courses, presents an important opportunity to study issues that are key in positioning library and information services organizations to be successful. However, marketing and the related area of public relations do not appear to comprise a significant area of study either on their own, in stand-alone courses, or as components of management courses. It might be argued that marketing principles can be addressed in the context of courses with content that is more broadly focused, but in which marketing concepts are relevant. The practical reality is that many LIS programs are not likely to offer elective courses in marketing. Thus, presumably, issues of marketing are most appropriately addressed in management-related courses. However, the general management courses must address a range of other issues, including planning, organizational change, organizational communication, financial management, and measurement and evaluation.

In addition, focus on these topics in other academic departments presents a number of concerns, including the issue regarding the extent to which the courses address the aspects of organizational culture, financial circumstances, and mission-driven foci that are specific to libraries. There is also the question of whether the limited discussion of marketing perpetuates a professional mode of thinking that suggests that librarians and information services are above marketing, unlike our competitors. This is of some concern, based on the documented connection between exposure to coursework in marketing and perceptions of the value of marketing in organizational operations. However, with the limitations associated with course offerings in LIS programs, the fact that students have the option of taking marketing courses elsewhere does provide the opportunity for exposure to the general principles of marketing in at least one way.

Ultimately, the success of organizations is tied closely to the ability of professionals to define and articulate the value of their products and services to their target audiences. The value of marketing in the work of information professionals has been articulated in a number of ways. Thus, there is the necessity for the educational preparation of future professionals to reflect the practical realities of the organizations of which they will be a part.

REFERENCES AND NOTES

1. Winston (M) and Hazlin (G E). Leadership competencies in library and information science: Marketing as a component of LIS curricula. *Journal of Education for Library and Information Science*. 44 (2). 2003: 177-187.
2. Teas (R K) and Grapentine (TA). Is your message getting across? *Marketing Research*. 14 (1). 2002: 34.
3. Marshall (N J). Public relations in academic libraries: A descriptive analysis. *The Journal of Academic Librarianship*. 27 (2). 2001: 116.
4. Weingand (DE). Future-driven library marketing. Chicago: American Library Association. 1998.
5. Jain (AK) et al., Eds. Marketing information products and services: A Primer for librarians and information professionals. Ottawa: International Development Research Centre; New Dehli: Tata McGraw-Hill. 1999.
6. Special Libraries Association. Competencies for information professionals of the 21st Century. Rev. ed. June 2003. Cited September 17, 2004. Available at http://www.sla.org/content/learn/comp2003/index.cfm
7. Wang (J). Promoting library services to campus administrative offices. *College & Research Libraries News*. 62 (2). 2001: 193-197. Germain (CA). 99 Ways to get those feet in the door: How to develop a public relations campaign. *College & Research Libraries News*. 61 (2). 2000: 93-96. Kirchner (T). Advocacy 101 for academic librarians: Tips to help your institution prosper. *College & Research Libraries News*. 60 (10). 1999: 844-846.
8. Wasserman (P) and Ford (G T). Marketing and marketing research: What the library manager should learn. *Journal of Library Administration*. 1 (1). 1980: 20.
9. Morgan (L). Marketing future libraries. *Computers in Libraries*. 18 (8). 1998: 50-51.
10. Pace (A K). Marketing our strengths. *Computers in Libraries*. 20 (8). 2000: 63.

11. Shontz (M L), Parker (J C) and Parker (R). What do librarians think about marketing? A survey of public librarians' attitudes toward marketing of library services. *The Library Quarterly*. 74 (1). 2004. Cited September 24, 2004. Available at http://www.journals.uchicago.edu/LQ/journal/issues/v74n1/740104/740104.html
12. Winston (M). Educating leaders: Challenges and opportunities in teaching human resources management. *In,* Simmons-Welburn (J) and McNeil (B), Eds. Human resources management in today's academic library. Chicago: Libraries Unlimited, 2004: 134.
13. Ibid
14. Ibid, p.133
15. Holley (R P). The Ivory Tower as preparation for the trenches. *College & Research Libraries News*. 64 (3). 2003: 173.
16. Ibid,1.p. 183.
17. Hallmark (J). Education for the successful geoscience information specialist. *Science & Technology Libraries*. 17 (2). 1998: 88.
18. Lathrop (I M). Continuing education needs of hospital librarians. *Bulletin of the Medical Library Association*. 74 (2). 1986: 110-114.
19. Davis (M). Marketing in librarianship courses in Australia. *The Australian Library Journal*. August 1988: 176-181.
20. Feehan (P) et al. Public relations 101: Learning by doing. *PNLA Quarterly*. 64 (4). 2000: 24-25.
21. Helfer (D S). Libraries in the new millenium. *Searcher*. 8 (3). 2000: 29-31.
22. Leonhardt (T W). Library education and the librarian. *Technicalities*. 19 (10). 1999: 1, 6-7.
23. Kniffel (L). Talking to ourselves about library education. *American Libraries*. 29 (6). 1998: 52.

EDUCATION AND TRAINING FOR MARKETING INFORMATION SERVICES IN THE UK

Sheila Webber

Abstract *This chapter aims to describe the extent to which training and education in marketing is available to the Library and Information Science (LIS) community in the United Kingdom (UK). The article starts by indicating the value that LIS practitioners attach to the area, goes on to describe the UK qualifications structure and the extent to which marketing is covered in LIS university curricula, and finishes by providing examples of how the Continuing Professional Development (CPD) needs of LIS practitioners are met.*

INTRODUCTION

There is ample evidence that UK LIS professionals think that marketing is an important topic. There are many articles about desirable skills for LIS professionals, and most of these articles include a reference to marketing skills. These are seen as necessary across all sectors, and I will highlight a few relevant articles which refer to these different contexts. Pedley [1] identifies 26 skills or qualities that employers have specified when advertising *business information* professional posts: these include marketing and communication skills. Urwin [2] states firmly that 'The skill that's most important to information professionals is the ability to market their information service to their customers. Without that, the rest is irrelevant'.

In her article about information professionals in *law firms*, Gibson [3] is clear that marketing is essential, and that it is not enough to know you ought to be doing marketing, you have also got to be good at it. Describing the results of an investigation into management of e-journals in *academic libraries*, Ashcroft [4] highlights the importance of marketing new media library services, such as e-journals, both in terms of market research and service promotion. Ashcroft also stresses the value of marketing knowledge for personal career progression.

Finally, Usherwood et al [5] surveyed employers, employees and students as part of a study of the UK *public library* workforce. When asked to identify the most important areas for training over the next two years, employers most frequently identified skills with Information and Communication Technologies (ICTs), but customer care-related skills were the second most popular choice.

In sum, it is difficult to find a list of "skills for LIS practitioners" that does not include marketing. One could therefore include that it is a subject which should feature in LIS curricula. Is that in fact the case?

This paper will describe the extent to which training in the subject of marketing information and library services is represented in Library and Information Science (LIS) university curricula in the UK, and covered by Continuing Professional Development (CPD).

QUALIFICATIONS AND TRAINING IN THE UK

In this section the word *course* is used to denote a complete undergraduate or postgraduate programme, and the word *class* is used to describe a discrete unit or module within such a programme. The term "information departments" is used since only two of the 17 university departments in the UK that offer courses accredited by the Chartered Institute of Library and Information Professionals (CILIP) have the word 'library' in their names.

In the UK there have been LIS courses at both the undergraduate and postgraduate level for some time. For those who are interested in exploring the history and characteristics of LIS education in the UK in more depth, Layzell Ward [6] provides a concise history of UK LIS education and an interesting perspective on recent developments. Candidates for professional posts in public and academic libraries in the UK would normally be expected to have an undergraduate or postgraduate qualification in LIS: it is now mainly a graduate (and in particular a postgraduate) profession. In other sectors it is possible that a subject specialism or business experience might be prioritised over LIS qualifications.

Information departments tend to have a portfolio of courses aimed at different market segments e.g. an undergraduate course in Information Management, MSc courses in Information and Library Studies and Information Management, and specialist Masters in an aspect of information management or informatics e.g. Health Informatics. In the UK students gain an MA or MSc in the appropriate subject, there is no specific "Masters in Library Science" as there is in the USA. CILIP accredits individuals, awarding them postnominal letters (MCLIP), if they fulfil membership criteria. Individual LIS **courses** (not Departments) may be accredited by CILIP, but as the prime focus is on individual accreditation, course accreditation is less important than in North America.

All UK higher education has for some years been subject to centralised review of teaching and research quality, in which the work of Departments is scrutinised systematically by a panel of peers (see Broady-Preston [7] and Elkin [8]). Each Department is given a score, and these scores help to determine levels of funding (therefore they are significant exercises). As part of the teaching quality process, documents have been drawn up by subject panels, outlining key areas for the curriculum. These documents are particularly important for undergraduate education, as Departments have to relate their own curricula to these "Subject benchmarks."

It is worth examining the LIS benchmark [9] for coverage of marketing. Four elements are listed as core to the LIS discipline, the fourth being: "The application of techniques for planning, implementing, evaluating, analysing and developing library, archive and information products, services and systems within the context of organisational culture, objectives and client base, professional statutory and ethical frameworks, and national and international legislation and regulations" (para 1.2)

Knowledge/ skill areas include:"The ability to identify, analyse and evaluate the information needs of different groups and make informed decisions to satisfy them."(para 2.6) and,

The most specifically relevant to marketing:"A grounding in the basic principles of the planning and management of services, including inter-personal skills, performance indicators, budgeting, purchasing, marketing of services, quality and liability issues and staff management and training, so as to enable the management of library and information services or archive organisations" (para 2.19)

Additionally, students are expected to be able to demonstrate a significant proportion of transferable skills, from a list which includes:"Recognise the significance of proactive marketing and promotion and demonstrate their impact on the achievement of organisational goals" (3.20)

WHAT IS TAUGHT IN INFORMATION DEPARTMENTS

In summer 2001 I carried out a survey on the extent to which marketing and quality management of library and information services were being taught in the UK. This was a companion study to ones on the situation in North America (researched by France Bouthillier at McGill University) and in Brazil (carried out by Sueli Mara S.P Ferreira of Sao Paulo University). We agreed the format of a questionnaire between us, and translated it into the appropriate languages. Full results from all three surveys are reported in [10].

I targeted all accredited courses: 21 undergraduate and 37 postgraduate. Questionnaires (one for each course) were sent to Heads of Department to each of the 17 institutions with relevant courses. Respondents were asked whether they regularly offered classes in marketing of library and information services, and the management of service quality. If the answer was *yes*, respondents were asked to supply further information. All respondents were also asked whether the two topics were covered in any other classes. Finally, respondents were asked to indicate how important they thought the topics were, using a scale of 1 (very important) to 5 (not important).

It emerged that two of the courses were not being offered that year, leaving a total of 56 potential returns. 18 questionnaires (a response rate of 32%) were returned by eight institutions. Eight of the completed questionnaires related to undergraduate courses (38% response rate) and ten to Masters (27% response rate). I will just give the key results for the marketing part of my survey.

For the eight undergraduate courses :

- Three courses were from one institution which offers an elective (i.e. optional) class *Marketing for information professionals,* on all three courses. Additionally, there is time devoted to Marketing in another class.
- On a further three courses there are no classes on specifically library/ information marketing, but there is a generic marketing elective class (not offered by the Department itself) and marketing is also covered to some extent in other classes.
- The final two courses have no class devoted to marketing, but marketing is taught as part of other classes.

Fig.1 Summarises these responses.

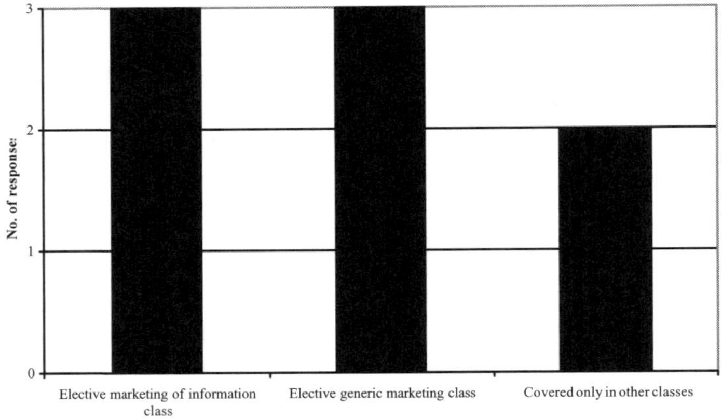

Fig. 1 : Extent to which marketing is taught on 8 undergraduate courses

Fig.2 Shows how respondents rated the importance of marketing.

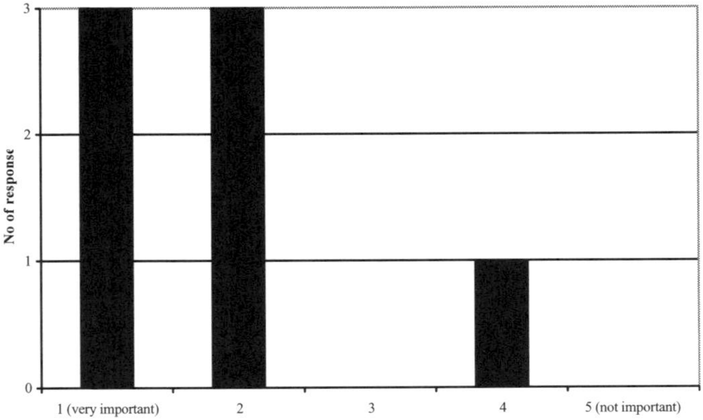

Fig. 2 : Value of marketing: undergraduate courses (7 responses)

For taught Masters courses, two out of the 10 courses had compulsory classes on marketing. Both were information and library studies Masters courses at two Scottish universities. At the other end of the spectrum, one course (an MSc in Information Management) has no specialist classes and no marketing taught in any other classes. The remaining seven courses have no specialist marketing classes and no agreements with other Departments to deliver marketing classes, but do have some coverage of marketing in other classes. Where timings were given, they showed that only a few hours was devoted to teaching marketing. Figure 3 summarises the position as regards teaching of marketing in postgraduate courses.

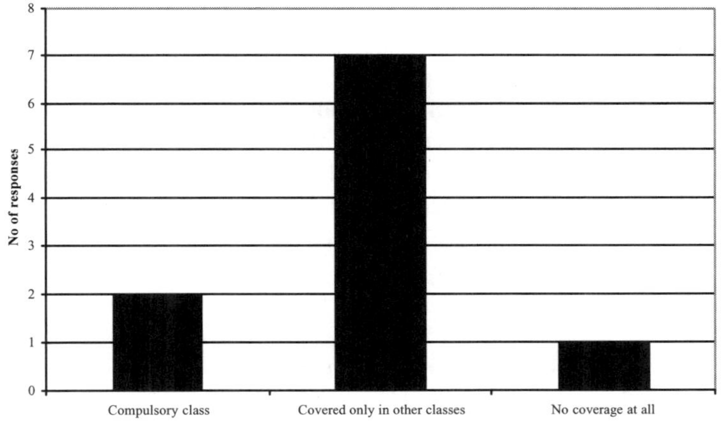

Fig. 3 : Extent to which marketing is taught on 10 postgraduate courses

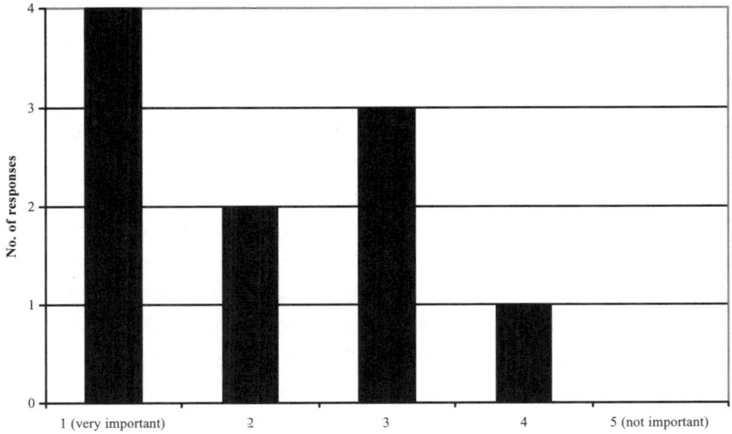

Fig. 4 : Value of marketing: postgraduate courses (10 responses)

Figure-4 shows the importance attributed to the subjects of Marketing by respondents. As with the undergraduate courses, no-one selected 'not important' (i.e. a mark of 5). The '4' grade was returned by the respondent who reported on the course which had no marketing elements at all.

WHAT HAS CHANGED BETWEEN 2001 AND 2004?

A follow-up survey has not been undertaken, however I have examined a sample of current course descriptions and consulted with academic colleagues. These investigations suggest that there has been no significant change since 2001 in terms of the amount of time devoted to learning about marketing. Management is still strongly represented in the curriculum, with marketing sometimes mentioned as one of the topics covered in a management module. A few specific marketing modules exist but, for example, one of the Scottish universities that had a separate Marketing module in my 2001 survey now offers a combined management and marketing module instead. There have been some changes within the marketing curriculum, reflecting developments in the field. For example, Customer Relationship Management, Relationship Marketing and aspects of internet marketing are now more likely to be taught.

DISCUSSION

It is likely that most UK LIS students nowadays will learn something about marketing: however, they will probably not learn very much about it. Students doing an undergraduate library/information course have quite a good chance of studying marketing, but may miss out on indepth study of information marketing specifically. At Masters level there tends to be less opportunity of studying the subject in depth, but students are more likely to learn something about information marketing (if not very much). Those students who choose a course with the 'library' word in the title, are more likely to study marketing. Since the trend in the UK is to remove the 'library' word from course titles, and focus more on the increasingly popular 'information management', this could mean that marketing will be learnt by fewer students in information departments in the future.

The relative lack of specialist marketing classes might indicate that information studies lecturers think the topic is of marginal interest for information and library students. However, the majority of respondents to my questionnaire did think marketing was a valuable subject of study. Therefore, there must be further reasons to explain why marketing does not feature more prominently on course curricula, and I will highlight some possible reasons.

The number of subjects that employers, students, professional associations etc. expect to be covered on information and library courses grows. At the start of this article I highlighted statements about the importance of marketing. But marketing is just one of the things mentioned on the lists of desirable skills for information professionals. There is even more pressure for universities to schedule Internet-related studies such as Web design, intranet management, and use of search engines. Management topics (people management, planning, budgeting, leadership etc.) also tend to come further up the agenda of potential employers. Previously unfashionable topics, such as classification and cataloguing, have demanded attention once more, in their new guises of taxonomy and metadata. In the academic library section, the focus on information literacy has led to demands to teach students about pedagogy. In the public library sector, specific areas of interest such as reader development have been given greater priority.

The Masters programme is a particular problem. Taught Masters courses in the UK normally last one year: the taught part of the programme will span eight months at most. Students will also expect some element of choice in these programmes. Information Management (IM) courses (distinct from e.g. information and library studies courses) generally have more emphasis on technical subjects and on information and knowledge management.

There are slightly different pressures on UK undergraduate courses, to account for the emphasis on optional marketing classes. There has been a big move to modularity: breaking courses down into one-semester modules, with ample choice of classes, so that students can choose their own pathway. One could argue that taking a generic marketing class, i.e. one offered outside an information department, is as useful as one taught by an information studies lecturer. However, it would also be valuable to learn about *information* marketing issues.

One result of this lack of coverage is that libraries may look beyond LIS graduates when recruiting people to market library services. Skeyes and Bedwell [11] reports on her experience in the London School of Economics (LSE) library, as someone with a marketing, rather than LIS, background. Her manager at LSE, explaining the rationale for Bedwell's appointment, notes that "we decided that if we as librarians tried to make the step change needed to improve our communications and income generation we would fail. What was needed was proper marketing expertise." Similarly, the British Library (the largest UK library) has looked outside LIS when making marketing appointments.

CONTINUING PROFESSIONAL DEVELOPMENT (CPD)

Until recently, the UK's professional LIS association, CILIP has not provided any real incentive for Continuing Professional Development for its members. This is changing with the introduction of a new Framework of Qualification, which will be introduced in 2005. This provides CILIP Members with the opportunity to revalidate their membership if they can provide evidence that they have participated in CPD and submit a personal reflection on the outcomes of the training they have undertaken. CILIP Members who achieve two Revalidation cycles will be eligible to become Fellows of CILIP. (see http://www.cilip.org.uk/qualificationschartership/FrameworkofQualifications/)

It will be interesting to see whether this influences the extent and type of training available. There already exists an active CPD scene in the UK, though, and this section will give examples of what is undertaken.

Firstly, experience is shared through CILIP's Publicity and Public Relations Group (PPRG), whose activities include a newsletter and an annual conference: in 2004, this focused on "evaluation for effective marketing". Presentations from previous conferences are available on its website (www.cilip.org.uk/groups/pprg/). This group manages (together with a sponsor: currently Farries Library Services) the annual Public Relations and Publicity awards. The Awards target promotional campaigns of different sizes, printed publicity material, web or multimedia publicity, sponsorship initiatives and personal achievement in the area [12].

Specialist groups and organisations are also active in the marketing area. For example, the "Marketing the National electronic Library for Health (NeLH)" campaign mobilises health librarians to promote electronic information services (many of which are available via the NeLH) to their customers in the National Health Service [13]. The NeLH *Digital Libraries Network* uses the web, including a weblog, to exchange information about the initiative (see http://www.nelh.nhs.uk/dlnet/default.asp). Reinforcing the recognition of the importance of marketing in this sector, an article on the 2004 Health libraries Group conference reports on a session in which "participants were invited to assess their own organisations and services against a list of 'hallmarks of market orientation' and critically consider their image 'How do we want to be seen?' "[14] Looking at a contrasting sector, the British Business Schools Librarians Group made marketing a key focus for its 2004 annual conference, with two workshops covering issues such as market segmentation.

CILIP runs an extensive training programme centrally (http://www.cilip.org.uk/training), mainly of one- or two-day courses. In the Autumn of 2004, these included events on "Producing effective promotional literature", "Customer Relationship management for library and information units", "Evaluating the impact of your service" and "Community profiling." Simmonds [15] has written about CILIP's training programme and delegates' needs. Commercial organisations also provide training. For example the one day courses regularly offered by TFPL (http://www.tfpl.com) include "Successfully marketing your information service" and "Transforming customer care in information services".

From these examples it can be seen that a spectrum of marketing issues are being addressed: not just promotion, but also marketing planning and research, marketing evaluation and customer relations. There is evidently a demand for training in marketing, and evidence that this demand is being met in events organised specifically for LIS practitioners. One problem for those outside the English capital is that London is the most popular venue for training events, both because there are a large number of LIS practitioners based in the London area and because London is a hub for transport connections. This can mean that, for those outside the South East of England, the training opportunities are not quite so rich as it might first appear. Some tailor-made marketing or customer care courses may be provided in-house for larger libraries, and larger libraries may also invite in external speakers for one-off talks, including talks in the marketing area.

However, online training for marketing LIS services has not developed significantly: comparatively, the UK is a small, densely populated country, and this has made virtual training less pressing than it is in some other countries. In terms of formal distance-learning courses for LIS professionals, The University of Wales Aberystwyth's MSc Econ in Information and Library Studies is probably the most successful, and this is one of the few courses to include a separate marketing class (http://www.dil.aber.ac.uk/dis/courses/default.asp).

The professional literature provides another "virtual" training medium, and the UK has an active professional press, including numerous newsletters and journals from specialist LIS groups. For example, a recent issue of *SCONUL Focus* [16], produced by the Society of College, National and University Libraries, included case studies on marketing at the University of Leeds and at University College Chester and a report on an initiative aiming to measure libraries' impact. There are books on information marketing published in the UK, including two recent general textbooks [17, 18]. There is not an open discussion list on marketing LIS, but the topic arises periodically on the general discussion list lis-link and more specialised discussion lists (these UK lists can be browsed and searched at (www.jiscmail.ac.uk).

CONCLUSION

40 years ago quite a few LIS practitioners viewed marketing with suspicion, and articles about marketing had to adopt an evangelical approach or be careful to preface any article with a careful explanation that "marketing wasn't just about selling". It has been a slow process of conversion, but in the 21st century there is far more widespread acceptance that marketing is good and necessary for LIS services. This is reflected in the way in which marketing is covered in the professional press and in CPD events aimed at LIS practitioners. As an LIS educator, I feel that marketing still deserves a more prominent place in the LIS university curriculum. However, I am also encouraged by the progress that has been made so far.

REFERENCES

1. Pedley (P). The information professional of the 21st century. *Managing information*. 8 (7). 2001: 8-9.
2. Urwin (S). Opinion going the virtual distance: Online training can keep information professionals up to speed. *Information world review*. April 2000: 21.
3. Gibson (M). Telling it like it is: A personal take on information. *Business information review*. 18 (1). 2001: 28-34.

4. Ashcroft (L). Developing competencies, critical analysis and personal transferable skills in future information professionals. *Library review*. 53 (2). 2004: 82-88.
5. Usherwood (R) et al. Recruit, retain and lead: The public library workforce study. London: Resource. 2001. (Library and Information Commission Research report; 106)
6. Layzell Ward (P). Professional education in Australia, the United Kingdom and the United States in the 20th Century. *In* Chapman (E A) and Lynden (F C), Eds. Advances in librarianship. 24. London: Academic Press, 2000: 103-137.
7. Broady-Preston (J). The Quality Assurance Agency (QAA) and subject review: The viewpoint of the assessor. *Libri*. 52 (4). 2002: 195-198.
8. Elkin (J). The UK research assessment exercise 2001. *Libri*. 52 (4) 2002: 204-208.
9. Quality Assurance Agency for Higher Education. Librarianship and information management. Gloucester: The Agency, 2000. Available at http://www.qaa.ac.uk/crntwork/benchmark/librarianship.pdf
10. Webber (S). Teaching of marketing and quality management in schools of library and information science in the UK: A review and report of findings. *In,* Savard (R) Ed. Education and research for marketing and quality management in libraries: Satellite meeting: Quebec, August 14-16 2001. Munich: KG Saur. 2002: 43-65.
11. Sykes (J) and Bedwell (K). Marketing the academic library: The LSE experiment. *In*, Brewer (S), Ed. Marketing strategy and research: Their role in library service development. Loughborough: Capital Planning Information. 2003: 1-9.
12. Public Eye. Congratulations to this year's winners of the CILIP and Emerald PR & Publicity Awards. *Public eye*. (61) 2003: 1-2.
13. Turner (A), Rosen (N) and Wilkie (F). Marketing the National Electronic Library for Health in 2003. *Public eye*, (62) 2004: 3-4.
14. Blagden (P). Sector shows evidence of healthy growth. *Library and information gazette*. 22 October 2004: 5.
15. Simmonds (P). Training and learning : Outcomes, not outputs. *Business Information Review*. 21 (2). 2004: 102-104.
16. *SCONUL Focus*. (31) 2004. http;//www.sconul.ac.uk/pubs_stats/newsletter/31/
17. de Saez (E E). Marketing concepts for library and information services. Ed.2. London: Facet. 2002.
18. Rowley (J E). Information Marketing. Aldershot: Ashgate. 2001.

EDUCATING FOR MARKETING OF INFORMATION SERVICES IN CANADA: AN ELECTIVE COURSE IN FIVE GRADUATE LIS PROGRAMS[+1]

Diane Mittermeyer

Abstract *Of the seven LIS schools in Canada offering an MLIS program, a Marketing course was identified in five programs. An examination of various documents submitted by each instructor (detailed course outline, reading list and description of assignments) led to the comparative analysis presented in this paper. From a standpoint of (1) Statement of Educational Objectives, (2) Course Content, (3) Reading List and (4) Assignment, the analysis summarizes commonalities and differences.*

INTRODUCTION

As foreseen, the content of these five LIS Marketing courses is comparable to a great extent. However, pertaining to objectives, readings, and assignments, each instructor demonstrates some distinctive priorities which are briefly exemplified. For purpose of analysis, the courses were regrouped in two groups + one. That is, one group of two courses taught on an alternate basis by Adjunct Instructors, and one group of three courses taught by full-time faculty members. The "+ one" pertains to the inclusion of an advocacy course, granting "advocacy is essentially the marketing of an issue." Finally, the state of development of a "public relations and advocacy" course in the 7th LIS school is briefly presented[1]. During Summer 2004, each website of the seven schools of library and information studies in Canada was consulted in search of a Marketing Information Services course being offered in their Master's program. Five Marketing courses were identified. They are:

LIBR 579D *Marketing*, School of Library, Archival and Information Studies, The University of British Columbia

LIS 646 *Marketing and Public Relations for Information Professionals*, Faculty of Information & Media Studies, Master of Library and Information Science, University of Western Ontario

BLT 6318 *Marketing des services d'information*, École de bibliothéconomie et des sciences de l'information, Université de Montréal

GLIS 624 *Marketing Information Services*, Graduate School of Library and Information Studies, McGill University

LIS 546 *Marketing Libraries and Information Services*, School of Library and Information Studies, University of Alberta

The purpose of this paper is to examine the content of these Marketing courses in order to identify, commonalities and differences, if any, among the LIS Marketing courses offered to students attending Canadian schools.

SOME PREVIOUS CONCERNS

In 2001, Bouthillier [2], conducted a survey of North American LIS schools "To gain more knowledge about the teaching of marketing and quality management..." Although this survey covers both Marketing and Quality Management, and encompasses 56 LIS schools in North America, she notes in her analysis that upon examining the Canadian schools separately "their websites reveals that 6 schools out of 7 (86%) offer a course in marketing." Three years later this number is 5 schools, that is 70%. The results of the last two questions of Bouthillier's survey are of interest, particularly the question pertaining to the importance of a marketing course in the LIS school's curriculum. While the survey's response rate is somewhat low with 22 questionnaires received out of 56 sent, the importance of the marketing course was rated by an even smaller group of participants. Only 17 answered this question. Of these, 6 respondents perceived the course as "very important". In fact, this represents scarcely 10% of the 56 North American LIS schools participating in this survey. According to Bouthillier: "One might even anticipate that marketing courses may become marginalized in a near future if they do not become more valued."

Given that in 1999, the Library Administration and Management Association (LAMA) issued some warnings regarding what seemed to be at the time, the devaluation of the teaching of Management courses in LIS programs in North America [3], and in light of the comment from a LIS school library director gathered by Bouthillier in her survey, to the effect that:

"Of course, it is important to market library services and to manage to improve the quality of library services. However, there are so many aspects of librarianship that must be covered in a two year sequence of courses that we can't possibly teach everything ourselves within one school. Everything is important. But in the great scheme of things, I would not eliminate a course in digital libraries or in reference or children's services, to add one in marketing or quality improvement..." [2]. But marketing should also be included in course curricula.

The author communicated with the instructors through e-mail to have update information of the courses on marketing in various library schools and have observation on the relevant issues.

FIVE LIS MARKETING COURSES + ONE

The development of a course being taught for the first time in fall 2004, in the Master program, at the Faculty of Information Studies, University of Toronto: FIS 2199H *Special Topics in Information Studies: Advocacy and Library Issues*.

In a communication from Wendy Newman, Adjunct Instructor appointed to teach the course, She specifies: "One of the wonderful things about doing this is that it is the result of a student-led proposal, backed up by their survey of the student body and a review of the curricula of the North American library schools. I think those students have already achieved something in advocacy."

As Newman mentions: "Since advocacy is essentially the marketing of an issue, there's a major connection." Is that to say that those of us interested in the teaching of LIS Marketing should be better advocates?

Given that the purpose of this analysis is to examine the commonalities and differences among the various courses identified, the first one to be examined appears to be the newest of the kind, namely FIS 2199H *Special Topics in Information Studies: Advocacy and Library Issues*. In most Canadian universities, a usual way of introducing a new course, sometimes on an experimental basis, is through the use of the course category: *Special Topics in*... As mentioned above, at the time of this writing, the course is being offered for the first time in fall 2004. While in essence the course is aiming at providing the students "with knowledge needed to understand the advocacy process and exercise professional leadership in the advocacy of library issues", a look at the more detailed outline reveals that effectively "marketing" is no stranger to "advocacy". Here are some selected examples of the topics being addressed:

Week 1	:	Advocacy defined (relationship to public relations, marketing)
Week 2	:	The environment of libraries in 2004
Week 3	:	Advocacy as the marketing of issues and positioning of libraries. The environment of public sector decision-makers in 2004
Week 4	:	Identifying and analyzing target groups for selected issues Stakeholder analysis: allies, bedfellows, opponents.
Week 5	:	Personal communications tools; mass communication tools
Week 8	:	Branding and advocacy: the "@ your library" campaign. Customizing the brand – types of libraries, types of services
Week 9	:	Fundamentals of library partnership development and maintenance
Week 11	:	Measuring and communicating impact

In terms of assignments, there are four assignments: (1) short written reports on selected readings, (2) one group presentation, (3) the preparation of one advocacy plan for a target group, and (4) one major paper. The readings are numerous, more than 60 items, plus video recordings and web sites. But, "There is no "textbook". The closest thing to a textbook is the CLA [Canadian Library Association] Advocacy Workbook, ... Although there are many readings listed in my reading list, much of the literature is not particularly helpful. The terms marketing, public relations, and advocacy tend to be used synonymously. Most of the articles in the library literature are actually about promotion rather than advocacy."

TEACHING LIS MARKETING ON AN ALTERNATE BASIS

The following two courses are examined first

This comparative analysis of LIS Marketing courses LIS 546 (Univ. of Alberta) and LIS 646 (Univ. of Western Ontaria), comprises four components:

Course Objectives: Upon completion of the course LIS 546 Marketing Libraries and Information Service, a student should know and understand:

- the critical role of marketing to the growth of libraries and the information professions;
- the major elements of a marketing approach to the provision of library and information services;
- how to evaluate the marketing experience of the for-profit sector and translate them into meaningful library activities;
- how various libraries have used marketing to their advantage.

The course LIS 646 will help students to:

- gain a solid grounding in the principles and methods of marketing and public relations targeted to identified client groups, and confidently apply these in formation settings;
- through discussion, critical evaluation and hands-on experience, develop an appreciation of professional design, production, packaging, distribution, and presentation of effective promotional materials for information products and services; and
- understand the positive impacts that marketing and public relations can have on user access, fundraising efforts, accountability, profitability, and volunteerism.

As can be seen, both sets of Course Objectives are geared at translating and applying for-profit marketing concepts to non-profit, service oriented library environments.

Content : Pertaining to Course Content, as foreseen there are definitely more similarities than differences. For example, although not necessarily in the same other, both courses address:

- The definition of Marketing
- The Marketing Mix
- Market research, Target Markets, Market Positioning
- The Marketing Cycle, the Strategic Planning Process
- Writing an Effective Marketing Plan
- Measuring Results, Evaluating Marketing Effectiveness
- Communication, Public Relations and Promotions

As for differences, while in both courses the various elements surrounding Communication are addressed in greater depth, including in one course (LIS 546) the topic: Writing for the Web, and in the other (LIS 646): Criteria for evaluating Internet sites, each course does present some unique aspects. For example, the course LIS 546 addresses "Advocacy" as a separate topic in two classes. This remains us of the fact that: "... essentially advocacy is the marketing of an issue..." On the other hand, "Marketing Yourself" as a complement to marketing your services and your organization, is the topic of another class. However, it may be argued that what may be perceived as a difference or unique to a course, may well rest on the terms used to specify the topic being presented. For example, the last class of the course LIS 646 addresses the topic of "Adopting the Marketing Mind-set" and "Issues/trends in library marketing and public relations".

Readings : A comparison of the reading lists provided reveals a rather limited number of duplications. While the course LIS 546 has a Required Text/Readings - Ries, 1993 [4], the course LIS 646 does not have such a requirement. However, in the Course Outline under Resources, one finds the following statement: "No required text. Readings and books placed on Reserve cover specific components of the course. Readings... please READ them! They expand class content and provide illustrative case studies or supportive material for assignments." On the other hand, it is interesting to note that out of a list of some 25 items in one course and over 40 items in the other, only 4 items are the same. These items are: SLA, 1997[5], Siess, 2003[6], Wallace, 2004[7], and Weingand, 1998[8]. Also worth mentioning, Karp,1995 [9] appears on the LIS 646 reading list, and *Karp, 2002 [10]* on the LIS 546 list.

Assignments: It is in the area of the Assignments that one finds the greatest diversity. The following summary presents an overview of the various types of assignments requested. LIS 546 Marketing Libraries and Information Services covers:

- Television Commercial Evaluation (25%)
- Presentation (Public Relations Topics) (25%)
- Major Paper (35%)
- Feedback Diary (5%)
- Class Participation (10%)

Whereas, assignment for course LIS 646 Marketing and Public Relations for Information Professionals include:

- Marketing Plan (30%) (Team Assignment)
- Short Essay (15%)
- Mining the News (5%)
- Media Plan/News Release and PSA (15%)
- Promotional Material (15%)

- Idea Generator – "Think Outside the Bun"©Taco Bell (5%) (Team Assignment)
- Participation (15%)

For purpose of illustrating the diversity of approaches in evaluating students learning, here are two examples. While the information provided is brief and the present summary may not do justice to the learning objectives of these assignments given that often further information is presented in class, the following two were selected for their requirements to look outside the box, so to speak. That is, to look at the outside world in order to compare and be in a better position to compete.

The first one is taken from the LIS 546 course and pertains to the Television Commercial Evaluation. As described this assignment's Objective is "To determine by watching TV commercials to what audience the product is being targeted." This is followed by a brief presentation of what needs to be done. The students are required to:

"Watch two hour-long programs on TV at two different times of day. Submit a written report, maximum length 2 pages (1 page for each program). The written report will include, for each program:

- Program name, day of week, time of day, and network
- Description of the likely characteristics of the program's viewing audience.
- The general slant or focus of the advertising.
- An analysis of how well the advertisements are targeted to the likely viewing audience."

Although such an assignment may seem straightforward and rather simple, most LIS Marketing instructors will recognize that there is much "more than meets the eye" in determining target audiences and advertising attributes.

The second example is titled "Mining the News" and comes from LIS 646. Such trendy title is sure to catch the students' attention. In terms of its out looking approach, this assignment requires the students to: "Identify a current story or article of interest to you (as a librarian) in the popular press that deals with any type of Market or Consumer Research, either stated or implied. (Look for items that include discussion of trends, survey results, forecasts, statistics, or customer preferences.)

With reference to the above item, briefly provide details on the following:

- Identify a type of library or information service that may see opportunities to use the content of this item in their marketing program.
- How the data or information be used with regard to a specific library product OR how this information help in planning for customer needs?
- After reading the article, is there an obvious action to be taken and if so, what?
- What other sources might one want to consult to supplement this information or to verify that it is relevant to a particular library, geographic, or other setting?

- Are there any dangers in using the information as stated?
- What might be appropriate timing for the library to act upon this information?"

It is further specified that this "mining" should not exceed one page and that while popular press can include national or community newspapers, various kinds of magazines, and even Internet sites, (a copy of the news clipping or first page of the article is to be appended to the assignment), articles from library journal or publication should not be chosen. Along with looking at the outside world in their approach, one will note that both instructors are sparing in their writing requirement: the length of each assignment - one page per analysis. There seems to be no time to loose over padding the work.

The last word goes to Della Paradis, the course coordinator of course 546. When asked if there were any aspect of Marketing on which she puts more emphasis, she wrote: "I think I emphasize developing a marketing mindset – i.e. customer focus, basing decisions on research/info., communicating benefits (rather than features), differentiating our services within a competitive environment." [6]

Teaching LIS Marketing – The Second Group

The three courses to be examined are: LIBR 579D (The University of British Columbia), BLT 6318 (Université de Montréal), and GLIS 624 (McGill University). As for the analysis of the first group, the same four components are examined here as below:

Course Objectives: For, LIBR 579D: Marketing, objectives include:

- understand the role and function of marketing in enabling the information agency to fulfill its mission;
- be able to apply marketing theory and concepts to improve customer service;
- be able to analyze macro-environmental opportunities and threats, and organizational and competitor strengths and weaknesses as a basis for determining opportunities and strategies;
- be able to integrate marketing strategies through the mix of product/services, place, promotion, price, people and politics;
- recognize marketing as an effective planning and resource allocation tool;
- be able to design effective advocacy programs through partnerships in the political process.

The objectives of course BLT 3618: Marketing des services d' information are:

- comprenne l'approche marketing adaptée aux services d'information;
- soit sensibilisé à l'importance et aux manières d'étudier le marché et les clientèles en marketing;
- sache comment établir une stratégie marketing en fonction de différents publics-cibles;

- connaisse les principales stratégies de communication marketing applicables aux services d'information;
- soit capable de planifier la gestion marketing.

The objectives of the course GLIS624: Marketing information services are:

- To understand the basic elements of the marketing process as applied to information services.
- To analyze the main features of marketing communication messages.
- To develop a marketing communication message.

In terms of similarities and differences, one will note that the instructors' approach to the statement of educational objectives is somewhat different. At one end of the spectrum (LIBR 579D), one finds a detailed list of objectives, while at the other end (GLIS 624), the list is succinct with a focus on communication. Furthermore, it should be mentioned that the detailed course outline of both courses LIBR 579D and BLT 6318 also present either a Course Goal (LIBR 579D) or the statement of a General Objective (BLT 7318). These are:

LIBR 579D: "To prepare professional librarians to design and evaluate marketing plans based on analysis, research and effective planning in order to improve customer service."

BLT 6318 : "L'objectif général de ce cours est de donner aux étudiants la base nécessaire qui leur permettra d'effectuer de façon efficace la gestion du marketing dans les différents types de services d'information. Il s'adresse aux étudiants de toutes les spécialisations, et est conçu en fonction de tous les types de milieux en science de l'information (bibliothèques, archives, entreprises, etc.)"

While the purpose of this comparative analysis is to describe and inform rather than evaluate, it is fortunate that the missing elements pertain to this author's outline. In light of my colleagues' contributions, the need to revisit the Goals and Objectives statements of GLIS 624 is, thus, acknowledged.

Content: Content wise, the three courses present a rather similar Marketing orientation. From Strategic Marketing Planning to the Marketing Audit, Market Research, Market Analysis and Segmentation, the Marketing Mix, and the Marketing Plan, one may conclude that "Marketing" is "Marketing". However, based on the documents provided (detailed course outline, reading list, description of assignments), in terms of content or topics being covered some differences could be noted. For examples: one topic being explicitly mentioned only in the course LIBR 579D pertains to "[Marketing] Applications to Advocacy and Lobbying"; while a topic being mentioned only in GLIS 624 is "The organization's distribution mix: the (virtual) place." However, as previously stated – what may be perceived as a difference or unique to a course, may well rest on the terms used to specify the topic.

Readings: As pertain to the reading lists, given that for one course (LIBR 579D) under "Required and Recommended Reading" one finds a statement inviting the students to select their own reading materials (one graduate marketing text and one library-based marketing text) without providing any further guidance, and given that another course (BLT 6318) addresses a French speaking audience, only one title, Kotler and Andearsen, 1996 [11] appeared on two reading lists (BLT 6318, and GLIS 624). It should also be mentioned that Walters, 1992 [12] on BLT 6318 and ,Walters, 1994[13] was found on GLIS 624. As for Required Readings, only GLIS 624 provides this information specifically. Along with Kotler and Andreasen's book mentioned above, two other titles are listed as required readings, namely Lovelock, 2001 [14] and Weingnand, 1999 [15]. When compared to the first group, only two titles were found to be the same on two lists. Both LIS 646 and BLT 6318 refer to: Rowley, 2001 [16] and Wallace, 2004 [17]. Finally, at least two French language publications, from the numerous listed on the BLT 6318 Reading List, should be mentioned: Muet, 2001[18] and .Sutter, 1994[19].

Assignments: As with the first group, it is definitely in the area of the assignments that one finds what appears to be the greatest difference between the three courses. In this particular case, one must admit that a summary presenting the overview of the required assignments may not do justice to the essence of the work to be accomplished. Based on the information provided, one course (LIBR 579D) presents rather different assignments profiles. These are briefly examined below.

Assignment for LIBR 579D: Marketing include: Project Management (10%); Seminar (20%); Marketing Plan and Presentation (60%); and Participation (10%)

Assignment for BLT 6318 Marketing des services d'information include:

1. Essai de définition du marketing (individuel; 3-5 pages) (15%)
2. Conception d'un outil de recherche marketing (équipes de 2) (10%)
3. Étude de cas en stratégie marketing (équipes de 2) (15%)
4. Présentation du contexte du projet de marketing (équipe) (10%)
5. Projet marketing :
   - présentation orale (10%)
   - rapport final (30%)
6. Participation au cours (présence, question, etc.) (10%)

Whereas, GLIS 624 Marketing Information Services includes:"A Visit to the Library: On-site or Virtual? (a matter of benefits and costs) (individual) (40%) "The Last Words Say It All" – A Large Ad on the boarding platform of the city public transit subway: a Poster session (team of 2) (45%0; and Participation in class discussion (15%)

As can be seen above, each of the three courses requires rather straightforward assignment work: essay papers, team projects, class participation. However, within the comparative framework selected for this paper, one must briefly signal the LIBR 579D rather distinctive teaching method. To do justice to the components which may illustrate best this course distinctness, here are a few quotes from the course detailed outline:

"Format of the course: This is a team-based course, conducted as a project management exercise. The course is based on the following principles of learning:

- Learning requires the active participation of the student;
- People learn in a variety of ways and at different rates;
- Learning is both an individual and a group process.

Consequently, a variety of strategies are used and group and individual responsibility are incorporated. This is also a problem-based course with assessment based on evidence. The instructor is available for assistance, clarification and support." *If at the end of this graduate course you believe that you learned as much or more from your colleagues as you did from the instructor, then the course will be considered a success.*"

Accordingly, each assignment reflects this team work responsibility, even when done individually such as leading a seminar. Ultimately, the evaluation is necessarily based on "both group and individual assignments, from team planning for the course to individual presentation." But such evaluation is ongoing and an important aspect of this process is "the strengthening of your own self-evaluation skills – learning the process of critical, non-defensive scrutiny of your own performance." Thus, as defined it appears that in this team-based course students learn more than Marketing principles and strategies, more than being an active team player, a good communicator, and a leader. According to Ken Haycock: "The better you are able to do this [self-evaluation], the more your professional growth will continue after you leave the course." To the best of our knowledge, the learning of such evaluation is seldom the focus of LIS courses, and in our opinion, this is somewhat unfortunate.

SOON... A SIXTH MARKETING COURSE

The readers familiar with the Canadian LIS scene will have noted that the School of Library & Information Studies, Dalhousie University, is missing from the present analysis. At the time of this writing, the course LIBS 6820 Marketing could be accessed from the Dalhousie School's web site. However, when the School was contacted, it turned out that the course had not been taught since 2000 and the instructor had moved to another Canadian LIS school.

Upon further inquiry, the Director of the School, Dr. Fiona Black, submitted the following information to our attention for the purpose of this analysis:

"Dalhousie's SLIS, as part of the Faculty of Management, offers several means by which students may gain appropriate knowledge concerning marketing of information services. Current and future course offerings in SLIS and in the School of Business and of Public Administration include BUSI 5104 Marketing Management and LIBS 6820. This latter course, currently called, simply, Marketing, is now being examined and will be offered as an advanced management course with a focus on public relations and on advocacy. (The goal of our Faculty as a whole is not to duplicate courses offered in any of the Schools in the Faculty.)"

Given that Professor Black teaches the core course LIBS 5570 Organizational Management and Strategy, she also mentions that she is likely to be the faculty member who develops the new public relations and advocacy course. So, hopefully by the time this report becomes available, the Canadian scene will comprised Six LIS Marketing courses + one, or depending upon Professor Black's approach Five LIS Marketing courses + two. In any case, the future looks promising and by 2005, no students attending a Canadian LIS schools will be without the opportunity to take either an LIS Marketing course or an LIS course advocating "essentially the marketing of an issue".

CONCLUDING REMARKS

The purpose of this paper was to identify and examine the content of LIS Marketing courses being offered in Canadian LIS schools in order to provide a summary picture of the Canadian scene. Through, essentially Internet communications (websites visits and exchanges of e-mails with numerous documents attached), we were able to demonstrate the importance and value attributed to Marketing in LIS education in Canada. With a ratio of 5 Marketing courses + one, out of seven schools, the presence of a certain level of importance and value should be acknowledged.

However, given that two of these courses are offered on an alternate basis and that "... in the great scheme of things..." numerous other calls are filling up the electronic (digital) information lines, this author's message to the Canadian readership is twofold: "If advocacy is essentially the marketing of an issue, then keep advocating the teaching of Marketing as The Issue."

Also, given that "Marketing is an attitude of mind", which should "... permeates an organization, and the entire staff"[11], MLIS students must be provided with the possibility to further develop and nurture such attitude of mind within the context of a recognized and values Marketing course, in order to enter the work place with the "right attitude of mind".

REFERENCES

1. Dalhousie University, School of Library & Information Studies, MLIS Programme. Course: LIBS 6820 Marketing. http://www.mgmt.dal.ca/slis/Courses/6820/index.html (Last consulted: 13 September 2004);
2. Bouthillier (F). The teaching of marketing and quality management in schools of library and information studies: The case of North America. *In,* Savard (R) Ed. Education and research for marketing and quality management in libraries: Satellite meeting: Quebec, August 14-16 2001. Munich: KG Saur. 2002: 21-30.
3. Library Administration and Management Association. *LAMA News.* 13(10) 1999: 230-235.
4. Ries (AL) and Trout (Jack). The 22 immutable laws of marketing: Violate them at your own risk. New York: HarperCollins. 1993.
5. Marketing matters: an SLA information kit. Washington, DC: Special Libraries Association. 1997.
6. Siess (J A). The visible librarian: Asserting your value with marketing and advocacy. Chicago: American Library Association. 2003.
7. Wallace (L K). Libraries, mission, & marketing: Writing mission statements that work. Chicago: American Library Association. 2004.
8. Weingand (D E). Future-driven library marketing. Chicago: American Library Association. 1998.
9. Karp (R S). Part-time public relations with full-time results: a PR primer for libraries. Chicago: American Library Association. 1995
10. Karp (R S). Powerful public relations: A how-to guide for libraries. Chicago: American Library Association. 2002
11. Kotler (P) and Andreasen (A R). Strategic Marketing for Nonprofit Organizations. Ed.5. Englewood Cliffs, N.J: Prentice Hall. 1996.
12. Walters (S). Marketing: A how-to-do-it manual for librarians. New York: Neal-Schuman. 1992.
13. Walters (S). Customer service: A how-to-do-it manual for librarians. New York: Neal-Schuman. 1994.
14. Lovelock (C H). Services marketing: People, technology, strategy. Ed.4. Upper Saddle River, N.J: Prentice Hall. 2001.
15. Weingand (D E). Marketing/planning library and information services. Ed.2. Englewood, C.O.: Libraries Unlimited. 1999.
16. Rowley (J). Information marketing. Aldershot, UK: Ashgate. 2001.
17. Ibid, 7
18. Muet (F) and Salaun (J M). Stratégie marketing des services d'information : bibliothèques et centres de documentation. Paris: Éditions du Cercle de la Librairie. 2001.
19. Sutter (É). Le marketing des services d'information : pour un usage de l'information documentaire. Paris: ESF Éditeur. 1994.

Websites

1. McGill University, Graduate School of Library and Information Studies, Master of Library and Information Studies. Course: GLIS 624 Marketing Information Services. http://www.gslis.mcgill.ca/MLIS_Courses_Complete.htm (Last consulted: 13 September 2004);

2. Library and Information Studies. Course: LIS 546 Marketing Libraries and Information Services. http://www.slis.ualberta.ca/546_outline.htm (Last consulted: 13 September 2004)

3. University of British Columbia, School of Library, Archival and Information Studies, Master of Library and Information Studies. Course: LIBR 579D: Marketing. http://www.slais.ubc.ca/COURSES/coursdes/libr/libr579d.htm (Last consulted: 13 September 2004);

4. University of Toronto, Faculty of Information Studies, Master of Information Studies. Course: FIS 2199H Special Topics in Information Studies: Advocacy and Library Issues. http://courses.ece.utoronto.ca/cgi-bin/main.cgi?cc=20049/fis2199hf (Last consulted: 13 September 2004);

5. University of Western Ontario, Faculty of Information & Media Studies, Master of Library and Information Science. Course: 646 Marketing and Public Relations for Information Professionals. http://www.fims.uwo.ca/mlis/courses/646.htm (Last consulted: 13 September 2004).

EDUCATION FOR LIS MARKETING IN INDIA

G. Mahesh
Dinesh K. Gupta

Abstract *In recent years, there has been enormous interest on the topic of marketing of library and information services. However, the number of libraries and information centres in India adopting marketing strategies are few in number. One of the barriers to marketing of library and information services is the lack of marketing skills in the library professionals, which could be due to the inadequate coverage of marketing in the LIS curriculum. The paper attempts to look at the importance of marketing in the LIS curriculum and looks at the University Grants Commission's (UGC) LIS Model Curriculum vis-à-vis the LIS curriculum of three leading institutions with respect to the marketing topics in their curriculum. The paper concludes that the coverage of marketing in the Model Curriculum of the UGC is inadequate, though institutions / universities have started inclusion the topic/ paper of marketing in its LIS courses.*

INTRODUCTION

Librarianship and libraries have been greatly impacted by the rapid developments in information and communication technologies (ICT) in the recent years. Traditional libraries are evolving into digital and virtual libraries, and the present day librarians are required to acquire information and communication technology skills to perform their roles effectively in a digital environment. The inevitable use of information and communication technologies in libraries has further consolidated the library's position as a cost centre. As such, libraries and information centres all over the world have been faced with decreasing budgets and escalating cost of resources. This and other factors have compelled libraries and information centres to undertake outreach and marketing activities.

Library and information science literature abounds with papers on marketing and there has been a steady growth of marketing literature in LIS over the years. A keyword search in Library and Information Science Abstracts (LISA) shows that during the period 1970 to 1975, there were just 30 papers on marketing while there were 1146 papers on marketing during the period 1996-2002. But despite the awareness of the importance of marketing and the fact that in the present day information or knowledge economy where information is of high value, library and information centres which are a repository of information are not able to literally capitalize on their resources. This brings us to ponder over the question of why library and information centres are not able to generate revenue by adopting marketing strategies. It has been reported that one the barriers to marketing of library and information services by libraries is the lack of trained manpower in marketing of library and information services [1,2].

EDUCATION AND TRAINING FOCUS IN LIS

It can be seen that in India, with the emergence of information and communication technology and its use in libraries and information centres, there has been a lot of focus on education and training in information technology aspects in LIS courses and programmes. However, the topic of marketing though important for not only generating revenue but also for promoting the libraries remains neglected. The erstwhile National Information System for Science and Technology (NISSAT) organized a number of short-term courses in information science as a part of its Manpower Development Programme in libraries. It is interesting to note that between the years 1986 to 2000, NISSAT had organized 208 short term courses and out of which 157 courses were on IT related topics and only 6 courses have been on marketing of library and information services [3].

In India, in fact, the importance of information technology in libraries was recognized as early as the 1970's with LIS curriculum in universities introducing the topic of information technology. The University of Delhi had as early as 1977 introduced the topic of computer applications to library and information centres in its Master's programme in library science [4].

As far as marketing is concerned there are only few library schools in the country which have given emphasis in their syllabi, such as University of Bangalore, University of Delhi, NISCAIR and IGNOU.

IMPORTANCE OF MARKETING IN LIS CURRICULA

Worldover, Wasserman and Ford[5] suggested a course of study in Marketing Management in information science courses and suggested a list of topics for inclusion in syllabi for the first time. Harmon's paper entitled *The importance of marketing in library and information science curriculum* quotes Schenk [6],which visualises curriculum for 2010 in 1960s, considers that "Is too much time given to learning cataloguing and other routines, and consequently too little to a consideration of methods of extending the use of the library by the public?" It is true that curricula involved several hours on cataloguing and other technical routines including too much emphasis on information technology related topics [7]. Rejean Savard prepared *Guidelines for Teaching of Marketing in the Training of Librarians, Documentalists and Archieves* under the General Information Programme of UNESCO [8].

These studies reflect the concern about the lack of marketing in LIS courses. Also needs for inculcating marketing orientation in library and information centres which is not an easy task and cannot be done overnight by just reading some *how to* books and manuals on marketing. Marketing concepts have to be learned systematically as a part of the course curriculum. In the absence of the topic of marketing in the regular curriculum, short term courses can help to a certain extent. In India, a number of national level institutions, and major libraries and documentation centres have been offering short-term courses. But efforts in this direction are limited to some NISSAT sponsored training courses on marketing that was conducted from time to time. The Indian Institute of Management, Lucknow is also known for its Management Development Programmes on Marketing in Library and Information Services.

Such short term courses and management development programmes are helpful in gaining insight of marketing concepts, but never comprehensive enough to educate and train the library professionals to have a holistic approach to marketing of library and information services. Therefore, the long term solution to the problem of inadequate trained manpower in LIS marketing is to include a strong marketing component in the LIS curriculum in the university education system.

MARKETING IN LIS CURRICULA IN INDIA

The need for serious efforts for including marketing in LIS courses in India was felt in 1982, as rightly pointed out "It is apparent that some serious efforts must be made to impart education relating to marketing techniques to students of information science courses, if the information profession is to grow"[9]. It outlines marketing syllabi in information science courses, including topics such as marketing concept, marketing segmentation, marketing environment, marketing research, identification of users needs and characteristics, marketing programme and implement, control and evaluation of the marketing programme.

The importance of marketing in the LIS curriculum in India was further discussed in 1988 wherein the significance of the topic of marketing in LIS and the need to introduce an elective course for students of MLISc courses were discussed by Gopinath[10] who suggested that a six-week condensed course on “Marketing of Information Service” to professional librarians who have already done MLISc courses may be introduced. He further suggested that "It can be made as an optional course in MLIS programme. Various methods of teaching such as oral, written, and audio visual, case study, clinical, and hands on experience methods of teaching can be adopted for this purpose. We can also build several simulation teaching packages to show the means and methods of teaching the impact of marketing methods". He outlined such a course comprising of four papers, viz,

Paper 1 : Information Economics
Paper 2 : Marketing as Social Activity

Paper 3 : Marketing and Management of Library and information Centre
Paper 4 : Information Products and Services

Similarly, in 1990, Gopalkrishnan [11] advocates that library schools should incorporate marketing as a module in the regular schedule of their programmes. He also outlines six module for training in marketing. Recently Gupta [12] envisions marketing as a new discipline of library and information science education in Asia. The article recounts the major developments in marketing of library and information services world over and in Asia taking India as a case.

This emphasises that LIS curricula should be suitably changed to widen the subject of marketing in greater detail giving importance to related concepts to equip future librarians.

THE MODEL CURRICULUM OF UGC AND MARKETING

In India, the University Grants Commission (UGC) was established for the coordination, determination and maintenance of standards of university education in India. Since its inception, the University Grants Commission (UGC) has envisaged keen interest in, and laid emphasis on development of University and College Libraries, together with formulation of Model Curriculum for different levels of Library and Information Science (LIS) courses conducted in Indian Universities, with a view to produce appropriate professional manpower for managing the work and services of different types and levels of libraries, by harnessing literature explosion with the aid of prevalent technology. The UGC accomplishes the task of constituting various committees, subject panel and Curriculum Development Committee (CDC) [13].

According to Kanjilal, most of the LIS schools in India follow traditional curriculum, which are inadequate to meet the demand of the emerging market. The existing curriculum of most of the universities is based on the recommendation of the Ranganathan Committee and the Committee set up by the University Grants Commission (UGC) in 1978. The recommendations made by these committees mainly for the Bachelors level courses which are quite outdated and irrelevant in the present day context. In order to restructure the curriculum and bring about a uniform national pattern of LIS education in India, the University Grants Commission (UGC) appointed the Curriculum Development Committee (CDC) in 1990. The Report brought out by the CDC was however found to be unsatisfactory and was not adopted by most of the universities [14].

A study of the model curriculum for the two years Master of Library and Information Science course shows that out of fifteen papers, the topic of marketing figures in Paper X on Information Analysis, Repackaging and Consolidation in the Unit on Information Products. This is highly inadequate and reflects how very little emphasis is given to the topic of marketing in the Model Curriculum for the universities to emulate and adapt. If we discuss the UGC's syllabi for National Level Test (NET) exam for eligibility for lecturer/ asstt. librarian in universities/

college librarians, there is an addition that a topic on marketing has been included in the course library management. Though, the UGC Model Curriculum does not lay emphasis on marketing, it is welcome that some universities and institutions have recognized the need for inclusion of the topic in its syllabi.

MARKETING IN CURRICULA OF DIFFERENT UNIVERSITIES

A full Paper at the University of Bangalore

As per the best knowledge of the authors of this paper, the University of Bangalore is the first and only university which has included "Marketing of Information Products and Services" as full paper for the master's Programme [15]. The objectives of the paper are:

- To familiarize the students about the changing philosophy of library and information services from free to fee based information services.
- To understand the economic value of information
- To have knowledge of principles, techniques of information products and services
- To impart knowledge in product planning, product pricing and also to understand the market behaviour.

Topics include

Unit1 : Information-its meaning and properties, information as resource, economic value of information, information marketing: basic concepts and global scenario.

Unit2 : Marketing of information and information services-Definition and purpose, economic models and their application to information industry.

Unit3 : Transborder data flow, barriers: access, economic, legal, linguistic and cultural.

Unit4 : Products and services: planning and development, marketing mix, product and services promotion-advertising, packaging, branding, etc.

Unit5 : Pricing of information products and services- objectives and importance, factors influencing prices, techniques of pricing.

Unit6 : Market research- techniques and tools, statistical tools, statistical tools forecasting models.

Unit7 : Strategic marketing, strategies for marketing of information products and services in different libraries, information marketing and new technologies.

Marketing in LIS curriculum at Delhi University

The Department of Library and Information Science of Delhi University was established by Dr. S.R. Ranganathan and Prof. S. Das Gupta, the renowned Indian librarians and teachers of library science in 1946. The Department during the past 58 years of its existence has played a significant role in library science education in India. Delhi University has recently introduced one complete course entitled Marketing of library and information services, products and management consultancy in its Masters programme in Library and Information Science. The paper covers various facets of marketing, including marketing research, marketing of services, advertising, sales, and public relations, among others as given as below. This is covered in Paper VI – Marketing of Library and Information Services, Products and Management Consultancy. Almost half of this paper covers the marketing related topics as mentioned below [16]:

- Marketing management, Philosophies, Challenges, Social Marketing
- Strategic Planning and the Marketing Process, Marketing Environment
- Marketing Research and Marketing Information System
- Knowledge, Information, LIS Service and Product as Commodity
- Consumer, Buyer Behavior
- Market Segmentation, Marketing Mix
- Pricing, Distribution Channels, Communication Strategy
- Advertising, Sales, Organisations, Persons, Places and Ideas
- Marketing Ethics, Marketing management and Librarianship: Past, Present and Future

Marketing in the AIS Course at NISCAIR

Yet another, Master's level programme is the Associateship in Information Science conducted by National Institute of Science Communication and Information Resources (NISCAIR) which was formed on September 30, 2002 following the merger of the Indian National Scientific Documentation Centre (INSDOC) and National Institute of Science Communication (NISCOM). The erstwhile INSDOC started offering an advanced training course in Documentation and Reprography in August 1964. In 1977, the course was renamed Associateship in Information Science keeping in mind the changing context of information requirements. The course has been revised from time to time in the last forty years to suit the changing needs of the country and to incorporate the expanding dimension of documentation and information science [17].

In this programme, the topic of marketing of information products and services is covered under the paper on Information Products and Services. The marketing topic begins with an overview of marketing in general. This is followed by the topic of marketing in libraries. Other lectures are on the marketing mix (P's of marketing), marketing plan and market research.

One session is devoted to an analytical case study that the students read and come to the class and which is discussed at length. Every student presents his or her view on the case and issues related to the case are debated upon. An invited lecture by a library professional actively involved in marketing of information products and services that ends with an interactive session with the invited lecturer is also included. Students also have to spend a few days at the Marketing and Customer Services Division of NISCAIR, where they have real time experience of interacting with customers and understanding the sales and marketing processes. The last section is a seminar on an aspect related to marketing of information products and services. Thus at the end of the topic, students have a clear understanding about the importance and need for marketing, preparing a marketing plan and also dealing with customers.

CONCLUSION

The need and importance of marketing of library and information services has long been recognized. However, the application of marketing in library and information centres has not been successful. Though there are indications that the topic of marketing of library and information services will evolve as a new discipline in library and information science education, the topic itself in the Indian LIS curriculum is grossly inadequate as has been reflected in the present study.

However, only a broad-based study that examines the LIS curricula of all the universities offering LIS courses will give a complete picture of the status of the topic of marketing in the LIS curriculum. Further, it may be worthwhile to have a brainstorming meet of LIS practitioners and teachers to discuss and debate on the topic of marketing in the LIS curriculum which could include aspects such as the need for the topic, its scope, extent of coverage, etc.

REFERENCES

1. Du (Yuanqing). Marketing of libraries and information centres in China: A case study. In Proceedings of the 63 IFLA General Conference. August 31 to September 5, 1997. http://www.ifla.org/IV/ifla63/63yuad.htm
2. Mahesh (G). Barriers to marketing of information products and services in libraries. *DESIDOC Bulletin of Information Technology*. 22(3). 2002: 35-38
3. Sarkar (B N). NISSAT manpower development program 1986-2000. *Information Today and Tomorrow*. 2001. http://itt.nissat.tripod.com/itt0102/mpd0102.htm
4. Mangla (P B). Master's course in library and information science. *In*, Mangla (P B), Ed. Library and information science education in India (Papers and Recommendations of an All-India Seminar held at the Department of Library Science, University of Delhi during 3-8 October, 1977). Delhi: Macmillan India Limited, 1981: 57-76.
5. Wasserman (P) and Ford (GT). Marketing and marketing research: What the library manager should Learn? *Journal of Library Administration*. 1 (1). 1980: 20.
6. Schenk (R). "The dread and terror" curriculum of 1910. *Journal of Education for Librarianship*. 1. 1960 :75-80.
7. Harmon (G). The Importance of marketing in the library and information science curriculum. *The Acquisition Librarian*. 14(28). 2002: 61-79.

8. Savard (R). Guidelines for the teaching of marketing in the training of librarians, documentalists and archivists. Paris: Unesco. 1988.
9. Thiagarajan (R). Marketing of information services by non-profit organisations. *NISSAT Newsletter*. April-June 1982: 8-17
10. Gopinath (M A). Curriculum and marketing of information services. *In* Papers of the13th National Seminar of IASLIC on Marketing of Library and Information Services in India. Calcutta: IASLIC. 1988: 125-129.
11. Gopalkrishnan (N K). Curriculum for marketing management for information professionals. *Library Sc.* 27. 1990: 129-135
12. Gupta (D K). Marketing of library and information services: Building a new discipline in LIS Education in Asia. *Malaysian Journal of Library and Information Science*. 8(2). December 2003: 95-108
13. University Grants Commission. UGC Model Curriculum: Library and Information Science, New Delhi: University Grants Commission. 2001.
14. Kanjilal (U). National information infrastructure: Education and training needs of information professionals in India. In Proceedings of the 63rd IFLA General Conference, August 31- September 5, 1997 [Available at http://www.ifla.org/IV/ifla63/63kanu.htm]
15. University of Bangalore, syllabi for MLISc
16. Delhi University. Department of Library and Information Science. Syllabi (Effective from Academic Session 2004-05), 2004.
17. NISCAIR. Associateship in Information Science 2004-2006. Prospectus and Syllabus

EDUCATION AND RESEARCH FOR LIBRARY MARKETING IN ESTONIA

Aira Lepik

Abstract *This article aims to provide an overview of application of the marketing principles to Estonian librarianship. This article describes the library network in Estonia with an overview of marketing principles applied to: training of the trainers', academic higher and continuing professional education of the information specialists. Also the articles on the topic of marketing in Estonian professional literature are analyzed, and an overview of relevant research is given. Sets future trends in LIS marketing in Estonia.*

INTRODUCTION

The concept of marketing has been analyzed in librarianship professional literature since 1970-s. The principles of marketing were accepted, and analytical relevant overview can be found by using the annotated bibliographies that contain secondary information since 1970 until 2000 [1, 2, 3, 4].

Analyzing the publications in 2000 concerning library marketing in professional literature M. Cox identified the following trends:

- increasing integration of the marketing and planning processes, emphasis or the need for marketing surveys, increasing usage of the pro-active management methods in librarianship;
- the continuous thorough analysis of the main concepts of marketing: the basis of marketing, the analysis of marketing and public relations, advertising; common and different in sale communication;
- increasing adjustment and implementation of the business world marketing methods in library marketing processes;
- Analysis of usage of new marketing methods and means in the development of library marketing strategies[3].

In this article the implementation of marketing themes in Estonian librarianship is analyzed, focusing on the training of information and library specialists and on the relevant articles and research.

LIBRARY NETWORK IN ESTONIA: A LOGICALLY GROUNDED COOPERATION

According to T. Valm, the key word that describes the network of the libraries in Estonia in 1990-s is changed. In order to evaluate the situation of the past ten years in the Estonian libraries T. Valm discerns the following trends:

- from an ideologically indoctrinated library system towards a democratic one;
- from close, inward oriented libraries towards the open, user-friendly information, recreation, education and cultural centres;
- from the safe state-founded library functioning towards the proactive, innovative and creative library paradigm;
- from traditional library education to the modern curriculum of library and information management;
- from deeply centralized decision-making to decentralized responsibilities for each library profile and performance[5].

A legal framework for the libraries is parallel to the general practice of library legislation in them. The Public Libraries Act (passed 1992, amended 1998) regulates the activities and functions of public libraries. The National Library activity is regulated by the National Library of Estonia Act (passed 1990, amended on 2002) and the research libraries follow the University Legislation and Organization of Research and Development Act (passed 1997, amended on 2001). The Estonian libraries network is coordinated by the Ministry of Culture and Ministry of Education and Research [6].

Today the network of Estonian libraries links 5 main levels: research libraries (National Library, universal libraries, university libraries, special research libraries); libraries of other higher institutions (private universities libraries, libraries in the state non-university level higher educational institutions, library in the private non-university level higher educational institutions); special libraries (government

Table-1: Estonian libraries in 2003*

	Number of libraries	Library-use			Documents in collection		Librar-ians
		Users	Visits	Loans	In total at the end of the year	Proportion of books	
Research and special libr.	80	170,142	1,795,275	2,248,319	60,168,550	17.0	1,023
Public libr.	573	449,354	6,779,909	12,963,104	11,236,515	98.0	1,350
School libr.	523	200,211	3,144,791	3,153,941	5,522,933**	97.8	658
LIBRARIES in TOTAL	1,176	819,707	11,719,975	18,365,364	76,927,998	34.6	3,031

* Research, special and public libraries data on 1st January 2004, school libraries data on 1st September 2003

** The number of items in main collections at the end of the school year 2002/2003

Source: *Research and Development Centre of National Library of Estonia [7]. Undoubtedly the library network will continue changing in future caused by economic changes and obvious need to improve library services.*

libraries, health service/medical libraries, libraries in the professional or learning institutions and associations, industrial or commercial libraries, libraries in the cultural institutions, other special libraries); public libraries (central libraries, municipal libraries, children libraries, community libraries, rural libraries, other public libraries); school libraries (elementary school libraries, basic school libraries, secondary school libraries, vocational school libraries, night school libraries and hobby-school libraries). The overview of some of Estonian libraries has been shown in Table-1.

TRAINING OF TRAINERS: HOW IT ALL BEGAN ?

The need to teach library marketing is critical due to the change of the library's position within the market, and knowledge and skills necessary for competing with other information organizations. At the end of 1980-s the guidelines for UNESCO were compiled by Canadian researcher R. Savard for teaching of marketing to the librarians, documentalists and archive workers [8]. The translation in Russian[9] reached Estonia in 1992 and had impact on implementing marketing in information science curricula. These guidelines contained the recommendations for the course structure, volume, content, evaluation methods and qualification of the lecturers.

The teaching of library marketing in Estonia was also impacted by the guidelines of M. Tees published for teaching of library management in 1993 [10]. At the beginning of 1990s by the initiative and with financial support of Nordic Council for Scientific Information/NORINFO the projects for trainers were started. During the project in April 1994 the training course "Library marketing and public relations" for the lecturers involved in library and information science education took place in Tallinn. The course was taught by J. Thorhauge from Royal School of Library and Information Sciences Copenhagen, Denmark, who emphasized the connections of library marketing with management and total quality management and recommended use of the case study method in teaching [11]. The seminar inspired the author of this article to present a conference paper same year, the emphasising the need for marketing surveys in analysis and evaluation of library activities [12].

Since the academic year 1993/1994 the themes on marketing have been included in the curricula of the Department of Information Studies in Tallinn Pedagogical University. The subject "Marketing in library work" has been taught by E. Rannap and A. Lepik. During the first years of teaching , the lecturers introduced little current professional literature for developing the subject. Meanwhile the students were showing increased interest to the subject.

In September 1994 in Tartu the seminar "Library public relations" was organized with the help of the colleagues from Finnish Library Association for the librarians. At the seminar library communication strategies were discussed with interested and target groups as well as the public relations [13].

In the mid 90s the interest in marketing increased by specialists in research libraries. In summer 1996 three workers of the National Library of Estonia and the author of this article participated at the international seminar "Marketing and library services: a new marriage" organized by the British Council in Cardiff (July 14-26, 1996, British Council Seminar 9647). The seminar provided a framework for understanding the key issues of services marketing – beginning with an overview of marketing and assessment of its relevance to the management of library and information services [14].

In 1995 the Centre for Information Management in the Department of Information Studies of Tallinn Pedagogical University established a 2-day training course, "Library marketing: Why? How? For who?". It was popular, especially in 1995-2000, when approximately 70 librarians from the university, National library, school and public libraries participated at the courses held in Tallinn in Tartu.

Thus the mid nineties were characterized by increasing interest in library marketing. This interest was fulfilled at training seminars and marketing was added to the information science curricula in Tallinn Pedagogical University.

LIBRARY MARKETING COURSES AVAILABLE IN ESTONIA

Among the institutions that prepare information professionals in Estonia, library marketing is currently being taught both in the curricula of Department of Information Science in Tallinn Pedagogical University and the curricula of Department of Librarianship and Information Studies in Viljandi Culture Academy. In Tallinn since academic year 1993/1994 there is a major subject "Marketing in library and information work" (2 credits, since 2003/2004 – 3 credits) and in Viljandi since academic year 1996/1997 "Library marketing" (1 credit) are offered. Since 2003/2004 at the master's level curricula Information management is also a major subject "The marketing of information services" is 3 credits taught in electronic environment IVA*.

Both major subjects "Marketing in library and information work" (TPU) and "Library marketing" (VCA) have a great deal in common; the main difference is in course coverage.

The teaching goal of the subject is to analyze the possible implementations and the need of marketing principles in library and information work. The students acquire the knowledge on marketing processes and experience to develop the library and information centre marketing plan.

The competencies and skills acquired are

- The ability to evaluate on what level the library services satisfy the users needs;
- The ability to design library services that meet the users demand;
- The ability to position the library in marketing environment;

- Knowledge and skills for planning and carrying on the marketing communication of the library and its services;
- Knowledge for implementation of marketing possibilities in different fields of library work;

THE CONTENT OF STUDIES

The subject content is divided in modules that comprised of sub-topics.

Module I. The basis of marketing and its implementation fields

This module consists of an overview of marketing goals, tasks, its basis, content and implementation.

1. Marketing: the concept, goal, basis, tasks. Marketing as philosophy and function of management of using marketing. The content of marketing. Marketing functions. Teaching marketing – need and multi-levelness.
2. Marketing: main concepts and terms, basis, need, fields of activity.
3. Marketing in services. Relationship marketing. Analysis of Groonrose concept. Marketing in non-profit field – the marketing of non-profitable organizations. Marketing and library marketing: the analysis of the concepts since 1970-s to the beginning of 21st century. Library marketing as a marketing of organization or service marketing.

Module II. Planning the marketing

This module is composed of how to analyze the marketing situation and how to manage market demand.

4. Steps and cycles of marketing process. The mission of the organization, its vision and goals. The market position of the organization, the defining analysis – SWOT & PEST.
5. Marketing surveys for carrying out the marketing processes. Primary and secondary surveys for gaining market information. Market information as internal and external organizational information. Prognosis of demand.
6. The market's concept and content. The ways of entering the market. Segmenting of the market. Usefulness, strategies, requirements of segmenting. Indicators of segmenting. Library and library services market.
7. Analysis of library market position: the marketing information from the library. The analysis and evaluation of library condition. The library marketing position using different analyzing techniques. Analysis of internal and external restrictions of the library.

Module III. Marketing collection in library

This module consists of an overview on marketing mix and designing of library offer.

8. Marketing mix or marketing collection "4P law and its development". 4 Cs law. Marketing environment (micro and macro environment). Analysis diagnosis of the environment.
9. Service as a marketing measure in library marketing. Life-circle of the service in library. Expected and actual service quality. Methodology of service quality analysis SERVQUAL, LibQUAL+.
10. Price as a marketing measure in library marketing. Price as a payment for using services. Price as a balancer of exchanging process. The main basic for the price design (expenses, demand, and competitiveness). Main factors of price designing. Using of cost-based price methods in defining the price of service in library.
11. Market place as a measure in library marketing. Library as a market place and environment. Market place - the choosing of market channels and management in library marketing.
12. Promotion as a measure in library marketing. Marketing communication: advertising, sale promotion, public relations, direct marketing, event marketing. Confidence and reputation in the library marketing process. Characteristics and motivation. Library company style and main elements.

The field of the marketing activity in any library is original but it is important in the training process to find a generalizable level where the knowledge from the learning process can be analyzed and adjusted to different types of libraries, needs and possibilities. The designing of the subject was supported by several courses in the curricula of European and American library schools. The concepts of J. Ellison and E. Daniel (USA) and S. Webber (UK) influenced this author's main areas of emphasis, previously [15, 16, 17].

The goal of the subject "Marketing of information services" (taught in TPU, 3 credits) is to analyze the adjustment possibilities of marketing theory in the marketing of information services being focused on relationship marketing and analyzing marketing strategy implementation in creating and assuring of competitive advantages.

There are different topics in the subject content that are divided in three modules:

Module I. Service and information service as a marketing measure

- The service concept and systematic;
- The impact of the service specifics on marketing activity.
- Services complex and principles of its design.

Module II. Marketing of information services as relationship marketing

- Formation of relationship marketing.
- The main processes of relationship marketing.
- Marketing of information services as implementation of relationship marketing.

Module III. Marketing strategies of information services

- Analysis of information services market position.
- Marketing strategy and basics for its choice.
- Strategies in Porter's concept (strategies of expenses advantages, strategy of differentiation and focusing).
- Marketing strategies in achieving the goals of marketing.

As far as the subject has been taught for the first time from academic year 2004/2005 and the conclusions has not been made, it is early to analyze the subject efficiency yet.

MARKETING AS A SUBJECT OF RESEARCH: CONCEPTS AND ARTICLES

The different aspects of marketing in the first half of 1990s found their implementation in different areas of library work and academic and continuing education as well as they were reflected in Estonian professional literature.

Since 1994 the marketing implementation possibilities have been regularly reflected in Estonian professional journal "Raamatukogu" (Library) where 17 articles of six authors on library marketing were published during 10 years. Analyzing thematically and contextually it is possible to differentiate the following trends:

- From casual representing at the seminars [11, 13, 18] to the articles based on research [19, 20];
- From the articles on analyzing marketing aspects e.g. public relation or price of library service as a marketing measure [21, 22, 23, 24, 25] to the complex problem analysis [26, 27, 28];
- The opening of rubrics annually in different fields of marketing. In 1999 – the rubric "Public relations" [21, 22, 23, 24, 29, 30], since 2001 - the rubric "Library success at the market" [15, 19, 20, 26, 27];

Estonian articles that analyze the different aspects of library marketing could be connected with characteristics of the different type of libraries, e.g. E. Koitmaa focused on the problematic of the public libraries. [19, 20], U. Tõnnov, I. Smuškina and T. Matsulevitš analyzed the specifics of the university library [31, 32], A. Lepik analyzed the meaning and importance of marketing in contemporary librarianship [33, 34] and in the context of library impact and value [35].

Connections of marketing with library and information activity have also been the interest of student research. In 1998 K. Mälton in her bachelor thesis analyzed the possibilities of implementation of public relation principles in different type of libraries [36], Mets gave the overview in internal communication in Estonian National Library [37], K. Eensalu found out the preconditions and possibilities of implementation of marketing principles in Estonian Business School Library [38], and H. Ruubel analyzed the role of information specialist in marketing process [39].

Connected with the marketing thematic in 2003, there was the first master thesis defended on marketing theme where E. Koitmaa found out and analyzed the implementation of marketing principles in the public libraries of Estonian rural areas [40].

Finally the articles are identified, where analysis of Estonian librarianship was presented to international audience. The papers of this article's author are mentioned, which were published in recent years and presented at the conferences in Europe [33, 34], North America [16] and Asia [41].

CONCLUSION

Marketing is not a new subject in librarianship yet at the same time it is not assumed to be skilfully used. Marketing is rather the method for implementing to the library mission and planning future techniques. The marketing activities are connected to distributive concepts. This article proposes basics of marketing can be applied to librarianship without changing the principles of both.

Marketing know-how in librarianship is critical for researchers as well as for the practitioners acting in the field in Estonia and all other countries which are seriously concerned with providing customer oriented library services.

REFERENCES

1. Norman (G). Marketing library and information services: An annotated guide to the literature. *Reference Services Review*. 10 (2). 1982: 69-80.
2. Norman (G). Marketing library and information services: An annotated guide to recent trends and developments. *Reference Services Review*. 17 (1). 1989: 43-64.
3. Cox (M). Library marketing research trends – a survey: 1988-1999. URL http://www.clmc.org/Research/ (20.12.2000).
4. Hamilton-Pennell (Ch). Bibliography of library marketing articles: 1999-2002. URL http://www.clmc.org/Research/ (08.01.2003).
5. Valm (T). Estonian library science in the past decade. *Nordinfo-Nytt*. 2. 2000: 19-34. URL http://www.nordinfo.helsinki.fi/publications/nordnytt/nnytt2_00/valm.htm (20.10.2004)
6. Valm (T). Raamatukogud silmitsi muutustega /Libraries facing changes. *In:* Nuut(K A), Ed. Raamatukogud ja raamatukogundus taasiseseisvunud Eestis 1991-2001. Tallinn: Eesti Rahvusraamatukogu. 2002: 9-20.
7. Library statistics in Estonia 2003. URL http://www.nlib.ee/inglise/lib/libstat.html (14.10.2004)
8. Savard (R). Guidelines for the teaching of marketing in the training of librarians, documentalists and archivists. Paris: UNESCO. 1988.
9. Savard (R). Guidelines for the teaching of marketing in the training of librarians, documentalists and archivists. (Russian Translation). 1992.

10. Tees (M). Teaching management to information professionals: Guidelines for instructors. *IFLA Journal*. 19 (3). 1993: 292-321.
11. Lepik (A). Koolitus seminar "Library marketing and public relations" / Training seminar Library marketing and public relations/. Raamatukogu. 3. 1994: 17
12. Lepik (A). Marketingiuuringud raamatukogus: vajadus ja võimalused / Marketing research in library: need and possibility/. *In*: Raamatukogu osast teaduslikus kommunikatsioonis. Konverentsi ettekannete kokkuvõtted, 5. -6. detsember 1994. Tartu: Tartu Ülikooli Raamatukogu, 1994: 13-14.
13. Riet (E). Seminar "Raamatukogu suhted avalikkusega"/Seminar "Library public relations"/. *Raamatukogu*. 5. 1994: 15.
14. Lepik (A). Marketing ja raamatukoguteenused: uued seosed ja võimalused /Marketing and library services: possibility for new relationships/. *Raamatukogu*. 5 1996: 13-14.
15. Lepik (A). Turunduse oskusteabest raamatukogunduses / *About Marketing Know-how in Librarianship/. Raamatukogu*.1. 2001: 27-28.
16. Lepik (A). Education for marketing management: profitable opportunities for information professionals in Estonia. *In,* Savard (R), Ed. Education and research for marketing and quality management in libraries. (IFLA publications; 99). Satellite Meeting, Quebec, August 14-16 2001. München: Saur. 2002: 134-142.
17. Lepik (A). Raamatukogumarketing: võimalus nõudluse ja pakkumise dialoogiks /Library marketing: a change for a dialogue between the demand and offer/. *In:* Acta Universitatis Scientarum Socialium et Artis Educandi Tallinnensis, Humanoria A 14. Tallinn: Tallinna Pedagoogikaülikool. 1998: 37-51.
18. Tõnnov (U). Avalikussuhted – mis need on ja mida neilt oodatakse /Public relations – what they are and what we are expecting from them?/ *Raamatukogu*. 6. 1999: 38-39.
19. Koitmaa (E). Suhtekorraldus rahvaraamatukogus /Public relations of public libraries/. *Raamatukogu.* 1. 2003: 17-18.
20. Koitmaa (E). Suhtekorraldusega tegeldakse sihipäratult /About public relations survey/. *Raamatukogu*. 4. 2004: 12-14.
21. Soone (T). Suhtekorraldus: jah või ei? /Public relations: yes or not?. *Raamatukogu*. 1. 1999: 33-34.
22. Soone (T). Enne Nuustakule, siis Pariisi /Before to Nuustaku, then to Paris/ *Raamatukogu*. 2. 1999: 32-33.
23. Soone (T). Suhted ajakirjandusega /Public Relations with Media/ *Raamatukogu*. 3. 1999: 36-37.
24. Soone (T). Kui meist huvitub ajakirjanik /If journalist is interested in us/ *Raamatukogu*. 4. 1999: 21-22.
25. Lepik (A). Raamatukoguteenuse hind turundusmeetmena /Price of library service as marketing measure/. *Raamatukogu*. 3. 1997: 20-22.

26. Lepik (A). Partnerlus raamatukogu turunduses /Partnership in Library Marketing/. *Raamatukogu*. 4. 2001: 28-30.
27. Lepik (A). Turundus ja kvaliteet /Marketing and Quality/. *Raamatukogu*.6. 2001: 25-27.
28. Tõnisson (K). Milleks meile marketing? /Why marketing in library?/ *Raamatukogu*. 3. 2002: 13-15.
29. Soone (T). Kriisijuhtimine /Crisis management/. *Raamatukogu*. 5. 1999: 35.
30. Soone (T). Turundussuhtlus /Marketing relations/. *Raamatukogu*. 6. 1999: 30-31.
31. Tõnnov (U). Avalikkussuhetest ja eriti ühest sihtgrupist – kasutajast /On public relations and one target group – library user/ *In:* Tartu Ülikooli Raamatukogu aastaraamat: 1999. Tartu: Tartu Ülikooli Raamatukogu. 2000: 155-162.
32. Smuškina (I). Matsulevitš (T). Vastukaja raamatukogu avalikkussuhetele / Responses to a user survey concerning public relations of the library/. *In:* Tartu Ülikooli Raamatukogu aastaraamat: 1999. Tartu: Tartu Ülikooli Raamatukogu. 2000: 163-167.
33. Lepik (A). Sharing success: marketing of reseach library services. *In:* Library as information gateway to the new millennium: Proceedings of the 6th Congress of Baltic Librarians. October 5-6, 2000, Vilnius, Lithuania. Vilnius: Lithuanian Librarians' Association. 2000: 256-259
34. Lepik (A). The Meaning of marketing for information specialists. In: Huma@n beings and information specialists. Proceedings of the 10th international BOBCATSSS Symposium on library and information sector. January 28-30, 2002. Ljubliana: University of Ljubliana. 2002: 124-132.
35. Lepik (A). Infoteenuse turuedukus raamatukogu väärtuse ja mõju kontekstis /Marketing of Information Services in Context of Value and Impact of a Library/. *In:* Usaldus. Vastutus. Sidusus. Eesti sotsiaalteaduste 3. aastakonverents, 22.-23. november 2002. Koost. Ü. Kaevats. Tallinn: Tallinna Tehnikaülikool. 2002: 117-122.
36. Mälton (K). Suhtekorralduse kasutamisvõimalustest raamatukogus: bakalaureusetöö /Possibilities taking advantage of public relations in libraries: bachelor thesis/. Tallinn: Tallinna Pedagoogikaülikool, 1998.
37. Mets (Õ). Sisekommunikatsioon Eesti Rahvusraamatukogus: bakalauseusetöö /Internal communication in Estonian National Library/ Tallinn: Tallinna Pedagoogikaülikool. 2001.
38. Eensalu (K). Turunduspõhimõtete rakendamine Estonian Business Schooli´i raamatukogus /Application of marketing principles in Estonian Business School Library: bachelor thesis/. Tallinn: Tallinna Pedagoogikaülikool. 2002.
39. Ruubel (H). Infoprofessionaali roll turundusprotsessis: bakalaureusetöö / Role of information professional in the process of marketing: bachelor thesis/ . Tallinn: Tallinna Pedagoogikaülikool. 2004.

40. Koitmaa (E). Suhtekorraldus Eesti rahvaraamatukogudes: magistritöö/Public relations in Estonian public libraries: master thesis/. Tallinn: Tallinna Pedagoogikaülikool. 2003.

41. Lepik (A). Marketing Plans for Libraries. *In,* Gupta (DK) and Jambhekar (A), Eds. An Integrated Approach to Services Marketing: A Book of Readings on Marketing of Library and Information Services. Mumbai: Allied Publishers Ltd. 2003: 151-160.

CONTINUING PROFESSIONAL DEVELOPMENT PROGRAMMES (CPDP) FOR LIS PROFESSIONALS IN MARKETING AREA : AN INDIAN EXPERIENCE

Roshan Lal Raina

Abstract *In keeping with the vision of its parent institute, and in line with its mission, the library at the Indian Institute of Management, Lucknow (IIML) has been conducting innovative continuing professional development programs for professionals engaged in the library and information sector, for the last ten years. More than thirty such programs, on areas like: (i) Quality Management, (ii) Marketing, (iii) Information Technology Applications, (iv) Human Relations, and (v) Communication, benefiting over five hundred top and senior level LIS professionals, have already been conducted. Giving a brief about the need of launching such programs from the library of a national level management school, the paper provides an overview of the programs conducted in the area of 'Marketing'. The overview includes a brief about the programme objectives, contents, schedule, delivery, participant profile and feedback.*

THE INSTITUTE

The Indian Institute of Management, Lucknow (IIML) is one of the six national level management institutes set up by the Government of India. The Institute's mission is 'to help improve the management of the corporate and the non-corporate sectors and also the public systems, through pursuit of excellence in management education, research, consultancy and training' [1].

OBJECTIVES

In order to respond effectively to the societal needs, the Institute aims at:

- Influencing management practices of the corporate enterprises through its postgraduate teaching programme for the young, prospective managers, training of corporate executives, consultancy and research. The research programmes are oriented towards developing management systems that are most suitable in the Indian context.

- Strengthening the management systems in the under-managed non-corporate organisations including the non-profit organisations and the public systems and exploring the possibilities of applying knowledge from the corporate sector in order to improve management practices in the non-corporate sectors.
- Helping enhance the managerial effectiveness of the educational and innovative systems with particular emphasis on the management of technology and devising mechanisms to facilitate application of research findings to solve ground level problems in business and society.

THE LIBRARY

In keeping with the vision and mission of the Institute, the library has been established "to facilitate knowledge generation and application through its effective dissemination" [2]. The library, named as Gyanodaya, therefore, acts as the main learning resource centre of the Institute and provides services and facilities to meet the requirements of the Institute's teaching, training, research and consultancy programmes.

In line with its mission, Gyanodaya operates with the following objectives:

- To support the learning process of its students through provision of knowledge/information.
- To meet knowledge/information needs of the faculty, to support their teaching activities.
- To meet knowledge/information needs of the faculty and research personnel to support their research activities.

To respond effectively, where possible, to the knowledge/information needs of the Institute's client systems. Gyanodaya stocks a rich collection of over 60,000 select learning resource materials in the discipline of management and related areas, in a variety of formats and operates from a 30,000 sq. ft. spacious, centrally located, air-conditioned building, built on most modern lines. Equipped with ergonomically designed furniture & fittings, managed by a highly dedicated team of professionals, the 24 hour library caters to the information needs of its highly demanding clientele, by offering a wide range of Information Technology (IT) based (and value added) services and products.

The library provides routine services like computer controlled circulation, current contents of periodical literature and current additions of books/report as a part of current awareness services, inter-library loan, bibliographic services, newspaper clippings, union list of periodicals, union catalogue of publications, audio-visual services, on-line access to 893 journals, CD-ROM databases, etc.

Besides catering to the diverse information needs of all its primary stakeholders,Gyanodaya is offering its services, of course under specified terms and conditions, to the clientele in the external environment, as well.

It is all the above aspects, taken together, that prompted the library to propose to its management about the conduct of CPDPs for LIS professionals.

WHY DID IIML GO FOR CONDUCTING CPDP FOR LIS PROFESSIONALS

The mandate of IIML being what has been stated in the beginning of this paper, thinking that emerged at the Institute was that in the present context of knowledge-based economy, institutions and organizations – be they in the corporate world, the academic world, the bureaucratic arena, the governmental as well as non-governmental context, all alike – will excel in achieving their desired goals and objectives only if they are backed up by adequate information support. For that to happen it was felt that the instruments – the libraries and information centres (LICs) – need to be managed well. It is in line with this scenario as well as to equip these LICs with professionally competent librarians and information managers (LIMs) that IIML took upon itself the task of organizing CPDPs for LIS professionals.

The second important reason being that Gyanodaya having achieved the status of a national level learning resource center in the field of management and related areas (as described in the preceding paragraphs), it was time for the team at Gyanodaya to share its rich experience with fellow professionals with a view to help them built much better information support centers and systems for their respective organizations.

Justifying specifically the conduct of CPDPs in the area of 'marketing', it will be apt to mention that the team and its management at Gyanodaya had observed that the resources, facilities, and services developed at Gyanodaya, over a period of time, were not being optimally utilized as long as their use was restricted to its primary members. At the same time it was also felt that there was acute need of access to such learning resources, facilities, and services from a good number of users in the external environment. To address both these concerns, it was decided to experiment with bringing in 'marketing' orientation at Gyanodaya itself. The experiment was successful in more ways than one. Not only did it help in enhancing the usage of Gyanodaya but it also helped in satisfying the long felt need of external users. Added to both these advantages was the by product – some amount of revenue generation. However, all this did not happen over night. Rich experiences and learnings were there and it was felt that the same need to be shared among all those engaged in the information sector.

CPDP ON MARKETING

With above in mind, five CPDPs have already been conducted by IIML and the fifth one scheduled during December 20-22, 2004.

Background, objectives, and contents of the programme as described in the announcement brochure and a brief about the programme schedule, programme delivery, participant profile and feedback is provided below:

BACKGROUND

Library and Information Centres (LICs) are now able to generate, by virtue of their using advanced computers and softwares, various kinds of information products and services in addition to their routine activities and services. However, it is a little unfortunate that these remain largely underutilized, or even, in cases, wholly unutilized. The reasons cited are several and include the following [3]:

i. Efforts in identifying and reaching out the target audience are inadequate.
ii. Information products and services are 'generator' driven rather than 'user' driven and in that there remains a "linkage gap" between the generators and users of such products and services; and
iii. Level and information awareness or consciousness is still low among the users and there is a need to raise it further.

PROGRAMME OBJECTIVES

Given the above scenario, efforts are being undertaken, through the present programme, to enrich the information environment of the potential clientele. An attempt is being made to equip the participants with adequate know how so that they are able to:

i. Identify and understand their potential users (internal as well as-external) in relation to their resources and facilities;
ii. Understand the information needs of such users more accurately and precisely;
iii Generate information products and services that are tailored to meet the exact needs of such users; and
iv. Remain cost-effective in the process of generating information products and services.

BROAD CONTENTS

The programme contents, which kept on getting modified as well as updated from one programme to another, was largely designed around the following themes:

a. Understanding the marketing process;
b. Marketing in the library and information context;
c. 4 Ps (Product, Price, Promotion and Distribution) of marketing in the context of information products and services; and
d Generating information products & services as sustainable sources of revenue generation.
e. Customer Relationship Marketing (CRM) Initiatives.

EXPERIENCE BASED CHANGE IN THE PROGRAMME CONTENT

The contents for the first programme were observed to be largely theory based with very little illustrations from the real life situations. Trying to make up for this deficiency in the subsequent programmes by introducing case method of teaching and learning, useful insight came through the 'feedback' that cases discussed be better from the library and information world. Having addressed all these concerns, one more useful insight came through the 'feedback' of the previous programme that the cases/case lets discussed be relevant to the Indian situation/ context and that is where we are trying to be up-to in our next programme.

PROGRAMME SCHEDULE

Final schedule for the three-day programme, got evolved and fine-tuned on the basis of experience gained (and feedback provided by the participants as well as the resource faculty) was worked out in such a manner that Day One was devoted to providing conceptual clarity on 'marketing' fundamentals, especially as related to 'service marketing' with special reference to their application in library and information environment. Attempt, in Day One, was also made to orient the participants to 'case' method of learning. Day Two would, through case-study based approach, attempt at bringing out clarity on the application of marketing mix (MM) elements in the context of library and information products and services and Day Three would continue with MM elements. The participants would then be, based on the SWOT analysis of their respective set-ups, advised to work out an action plan for their respective set-ups. The Action Plan would be firmed up under the guidance of the resource faculty towards the end of the Day Three and that would be the key take from the programme..

Outline of a typical programme schedule is shown below:

DAY	SESSION-I	SESSION-II	SESSION-III	SESSION-IV	SESSION-V	SESSION-VI
One	10.00–11.00 About the Programme	11.00–12.00 Marketing :A Conceptual Framework	12.00–13.00 Service Marketing Fundamentals	14.00–15.30 Marketing in LIC Context	16.00–17.30 Case Method of Teaching	18.00–19.30 Experience Sharing
Two	10.00–11.30 Marketing Concepts Case: VC	11.30–13.00 Marketing Mix (MM) Product Offering Segmentation Case: INDMARK (A)		14.00–15.30 MM: Processes Physical EvidenceCase: INPRS	16.00–17.30 Experience Sharing	18.00–19.30 MM: Pricing Cases: INDMARK (M) The Information Bank
Three	10.00–11.30 MM Promotion & Distribution Case: ADC	11.30–13.00 MM New Product Development Case: HHP (C)		14.00–15.30 MM: Marketing Strategy Case: The News Paper	16.00–17.30 Action Plan (AP)	18.00-19.30 Firming up of Action Plan, Feedback Valediction

PROGRAMME DELIVERY

All the technical sessions were handled by a faculty mix of experienced academics as well as practitioners in the field of 'service marketing' and library and information marketing. As stated under the 'schedule' above, case study based approach was followed all through with examples and illustrations from the information world, both in Indian as well as foreign environment. Experience sharing sessions among the participants proved to be an enriching component of the programme as their active participation in the sessions, moderated by the Programme Director, provided very useful insights into their success as well as failure stories on the subject.

PARTICIPANT PROFILE

The five programmes saw participation of more than one hundred top and middle level qualified professionals, engaged typically in reference and information services and other user services in their respective set-ups. Of course, some had also been involved in designing, developing and delivering value added information products and services. It is worthwhile to mention here that the then INSDOC, DESIDOC, the British Council had been regularly sending sent their nominees to the programmes. Needless to mention, all these great institutions have been the only institutions of their kind (in the country) that have been involved with the activity of marketing of their information activities, products and services. Yes, the participants to these programmes came from other academic institutions, government departments, research labs, industrial out-fits, but they were predominantly from scientific/industrial research and training institutions.

PROGRAMME FEEDBACK

Going by the participants' feedback, obtained from them with the help of a structured questionnaire designed for the purpose, as well as through other formal (participants' reactions in the valedictory sessions) and informal modes (grape-vines, etc), the programmes were reported to have been very well received by them. Formal 'feedback' instrument administered to the participants at the end of the programme, was very useful in soliciting their pointed 'feedback' on a 5-point scale on areas like: (i) achievement of the course objectives, as mentioned in the announcement brochure/s; (ii) relevance and usefulness of the course to the participant's area of work; (iii) programme duration; (iv) programme contents; (v) applicability of concepts discussed; (vi) conduct of the programme; (vii) programme design in terms of extent of coverage, conceptual clarity, orientation to practical problems, methodology; (viii) faculty mix; (ix) course material/lecture notes; (x) interaction with fellow participants; (xi) extent of useful knowledge acquired from the course; (xii) any session found particularly useful or could have been dropped; (xiii) training methodology in the context of presentations by the resource faculty, case preparation/discussion, group interaction; (xiv) resource faculty assessment; (xv) hospitality in terms of boarding, lodging, transportation; (xvi) overall assessment of the course; and (xvii) general comments and suggestions. Specifics that came from the feedback include: (i) cases used by library and information specific; (ii) cases be situation specific in the Indian context; and (iii) examples used to illustrate 'marketing concepts and strategies' be more oriented towards library and information world. As stated earlier, all these useful inputs and many more such were duly taken note of and needful done as appropriate in the subsequent programmes. Some other positive comments were "very useful programme in the present context"; "right step in right direction at right time"; "case orientation towards librarianship" very useful; and so on.

CONCLUSION

It is not to submit here that the exercise initiated by IIML has been the only effort of its kind from India to bring in marketing orientation in the context of Indian libraries, but it, certainly, has played a catalyst role in changing the mind set of not only the professionals engaged in this sector but also of all those who are responsible for building such facilities in the country. Today all concerned seem to be talking in terms of 'cost-benefit' as well as 'cost-effectiveness' as against 'free service' when it comes to the question of developing and maintaining such systems and their services.

REFERENCES

1. In quest for excellence. IIM Lucknow. 2004:1.
2. Library guide. IIM Lucknow. 2000:1.
3. Raina (R). Marketing of library and information products and services. *University News*. 33 (33). 1995: 8-9, 12.

RESEARCH FOR DESIGN AND TESTING OF INFORMATION PRODUCT

Abhinandan K. Jain
T.P. Rama Rao
(Late) Ashok Jambhekar

Abstract *Information Bulletin on Management (IBM), a value added product, is being brought out every quarter by National Information Centre for Management (NICMAN) located at Indian Institute of Management, Ahmedabad (IIMA). IBM has had a subscription base of above one hundred over the last three years and has achieved cash break even. Required research was carried out to conceive the concept, design and test the IBM, and design and test a marketing plan for the launch of IBM. This paper is a brief description of the research. It also provides suggestions for improving research efforts to conceive, design, and introduce new value added products from libraries and information centers.*

CONCEIVING IBM

The major step in the process of conceiving IBM was the project "Market research on the Utilization of Management Information in India" conducted at IIMA with the support of International Development and Research, Canada (IDRC). The objectives of the project included, among others, "identify useful and acceptable new products/services" that could be introduced in the country for the benefit of managers and academicians from the libraries of leading management schools in India. The process included

i) a workshop,
ii) an exploratory research,
iii) a descriptive research, and
iv) decisions on the ideas for designing product/ service concepts.

Besides describing the above steps, this section also provides suggestions for conducting research to generate ideas about value added information products and services.

WORKSHOP

As a part of assessing the market opportunity for information products and services that could be offered by libraries of leading management institutes in

India, a workshop was held at IIM Ahmedabad. The workshop participants included the librarians of the four IIMs (at Ahmedabad, Bangalore, and Calcutta), of All India Management Association (AIMA), and library professionals from sectoral management organizations and local libraries (at Ahmedabad). The workshop was assisted by marketing and information technology experts from IIMA and an observer from IDRC. With the help and guidance of marketing and information technology experts from IIMA and an observer from IDRC, the group worked out methodology for: (i) identifying the target segments (and sub-segments), (ii) identifying needs of the target segments, (iii) developing new information products and services, (iv) assessing the overall viability of introducing information products and services from libraries of leading management institutes..

EXPLORATORY RESEARCH

The purpose of exploratory research was to re-confirm the identification of sub-segments, classify the information requirements of the target segments into meaningful categories, and prepare the ground for descriptive research. Exploratory phase was conducted through in depth interviewing of respondents in each sub-segment. A total of 216 respondents in academic (73), business (80) and government (63) segments were interviewed. The instruments used in the exploratory research collected the data related to decisions and tasks performed by the respondents such as: information used, sources of information, assessments of information used, and improvements requirements of improved information. The data was analyzed to identify and classify tasks, decisions, and nature of information required by each user group. The segments and sub-segments identified through the workshop and reconfirmed through the exploratory research are presented in the table below:

S. No.	Segment	Sub-segment(s)	Description of Respondents
1.	Academic	Students Faculty	MBA and Ph.D Primarily research and teaching oriented in Indian Institutes of Management, University Departments and Sectoral Management Institutes.
2.	Business and Industry	Size and Ownership Type	Functional area and Level of management
3	Government	Government	Department and Level of management
4.	Service Sector		Level of management

Information required by the above segments was classified as:

a. Conceptual / Theoretical
b. Cases / Experimental
c. Statistical Data
d. Reports (both textual and statistical)

The exploratory research also provided further guidelines for designing the descriptive research.

DESCRIPTIVE RESEARCH

Objectives of the descriptive phase of the research project were to:

i) Prioritise the nature of information needed to perform the job by the respondent
ii) Assess the level of satisfaction with and the improvements needed in the information products and services used
iii) Assess the acceptance of some basic information products, including their format and frequency, for determining demand for information products and services
iv) Identify the products and services required to fulfill information needs
v) Assess the libraries of the leading management institutes for offering the needed information products and services.

The descriptive research was a nation wide study conducted through structured questionnaires among respondents in academic, business and industry, and service sector segments. Separate instruments were designed for segment and sub segment if needed. Each instrument was designed to assess the objectives of the research viz. need for management information, use and satisfaction level with current information products/services, desired improvements in current information products and services, and assessment of demand for specific information products. The demand assessment was made for 11 products and services (basic information products 5 Current Contents and 5 Index of Management Literature - one each for the five functional areas - General Management, Finance, Marketing, Production/Material and Systems and Personnel and Industrial Relations and one Index of Management News). Each of these products was designed by library staff under the supervision of librarian for getting the assessments from respondents. A well known method, Benefit Structure Analysis 1, for developing new products was used to identify the desired improvements in the existing management information products by the respondents in the business and industry and service sector segments.

A two stage sample plan was prepared and implemented. Stage one consisted of identification of organizations and the second stage was for selecting individuals. The final sample of respondents achieved is presented in the table below:

S.No.	Segment	Sub-segment	Sample size
1.	Business and Industry	Executives	535
		Librarians	38
		Information Officers	41
2.	Academic	Faculty members	121
		Students	281
		Librarians	23
3.	Service Sector	Executives	98

Analysis of data revealed significant and growing opportunities for basic information products and services like Current Content (CC) and Index/bibliography of Management Literature (IML) (of different functional areas) in academic, business and industry and service sector markets. The data also revealed a significant interest in value added products like management digest among managers and academics. The analysis also revealed that the libraries of the leading institutes were perceived as capable of providing the needed products and services2.

Decision on Ideas

A workshop was held to discuss the findings of the research project. The workshop also discussed and decided on the methodology to be used for testing the viability and sustainability of the identified products and service. Encouraged by the results, the workshop participants discussed and evolved the following three dimensions of information products and services to generate new product ideas/concepts:

Dimension 1: Products/Services using: any one or more of the available base materials i.e. published materials like journals and books and un-published materials like cases, dissertations, research reports, and working papers.

Dimension 2: To be offered as: current content (CC), literature index, annotated index/bibliography of management literature (IML), abstracts, executive summary and full text.

Dimension 3: Through the medium of: hard copy, floppy / cartridge, local area / wide area network through email / direct access.

Any combination of each of the three dimensions could provide a new product/service idea.

On the basis of the distinctive strengths of IIMs, in terms of resources (particularly, cases, research reports, and other materials and research output), the group prioritized the basic source materials for generating products and services:

(i) cases and (ii) Management journals both Indian and foreign. The workshop decided to design and test a value added product, Digest of management literature for executives in Business and Industry, besides testing the traditional library products like CC and IML.

The experience of IDRC and other participants had shown that good products and services from libraries were easier to design but most difficult to achieve success in the market place. This usually led to unsustainable situations and ultimately stoppage of such products and services. Therefore, the workshop participants recommended a second research project to design and test the products and design and test the Marketing programmes on the target customers. A new project "Products Design and Test Marketing of Management Information Products and Services" was undertaken at IIMA with the participation of IIMs at Ahmedabad, Bangalore, Calcutta and AIMA, Delhi for achieving the purposes and decide whether to launch the products and services3.

Suggestions for Improved Research to Generate New Concepts

- Use informal and exploratory research to identify the relevant type of customers (segments) and the nature of products required by them to perform their tasks/ solve their problems/ achieve their objectives (mission). This research gained immensely with this step in identifying both through the methods advocated.
- Conduct descriptive research using some methodology like the benefit structure analysis 1 to assess the strengths and weaknesses of existing products and services as well as obtain suggestions for new ones to help the respondents in achieving their tasks/ solve their problems/ achieve their objectives.
- Identify key dimensions along which the new requirements could be grouped and use them to generate new ideas which cover the requirements of the all types of customers. The understanding of the three dimensions (of type of resource materials, specific product contents and forms, and the mode of delivery) enabled a fuller specification of new product ideas.

DESIGNING AND TESTING IBM

The three key issues in design and testing of IBM were: defining the product concept, testing a typical entry, and designing and testing of the complete product.

Defining the Product Concept

The first step in arriving at the product concept was to anlyse available products like abstracts, annotated abstracts, and digests. The conclusions emerging out of the above step, were that the concept should:

- Help target customers to identify whether an article could be of interest to them

- Provide broad understanding of the article and what it could be used for,
- Have language and format appealing to a generalist rather than a specialist of the subject

To carry out the process, the researchers first selected an article of likely interest to both managers and researchers: "Do you want to keep your customers forever", HBR, March- April 1985, pp 103- 114. Four different types of entries (abstracts) were prepared. The primary purposes of testing were to test index terms, body, format, and layout of the text.

Testing a Typical Entry

The research method used to test was focus group discussion. The participants attending short and long duration programmes at IIMA were selected for the purpose. They represented both academic and industry market segments. A total of four focus group discussions were conducted. Two of these groups were from industry and the other two from academics. Among the academics, one of the groups was from Common Wealth countries. On the basis of these discussions, one of the four versions of the entry was selected for further research.

Preparation of Complete Product

This involved preparation of entries, design of hard copy features, and testing of the complete product. Selection of the journals to select the articles was carried out by librarian of IIMA. These were then finalized with the help of three faculty members and three senior managers for being used in the preparation of IBM on a regular basis. A rigorous methodology was followed for this purpose. Relevant articles were then selected for developing the abstracts to be included in the complete product. A total of 55 articles were selected for inclusion in the product. Abstracts were prepared by an experienced professional preparing abstracts for a leading management journal (Vikalpa, published by IIMA). The professional was trained by the researchers and prepared the abstracts under the guidance of Librarian, a co researcher of the project.

It was decided to include an author and subject index in the IBM. The other elements of the product design included selection of paper, font, size of letters, size of issue, cover page, and envelop for the issue etc.

Testing of Complete Product

The issue was tested on 75 senior managers from business/industry from all parts of the country who attended a 3-week General Management Programme at IIMA in August 1997. The testing procedure followed was as follows:

- The participants were sent a letter, an 11-item instrument, and a copy of the first issue requesting them to assess the IBM. The instrument included questions to elicit response on three price levels i.e. Rs.1,000, Rs.1,250 and Rs.1,500 per year.

- Those responding were offered a personal copy of any one of the articles abstracted in the issue free of charge.

The inferences made from analysis of data from testing of the complete IBM were:

- The accepted format of entry included references/index words, specification of audience to whom the article would be useful, and the main theses and highlights of the articles.
- The quarterly frequency was acceptable. Earlier tests indicated the size of each issue as 40 to 60 abstracts.
- The usefulness of the issue was on account of providing a good summary of the articles and thus keeping the management informed.
- IBM was found to be "very useful" (Eight out of Eighteen respondents), "very convenient to use" (12 out of 18 respondents), and "unique' (10 out of 18 respondents). These were very promising findings.
- At least 10% respondents expressed definite interest in subscribing to the product at prices ranging from Rs.1, 000 to Rs.1500 per year.
- The Product might also be acceptable to academics.

The product test clearly demonstrated the suitability of IBM for business and industry segment. A penetration level of 10% plus could definitely be realized. The test also suggested that a price of Rs.1, 500 should be set. Some improvements in coverage could increase the usefulness. Other specific products for Industry/ business sector could have significant potential. Alternatively similar topics should be included in the current product itself.

Suggestions for Improved Research to Design and Test New Products

Suggestions on the research process of product design and testing of IBM, which could be applicable to other similar decisions, are:

- Specific concepts should be chosen which are beneficial to customers, distinctive from competitors, and feasible for the library / information centre. They should also have the potential of economic viability in the long term.
- Selection of source material (journals, etc) should be made in consultation with serious users and experts in the specific area of the subject like marketing professors for designing IBM for marketing professionals.
- The design of each entry / document, which is crucial for the acceptance of the product, should be on the basis of a) requirements of representative customers and b) distinct and superior to competing Products. Therefore, subject experts who have knowledge about client requirements, like senior managers and marketing consultants for IBM Marketing, should select the articles and guide the professionals preparing the entries/ documents.
- Testing of each entry/ document could be done through a series of in-depth group and/ or personal discussions. Testing should be continued till a suitable final version was arrived at.

- Library (information) professionals should be trained for preparing the entries/ documents. Both content and language editing should also be done to make sure of consistency of contents and their adherence to the position chosen for the product.
- All elements of the product design should be thought through like brand name, frequency, price, size of document, etc.
- The complete issue so prepared should be tested with relevant target segment by placing it with them. Research should be conducted for assessing the strengths and weaknesses, liking and disliking of the target customers, and their level of overall acceptance of the product with out and with price knowledge.

DESIGNING AND IMPLEMENTING THE MARKETING PLAN FOR TESTING

This section includes design of an appropriate marketing plan for testing, implementation of the plan in a test market, and analysis of results to decide whether and how to market the product.

Design of Marketing Plan

After testing the product and its price, a marketing plan was prepared for test marketing the offer. The plan consisted of decisions on target market segments, position, product, price, promotion, and research and feedback.

Target Market Segments: While the target market segments were business/ industry and academics, IBM was likely to appeal more to business/industry.

Positioning: The position of the products was decided on the basis of key consumer perceived benefits of such products, comparative position of the products in relation to competing products, and the long run sustainability of the chosen position by the marketing organization. A sober, academic position was chosen for IBM. The position was "High Quality Information from IIMA, the Leading School of Management." Any element that contradicted this position was to be avoided.

Product

The contents of product were designed and tested as reported earlier. The brand name was selected on the basis of being academic sounding, appropriate for the product, and extensible to different functional areas/sectors if such products were to be added later in such areas/sectors. Thus the name selected, even before the product testing was done, was Information Bulletin on Management IBM.

The specific design of the product was to cue the academic (not business) emphasis, and value for money (not high price), and the sober image of IIMA. Selection of colour of envelop (white/blue printing/block printing), brand name (academic sounding), cover design to include IIMA logo and NISSAT logo, etc., in the judgment of IIMA team strongly supported the positioning statement.

Pricing: For achieving viability of operations, pricing was a major decision. Major inputs in pricing were the costs of production and marketing the product, likely market response as assessed through product testing and coverage of cost at different penetration levels of the market.

The one-year subscription for industry was fixed at Rs.1, 500 for IBM. The price was modified to adjust for individual subscriptions and for two and three year time period. For individuals and for additional year it was decided to give a 50% discount over the organizational subscription rate. At these prices, the team was confident of the break-even.

Promotion

The key choices made in promotion were target audience, media, message, and budget. The target audience for management literature was likely to be professional managers in business/industry and academics in management institutions. The product tests and discussions indicated that IBM was likely to appeal more to managers than academics. To match this audience profile, the general business media was ruled out for creating awareness because of exorbitant cost.

Advertisements in alumni magazines and journals of management institutions were to be used for creating awareness among target audience. Direct mail with brochures and sample copy (ies) of products was to be used for creating interest and inclination to buy the product. Wherever possible, presentations were made to managers in programmes run by leading management institutions to build image among and get subscription from the most relevant target audience. All these efforts were to be supplemented with advertising on IIMA website.

The budget for test marketing was arrived at by aggregating the cost of above media plan.

Implementation of Marketing Plan for Testing

Ahmedabad and Pune cities were selected as the test markets. They were medium size cities as far as the market for information products was considered. The benchmark for success was set at 10% market penetration.

The project staff designed the product, direct mailer, envelops, and advertisements. Separate staff was hired for preparing abstracts for IBM and entering the data into the database. The list of addresses maintained by IIMA was used as the primary mailing list. To supplement, independent local research agencies were employed to generate the required number of addresses.

The response to direct mail was collected through tracking enquiries and subscription orders after each issue was published and mailed. Research was also done to get feedback on product and marketing plan as well as suggestions for improvement through both mailed questionnaires and personal interviews. At least five respondents were contacted personally to seek response by mailing a questionnaire to all subscribers and an equal number of non-subscribers, (who were sent a direct mail). At Pune a professional researcher-cum-manager and at Ahmedabad the library staff and consultants did the interviews.

The planned and actual achievements of promotional activities are presented in the table below:

Product: IBM	**Markets**			
Total	Business / Industry		Academic	
Target	Planned	Achieved	Planned	Achieved
138	37	23	20	230

The shortfall in the business/industry market was primarily for lack of adequate number of addresses. The research agencies also failed to provide addresses because of the refusal of potential clients to provide their addresses. The academic segment's over achievement was because of tapping the market beyond Pune and Ahmedabad.

Some of the difficulties faced in implementing the plan included non-availability of regular staff, non-acceptance of bulk-mailing by dispatch/post office, and, of course, non-availability of adequate addresses.

ANALYSIS OF RESULTS TO DECIDE WHETHER AND HOW TO MARKET IBM

Subscriptions: Till 25 March 1998, subscriptions for IBM from different segments were as follows: Institutions (23); Industry (11); Individual (15); Total (49).

Of the 49 subscriptions to IBM, 26 were for three years, 19 for one year, and four for two years. In addition, there were enquiries for invoices to process subscription to IBM from six institutions.

Sample copies of IBM were sent to 60 business/industry organizations and 230 academic organizations. In addition, brochures of IBM were mailed to 100 business/industry organizations. The response was as follows:

		Business/Industry	**Academic**
1	Subscriptions	11	38 (+6 Invoices)
2	Sample copy sent to	60	230
3	Brochures sent to	100	-
4	Responses to brochures (1/3) %	11	NA
5	Response to sample copy (1/2) %	18	17 (20)
6	Range of response %	11-18	16-20

The response of 11 from business/industry was made up to about half. Five subscriptions were from a single organization in Ahmedabad. There were indications that large organizations may not mind subscribing to IBM. However, this needs to be still watched.

A large proportion of the subscriptions of more than one year might be on account of both a steep discount as well as the IIMA image. The discount beyond one year was 50%.

Analysis of results showed that IBM would have good response of about 15 to 20%, if promoted with a sample copy, from both industry and academics. This volume would be economically viable.

Suggestions for Improved Research to Test Marketing New Products

- Design a marketing plan consisting of target market (consumers), position, product, price, distribution, promotion, and the organisation involved in producing and marketing the product.
- Identify areas/ consumers who are representative of the average market characteristics where the plan could be tested. Plan for implementing the plan after assessing the feasibility of the implementation. It should not happen that the plan is not implementable. This happened in case of the industry segment in case of test marketing of IBM.
- Specify the targets of inputs that are in line with the ultimate marketing plan. Also, specify the benchmark for deciding to market or not market the product after the testing.
- Implement the plan and collect information to assess the results. Analyse the information to decide whether to go ahead with launching with the same plan or with an altered plan or not to go ahead.

PROGRESS TILL 2004

Normal efforts of promotion as envisaged in test marketing plan were continued till 2002. After 2002 there was no effort really to promote. However, IBM has continued to remain strong with a membership of over 100 for each of the years as can be seen from the statement below:

Statement of Nicman Publication: IBM
Period: 2000-2004

Year (Jan. - Dec.)	Individual Subscription	Institutional / Organizational Subscription	Total Membership
2000	49	74	123
2001	48	71	119
2002	36	80	116
2003	32	74	106
2004	37	70	107

SUGGESTIONS FOR FUTURE RESEARCH

- Use informal and exploratory research to identify the relevant type of customers (segments) and the nature of products required by them to perform their tasks/ solve their problems/ achieve their objectives (mission). This research gained immensely with this step in identifying both through the methods advocated.
- Conduct descriptive research using some methodology like the benefit structure analysis 1 to assess the strengths and weaknesses of existing products and services as well as obtain suggestions for new ones to help the respondents in achieving their tasks/ solve their problems/ achieve their objectives.
- Identify key dimensions along which the new requirements could be grouped and use them to generate new ideas which cover the requirements of the all types of customers. The understanding of the three dimensions (of type of resource materials, specific product contents and forms, and the mode of delivery) enabled a fuller specification of new product ideas.
- Specific concepts should be chosen which are beneficial to customers, distinctive from competitors, and feasible for the library/ information centre. They should also have the potential of economic viability in the long term.
- Selection of source material (journals, etc) should be made in consultation with serious users and experts in the specific area of the subject like marketing professors for designing IBM for marketing professionals.
- The design of each entry/ document, which is crucial for the acceptance of the product, should be on the basis of a) requirements of representative customers and b) distinct and superior to competing Products. Therefore, subject experts who have knowledge about client requirements, like senior managers and marketing consultants for IBM Marketing, should select the articles and guide the professionals preparing the entries/ documents.
- Testing of each entry/ document could be done through a series of in-depth group and/ or personal discussions. Testing should be continued till a suitable final version was arrived at.
- Library (information) professionals should be trained for preparing the entries/ documents. Both content and language editing should also be done to make sure of consistency of contents and their adherence to the position chosen for the product.
- All elements of the product design should be thought through like brand name, frequency, price, size of document, etc.
- The complete issue so prepared should be tested with relevant target segment by placing it with them. Research should be conducted for assessing the strengths and weaknesses, liking and disliking of the target customers, and their level of overall acceptance of the product with out and with price knowledge.

- Design a marketing plan consisting of target market (consumers), position, product, price, distribution, promotion, and the organisation involved in producing and marketing the product.
- Identify areas/ consumers who are representative of the average market characteristics where the plan could be tested. Plan for implementing the plan after assessing the feasibility of the implementation. It should not happen that the plan is not implementable. This happened in case of the industry segment in case of test marketing of IBM.
- Specify the targets of inputs that are in line with the ultimate marketing plan. Also, specify the benchmark for deciding to market or not market the product after the testing.
- Implement the plan and collect information to assess the results. Analyse the information to decide whether to go ahead with launching with the same plan or with an altered plan or not to go ahead.

REFERENCES

1. Myers (J H). Benefit structure analysis: A new tool for product planning. *Journal of Marketing*. October 1976: 23-32.
2. Jain (A), Rama Rao (T P) and Jambhekar (A). Marketing of management information: Research at IIMA. *In,* Jain (A), et. al, Eds. Marketing of information products and services. Ahmedabad :Indian Institute of Management. 1995.
3. Jain (A), et al. Product design and test marketing of information products and services. New Delhi: Oxford & IBH Publishing Co. 1999.

Appendix-I
Methodology for Need Assessment

The executives were asked to:

1. Indicate 'criticality' at least two of the four types of information for better performance of their job/task.
2. State whether they received the particular type of information through any source.

The types of information covered were:

a) conceptual/theoretical
b) cases/experiments etc.
c) statistical data
d) reports

The 'criticality' of information was assessed on a five point scale (see table below).

The level of need of a particular type of information was assessed by finding:

i. The percentage of respondents who consider the information as essential, very essential, and absolutely critical. This would provide a measure of total potential of the information type.

ii. The percentage of respondents who do not receive any information among those who consider the information as essential, very essential, and absolutely critical. This would provide a measure of unfulfilled potential for the information type.

Appendix-II
Method for Assessing Demand: Type of Company Basis

The intention to subscribe to Current Contents and Index of Management Literature was found to be independent of functional area of the respondent. The following method was adopted to arrive at demand estimates:

Step - 1: Derive proportion of subscribers (to total sample) for each of the three products across functional areas irrespective of company/ industry type (P1).

Step - 2: For each of the company type, the proportion of companies (P2) having specific functional areas was derived from the sample of companies which were organised function wise. This was superimposed on all companies i.e, the existence of functional areas was assessed to be the same in companies having divisional structure.

Step - 3: The multiplication of P1 and P2 for each company type was used to get a composite multiplier = (M) for each company type.

Step - 4: Multiply the number of a type of companies (No.) in the universe with the multiplier found in step 3 to obtain an optimistic demand assessment in a functional area.

Step - 5: Find the number of organizations who had a potential need for Conceptual/Theoretical Information (Np). For finding a pessimistic estimate of demand it was assumed that the response to the test products may be influenced by potential need for Conceptual / Theoretical information as derived from criticality of the information for particular type of companies.

Step - 6: Multiply the number of companies found in step 5 (Np) with the multiplier obtained in step 3 (M) to derive a pessimistic demand assessment.

Step - 7: For each functional area, add the optimistic estimate and the pessimistic estimates across company types to get total optimistic and pessimistic estimates of demand.

APPLICATION OF THE CONJOINT ANALYSIS AS A MARKETING RESEARCH TOOL FOR THE DEVELOPMENT AND CONTROL OF FUTURE ACADEMIC LIBRARY SERVICES: THE ProSeBiCA- PROJECT

Antonia Hermelbracht
Erik Senst

Abstract *The paper at hand presents the contents and goals of the DFG-project ProSeBiCA, which is currently conducted at the Bielefeld University in Germany. A main focus of the project is to involve the consumer perspective in operative and strategic planning of future library services and profiles. We are going to develop a comprehensive analysis and simulation framework for academic libraries that systematically enables a strategic planning of future service design on the basis of preference measurement (using Conjoint Analysis). Here, we take into account services that are already available as well as potential ones that do not exist yet. The empirically deduced statements will be maintained by consumer surveys at a wide base in German and USA libraries. These surveys will be implemented by means of an adjusted model for the measurement of user preferences.*

INTRODUCTION

The issue of the future orientation of academic library services is nowadays more up-to-date than ever. Indicators of this development are current discussions considering the enhancement of digital library services and the reorientation of the scientific publication process in terms of open access to scientific information. A new common issue, especially in Germany, is the adoption and extension of a more customer orientated point of view as the future development of German libraries should be answered not only by librarians, but also by the library users.

There are different ways to develop library service offerings, which are based upon user needs and preferences. One appropriate way is the application of practice-proven methods of marketing research and planning. The complexity of the problem and the high degree of innovation argue for the implementation and superiority of this way. The strengthened competition in the field of information services especially offered by private Internet providers is also a reason for the necessity of a systematic and scientific treatment of the problem.

Although the development of academic libraries today is based to an increasing degree on practice-proven marketing methods for measuring and valuating of library services, these instruments are mostly confined to controlling relevant aspects like measuring of effectiveness, costs and quality. Mostly, the already existing services are subject of examination and not the new and up to now not-existing services.

The current project *ProSeBiCA1* (This is an abbreviation of the German translating of "Prospective control of the services of academic libraries by means of Conjoint Analysis". The project is funded by the DFG , i.e. German Research Foundation; Deutsche Forschungsgemeinschaft). ties up to the already existing rudiments of marketing methods in libraries and pursue the aim to define a spectrum of future relevant academic library services, using the methods of Conjoint Analysis[1]. The project is based on a cooperation between the Bielefeld University Library and the Department of Economics and Business Administration at the Bielefeld University, particularly the Marketing chair (Germany). It aims at the development of a widespread analysis and simulation framework for academic libraries serving as a guideline for other libraries. The usage of Conjoint Analysis as an approved marketing research method for new product development makes the project forward-looking and confines it from other methods for measuring and valuating of academic library services. Subject of examination are both already existing services and up to now not-existing, new services. However the main focus concentrates on new and innovative services.

Against the background of shrinking budgets and rising costs the development of the "right" products becomes increasingly important. The current process of restructuring and changes in the public sector in Germany signalises here a clear call for action. In addition, this process offers the chance to go for new and, so far, perhaps rather unusual ways. The aim of the ProSeBiCA-project is to deliver appropriate answers for designing the "right" range of services in an academic library. The exploration of the new ideas for general and especially digital library services will be maintained by online-surveys at the University Libraries in Bielefeld, Cottbus (Germany) and at the Johns Hopkins University, Baltimore (USA). Subsequently a brief review of the individual steps of the project should be given.

GENERATION OF NEW IDEAS FOR LIBRARY SERVICES

The first step in order to develop new products and services is the scanning of the relevant environment and the generation of plenty of possible ideas for desired modernisations. This step is to insure that no relevant aspects are neglected. That's why this stage is very important for the success of a project and should be processed with adequate dedication.

First of all we should perceive innovation possibilities using methods like environmental scanning[2], which includes the systematic acquisition, analysis and adoption of environment information for the organisation. Otherwise we can use perceptual maps, which visualise the common situation regarding selected services from a target group point of view. An innovation can be a slight variation of an existing product (e.g. the extension of the opening hours), an eminent modification (e.g. the implementation of a scientific search engine) or a revolutionary invention in the treated area (e.g. the development of the internet). The best sources for generating new library service ideas are the users of these services, the own staff and other libraries.

Within the ProSeBiCA-project different sources and techniques were used to generate new ideas. A comprehensive analysis of secondary data, relevant literature and information databases on the internet about innovative new services (for libraries as well as for other organisations) build the basis of the examination. In addition business administration students generated new library services within a project oriented course at the Chair of Business Administration and Marketing at the Bielefeld University. Furthermore a series of workshops with scientific staff and librarians were held, applying idea generation methods like brain storming. These were conducted at the Bielefeld University, the Brandenburg University of Technology Cottbus and the Kansas State University. The result is a list with more than 250 different ideas for new services. They may represent a small detail of an existing service on one hand, as well as complex new service area on the other hand. Some of them are easy to implement, whereas others look wide ahead. Independent from the level of complexity we subsequently present some examples for new ideas for scientific library services:

- translated basic-info packages for foreign library users
- unique user-card (for all electronic systems available to the members of the university)
- home delivery service for books
- media workstations in the library
- virtual "ask-a-librarian"- agents on the web
- information about the loan account via SMS on the mobile phone
- online auctions with used old books from students
- water dispensers within the library
- carrels with extended technical communication capabilities (video conference)
- loan of technical equipment like notebooks or memory sticks
- W-LAN-accessibility
- video-mediated book-view
- online self-administration for user accounts
- 3D multi-modal search engine
- support for voice-enabled-browsing
- webcam communication with librarians
- open access platform for scientific publishing etc.

VERIFICATION OF NEW SERVICE IDEAS

The next step of the development of new service offerings is the testing of the new service ideas concerning their acceptance by the library users. There are different methods to inquire the opinion of a target group concerning an issue, but a comprehensive type of survey is the best way to detect the customer preferences. In the marketing research one special method has achieved a leading position and is preferred by enterprises in order to develop new products or services (3-4). This method is Conjoint Analysis, which is based on the joint rating of more than one characteristic of a product (see Figure 1).

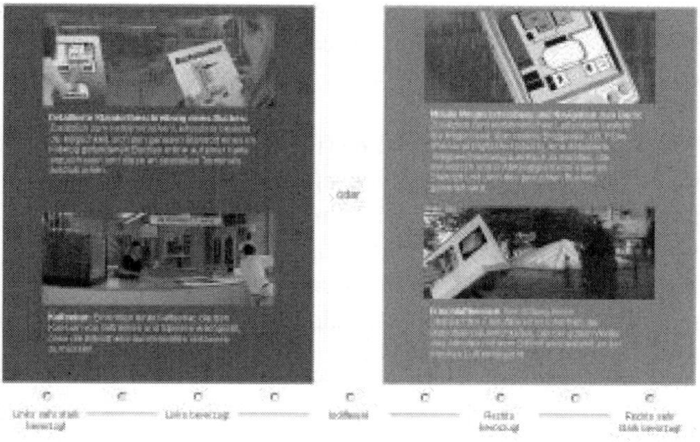

Fig. 1: Paired comparison of two products with two characteristics

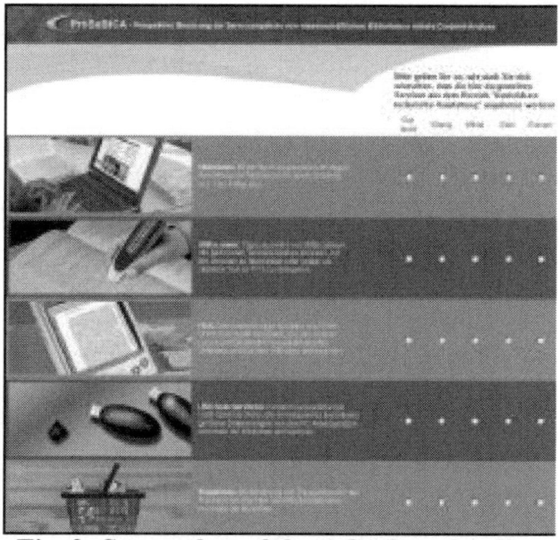

Fig. 2: Screenshot of the ACA based online survey

Librarians in the United States detected the Conjoint Analysis for their purposes a long time ago. Theoretical and empirical papers dealing with Conjoint Analysis for library services were published in the 1980s [5-7]. These and later studies handle only with one small area of the whole range of possible library services, that is to say mostly with the reference services and their possible characteristics [8-9]. The achieved samples at that time contained about 100 students and library users.

Within the ProSeBiCA-project we try to valuate the complete range of services in terms of new developments, using an adjusted version of the Conjoint Analysis. The most commonly used commercial software for computer based analysis is deployed for selecting the data. The data pool is collected within separate online surveys at the Universities of Bielefeld and Cottbus and in the USA. This approach should guarantee a high expressiveness of the data. In these online-surveys the services are presented with text and image or animation (see Figure 2). The user assesses which advantage the described services have got for him personally and makes his choice.

To shorten the time needed for filling out the forms the number of questions was reduced by dividing the whole range of possible library services into four different main categories:

- Provision of media and information (for example: collections and catalogues, supporting enquiry, lending, pick-up and delivery of media)
- Supporting learning and working in the library (for example: orientation within the library, working places and carrels, interior design)
- Communication with the customers and between the customers (for example: announcements, training and tutorials, ask-a-librarian, help and information)
- Extra services (for example: handicapped accessibility, entertainment and activities, convenience)

The participant will coincidentally be asked about services in only one of these four categories. Therefore the total amount of time for completing the online-questioning is only between 20 and 30 minutes.

In order to motivate the users to join the survey, which is a crucial factor for its success, several different activities were initiated in parallel. On the intrinsic level of motivation, we wanted the participant to get emotionally connected to the questioned issue. Therefore the survey begins with a short animated introduction sequence, which shows the participant, that his personal support and his opinion is needed for developing the *library of the future*. Furthermore we try to support the extrinsic level of motivation by the offering of (sponsored) high quality prizes, which can be won by joining this survey. To avoid that the respondents leave the online survey without completing all questions, the raffle is positioned at the end of the questionnaire and not at the beginning. This way the respondents have to answer all questions before they are able to get to the page, where the form for the raffle is implemented. In addition to this virtual campaign students are animated proactively by our staff, who addresses the library users personally (face-to-face) and by poster and flyer publications.

Another, until today, rather unusual and interesting aspect of this conjoint based study is the already mentioned usage of images and animation in addition to text for describing the different service ideas. Usually pure text is the most implemented form of stimulus presentation. The images in this survey have the function to visualise the text. This approach is particularly adequate, because most of the presented services do not exist until now. Therefore the pictures do not only help to explain the text, but also help to *imagine* the future usage and possible benefit of the described services in the context of the familiar environment of their own library (through photomontage). Furthermore, the described use of images follows the assumption that the cognitive load of picture processing is smaller than the cognitive expenditure while processing text media, which can have an indirect or direct influence on motivation, concentration, comprehension and decision-making of the respondent and therefore on the goodness of the results. New empirical examinations argue clearly for a higher validity of conjoint surveys based on picture visualisation (10).

APPLICATION AREAS FOR THE PROJECT RESULTS

The project is currently (November 2004) situated at the described stage of data collecting at the Bielefeld University. A follow-up Choice-Based Conjoint Analysis (CBC, A software package from Sawtooth Software is available for the appliance of Choice-Based Conjoint-Analysis : http://www.sawtoothsoftware.com/cbc.shtml). survey based on the results of this first Adaptive Conjoint Analysis (ACA, Adaptive Conjoint Analysis is also a product of Sawtooth Software and takes the second placed after CBC accounting the number of implementations concerning the available Conjoint Analysis software: http://www.sawtoothsoftware.com/aca.shtml). examination will be executed in the beginning of 2005. Parallel surveys at the Brandenburg University of Technology Cottbus (Germany) and at the Johns Hopkins University (USA) will complete the study until March 2006.

The analysis of the locally collected data-packages will show the services with a high benefit for the users of the considered library.

Comparing the data of the different surveys, the deduction of universally valid statements for the libraries in Germany (and their comparison with the USA) will be possible. This way other libraries in Germany can benefit from the results of the project by using them as an orientation for their own strategic planning.

As another result of the project, a guideline (including the rating and evaluation methods) and a database (including the list of ideas for new services) for other libraries will be provided in order to enable further implementations of this analysis method on a global basis. Both, the searchable and categorized idea database as well as the guideline for executing conjoint based analysis will be published online and for free usage.

To sum up, libraries can benefit from the achievements of this study by using the empirical results as basis for their own strategic service planning, or they can follow the published guideline and execute a conjoint based study on their own. In either case (usage of general statements or execution of conjoint study) the results (services with a high benefit) have to be checked concerning the own strategic planning, the organisational feasibility and the availability of personal, technical or financial resources. For this purpose further marketing techniques (e.g. the *Quality Function Deployment*) [11] should be implemented.

CONCLUSION

Although the project is still at the beginning stage, our practical experiences until now argue clearly for the fact that the conjoint analysis seems to be an adequate tool for measuring the acceptance of library services, as well as it proved its superiority as a marketing tool in the industry and product oriented sector. Nevertheless a clear difference can be seen between the benefit measuring of products and services. Products often can be categorised in a better way and can be described on a lower level of complexity. Products (e.g. laptops) have different material and/or technical properties, that can be divided clearly from each other (MHz, RAM, weight, extra devices etc.), whereas service categories need much more complex descriptions. The described usage of images can help to explain these complex ideas as an addition to the textual presentation.

REFERENCES

1. Decker (R) and Hermelbracht(A). Gestaltung zukünftiger Bibliotheksangebote mit Methoden der Marketingforschung - Ein neues DFG-Projekt des Lehrstuhls für BWL und Marketing und der Bibliothek der Universität Bielefeld, *Bibliotheksdienst*. 38 (5). 2004: 611 – 626. http://www.zlb.de/aktivitaeten/bd_neu/heftinhalte/Betriebsorganisation0504.pdf
2. Aguilar (FJ). Scanning the business environment. New York: Macmillan. 1967
3. Wittink (D R) and Cattin (P). Commercial use of conjoint analysis: An update. *Journal of Marketing*. 53 (3). 1989: 91 – 96.
4. Wittink (D R), Vriens (M) and Burhenne (W). Commercial use of conjoint analysis in Europe: Results and critical reflections. *International Journal of Research in Marketing*. 11 (1). 1994: 41–52.
5. Halperin (M) and Strazdon (M). Measuring students' preferences for reference service: A conjoint analysis. *Library Quarterly*. 50(2). 1980: 208 – 224.
6. Halperin (M). Determining user preferences for information services. *Drexel Library Quarterly*. 17(2). 1981: 88 – 98.
7. Ramsing (K) and Wish (W R). What do library users want? A conjoint measurement technique may yield the answer, *Information Processing & Management*.18 (5). 1982: 237 – 242.
8. Crawford (G A). A conjoint analysis of reference services in academic libraries. *College & Research Libraries*. 55(3). 1994: 257 – 267.

9. Joseph (V) and Binwal (J C). Conjoint analysis: Technique for assessing customer's preferences on library products and services. *Journal of Library Information Science*. 19(2). 1994: 75 – 85.
10. Brusch (M) and Baier (D). Multimedia stimulus presentation methods for conjoint studies in marketing research. *In,* Schader (M) et al., Eds. Between data science and applied data analysis. Berlin: Springer. 2003: 530 – 537.
11. Call (G). Entstehung und markteinführung von produktneuheiten, Gabler. Wiesbaden. 1997

Section - V
EXCELLENCE IN MARKETING

Section - V
Excellence in Marketing

It is a world of perfectionism, of being an ideal, *a paragon, the ne plus ultra, beau ideal, non-pareil, the crème de la crème,* and the ultimate. Awards given to promote marketing in libraries aim to recognize and reward the best practices and reward the valuable works which bring library services to the community. These awards are in no way a deterrent to those who did not achieve these but an inspiration to further their endeavours and reach the zenith of human achievement.

Various awards recognize excellence in LIS marketing, has been demonstrated in brief in the following table:

Name of the Award	Year of Inception	Frequency	Award consists of	Emphasis of Award
IFLA-3M International Marketing Award	2001	Yearly	A trip to main conference & cash award of US$ 1000	Recognize best marketing practices at international level
John Cotton Dana Library Public Relations Awards (6 categories)	1946	Yearly	Each winner US $2500	Outstanding library public relations.
CILIP Public Relations and Publicity Awards for different six categories		Yearly	Gold award Silver Award Bronze Award	Recognize and reward this valuable work, which brings library services to new audiences and develops and publicizes an extensive range of new activities to existing users
Best Practices in Marketing Academic and Research Libraries @your library® Award	2004	Yearly	$2000 for first place winner and $1000 for second place winner	Effective marketing practices in academic and Research Libraries
AALL/West Excellence in Marketing Award for five different categories		Yearly	Winners receive a plaque issued by AALL & monetary award from West recognizing their outstanding achievements	Honouring outstanding achievement in public relations activities

This section covers writings on some of the marketing awards and the details of the award winning programmes in award winners' own words.

Christie Koontz in her paper *Excellence in marketing* gives an outline of the IFLA-3M International Marketing Award which recognizes best practices in marketing of library and information sector worldwide. The award was introduced in 2001 and has been given to libraries of USA, Spain and Australia for their unique marketing initiatives. She gives full details of the award, award winners, and applicants during the three years.

Muhudien Mohammed, the winner for the 2004 IFLA –3M award, in his paper *I Came, I Saw, I Read: Marketing Initiative for Refugee Children* shares the success story of serving immigrant students through the well designed programme called "I can see further by standing on my books" in an Australian school library. Similarly, Andrea Lepsley, the first year's winner of the award for 2002, in her paper *The Power Card Challenge: Marketing the Houston Public Library* makes distinction about "Power card challenge" programme to increase user population in the Houston Public Library. Mireia Sala, the winner for the year2003, in her contribution *Literary Pathways: Approaching literature through Literary Landscapes* talks for the "Literary Pathways" as programmes to raise awareness of the Barcelona's library network among the non-users to have library experiences.

Antony Brewerton, the CILIP/EMERALD Public Relations and Publicity Award winner for the 2003, in his contribution *Marketing Academic Libraries in the UK: The Oxford Brookes University Library Approach* reports how Oxford Brookes University managed its marketing activities to attract new customers and establish customer contacts and assessing their needs, branding and re-branding, reviewing publications, developing displays and using fairs for campaign, etc.

EXCELLENCE IN MARKETING

Christie Koontz

Abstract *Librarians around the world who are identifying customer wants and needs, and delivering products and services to fulfill those needs, are by definition, successfully marketing. To recognize those libraries that develop and implement effective marketing programs, the Management and Marketing Section of the International Federation of Library Associations (IFLA) and 3M Library Systems joined in 2001 to create the IFLA/3M International Marketing Award. The paper gives an overview of the same and details winners of the award during 2002-2004.*

AN AWARD FOR SUCCESSFUL LIBRARY MARKETING

Since 2001, IFLA Section on Management and Marketing in collaboration with IFLA's Gold Partner 3M gives every year "IFLA-3M International Marketing Award" to recognize the best marketing project in any kind of library worldover. The award was based upon the success of the American Library Association's Library Administration and Management Association's, John Cotton Dana Library Public Relations Award, first presented in 1946, to honor outstanding library public relations programs that support a specific project or activity, or a sustained ongoing program (e.g., the promotion of the summer reading program, a year-long centennial celebration, or fundraising for a new college).

The IFLA 3/M award honors outstanding application and understanding of all four basic steps in a marketing model: marketing research: marketing segmentation; marketing mix strategy; and marketing evaluation.

First, second, and third prizes are presented at the IFLA Annual Conferences. The last three included: Glasgow, 2002; Berlin, 2003; Buenos Aires, 2004. The second and third place winners receive certificates and notification at the IFLA closing ceremony, while the first-place winner receives same, and airfare, lodging, and registration for the IFLA General Conference, and a cash award of $1,000 (U.S.) to further the marketing efforts of the library.

CRITERIA AND APPLICATIONS

Over the three year history of the award there have been 104 applicants from five continents. The application is available in the five official IFLA languages (English, Spanish, French, Italian, German) on the Web sites of both sponsors, IFLA and 3M.

Applicants are judged on such criteria as the creativity and innovation as demonstrated by solutions to marketing challenges, effectiveness of marketing goals, and an ongoing commitment to marketing (For a full review of the application, see the URL at end of this article).

The applicants (thus far) are judged on the following criteria

- Strategic approach to marketing communications, indicated in the research and planning stages of a submitted project.
- Creativity and innovation as demonstrated by the originality of solutions to marketing and communications challenges.
- Potential for generating widespread public visibility and support for libraries, irrespective of the kind or amount of resources employed.
- Effectiveness illustrated by efforts to emphasize the organization's communication and marketing goals.
- Commitment to ongoing marketing and public relations activities
- The project had to have taken place no more than three year older.

The committee continues to revise the criteria and simplify the application to facilitate participation by a broader range of countries, and specifically to recognize marketing efforts by developing countries with fewer resources.

SOME BACKGROUND ON MARKETING AND LIBRARIES

When marketing was first introduced to the library field in the late '70s, there was much confusion between marketing and publicity. Over the past 20 years the field focused on understanding and applying systematic marketing activities that embody four main steps: 1) identifying customer wants and needs, 2) grouping customers with similar wants and needs, 3) developing a product with the right price, distribution place, and promotional message for those customer groups, and 4) evaluating the marketing program. Publicity is of course only one activity (ultimately free press coverage or public awareness) that is part of the promotion category. It has taken almost 25 years to straighten out the difference in meaning, but, as illustrated by the applicants for this award, it can be said that libraries are now embracing true marketing. Over the course of the award, the winning libraries all marketed in a systematic way. By telling their own stories, the people who apply for this IFLA/3M International Marketing Award provide insight into the colorful behind-the-scenes daily business of modern libraries.

WINNERS IN REVERSE CHRONOLOGICAL ORDER

WINNERS IN 2004

This year, altogether there were 52 applicants from all five continents, sent in from 17 countries including: Russian Federation, Australia, Spain, Nigeria, New Zealand, India, United States, Canada, Ivory Coast, Philippines, Cuba, United

Kingdom, Sweden, Romania, Indonesia, Argentina and Chile. Any library, agency, or association in the world that promotes library service was eligible to receive the award.

First Place: "I Came, I Saw, I Read," Australian Islamic College (AIC)

Overview of the Program: The programs was designed to develop computer-based reading and computer literacy as well as cultural amelioration for 300 refugee children who recently migrated to Australia from Afghanistan, Iraq and Somalia and joined the school at the end of 2001. While the Accelerated Reader Program is commercial, the motivational writing and research programs, "Cyber Camp," and "Yes! I Can Write!" were developed in the library to enable new-arrival students to develop the skill of writing and research in literature-based programs, and explore their new culture.

Objectives: The top three objectives out of a list of nine, which are measureable and can be evaluated are:

1. Integrate children who came from war torn countries with the mainstream students through this program.
2. Introduce refugee children to Australian culture through reading and discussion.
3. Promoting the library and its work and encourage the use of library and information services by new immigrant students.

It was noted in the application that most of the children had little or no computer skills; almost all were first time English book readers; many of the children had never been in a library in their whole life; most never attended school with the other sex; most never had foreigners (people who do not speak their native language) as teachers and librarians; and many were traumitized, with fears of anything foreign. The challenge was for the library to overcome these barriers to service.

Key to Excellent Marketing

The first tenet of successful marketing is to identify customer wants and needs, and meet those needs within the resources and mission of the organization. The winning programs developed by the library, are based upon information gathered after the library provided services for Bosnia refugee children in 1999.

Step One-Marketing Research: This is step one in the marketing process, gathering customer research data to identify what is wanted and needed). In 1999, the library received complaints from students and their families about poor library service. Based upon this, the library then decided to survey 20 parents and children of the Bosnian group who remained in Australia, as well as former migrant students to get a better idea of what was desired by the children and their families. The survey results indicated that many students perceived the library as 'one of the boring and idle places of the school', and they (and their parents) did not understand the library's role or what it had to offer. Many said the formal English as a Second Language (ESL) classes helped students read-but not form the reading habit. Based upon this information, and knowledge of the children's likelihood of limited experience with foreign cultures, the library decided it would develop new programs to overcome these obstacles for any future groups of refugees, and help acculturate the children, and facilitate a love of reading. In 2001, when the 300 refugee children came to the school, the library was ready.

Step Two -Marketing Segmentation: The library saw a need to identify and prioritize customer groups to provide unique services with the funds available. The primary target market identified was the 300 refugee children, and secondary markets were identified as primary students from the main stream classes, and parents of refugee children. This step two in the marketing process, is market segmentation, gathering individuals with similar needs into groups, and prioritizing the groups for optimal resource allocation.

Step Three-Marketing Mix Strategy 4P's: The library then designed programs and services to meet the objectives set. Through utilizing the Accelerated Reader Program (ARP), from Renaissance Learning they offered motivational writing and reading programs. AIC developed a Cyber Camp where students could travel and explore virtual forest and animals. A student could also learn about plants and animals that live in the forests of Asia, Africa and Australia. The library also offered incentives such as 'Best Writer of the Month,' 'Book Worms of the Week' and ARP awards. These products all had consideration of price from the users point of view, such as number of hours required in library or at home. The promotion of the products was on a weekly TV program that the school broadcasts, posters and brochures, weekly reports aimed at parents, school assembly, display boards, and School Library Friends network. All activities were organized in the library, which is open 8 am to 5 pm, Monday through Friday.

Step Four-Evaluation: Did We do What We Said We Would Do? The library then proceeded to develop ways to measure the success of the new programs through evaluating reading test results, surveying teachers and parents regarding individual child development, online suggestion boxes for students, and monitoring if budgetary requests were successful or not.

The results were positive. Awareness of the library by parents increased 70%; circulation of library resources by new students increased 85%; desire to use the computer for research purposes by new students increased 70%; and new students performance on state level literacy tests improved by 20%. The management recently increased the library's budget. A sure sign of excellent marketing.

These remarks were received from Muhudien Mohammed, who is the head librarian after his receipt of first place for the IFLA/3M International Marketing Award.

"When I started the program I had this big dream of changing children's lives and making a difference in the lives of refugee children. I didn't realize that the program would also cause me to share my family time (increased workload!) and I did not realize that the books could become a flash point for cultural misunderstandings and mistrust. For the last two years I met with angry parents who accused me of allowing kids to read "Harry Potter' or books that contain a few words of profanity. I listened to the lectures of religious teachers about the importance of censorship. Anyhow, the last two years were roller coasters, at times I touched the sky with joy and happiness, and other times I touched the bottom of the earth on desperation and anger. However, getting IFLA's recognition was unexpected and beyond my imagination. Thank you again for selecting me for this wonderful award."

As western countries and their professional librarians lament the digital divide and consider how libraries can help bridge that gap, this project helps other professionals to realize that most of the world is dealing with growing numbers of diverse and changing population, with limited resources or restrictive cultural norms. For more information see full paper on this project in this volume.

Second Place: "Remedy for the Soul" Krasheninnikov Regional Research Library, Kamchatka, Russia

Description of Program :The library has many years of experience dealing with socially disadvantaged population in the region, and working with local government and charitable organizations in partnership. In the past in-home books were delivered to the disabled and the elderly and library services and activities were offered to the same population such as computer training, and special exhibitions and programs to enhance leisure time. The library's goal for this new program was to develop an information and referral center for the socially disadvantaged. The program would facilitate access to important social services, and leisure-enhancing information, and include a summary database of organizations and institutions which offer 'help services' called 'Ask and You Will Get Help.' This was an impressive program which included systematic marketing.

For more information contact Ivanova Bella Solomonova, Director, bella@library.iks.ru

Third Place: "Current Contents at WARDA" West African Rice Development Association Center in Abidjan, Ivory Coast, Africa

The National Agricultural Research System (NARS) of West Africa, identified the growing need to provide current information to agricultural researchers to 'strengthen' their scientific research capabilities through provision of tables of contents of recently acquired journals, worldwide access to agricultural literature particular to rice; and provide photocopies of articles in the *Current Contents Bulletin* without charge to users. These needs were identified at a WARDA meeting at which NARS members presented their needs, and inability to singularly subscribe to current journals. The organization WARDA, also identified price as cost of user's time to fill out forms of request. Direct mail and conference presentations are being used to disseminate the new services. This program offered many successful components of a marketing plan, and came through great effort from a developing country in West Africa, amidst civil war. For more information contact Thomas Adigun, t.adigun@cigar.org

WINNERS IN 2003

Altogether there were 15 applicants from 7 countries (4 from Spain, 4 from USA, 3 from UK, 1 from India-Tanzania-Serbia-Thailand.)

First Place: "The Marketing Campaign: Literary Pathways." Concorci de Biblioteques de Barcelona (CBB) Spain

The public library system of Barcelona, Spain, is developing non-users into users through a program called "Literary Pathways". This is a program featuring actors or guides leading tour participants and reading selections of works, into neighborhoods in which famous authors lived, or were portrayed in their writings. The library requires the literary travellers to register for a library card. The nearest library is often a stop on the tour as well. The library encourages families and children to participate together, thereby creating a basis for a whole new generation of library users.

Subjects of tours include foreign writers living in Barcelona, such as, George Orwell, author of 1984 and Animal Farm who once spent time in the late night neighborhoods. Other topics included famous poets, children's authors, and even a ghoulish tour of a cemetery where authors lie in rest.

The campaign is supported by a variety of communication media from posters in bakeries, to publicity articles in speciality magazines and local newspapers. Brochures and buttons were developed as well as point of purchase displays in the libraries. For more information contact: Mireia Sala, director, msalaf@mail.bcn.es

Second Place: "CU e-Intellectual Property" Center of Academic Resources Chulalongkorn University, Bangkok, Thailand

The second place winner is from Bangkok, Thailand and the 1999 site of an IFLA marketing workshop, sponsored by the Management and Marketing Section.

The Center of Academic Resources within the university, offered a full text in house database of graduate theses which was well accepted, but little used. To increase use and better serve the academic community, the library added in faculty research data. Yet use of the database still did not increase at the rate planned. So during a time of increased need to show the value and impact of the library, staff created a well-developed marketing plan to increase use of the database by 10%. The second objective was to provide easier access to the database at anytime from anywhere. These objectives were to be met within 18 months. The campaign used all the tenets of marketing, including customer identification and segmentation, marketing strategy and evaluation. The database was renamed to "CU e-Intellectual Property." For more information contact Ms. Yupin Chancharoensin and Ms. Supaporn Chaithammapakorn, yupin.c@car.chula.ac.th

Third Place: We Got News for You!" Newman College of Higher Education Library and Learning Resource Centre, Birmingham, UK

Newman College Library designed a campaign to communicate changes in the library's staff, programs and services. The library staff identified primary target markets, as academic staff and students. The goal was to make the markets more knowledgeable about the 'new' and larger library, and to increase use of a growing array of virtual services. The library created a newspaper "The Library Times," which is published and available on campus and available on the college's intranet. The paper is 'packed' with library news and information-and students are encouraged as columnists. The library is also holding on-site quarterly showcases which illuminate new services and products. The winning features of this application were again the identification of customer groups, the precise and systematic communication to those groups through various and sundry media, and evaluation based upon measurable objectives. For more information contact Janice Bell and Maureen Carter, library@newman.ac.uk

A Review of Some of the Other Applicants

Excellence in Library Marketing from Tanzania to India
University Library Campaigns

University campaigns included: increasing use of a special map collection, combining manuscript and electronic information into one project, through promotional strategy; promoting a positive image of the library and services through development of a new online catalogue; a campaign to foster user interest in improving library skills, with distribution of a promotional product, a toothbrush, imprinted with a slogan, "Brush up on your Library Research Skills;" promotion of a historic collection both physical and virtual to a wider user audience; a strategy to develop classroom bibliographic instruction to increase use by specific student populations; utilizing publicity for promoting the acquisition of the 1.5 millionth volume, to build relationships with key funders; and a marketing plan to overcome customer dissatisfaction with the physical library facility.

Special Library Campaigns

A unique array of campaigns were entered by libraries representing governments, agencies and special institutes including : a US state library and a state library association developing partnerships to foster public libraries in an eastern European country; promotion of an information system to improve decision-making skills of students and management practitioners; a campaign to promote use of the library as a meeting point for discourse and information by a community recently experiencing severe civil war; and a new employee campaign to promote knowledge of the information center's resources and services through tours, open houses, personal contacts and a graduation card.

A special note in this category, regarding the late Ashok Jambhekar member of the M&M committee, who passed away in May, 2003. Mr. Jambhekar was an applicant for this year's award and a strong contender. He was head librarian of the Indian Institute of Management, and a proponent of marketing practices for libraries. His application and contribution to this award and process is acknowledged. Ashok is missed, and the committee aspires to carry on his high standard of marketing.

WINNERS IN 2002

Altogether there were 37 applicants from four continents, sent from 14 countries: Argentina, Benin, Brazil, Bulgaria, Canada, Colombia, Congo, Germany, Italy, Kenya, Poland, Romania, Spain, and the U.S.A.

First Place: "The Power Card Challenge: A Long Term Marketing and Public Relations Plan to Increase Library Card Registration and Use by the Children of Houston"

Description of Program: The goal of the Houston Public Library was to increase the number of children accessing library materials, both to improve their schoolwork and to develop lifetime readers, thereby ensuring educated and productive future generations. The 3-year campaign set specific goals for juvenile registration and circulation each year, with the final numerical goal of increasing juvenile registrations from a little over 100,000 to 303,000, and increasing juvenile circulation by 30 percent.

Objectives of Program: First-year objectives: Give temporary library card (an application/informational flier with the new library card design) to every school-age child in Houston (approximately 500,000). Encourage all kids to "activate" their "card" which could raise the number of juvenile cardholders to 200,000 by

June 30, 1999. Increase juvenile circulation at least 20 percent from July 1998 to June 1999.

Second-year objectives: Increase the number of juvenile cardholders to 240,000 by June 30, 2000. Increase juvenile circulation by 10 percent from July 1999 to June 2000. Increase use of juvenile electronic resources and youth Web pages by 10 percent.

Third (final) year objectives : Increase current juvenile cardholders to 303,000 by June 30, 2001. Increase juvenile circulation by 5 percent to 2,960,000 items. Increase the number of juvenile borrowers with items checked out to 45,000, based on a monthly average. The benchmark in FY2000 was 41,000.

Program Plan : According to research done for the library's Strategic Master Plan, the number of children under age of 15 in Houston exceeds the national average by 20 percent. Additionally, the research shows that Houstonians are somewhat below national averages in library usage, library card ownership, and frequency of use. Hispanic Houstonians are the most underserved compared to their numbers.

Target Audiences Identified were : All school-age children in Houston, 500,000 (nearly 30 times the 17,000 targeted in a 1997 library card sign-up campaign) Parents, grandparents, teachers, and caregivers of such children, so that the required signatures could be obtained and the applications returned to the library Potential partners: community organizations, businesses, schools, city government, and the media to extend the reach of such an ambitious campaign The underserved Hispanic community

Summary: With the Power Card Challenge, Houston Public Library created a 3-year program that redefines library card campaigns, gave the library a brand and identity in the community through a new library card design and graphics, ran a well-defined marketing/publicity campaign, and provided a model for other communities to replicate. A full paper has been included on the Power Card Project in this volume.

Second Place: "Rediscover Your Calgary (Public) Library," Western Canada submitted by Grant Kaiser

Description of Program: The Calgary Public Library's research identified clear demographic gaps in its customer base. A plan was developed to use television advertising to target groups that did not use the library, but might. It would be the first time that television advertising was used to promote a library anywhere in Western Canada. Three "hot buttons" were identified: 1) high costs of books, music CDs, and magazines, 2) the love of, and need for, convenience and easy access in everything, and 3) the confusion over the volume of information available in the world today, and the accuracy of that information. For each point, 15-second television commercials were produced. Evaluation benchmarks were established, and a 2-week TV campaign ran in September/October of 2001.

Objectives : There were three objectives to the "Rediscover Your Calgary (Public) Library Campaign." The primary objective was:

1. Increase the top-of-mind awareness of the Calgary Public Library: When someone has a question they need answered, or wants a book to read, the library is one of the places they consider going to. The Calgary Public Library believed that progress on this objective was essential for any of its communications or marketing activities to be effective.

Two secondary objectives were also established:

2. Increase circulation.
3. Increase the number of new library memberships issued.

Summary : The results were positive. The library saw a substantial increase in top-of-mind awareness (43 percent), and in new library memberships (21 percent), and also a strong increase in circulation (three times growth trends). The program ran from July 2001 through November 2001.

For more information contact Grant Kaiser, grant.kaiser@calgarypubliclibrary.com.

Third Place: "The Opening and Promotion of the Flushing Library," Jamaica, NY (U.S.A.)

Description of Program: The Flushing Library is one of 62 branches of the Queens Borough Public Library, which is one of New York City's three independent systems. The new 76,000-square-foot, state-of-the-art public library opened in June 1998. The marketing campaign leading to Opening Day was designed to stimulate awareness; to relieve irritation of customers who had been getting library services from an undersized temporary storefront during construction; and to reinforce Queens Borough Public Library's name with patrons, legislators, and donors.

The concept of the Flushing Library Public Relations Plan was to stir broad-based citywide and national attention and support for this new facility, the largest branch library in New York State. It was hoped that the Flushing Library would be a springboard from which publicity for the Queens Library system as a whole could be generated.

Staff enthusiasm was also of paramount concern in designing the public relations plan. It would take months of gruelling labor to get the branch ready to open. There were no funds for additional staff, so "bodies" would have to be borrowed from all over the system to get the building open and books on the shelves. That was going to leave difficult staff shortages all over the library system. It was imperative that the whole staff get behind the project all the way. Without full support, it simply could not happen.

The target audiences included legislators, community leaders, business leaders, the education community, Queens residents/non-library users, donors and potential donors, and print and broadcast media, including ethnic outlets.

Goals and Objectives : To generate awareness of the Flushing Library as a unique resource in Queens and in New York City. To generate awareness that the library is not only an archive but that its information can be used on a daily basis to do business, to further education, and to assist in daily living. We want people to be aware that it has a vital role in the economy in Queens. To generate publicity for the name "Queens Borough Public Library" as being distinct from its two sister systems in New York C Brooklyn Public Library and New York Public Library. To create awareness that much of the best that New York City has to offer is not necessarily in Manhattan. To generate and sustain traffic in the new facility. The goal was to rival the traffic in Queens' Central Library, reported to be the busiest library building in New York State with 2,500 to 3,000 visitors a day. To validate the generous amount of money allocated to this facility. To make all the members of the community feel welcome. To create an opening event worthy of the jaded New York City media's attention (always an uphill battle). To bring in an impressive crowd of library customers for the opening. (The old library had 1,500 visitors on a busy Saturday in 22,000 square feet. Allowing for the 350-percent increase in size, we hoped to double attendance, setting our goal for 10,500 visitors on opening day.) To use the opening as a theme for a fundraiser, to be held by the Queens Library Foundation.

Summary: The opening of the Flushing Library created a lot of media attention. The pre-launch campaign was considered ultimately successful. On opening day, June 20, 1998, about 16,500 people walked through the doors of the library, attending one of 17 programs and borrowing 8,500 items, achieving150 percent of its goal. During the final 9 days of the fiscal year, the library had circulated more than 55,000 items, registered 900 borrowers, and welcomed 78,000 visitors. Positive relationships were established with community groups and support was garnered by local legislators.

The library continued to book the best of its program schedule there to keep the momentum going. It also continued to foster Flushing Library's reputation as a valuable resource for international information. Symposia on topics such as "Doing Business with China in the 21st Century" have been held there. Eventually the attention the Flushing Library received was turned toward other library programs and services. For more information contact Gary Strong, gstrong@queenslibrary.org.

NEXT YEAR'S APPLICATION

It is significant that 3M, a major international business, would partner with the library field to award best marketing practices. "Effective marketing is vital to a library's success. We are proud to continue our support for this award," says Don Leslie, Business and Government Relations Manager for 3M Library Systems and coordinator of the program.

The Commitment to Marketing

Both sponsors-IFLA's Management and Marketing Section and 3M Library Systems-share a strong commitment to increasing awareness about the value of libraries marketing their services. This shared commitment serves as the foundation for the partnership between IFLA and 3M, and led to the creation of the IFLA/3M International Library Marketing Award. The M&M Section hopes to provide a continued forum through this international award so that libraries in all countries can share just how they are bringing customers what they really want and need, and information that people can use to enhance the quality of their lives.

Applications will soon be available for the next year's award at http://www.3M.com/library/events/IFLA_app.doc or through the IFLA Web site, http://www.ifla.org/.

New Partner Collaborates

In late 2005, the new partner SirsiDynix joined the Award in place of 3M. The IFLA Section on Management and Marketing in collaboration with SirsiDynix announced applications for the award for 2006 in the changed name "**IFLA International Marketing Award**"

CONCLUSION

This annual international award was created to identify best marketing practices. The award, through the voices of its many applicants, can best communicate the types of marketing activities that libraries successfully engage in, not only to colleagues around the world, but also to people who use libraries or may want to use libraries, or those in charge of providing funds for library services. This award at the time of this writing is now in its fourth year, continuing to offer opportunity for all types of libraries to showcase marketing campaigns and programs, rather than simple publicity efforts.

I CAME, I SAW, I READ: MARKETING INITIATIVE FOR REFUGEE CHILDREN

Muhudien Mohammed

Abstract *'I can see further by standing on my books' is a reading and computer literacy program designed for about 300 primary school children who mainly came from non-English speaking migrant families. It is a computer based reading and writing assessment program, designed to promote reading and research among migrant students. The whole marketing process was comprised of four different programs : Accelerated Reader a computer based reading assessment program developed by Renaissance Learning, Yes, I can write a computer based writing program developed by AIC library staff, Cyber camp, a simulated online camp designed to engage students in discussions on ideas of nature and culture, and book fete, a discussion forum designed to engage students in formal and informal face to face discussions. Before it became the main stream part of the education program in the middle of 2004, the library had run the program for two and half year as a pilot project. This paper investigates and indicates the social dimensions of reading, collaboration, group work, and the importance of information technology on the assessment and development of children's reading habit, and tries to indicate how these relate to meeting the needs of children in the library.*

INTRODUCTION

Australian Islamic College (AIC) is a community-based school that caters to the educational need of students from Kindergarten through to year 12. The school has three campuses and provide an educational service for more than 1500 students. Most of the students in the school came from Non-English speaking migrant families. According to the recent school statistics 60% of the students are born outside Australia, and 30% of these students passed thorough the school ESL system before they joined mainstream classes. Like many schools in Australia developing students literacy level, in reading and writing is one of the major challenges faced by the school. As Richardson indicated "literacy would appear to be one of the few elements of education that everyone agrees to be a necessity for modernity." When it comes to literacy AIC's case was not an isolated issue, but the situation was unique because of the fact that many of the students came from the non-English speaking backgrounds.

The recent influx of migrants from ASI to Australia increased the number of the first generation of migrants in AIC and has raised the question on the methods and approaches used to address literacy and numeracy problems. Traditionally the school addressed any numeracy and literacy related issues by opening more ESL classes or by developing literacy classes that run in parallel with mainstream classes. ESL classes as their name indicates cater for the development of migrant students literacy and numeracy development through interaction, discussion and using various technologies. The school used "parallel literacy classes" in the belief that combining students who recently finished ESL classes with main-stream classes would develop interaction and discussion among students and in the way develop new students moral steam and confidence.

Sadly most of these initiatives were teacher and class oriented that didn't include the resource centre as part of a solution to literacy and numeracy problem. When the idea to use the resource centre as part of the literacy and numeracy program, especially the shifting from class based literacy classes to library based literacy program came into existence the school got a grasp on the depth of academic and behaviour problems of students created because of the lack of proper literacy and numeracy skills. When the library was assigned to lead the trial literacy program in year 2000 with 300 ASI students the first thing we did was organised a team for the program, develop detail running programs, and put down any problems we thought we might encounter and their solutions. We used the theme "My Vision: I can see further by standing on my books" as the general theme of the program. Before we started to run the program we came up with the idea of using Napoleon's slogan "I came, I saw, I conquered" but modified to " I came, I saw, I read" as a slogan to the over all program.

OVERVIEW OF THE PROGRAM

My Vision : I can see further by standing on my books is a reading promotion and computer literacy program designed for children who, at the time, recently migrated to Australia from Afghanistan, Iraq, and Somalia and joined the school at the end of 2001. It was a computer based reading and writing assessment program, designed to promote reading and research among migrant students. The reading program, The Accelerated Reader Program, was acquired from Renaissance Learning, however the motivational writing and research programs, "cyber camp and Yes! I can write", later called 'audio book' have been specially developed in the library, to enable new-arrival students to develop the skill of writing and research in literature-based programs.

TARGET MARKETS

The program was first targeted:

- The 300 refugee children
- Primary students form the main stream classes
- Parents of the refugee children

Objectives of the program

- To integrate children who came from war torn countries with the mainstream students through reading.
- To introduce refugee children to Australian culture through reading and discussion.
- To promote the library and its works and encourage the use of library and information services by new migrant students.
- To promote refugee students work and to provide access to information and ideas that will prove useful to them.
- To involve the parents of these children in reading promotion, library activities and competitions.
- To provide a place and equipment for migrant students to work with mainstream students in library oriented teamwork projects and activities.
- To monitor students' literacy progress and identify learning difficulties that students might encounter.
- To modify, monitor and evaluate the success of this program at periodical intervals.
- To develop more library and information oriented programs in the library that will stimulate and involve more students.

GOALS

- To promote the importance of reading in a modern society and to create awareness among migrant.
- To make refugee children independent learners and decision makers.
- To create awareness among refugee children about different cultures, people, and customs through reading and research.
- To encourage children to stay in school and finish high school and enter colleges and universities.
- To encourage refugee children to talk about their problems, worries and hopes thorough the program called "book fête" and guide them to overcome their fear and misconceptions.
- To encourage migrant children to develop public talk and discussion

SITUATION ANALYSIS

- Most of the children have little or no computer skill
- Almost all the children are first time English book readers

- Many of the children have never been in to a library in their whole life.
- Many of the children have never been attended schools where by boys and girls are integrated.
- Almost all the children never attended school where foreigners (people who don't speak their mother tongue) are teachers, librarians and administrators.
- Many of the children are traumatized and have a fear of anything foreign.
- Many of the parents were starting to build their lives from scratch in a new country and foreign culture and, who ran every day to meet ends was very difficult and disappointing at times.
- Marketing a library program, which involves a voluntary cooperation, willingness to involve and be part of something new, to people who have been told all their life what to do and not to do by their governments, tribal or clan leaders, was a very difficult and challenging.
- Simple things such as progress reports, meetings, and enquiries at times were translated to three four languages before we sent them to parents and in the process, these reports lost their content and created big frustration to library staff.

STRATEGIES

- Library has an enthusiastic and talented library staff
- The school administration and the principal have supported the program
- The library has enough time to promote its products and services
- The library can organize a separate room with 12 computers for the program
- ESL teachers have been showing great interest to the program
- We have got enough budget to run the trial program
- Our web page developer work full time to improve and modify the program as suggested by the head librarian

TECHNOLOGY

- We have enough computers to run the program
- We have all the software required to develop the program
- The school network system is reliable and easy to access

WEAKNESS

- The school web site doesn't have adequate representation somewhere on the site for all services that are developed in the library
- Lack of Internet space won't allow us to run the program online
- Running the program on the intranet won't allow participating students to get access to the sites from other places
- We don't have staff who can follow up reports, communicate with parents in a regular bases

PRODUCTS

- Cyber Camp
- Accelerated Reader program
- Yes! I can write
- Book fête

All the 300 and other mainstream students who participate in the program will spend 3 periods a week (3*45min.) in the library. The library has already transferred the former teachers corner (a separate room in the library) to a room called " Destination Decipher" The set up of this room is changed every week based on the team of the program and the week.

Cyber Camp is a virtual camp designed and developed by library staff to encourage kids to interact with computers, and to help them to develop the skill of reading and writing through listening and interaction. The cyber camp is the same as any camp except the fact that it is an online camp. During the session of cyber camp the library staff change the set up of our special room to look like a holiday destination. Every week, as much as possible we try to make the room to look like the destination of the cyber camp. For instance if our students plan of destination is Africa, we put different pictures and costumes of Africa in the room, we invite children to bring something of African origin, costumes, books, artefacts or anything African to the library. In the cyber camp students are allowed to adopt an animal from the week's destination continent. Besides that the cyber camp program provides students with a brief description of the selected animal, a three minute digitized video about the animal and its environment, and different sounds of the animal. At every session children are asked to register and give their detail before entering to the camp and they are required to discuss and share stories after the end of each session of the virtual tour. At the end of the tour students are provided with quizzes, these weekly quizzes are varied from listening the sound of an animal and writing its name to writing a short paragraph about their adopted animals.

Cyber camp allowed students of ESL and main stream classes to work together, to discuss issues related with environment, ecology, and animal rights. The program created a big discussion point, even at times confrontation between students. However, the close availability of library staff and teachers as moderators helped students to understand each other cultural differences, and help them to learn to respect each other views.

In the **Accelerated Reader program** students are required to select a book of their choice every week based on their reading level, and by the end of the week they are asked to answer computer based multiple choice quizzes. All the quizzes are based on the books the children read, and the computer generate different reports based on their results. By the end of each session students are automatically notified of their results and every fortnight the library sends a letter and diagnostic report to parents. All parent reports are translated to the language of the child's parents. Based on their results children are passed to the next level of reading or asked to stay on the same level until they improve their reading skill. Children who score above 90% on every week quizzes are rewarded with the specially designed "reader of the week" pencils, pens and notebooks. Children who pass their quizzes regularly and reach the targeted goals are rewarded with certificate and special prizes in front of the whole school. A class that scores the highest mark in a week would be rewarded with a basketball and the readers of the week banner and their class picture is displayed on "bookworms of the week" display board.

Yes! I can write (Audio book) is also a computer-based program. The program is designed to teach refuge children the importance of bibliographic records and encourage them to develop their writing skill. Once children finished their accelerated quizzes, they are asked to write the author's name of their book, the title, the publication date, page number of the book, the names of the main characters of the book, and they are required to prepare a brief summary of the book. Once they finished the writing program they are allowed to play selected computer and cardboard games as a reward.

Book fête is a program designed to encourage refugee children to talk to each other and with other mainstream class children about books. There is no formal preparation for this program; children are allowed to sit with whomever they want to and allowed to talk about any books they wanted to. Groups are allowed to interact with other groups and encouraged to talk about anything they wanted to. The library is organized a forum and a place for discussion based on the most popular books of the week. For instance Gizmo's corner or A cat in a hat corner, and children are encouraged to dress as the characters of their books.

THE MARKETING PROCESS

Background study

One way of looking at the overall productivity and importance a service, such as a library is to look for evidence of the need for it and use made of it. Before we have embarked on the process of marketing our new service we have assessed the same kind of program offered to other migrant students a year earlier, and analysed its outcome in the general information behaviour students involved in the program. The library had provided a service for Bosnian refugee children in 1999, however at the end of that year many children and parents complained about the poor library services offered, and also indicated the difficulties they had faced to understand the library rules and regulations.

Before we started the new marketing project we surveyed about 20 parents and children of that group who remained permanently in Australia and also sent out a questionnaire to many former migrant students. The questionnaire and the survey results indicated that many students felt that the library was one of the boring and idle places of the school, many of them left school without much understanding of the role of the library in the school. Many students also replied that their formal ESL classes had helped them to develop their reading skills, but failed them in developing the habit of reading. Half of the former students that surveyed said that they don't consider themselves as a very good book readers, and the other half, mainly boys, replied that they don't read novels at all. These surveys also helped us to find out that many of our students used our library when teachers pushed them, or when teachers told them about the information sources available in the library.

CUSTOMERS

Our potential customers are the 300 refugee children, their teachers and parents, however we have been involving different classes each term from different year groups of the mainstream students.

OUR MARKETING PLAN AND PROJECT

Objectives

- To create greater awareness about the importance of the school library among students and parents
- To bring more students to the library, especially new students
- To form a better affiliation with teachers, school administration and parents
- To get a place and a voice in the future decision making processes of the school
- To get a better budget, technology and infrastructure from the school administration
- To inform students and teachers that library is not only a place of reading, but also a place for research based informative learning, a place of activities and discussion
- To change the image of the library from a place of lending and borrowing to a place of active learning

PRODUCTS

The literacy and information service Programs

- Accelerated reader program
- Guidance on the development of written communication skill
- A computer training program for all participants of the program
- Software usage coaching
- Teach students how to search and find information from print resources
- Internet information search technique training

Social programs

- A place of interaction among fellow students
- Guidance on the development of public speaking and debating
- Develop theatrical skills

Others

- Develop a skill of camping and tour
- Learn about cultures and environments of different continents
- Learn about habitat and nature of different animals

Price

- Each student will spend a minimum of 135 minutes a week in the library
- Each library staff spends a minimum of 30 hours a fortnight to run this program
- Money needed to hire a casual staff that follow up student's results, send weekly progress reports to parents and administration.
- Initial cost to acquire the Accelerated reader program, books, prizes and promotional materials

Promotional Tools

- Getting a spot for Bookworms of the week on the weekly TV program of the school (Breaking Barriers)
- Posters and brochures prepared by the library
- Students and parents weekly reports
- The school assembly (once a week)
- Using the School library friends club network to spread messages and programs
- Display boards prepared for this program
- The main board of the school- to display the picture of students that reached a classical reader stage

Place

All activities are organized in the library. The library is located at the centre of the school and provides a service from 8:00 Am-5:00 PM.

The library has already set-up a new computer laboratory for this program and all books and other materials related with this program are separated from the main collection. Students who directly participate in this program have full access of this place through out the day.

Cyber

The school intranet net program has been used to run the program, to get suggestions and comments form teachers, students and parents.

PARENT STUDENT NIGHT AT THE LIBRARY

The library has been organizing the parent and students nights in the library for the last year and half, it has been one of the successful parent nights and helped us a lot to communicate with parents

Evaluation

- Assessment of Accelerated Reader Program results. The weekly results indicate whether students' literacy skill is developed or not, how many books are circulated, which books are popular and students tendency towards reading
- Teachers Survey-by the end of each term we send questionnaires to teachers to investigate the development of each child in their class, how the program affect their educational goal, and the benefit they got from the over all library program
- Interviewing parents-we have been organizing end of term parent and students nights in the library and at all these occasions we have interviewed parents about the behavioural changes of their children since they started to involve in the program, and how we can improve the program.
- Parents attendance sheet-from term to term parents attending the parent and student night have been improved since we started the program and this improvement showed us parents interest towards the program.
- Online suggestion boxes-students are allowed to send any comments and suggestions they might have regarding the program through the library address and so far all students suggestions indicated the program is popular among students
- Increased budget for the program in academic year 2002/2003. The school management decision to increase our budget request has indicated us the acceptance and success of the program.

According to our survey consisting of, questionnaire and interviews of 2nd term of academic year 2003 (June 2003), the following were the result:

- Awareness about the importance of the library by parents improved by 70%
- Circulation of library resources by new students improved by 85%
- Desire to use the computer for research purposes have been improved by 70% among new students
- New students performance on state level literacy tests have been improved by 20%

CONCLUSION

The marketing program designed to promote literacy was successfully finished in June 2004 and since then it became an integrated part of the primary education program. Nothing was as easy as we put it on the paper, there were times we came closer to abandon the program, at times staff at the library were frustrated and angry and at other times we were so happy that we achieved something. One of the greatest problem in our side was, we gave less credit to the influence that culture has on the reading habit and interest of our customers, we didn't realize at the time that some reading materials would be a flash point for cultural differences.

In our wildest imagination we thought that having any reading material would be much better than not having it. However, we paid dearly for our ignorance of cultural sensitivities. In some cultures some things are not said openly, especially when it comes to relationship between sexes, and some words of profanity. People want discretion and we failed to understand these things.

Over all we were so successful that by the end of the program the school management increased our budget, we got a permission to change the set up and interior design of the library, which cost a fortune to the school. Nothing would have been possible without the successful achievement of the marketing initiative, and the consequently winning IFLA's Marketing prize.

MARKETING ACADEMIC LIBRARIES IN THE UK: THE OXFORD BROOKES UNIVERSITY LIBRARY APPROACH

Antony Brewerton

Abstract *This paper focuses on how marketing is managed at Oxford Brookes University Library, specifically the work of the Library's Marketing Group. After reviewing the administration of the Group, the main body of the report considers the Group's successes from the last four years in establishing customer needs, branding (and re-branding), reviewing publications, developing displays and working with colleagues University-wide to promote the Library and its services. A key success has been in the field of outreach to new students, in particular the Group's Freshers' Fair campaigns. It was for one of these campaigns that the Group was awarded the CILIP/ Emerald Award.*

INTRODUCTION

Marketing libraries has become a hot topic in the United Kingdom, with the theme dominating conferences, workshops and professional publications. A recent issue of the SCONUL (Society of College, National and University Libraries) journal focuses specifically on the challenge of marketing academic library services and gives overviews from some of the key players in the field [1]. One of the centres of excellence profiled is Oxford Brookes University Library. The Library's Marketing Group was the winner of the CILIP (Chartered Institute of Library and Informational Professionals)/Emerald Public Relations and Publicity Award for its imaginative "Inspiration" campaign.

MANAGING MARKETING AT OXFORD BROOKES UNIVERSITY LIBRARY

The key to (our) success in marketing the Library at Oxford Brookes University is a co-ordinated, business-like approach. Although everyone in the Library has a marketing responsibility (we all have customers, we are all ambassadors), the marketing *function* is managed by the Library's Marketing Group.

This Functional Group was set up in 2000, alongside a number of other "Fun" Groups (as they as known) to manage some of the more traditional aspects of our work (such as the areas taken on by the Information Skills Group, the Web Group, the Enquiry Services Group and the Collection Development Group) plus explore new departures for Oxford Brookes University Library: special collections; virtual learning; increased research support; raising disability awareness issues; and so on. Employing a matrix management approach, these groups took staff from the Library's departmental teams to develop new services and take the Library's portfolio forward.

The aims and objectives of each Group are set down in the Group's remit. For the Marketing Group they read thus:

- To take responsibility for the co-ordination of marketing at Oxford Brookes University Library and its services, focusing particularly on: staff training, publications, marketing programmes, and PR initiatives;
- To identify the needs of different groups of Library stakeholders and develop services (in conjunction with appropriate colleagues) to meet these needs. Particular use will be made of: focus groups, suggestion forms, questionnaires, and informal feedback mechanisms;
- To improve communication with all the Library's stakeholders, using various methods including: Library newsletters, targeted communications, electronic publications, and informal networks;
- To raise the profile of the Library within the University and the wider LIS/ HE sector by publishing and promoting the Library in appropriate form;
- To keep abreast of developments in the field of marketing and to feed these into the Library's working practices as appropriate.

The Marketing Group first met in January 2000. Although there have been changes in personnel over the last four years, some things have remained constant. The Group is not just made up of our main site staff: all sites and departments are represented. It is not just made up of 'front of house' staff: subject staff and the Lending Services Librarian work alongside the Head of Cataloguing and colleagues in Acquisitions. Probably most important of all, it is not just librarians in the Marketing Group. At Brookes there is not a huge divide between the work of librarians and library assistants. Library assistants are invariably seen as just as important in developing services as the (so called) 'professional staff'. This is particularly the case with marketing. If true marketing is customer-focused, library assistants are often better placed to be customer-focused than some other staff, simply because they spend more time *with* the customers.

SO HOW DOES THE MARKETING GROUP AT BROOKES ENSURE ITS REMIT IS FULFILLED?

The Functional Groups–just like the Library's Departmental Teams- operate a planning cycle approach. At the beginning of the year we compile an Operational Plan, outlining all the things we hope to achieve over the coming twelve months. At the end of the year, we look back at the Plan, reflect on (and celebrate) our successes in an Annual Report, and carry anything that has not been achieved over into the Operational Plan for the following year. In between these milestones, the Group has regular (formal) meetings and on-going (less formal) pushes to take our business forwards.

The other thing we have is a budget. In our first year we had no funds allocated to marketing and "made do" with petty cash. We were relatively successful with this approach but we felt we could do better if we had some monies that we knew we could devote to marketing initiatives. Hence, for Year Two we made a case to Senior Management for an annual allocation. This proved successful so we now receive a modest–but essential- budget of £600 pa.

All of this–the allocation of staff time (Functional Group work appears as a line in job descriptions), a specified budget and a planning cycle approach- has helped make the Marketing Group the success it is.

SUCCESSES TO DATE

Establishing customer needs

True marketing is all about having a customer-focus. The textbook definition of "marketing", from the Chartered Institute of Marketing reads "Marketing is the management process that identifies, anticipates and supplies customer requirements efficiently and profitably"[2]. Note: "*identifies*". More specifically, Baker's 'four essential features' of marketing are:

1. Start with the customer
2. A long-run perspective
3. Full use of all the company's resources
4. Innovation [3]

By its nature, the Marketing Group (with its planning approach, budget and sparky staff) aims to supply points 2, 3 and 4. But point 1 is most important of all and that is why it features so prominently in our remit.

Although we have run polls and provide an on-going suggestions service, successes in establishing customer needs have been largely focused-to date-on focus groups. Some of these have been general (promoted to staff and students at all levels and covering the spectrum of library services) whilst others have been subject-specific, sometimes tied in with quality assessment programmes or aimed at particular segments of our customer-base (e.g. researchers). Service enhancements that have come directly from customer comments include the repositioning of the photocopier card re-charger machines and the re-subscription to *Art Abstracts* (a particular concern raised at a Fine Art focus group).

In 2003, a Learning Resources-wide (the Library and Computer Services are a converged service at Brookes) Customer Care Group was set. Part of the Group's remit concerns market research, and this is how we will take this forwards. A questionnaire was launched recently, with focus groups planned to pursue identified "hot topics" further.

Branding ...and re-branding

One of the first things the Marketing group did was consider the Library's brand. The old Library "logo" was composed of the word "Library" repeated five times in a box (Fig. 1).

Fig. 1 : The Old Library logo

This was starting to look a bit tired so in 2000 we set about establishing a new brand. To encapsulate our hybrid future (part e-delivery, part traditional) the Group came up with a new logo made up of the word "library" from our URL ("/library/") surrounded by a bookshelf motif (Fig. 2).

Fig. 2: The New Logo...

This was used in all publications, with a blue version for general guides, a green one for subject guides, a pink variety for journals lists, plus an adapted header for the Library News (Fig. 3).

Fig. 3: ...on The Library News

The logo was also adopted on our Web site (with a new "Welcome to the Library" front page (Fig. 4)), used on pens promoting our URL and provided the sign that appears over the front door of our Headington Library (Fig. 5).

In 2003, the University as a whole went through a re-branding exercise so it was all change again. The Marketing Group worked with colleagues in the University's Corporate Affairs Department to

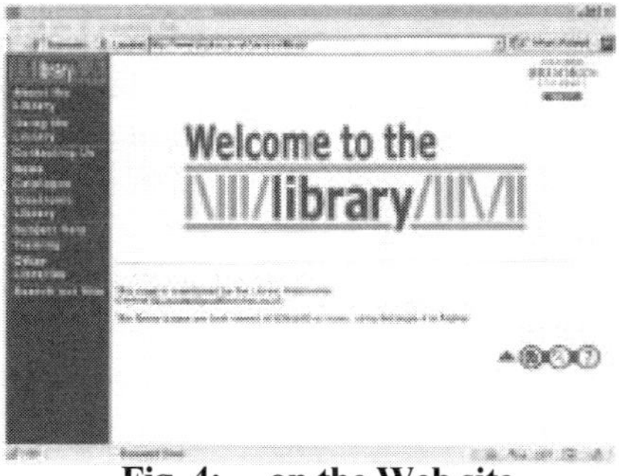

Fig. 4: ...on the Web site

Fig. 5: ...on the Library sign

develop new branding within University guidelines and then promote (correct) use by colleagues Library-wide.

Consistency of Style

But branding is only half the story. To give a professional impression, there must be a consistency of style in everything an organisation produces. Even after newly branded paper was produced in 2000, we could still find a variety of styles at play in the Library. Some guides were in Ariel font, others were in Times New Roman. Some were justified, others aligned to the left. Some had titles in bold, minimum caps, whilst others screamed in underlined capitals. Something had to be done!

The Marketing Group compiled a Style Manual. This guide to good practice covers typography and terminology, with guidelines illustrated by annotated examples. Colleagues who found header sizes a headache, were never bold enough to use bold or always queried whether it should be the Enquiry Desk or Information Point, have taken this to heart and publications now have a more consistent, corporate feel.

Revitalising Publications

Whilst we are on publications, one of the Marketing Group's most practical achievements came with the establishment of a Publications Sub-Group which set about revitalising Library publications in 2003. The Sub-Group did two simple – but essential-things. Firstly, it reviewed the management of publications. In the past there was no central organisation overseeing supply and demand. As a result, some guides would be constantly running out, with emergency copies being produced whilst we waited for the University's Print Room to supply a new batch. Alternatively, some guides would be printed at the beginning of the year, sit on the shelves and then be destroyed (once information had become out-dated) at the end of the year. The Sub-Group reviewed administration and monitored *actual* demand on a title-by-title basis to provide a truer picture so print runs could be increased (or reduced) for the following year.

The other thing the Sub-Group did was to compile a master list of all publications produced by the Library (no mean feat!), number them, and then review what was relevant, what could be dropped, what could be augmented and what could be pruned. Our Lending Services Librarian proved particularly fierce with her blue pencil! As a result, although we developed some new guides (like the newly branded all-in-one student guide (Fig. 6), overall we trimmed our portfolio, leaving it more lean, mean …and read.

Fig. 6: The newly re-branded student guide

Developing Displays

Displays are one of the cheapest– and most effective-marketing tools open to libraries. Our Library has always had display space but this has been woefully under-exploited.

To promote use, the Marketing Group has developed a Displays Calendar. This guide fulfils two functions. Firstly, it provides booking sheets for all the display areas in the Library. Not only does this enable us to avoid clashes, it also places a "value" on display space. Secondly–and more importantly- the calendar offers *opportunities* for displays. We already knew about-and made good use of-the obvious dates (Valentines Day allowed us to promote our poetry collections, World Aids Day the 616.9792 stock) but we felt that we may be missing out. In August 2002 we put a plea on the UK library discussion list lis-link (lis-link@jiscmail.ac.uk) for help. We were inundated with useful suggestions and compiled a list of sources of inspiration [4]. Nowadays,

National Bike Week, Farmhouse Breakfast Week and even British Cheese Week are all suitably celebrated. Not only does this make the Library look a lot brighter (Fig. 7), it means the stock gets promoted and used. At the bottom line, this is what marketing libraries is largely about.

Supporting Other Functional Groups

But it is not just about books. Why develop new services if they do not get used? The success of the Functional Groups can be largely measured by the new services they now offer: rejuvenated induction tours, subject surgeries and research sessions from the Information Skills Group; a new, improved Web site from the Web Group; newly accessible special collections managed by the Special Collections Group; and so on.

The Marketing Group has worked with these colleagues to help promote theirgood works. For the Information Skills Group, we produce displays, flyers

Fig. 7: Library Assistant Maureen Davies surveys a display to promote a new Film Studies course at Brookes

and newsletter entries to promote induction tours, generic surgeries, dissertation workshops and research sessions. Attendance at each of these continues to increase, rising from a mere handful to room capacity for some recent sessions.

We worked with the Web Group on our award-winning "Inspiration" campaign to promote our re-launched Web site in 2001[5]. Since then, we have used pens, posters and (re-branded) publications to keep promoting our URL. The hit rate for the site continues to increase, doubling in hits with a high-profile re-launch and markedly growing each year with further promotion to Freshers. Over the last year, the site has regularly received over 300,000 visits per month.

Fig. 8: Library "beer mats"

Latterly, we have started to work more with the Special Collections Group. Space in the Library is at an absolute premium. If these collections of old books, letters and other ephemera are to earn their shelf space they need to be used. We now find ourselves marketing them to internal customers (special collections are a standing item in the *Library News*) and external customers. Beer mats/coasters used to promote the Library at the 2003 Freshers' Fair have the dual purpose of also promoting one such special collection, the National Brewing Library (Fig. 8). Cheekily we sent beer mats to a variety of brewing trade journals. Intrigued by our approach, the Institute and Guild of Brewing's *The Brewer International* and Campaign for Real Ale's *What's Brewing* have run stories on our campaign resulting in a lot of approaches from professionals wishing to use the NBL (…not to mention a few requests from landlords for beer mats!)

INCREASING AWARENESS AMONGST LIBRARY COLLEAGUES OF THE NEED FOR MARKETING

One small–but hugely significant-change is the attitude of colleagues to marketing. There is invariably still some hostility/coolness to marketing concepts in the Library world. Colleagues are not always comfortable with the "m" word.

At Brookes, I am pleased to say such reticence has largely melted away. Admittedly, some colleagues are less keen on us using the "c" word when referring to our readers/users as "customers", but the general principles of marketing are embraced and "we must, of course, market this" is now a regular cry at meetings.

USING PR EVENTS TO PROMOTE THE LIBRARY INTERNALLY: FRESHERS' FAIR CAMPAIGNS

Fig. 9: The author enjoys a quiet afternoon at Freshers' Fair with Marketing Group colleagues Ruth Wilkinson and Linda Dixon

The Marketing Group's greatest success, though, must be in the field of Public Relations activities, notably our Freshers' Fair programmes.

For perhaps the obvious reasons, academic librarians have been slow to grasp the opportunity offered by Freshers' Fair. For the uninitiated, Freshers' Fair is typically held at the end of Freshers' Week, the period set aside by British universities to induct new students into the ways of university life. After registration and enrolment, sorting out timetables and finance, students are given time to turn their attention to what really matters at Freshers' Fair: how they are going to fill their non-timetabled, non-working life. Of course, societies, clubs and pubs tend to dominate Freshers Fair. But why should libraries not also compete for the students' valuable time?

Our first foray into this world came in September 2000 when we employed a Dracula campaign (Fig. 10) to: market the Library generally; highlight the network of subject support available from the Subject Teams; and promote the Library's enhanced induction tours programme as developed by our Information Skills Group.

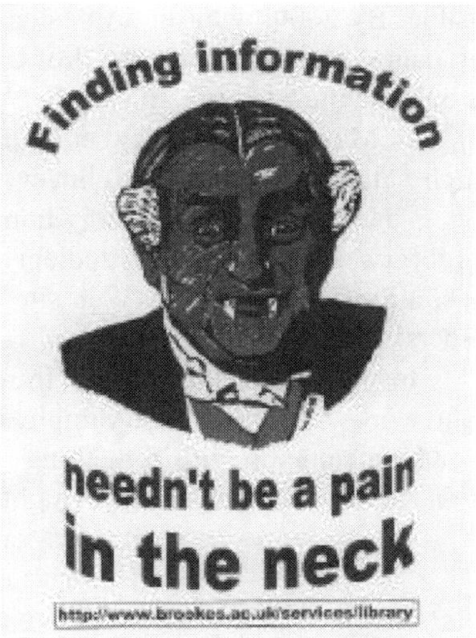

Fig. 10: The Library's Freshers' Fair poster campaign for 2000

Despite initial reservations by the Group (would students really be interested in visiting a Library stand when we were competing with the Dangerous Sports Club, free drinks from the local night club promoters and cheap posters of Brad Pitt and Madonna?) we felt the stall proved a success. In less than five hours we spoke to between 500 and 600 potential customers, many of whom would not normally attend a Library induction tour. This seemed a cost effective way of promoting services and making it clear that the Library is an integral part of the whole Brookes experience for a student. We were hence keen to make Freshers' Fair a regular part of our marketing programme.

THE KEY THINKS WE LEARNT FROM OUR FIRST APPEARANCE

Abstruse campaigns are good – Opting for a Dracula display rather than an earnest "Library" display (which would have been actively avoided by most students) worked well.

You need something to give away: you need "freebies" – Freshers' Fair is partly about getting a bag full of goodies, mementoes to remind the student of their whirlwind visit. In 2000 we gave away bookmarks. These worked well ...but you expect a librarian to give you bookmarks. Something less obvious, more memorable was required for 2001.

As anyone familiar with the '4Ps' of the marketing mix knows, "product" is essential ...but what product? - Despite giving out handfuls of flyers for tours we found that, by the time Freshers' Fair had come around at the *end* of Week 0, most of the students who were going to take a tour of the University Library had already done so. For 2001, then, a different product was required.

So what should we promote in Freshers' Fair 2001? In truth, we did not have to think too long and hard about this. As with most academic libraries, Brookes has invested heavily in providing Internet solutions to meet our customers' information needs, offering off-site access to databases and e-journals wherever possible. By 2000, with the explosion of information available via the Library's Web pages, a complete overhaul of the site was required. As mentioned earlier, this became the key objective of the Web Functional Group.

In May 2001, the new site was launched. There had been a successful launch campaign at the time, but we felt more could be done to promote the service. New students–some of whom might not always want to *physically* visit the Library-would be an ideal audience to hear about just what our new, improved site could offer. Hence our Web site became the product we would promote at Freshers' Fair 2001.

Inspiration for the theme of the campaign came quickly one morning on the way to work. After last year's vampires we wanted something a bit more subtle. In the end we came up with something very simple that felt like a cross between a Calvin Klein perfume advert and a night club flyer. Newton's apple, Rodin's Thinker and various other striking, thought-provoking images (to be photographed against a plain white background) would simply accompany the legend "inspiration ...available now from the library" and our URL, www.brookes.ac.uk/services/library.

These images appeared on posters (alongside the other designs (Fig. 11)).

Fig. 11: The "Inspiration" campaign posters

The Library Web site, the front of the *Library News,* and Freshers' Fair T-shirts (Fig. 12).

As well as posters, we decided that we should add "freebies" to give away to our 2001 portfolio. As well as the (tried and tested) bookmarks from 2000, the Marketing Group decided it needed to continue with the apple theme. One of the University's strategic priorities is to promote healthy living. What could be more healthy than giving out apples? Our initial plan was to give them away with special stickers attached promoting our URL. Sadly, despite much detective work and perseverance, we were unable to do this. In the end we produced stickers to stick on humans (in red and green, very much in the style of their fruit-affixed sisters) with drawings of apples, our URL and the message "be inspired" (Fig. 13).

Fig. 12: The author models the campaign T-shirt at the Library's Freshers' Fair stall

Fig. 13: The Campaign Stickers

Freshers' Fair fell on Saturday 29 September 2001. Five members of the Marketing Group spent two hours each timetabled throughout the day promoting the Web site and other Library services to as many students as possible.

So was it worth it? This was without doubt a highly effective and highly cost-effective campaign. The outlay was a limited amount of staff time (in the summer vacation when pressures are generally less on Library staff) and a financial investment of less than £400 (see Table-1). Take-up on the day was impressive. Again we managed to speak to c.600 people in a few hours. The apples were immensely popular: we could have easily given away 500 instead of the 250 we had procured (and had to effectively ration to see us through the day). The stickers proved popular also and beneficial in ways we had not anticipated: they provided a good ice-breaker; they allowed us to see whom we had already spoken to; and they made the "bright young things" a walking billboard for the Library.

Table-1 : Costs for the 2001 campaign

Expenditure	*Cost (£)*
Posters (quantity: 60)	90.00
T-shirts (5)	64.95
Stickers (1,000)	145.00
Apples (250)	28.50
Stall rental	50.00
Photographs (for artwork/post-event publicity)	10.98
TOTAL COST	**£389.43**

But did the campaign achieve its objective of promoting the Library Web site? The new-look Web site proved a massive success with our customers, with a huge increase in hit rates recorded following the launch campaign (May 2001) and especially following the "Inspiration" campaign (September 2001 onwards). The launch of the new look site (on 8 May) saw the number of hits virtually double "over night", shooting up from 73,000 in April 2001 to 133,600 in May. Since then there has continued to be a huge month-on-month increase in visits to our site compared with the previous year, reaching a massive 180,927 hits for October 2001 –the month following our "inspirational" Freshers' Fair appearance- three times that of October 2000's total (65,192).

USING PR-EVENTS TO PROMOTE THE LIBRARY EXTERNALLY: AWARDS

Hosting the stall on 29 September was not the end of the campaign, though. As stated above, one of the objectives of the Marketing Group (Point 4) is "to raise the profile of the Library within the University and the wider LIS/HE sector by publishing and promoting the Library in appropriate fora." Following our success at Freshers Fair we ran a follow-up story on the front of the *Library News*/Library Web site thanking students for visiting the stall and reinforcing the messages we were trying to get across on the day. In the wider LIS sector we submitted news stories/photo stories about the Inspiration Campaign to *The Bookseller* and the *Library Association Record* [6]. Once the effects of the campaign had become apparent, fuller articles covering the planning process and results were put together for the *SCONUL Newsletter*, *Managing Information* and *Public Eye* (see Publications list below). Details of the campaign have also subsequently been covered in workshops ran by the author (see list of Papers Presented, below).

When the CILIP/Emerald Public Relations and Publicity Awards were announced we saw this as another good opportunity to tell colleagues about the good work Oxford Brookes University Library's Marketing Group is doing. The entry required four elements:

Part 1 : promotional objectives of the campaign

Part 2 : how these objectives were met

Part 3 : project budget

Part 4 : printed materials

As well as providing text under these headings, artwork (in A4 and laminated A3 posters), photographs, articles and internal documents were supplied to give a fuller picture of the campaign.

It was with great honour (and some surprise) that we received the Award for a "promotional campaign with a budget under £500" from Sheila Corrall, President of CILIP at the Landmark Hotel in London on 1 November 2002 (Fig. 14).

Fig. 14 : The author and Linda Dixon of the Marketing Group receive their CILIP/ Emerald Award

As a result of the Award, the Marketing Group received coverage on the front of the University's staff newsletter, in the local newspaper, the *Oxford Mail*, the *Times Higher Educational Supplement*, *CILIP Update* and the CILIP Web site, the *SCONUL Newsletter* and *PR Week* [7]. The author was also invited to lecture further on the campaign and write a piece for *New Library World* [8].

FUTURE PLANS

As is beholden on a marketer, I hope I have highlighted our successes and blown the Marketing Group's trumpet suitably hard. But a marketing librarians' work is never done and already the Group is making plans for the future. We have just embarked on a relationship with a UK promotions company, You[th] Media, to produce bookmarks (Fig. 15) and carrier bags (Fig. 16) to promote our services. Special collections are likely to take up even more of our time and we alr eady have some pretty exciting plans to promote some of our history of medicine collections. Overall, though, we also need an annual report to bring records of all our successes together in one document. After all, marketing is partly about showing people just what a good job you are already doing ...as I hope this article has shown!

Fig. 15 : Bookmarks advertising self-service facilities

Fig. 16: Our latest carrier bag design

REFERENCES AND NOTES

1. SCONUL Focus, Spring 2004, issue 31 is available via www.sconul.ac.uk.
2. Chartered Institute of Marketing, see, for example, www.cim.co.uk/cim/ser/html/infQuiGlo.cfm?letter=M.
3. Baker (M J). The marketing book. Oxford: Heinemann. 1987 : 8.
4. These were summarised for the list ("Happy Days are here again", posted 23 August 2003) and can be found at http://www.jiscmail.ac.uk/cgi-bin/wa.exe?A2=ind0208&L=lis-link&P=R13222&I=1.
5. Brewerton (A). Making our Web site a hit: How Oxford Brookes University weaved a Web marketing programme. *Managing Information*. 9 (1). January/February 2002 : 34-35.
6. *Library Association Record*. 103 (11). November 2001: 649.
7. Library cash. *Oxford Mail*. 22 November 2002: 4; Thinker helps Website to win PR award, *Times Higher Educational Supplement*. 8 November 2002: 2; "Public relations and publicity", *CILIP Update*. 1 (9). December 2002: 11; see also Libraries lead the way in innovative and imaginative marketing and publicity: www.cilip.org.uk/news/021101d.html ; The CILIP/Emarald Public Relations and Publicity Awards, Category 1: Promotional Campaigns with a budget under £500: www.cilip.org.uk/practice/awards/prpa/cat1_2002.html; *SCONUL Newsletter. 27.* Winter 2002: 94; News in brief: libraries. *PR Week.* 8 November 2002: 5.
8. Inspired! Award-winning library marketing. *New Library World*. 104 (7/8). August 2003 : 267-277.

THE POWER CARD CHALLENGE : MARKETING THE HOUSTON PUBLIC LIBRARY

Andrea Lapsley

Abstract *With the Power Card Challenge, Houston Public Library created a program that redefined library card campaigns, gave the Library a brand and identity in the community through a new library card design and graphics, a well-defined marketing/publicity campaign, and provided a model for other communities to replicate. This article takes the reader through the formation of the campaign, goals, partnerships, budgets and much more.*

INTRODUCTION

For the Houston Public Library, marketing is defined as the integration of a wide variety of disciplines, such as market research, public relations, advertising, promotion, publicity, and customer service into a single plan which creates the action that draws the consumer into the library, creates a patron out of them and keeps them coming back. The Power Card Challenge allowed the entire Library to use all these elements in launching an exciting library card registration campaign.

The campaign was also successful because the Library was able to blend the characteristics of a market driven yet mission-based organization. Those being:

- Know the Markets: We realized that markets extend beyond just the people we currently serve. We identified, quantified, and targeted the markets that we wanted to serve.
- Treat Everyone Like a Customer: Funders, board, staff and people that receive services were all thought of and treated like customers. Customer service and rapid response became a top priority.
- Have Everyone on the Marketing Team: We worked work to develop the attitude that everyone, every staff person and every volunteer was crucial to the success of the organizations' marketing, its customer service and its competitive edge.
- Ask, Ask, Ask, and then listen: We shaped our services to meet customers needs, and then constantly asked customers in order to stay in tune with how those needs changed and developed.
- Innovate Constantly: To respond to changing market conditions and customers needs we became extremely flexible with staff encouraged to take reasonable risks on behalf of the people that they serve.

Results of being market driven are

- You will have happier markets. If you ask, listen, and then make reasonable effort to accommodate the wants people have, they will have a better feeling about you.
- Your organization will have a better image in the community. People will associate your organization as one that is using their money in a more efficient, effective manner. You will have a higher visibility because you will be out there asking all the time. You can gain a reputation as being a responsive organization.
- You will retain your current markets. By doing good marketing now, not after the competition has shown up, you will cement long-term relationships with your core markets.
- Your organization will be more efficient and effective in providing services. You will be doing things that your markets want, not what they don't want. You can be more focused with dollars and staff.
- You will develop new revenue sources. Success breeds success.

THE CHALLENGE

So what led the Houston Public Library to put all their talent and resources into a library card registration campaign and how was it structured? At his inauguration in 1998, Mayor Lee P. Brown stood before Houstonians, dedicated his administration to the children of Houston and said:

> *"... Books were the first rungs on the ladder I, like many others, used to climb out of poverty ... Now, it is my goal to see that every school- age child in Houston gets a library card."*

Although Houston Public Library had previously promoted Library Card Sign-up Month, Mayor Brown's campaign promise challenged the Library to achieve unprecedented results. This meant reaching new customers, redefining how we did outreach to our community, examining the roles of each staff member, emphasizing customer service at all levels and identifying how we would market and brand our Library. With one statement from our Mayor, the Power Card Challenge was set into motion and three years of hard work began.

Quickly a committee of key staff members was formed to oversee this ambitious project. The members included the Assistant Director of Library Operations, the Assistant Director of Marketing, the Manager of Youth Services, the Manager of Programming, the Chief of Technical Services, the Public Information Officer, and a project manager. Other staff members joined the core group as needed over the course of the project. A review of professional literature provided no examples or models for a project of this magnitude. This group was charged with designing the blueprint for success.

ANSWERING THE CHALLENGE

Goals for the campaign were immediately set: the first, to increase the number of children with library cards accessing library materials to improve their school work; and second, to develop lifetime readers, thereby insuring educated and productive future generations. The three-year campaign set specific goals for juvenile registration and circulation each year with the final numeric goal of increasing juvenile registrations from a little over 100,000 to 303,000 and increasing juvenile circulation by 30 percent.

Setting measurable objectives for each year was critical not only in setting our course, but for us to create a marketing and promotion plan to ensure that the objectives were met. Objectives for the first year were as follows:

- Give a temporary Library card (an application/informational flier with the new Library card design) to every school-age child in Houston, approximately 500,000.
- Encourage all kids to "activate" their "card" and double the number of juvenile cardholders to 200,000 by June 30, 1999.
- Increase juvenile circulation at least 20% from July 1998-June 1999.

Objectives for the second year and third years were as follows

- Increase the number of juvenile cardholders to 240,000 by June 30, 2000.
- Increase juvenile circulation by 10% from July 1999-June 2000.
- Increase the use of juvenile electronic resources and youth web pages by 10%.
- Increase current juvenile cardholders to 303,000 by June 30, 2001.
- Increase juvenile circulation by 5% to 2,960,000 items.
- Increase the number of juvenile borrowers with items checked out to 45,000 based on a monthly average. The benchmark in FY00 was 41,000.

It was quickly evident that the Library budget could not absorb the cost of the campaign. When the campaign was announced, the Library was already half way through the fiscal year. Funders and partners at all levels would have to be secured and the Mayor would have to back up his words with action. He followed through with a 13 percent in the operating budget with funds allocated for more staff, equipment, materials, printing and promotion.

Although the target audience was children, it was unrealistic to believe that we could reach every child in the Houston area in a three-year period. In order to be successful we decided to concentrate on children in our largest school district, Houston Independent School District (HISD). According to research done for the Library's Strategic Master Plan, Houston exceeds the national average by 20 percent in the number of children under the age of 15. Additionally, the research shows that Houstonians are somewhat below national averages in library usage, library card ownership and frequency of use. Hispanic Houstonians are the most underserved compared to their numbers. Approximately 55 percent of all HISD students are Hispanic. It was also clear that we would have to translate our materials into Spanish and customize our plan to reach the Hispanic market.

When the planning began for this program, demographic research determined that there were 512,717 children living in the areas served by Houston Public Library's (HPL) 34 branches and Central Library. In 1998 as the campaign started, a little over 100,000 children held library cards with the Library traditionally registering 45,000 new juvenile library cards annually. To move from 100,000 to 300,000 in three years required a new way of doing business.

Other target audiences identified were parents, grandparents, teachers and caregivers of such children, so that the required signatures could be obtained and the applications returned to the Library. A list of potential partners including community organizations, businesses, schools, city government and the media was created to help the Library extend the reach of such an ambitious campaign.

The next order of business was to agree on the strategies needed to accomplish the objectives. These were:

- Create a "product" with name brand identity that would appeal to the targeted markets.
- Identify and recruit several key players to augment the campaign and encourage others to follow suit, adding "value" to the product whenever possible.
- Lobby City Council to waive the non-resident fee, at least for children, in the areas surrounding the Houston City limits.
- Launch a massive public relations campaign to establish and reinforce the message.
- Increase the kinds of materials that would appeal to kids in sufficient quantities, so they will be attracted to the Library and effectively market the collection in-house.

CREATING THE POWER CARD

With our work plan in place the Power Card Challenge came alive. The next step was to create a new library card. The current Library card was simple, on tan paper, and had no graphics other than the Library's logo. Certainly that would not do for this energetic and ambitious campaign. The Library wanted to create a card and brand that would set this Library apart, identify with the power of information and the powerful resources located within each Library, and be something that children would want to have. In thinking about potential sponsors the local power company, Reliant Energy (providing both electricity and gas), came to the forefront. Our first and most successful partnership was secured. Reliant Energy's creative staff worked with HPL to create a new Library card and give it a new name, the Power Card. The brightly colored contemporary swirl design, implying energy and excitement, was designed to appeal to kids. On the card, Reliant's designer created a generic, politically correct image, the Power Card Critter, a running, winking eye holding a book. Both images, the colorful swirl and the Critter could be used together or separately. The slogan "Pack the Power" was chosen, with the sub line "Small enough to fit into your wallet, big enough to change your life." Everything that was produced, print, electronically, on the Web, or other formats all included these new elements. Applications, event fliers, T-shirts, stickers all sported the logo and colors. Even documents such as fax cover sheets, stationary, etc. carried the logo. The Power Card became a new product and the brand of the Houston Public Library.

THE CAMPAIGN

The campaign was kicked-off with a high-energy press conference followed by a celebratory partner appreciation breakfast and press conference a year later. After the third year, a huge celebration in the Central Library touted our success. For the final celebration a huge balloon arch was formed with the numbers 303,000 on the top. Mardi Gras bead necklaces were purchased in Power Card colors to have a strong visual to remind the media, our partners and our staff just what a remarkable accomplishment this number was. The beads were counted on a single necklace and enough necklaces purchased so 303,000 beads were hung over the second floor balcony, with each bead representing a juvenile Power Card holder.

The Mayor became the key spokesperson for the Power Card Challenge in speeches, Public Service Ads (PSAs), and press conferences, and was the subject of photos used in brochures and a life-size cut-out of himself. In all his speeches, Mayor Brown reminded the audience that "knowledge is power" and he proudly took his Power Card from his suit pocket and announced that he "Packed the Power" and challenged the audience to do the same. The High Impact Squad, a team of acrobatic, slam-dunking super heroes, was featured in PSAs and many events. Local media figures made celebrity appearances and supported the Power Card on the air. All printed materials were produced in both English and Spanish.

To facilitate outreach to youth throughout the Power Card Challenge, Mayor Brown supported the waiver in July of 1998 of the non-resident fee for library cards for children 18 years of age and younger living in Harris and the contiguous counties, Brazoria, Chambers, Fort Bend, Galveston, Liberty, Montgomery and Waller. This was remarkable for several reasons. The City charged $40 a year for a Library card to non-residents. The waiver of this fee meant reduced revenue for the City. By extending the waiver to children in the surrounding counties, the Mayor made a clear statement on how important Library services were to this community. This waiver was successful for registering children, but still provided some obstacles. Children needed their parents to bring them to the Library. That was not happening if the parent could not get a Library card. Families wanted to use the resources of our Library. So a year later, in July of 1999, the City Council waived the fee for adults in the same eight county area, allowing Houston Public Library to serve the larger regional economic area. This enabled anyone with a Power Card and access to a computer to go to our Web site and use our databases and resources. Even though they might not drive to one of our locations they could now access us remotely.

In order to achieve the large number of registration necessary the Library conducted unprecedented outreach in the community. We started with the schools. Power Card applications and a letter from the Library Director were included in the "first day" school packages for all HISD students, along with permission slips and school information parents received Power Card applications. Teachers and school librarians were not required to collect applications, but asked that students and parents visit the Library to get their Power Card. Staff from HPL did follow-up with the schools and also did hundreds of onsite registrations.

After HISD, other local schools became a primary target for Library outreach. Within its boundaries, Houston has eleven different school districts. Private and parochial schools were included in the campaign. The target audience from these school districts and other schools was an additional 120,000. Staff attended assemblies, in-service workshops and school special events. During Read Across America Day, staff members from every branch visited at least one school to promote the Power Card. Banners proclaiming "Our School Packs the Power" were created for schools who achieved signing up 90 percent of their students with a Power Card. A healthy competition began between schools and they started challenging each other and creating their own Power Card registration events. School librarians and administrators were real champions and allies of the Power Card Challenge.

Schools were not the only avenue to reach kids. Library staff manned sign-up booths at Houston Astros (baseball) games, the Houston Livestock Show and Rodeo, community festivals, summer lunch programs, health fairs, grocery stores, and shopping malls. Corporations offered Power Card sign ups for their staff. Groups such as the Girl Scouts, Boy Scouts Boys, and Girls Clubs and many others distributed applications and promoted getting a Power Card through their newsletters. The Library sent out a mailing to more than 350 social service agencies in Houston that served youth asking them to answer the Power Card Challenge. Contests, parade participation, and tie-ins to existing Library events further touted the Power Card. Citywide festivals were some of the most successful in terms of registrations. Participation in more than 500 outreach events took the Library message to the community. Where people were gathering, the Houston Public Library was there touting the Power Card and Library services.

PARTNERSHIPS AND PROMOTION

Partnerships became critical in getting our message out to the public and to assist with funding. Partnerships with other city departments abounded. Juvenile court offenders were required to get Power Cards, members of the Houston Fire Department did storytimes, applications were handed out in the Houston Police Department's anti-drug program, the Parks Department signed kids up for Power Cards at community centers, and the Health Department hosted sign-ups at clinics. Corporate partners ranged from the title sponsor, Reliant Energy, to individual branch partnerships with local businesses. Cultural organizations joined in, as the Museum of Fine Arts and the Children's Museum of Houston offered free admission for Power Cardholders. With Mayor Brown's support, the Challenge has involved businesses, schools, community groups, cultural organizations, city departments and staff to make library services to youth a top priority for all.

During the three-year Power Card Challenge, nearly 300 partnering organizations participated, contributing more than $1,535,000 in donations and in-kind services. Banners were created and hung in the lobby recognizing out partners and their contribution to this important project and they were recognized on the Web site.

Besides the usual press releases, brochures, posters, newsletters and fliers, the Power Card Challenge was featured in Reliant's Power Page bill insert, reaching more than 1 million customers two separate times. The Library used billboards for the first time as a way of getting the message out into the community. Over the course of the campaign, two separate sets of billboards were produced in English and Spanish. The first message was "Get a Library Card." The second message was "Get It. Got it? Use It!" Each billboard featured the image of the Power Card, the Library's phone number and the Web address. The major daily newspaper ran editorials in support of the Power Card, feature articles and the application form. Neighborhood newspapers ran photos and stories. A monthly newspaper for kids, Kid'n Around, featured the Power Card in each issue. Library publications all took on the Power Card look with the colors, the logo, or using the word " Power." Partners routinely ran articles on the Power Card Challenge in their newsletters, membership fliers, and their Web sites were linked to the Library. Materials were produced in Spanish to reach Houston's large Hispanic population.

Media partnerships created six new PSAs for television. Radio campaigns tied the Power Card to paid advertising by corporate sponsors such as Coca-Cola and McDonalds. The Power Card was featured on school book covers and bookmarks, promoted on the local ABC Channel and distributed at Kroger Stores as part of ABC's "Children First" campaign. This marketing approach represented a new way for a City agency to "do business" by developing true partnerships. The Power Card was the topic of one segment of Houston's public access television show, "Today's Library," and was integrated into the others. Time Warner Cable created PSA's and ran them on their more than 50 local channels. A large section of the Library's Web site was devoted to the PCC and listservs were set-up to keep staff and partners informed. Web pages were created to document every step of the Power Card Challenge. Photos were posted. Programs, services and materials were touted. The current registration count was listed as well as funders and partners being acknowledged. A Power Point presentation and a companion video were produced for community outreach and presentations.

Merchandise was yet another vehicle to get out message out that had not been tried before. T-shirts were created with the Power Card Critter and given to all staff, media, and local partners. Everywhere in Houston the bright orange color, the swirl design or the Critter was showing up. Watches were purchased with the Power Card design on the face and given to partners. During the third year of the campaign the T-shirts, watches, caps and polo shirts were made available for purchase to the public through the Library and as part of the merchandise in the City of Houston's Convention & Entertainment store.

Another promotional item created over the span of the campaign was 1 million stickers. Each sticker was the colorful Power Card swirl. These were used at outreach events, used in craft projects, on Library displays, etc. Children and staff created earrings, necklaces, bracelets, covered pencil holders and other unique items using these stickers and other craft materials.

TIME LINE AND LOGISTICS

The plan called for Phase-I to begin in the spring of 1998 with school outreach for the Summer Reading Program. Phase-II was to focus on the school campaign, from September 1998 through June 1999. Phase-III as follow-up beginning in July 1999, picking up those not reached through the previous two phases and continuing until June 2001. In reality, lead-time for development of the campaign, recruiting partners, the design and production of the print materials, and the hiring of additional key staff, eliminated Phase-I. The campaign began with a kick-off press conference on July 30, 1998, prior to the beginning of school. Phase-II began the second year, July 1999 with new goals and Phase-III in July 2000. The campaign ended June 30, 2001 successfully meeting all goals. The final press conference celebration rally was held August 28, 2001.

As the campaign and marketing program grew in the second and third years, it was evident that the seven initial team members needed additional support. After the first year an evaluation form was sent to each staff member and a full day retreat was held with 25 staff members to evaluate the progress and gather staff input before moving forward in the second year. It was clear that staff liked the campaign, felt good about the results and what they were doing, and wanted to take more control of the campaign within their unit. The Power Card Challenge had stretched the staff, but provided opportunities for creativity and a real connection with the community. Power Card teams were created in each of the Library's six regions. These teams consisted of six to 10 staff members from the branches in each of the regions. The teams set local goals for each branch, handled neighborhood outreach events, and customized Power Card activities suitable to each neighborhood. The steering committee continued to monitor the overall goals, ensure that the team activities supported the campaign, recruit additional partners and to oversee the promotion and publicity of the Power Card Challenge.

BUDGET

As stated, the Library's existing print budget was not enough to cover the many expenses and large quantities required for this campaign. The first printing of Power Card applications alone was 1 million copies. Additional books and materials were also needed for our new customers and staff was needed to select and process these materials. Additional City funding was requested in fiscal year 1998 and 1999. The total funds approved in FY98 $284,000 and $1,252,628 for FY99. No additional City dollars were requested during the final years of the campaign. As mentioned previously, cash and in-kind contributions from corporations and community organizations were more than $1.5 million, which included print materials, airtime, and incentives.

Overall city budget summary:

	FY98-99	**FY99-00**
PR Campaign	$ 34,000	$ 53,350
Library Cards	$ 15,000	$ 15,000
Books/Materials	$200,000	$500,000
Staff		$606,278
Equipment		$ 40,500
Postage		$ 2,500
Display Fixtures	$ 35,000	
	$ 284,000	**$1,252,628**

Overall Marketing/PR Budget

Applications	$ 27,289
Fliers	$ 5,851
Posters	$ 3,173
Banners	$ 3,500
Bookmarks	$ 1,000
T-shirts, watches	$ 14,600
Stationary, press kits	$ 2,405
Stickers	$ 3,900
Media Events/Photo	$ 9,869
Billboards	$ 23,000
Incentives	$ 21,287
Donor Recognition	$ 10,483
Misc	$ 872
	$ 127,229

EVALUATION

Evaluation began early and was an ongoing process as the Library continually monitored its communications and registrations. The messages and tools were fine-tuned for better communications. We discovered early that people didn't understand what a Power Card was, that it is the NEW Library card. Later, people began to think that it was just for kids. With adjustments in the message via press releases and speaking points and in media interviews and PSAs, the public understood and embraced the Power Card.

Another thing the steering committee discovered was that, initially, we had failed to include staff as a target audience. In a large system with more than 35 locations, it became imperative to make changes. Lines of communications were clarified, emphasizing the importance of the message to ALL staff. Managers were encouraged to include everyone on their staff in the program. Polo shirts initially meant for dignitaries and partners were awarded each month to staff members who had made outstanding contributions. This honor became known as the "Polo Club."

Clearly, measuring the success of the Power Card Challenge is in the numbers. A ten-foot tall stack of faux books in the lobby, the Tower of Power, showed how the numbers grew each month. One of the Power Card symbols, the "Critter," was moved up the stack each month to reflect the current number of juvenile registrations. This ceremonial moving of the "Critter" to indicate our progress was another source of pride and a PR opportunity. Sometimes staff members moved the "Critter", other times partners, or teams of staff members. Each was photographed and placed on our Web site and Intranet.

Houston Public Library met an overwhelming challenge and with the help of many enthusiastic partners exceeded the measurable objectives. Through monthly reports registration and circulation figures were monitored and measured. The waiver of the non-resident fees was certainly a factor in achieving the registration increases.

Recognition by colleagues in the library and public relations profession is certainly an indicator of success. In 1999, the Power Card Challenge was recognized as the Texas Library Association Project of the Year. The International Association of Business Communicators honored the innovative Power Card design with the First Place Bronze Quill Award for Illustration. Mayor Brown was honored by the Library Journal in 1998 as "A Politician Who Made a Difference" and then in 1999, took their ultimate honor, Politician of the Year, complete with a cover photo and feature story. In 2000 the Houston Press called the Power Card "the best thing any government agency has done for anybody in a long time." In 2000, the Public Relations Section of the American Library Association awarded the Power Card Challenge the prestigious John Cotton Dana Award. In August 2002, the campaign was honored with the first IFLA/3M Marketing Award at the IFLA conference in Glasgow, Scotland.

Media support was overwhelming, with radio and television pro bono airtime estimated at $300,000, well above the initial PR goal of $75,000. Six new PSAs were produced at no cost to the Library and were aired many, many times. The Hispanic media was very helpful, with about 33 percent of the overall coverage provided by the Hispanic media. The Power Card became the "feel good" story of the three-year campaign, with people clamoring to be affiliated with HPL as the successes grew.

One of the greatest indicators of success of the number of inquiries the Library has received about how to replicate this model for other communities. More than 100 cities have requested information and materials. Many have begun their own campaigns using the elements of the Power Card Challenge. Library staff has made presentations on the project at the American Library Association conference, the Public Library Association conference, numerous state conferences and for individual library systems. Articles have been written for numerous professional publications. A book by Neal-Schuman Publishers *How to Run a Successful Library Card Campaign* features the Power Card Challenge. The Neal-Schuman book, *Marketing for Libraries,* has just been updated and includes an entire case study of the Power Card Challenge.

Much less easy to measure is the growth in the community's pride in its Library. You see it in the little things: the excitement in a child's face as he pulls his Power Card from his wallet and reaches up to proudly hand it to the circulation clerk, or the sound of a child's voice across a crowded grocery store, "Look, Mom, It's the Power Card people!" The children of Houston are proud to own a Houston Public Library Card, the key to the powerhouse of information, the Library. Indeed, they "Pack the Power" with pride!

This was a project that truly united and energized staff and brought the Library to a new level within our community.

BEYOND THE POWER CARD CHALLENGE

The Houston Public Library's success with the Power Card Challenge moved the Library's marketing and public relations efforts to a new level that is continued today. The media partners recruited for the Power Card Challenge continue to support the Library and our many services. The media alone now donates more than $250,000 for the Summer Reading Program. The Library continued its success with billboards and placed more than 125 billboards in neighborhoods in 2003. Due to a reduced City budget no funds were allocated for billboards in the present budget. Thanks to the Power Card Challenge we created Power Plus Programs with local cultural organizations. The Power Card continues to give free juvenile admission every Saturday and Sunday at the Museum of Fine Arts, Houston. Free days are offered several times a years at the Children's Museum and a Power Card gives children free admission to the McGovern Museum of Health and Medicine any day of the week. The partnerships begun or strengthened by the Power Card Challenge continue to grow and expand. Even though the challenge of library card registration is over, the Library continues to work with these partners to enhance and strengthen programs. Not only do we want children to have a Power Card, but also we want them to come into the Library to use our resources and participate in educational programs. The Library was seen as an organization that could handle a major initiative and effectively reach the community. We are now sought out as a partner by other organizations. Our partners continue to help us get the message of the Library out into the community.

The Power Card Challenge really brought the Library to the forefront of local media. In the past year, media contacts have increased by 38 percent and media placements have increased by 25 percent. Our Web page is playing a stronger role in our marketing activity. Remote customers need the same information as customers who walk through our doors.

Private donations are more than $1 million annually. The Power Card Challenge showed the community the strong and important role the Library plays in the life of all citizens. Editorials continue to be written about the importance of the Library for quality of life in Houston. And urge citizens to support the Library with contributions of time and treasure.

Have we been able to maintain high number of juvenile Power Card holders? Truthfully, no. The Power Card is good for three years and then must be renewed. Since the Power Card Challenge ended in August 2001 we have lost approximately 40,000 of the more than 200,000 children we signed up with Power Cards. What were the reasons? Some of the children living outside Houston and using the Library remotely failed to renew their card. Many have moved away from the City. Since 2001, the City of Houston has gone through difficult financial times. The

Library budget has been cut by almost $4 million dollars and staff has been reduced. Our materials budget has been severely reduced. Hours of service have also been reduced. The combined effect has been limited community outreach. Some outreach is still done by our branches, but the strong school outreach and onsite registration efforts that were trademarks of the Power Card Challenge have been lost over the past two years.

The marketing and public relations efforts have still continued, but they cannot replace personal contact and customer service. Inviting someone to get a Power Card and telling them about all the exciting things the Library has to offer has been lost. Even in these difficult times, the Library has come back to placing increased emphasis on outreach in its goals for this year. During the goal setting process for this year, much discussion was centered on outreach, its importance and re-establishing this as a priority. The lessons learned from the Power Card Challenge have not been lost. Even though we are open few hours we will take advantage of the time we are closed to the public to do outreach and visit schools. Getting back into the schools on a more consistent basis and attending community events head the list of activities targeted for increasing registration. A small team of staff from the Central Library and branches now review the requests for outreach and the Library presence at community events and manage the staffing of these events using personnel throughout the Library system. Outreach with the community and library card registration is now everyone's responsibility.

CONCLUSION

Because of the success of the marketing/public relations campaign begun with the Power Card Challenge the Library has a true identity in the community. Our partnerships increase annually and our media contacts grow. As the Houston Public Library celebrates its Centennial year this year, we are getting back to the basics and inviting our community to "Pack the Power" and become Power Card holders.

LITERARY PATHWAYS: APPROACHING LITERATURE THROUGH LITERARY LANDSCAPES

Mireia Sala

Abstract *Literary pathways are walks that link parts of the city of Barcelona (Spain) with literary works and authors. A guide and an actor performing or reading pieces of the different authors involved help the walkers to appreciate the relationship between the author and the site. They are taking place from 1998 as a very effective tool for raising awareness of the city's library network especially among the library non-users, who often become users as a result of their experience. Residents who are not library users must pay a visit to a library and to inscribe there. After the walk they have the opportunity to attend a set of conferences and participate in reading clubs about the authors involved. A promotion campaign is organised with leaflets, programmes, advertisements on the media, website promotions, etc. IFLA awarded the Literary pathways with the 2nd IFLA/3M International Marketing Award because of its creativeness, originality, tight budget and ability to attract new users.*

INTRODUCTION

Barcelona's libraries have been organising literary pathways since 1998. The aim of this activity is promote reading by giving residents the opportunity to delve into the world of authors in an entertaining way. They also offer a different angle for discovering libraries , though the authors and through the possibility of seeing the city in a different light.

Literary pathways are literary walks that link parts of the city with literary works and authors. Participants find out about authors by visiting areas that are related to them in some way or that have featured as fictitious scenes in their novels (bars, houses, parks, theatres...). The areas visited on the walks are not normally open to the public, which makes the activity even more attractive.

Explanations by a guide are alternated with performances by actors who read excerpts of the works in the areas visited on the walk. The guide provides the biographical part, literary information and historical context, while the actors offer a closer, more emotive element by interpreting texts by the author or fragments from works by other writers to help him interpret the author's works.

This initiative invites readers to discover literary works in a very hands-on way with its use of a format that is different and attractive to residents. Both works and authors form a part of universal literature.

Another of the aims of these walks is to raise awareness of the city's libraries and the services they offer by means of an activity that takes place out side of the library building to reach members of the public who are not library users. The itineraries are always carried out with media publicity (radio interviews, opinion columns...) to support their goal.

Itineraries are therefore a very effective tool for raising awareness of the city's library network, allowing us to reach new segments of the public who are not familiar with libraries and who become users as a result of this experience. They encourage people to read by promoting literature in a pleasant, original way, and contributing to the cultural education of residents through entertainment.

One of the requirements for those who wish to take part is that they have a library card. Residents who are not library users must therefore pay a visit to a library before going on the itinerary. Bookings are made by calling a library in advance. Each itinerary is based at a different library.

To link this initiative to activities held inside libraries, the itineraries coincide with 'formal' discussions held inside the libraries. The itineraries offer a different view of the author: their specific relationship with Barcelona.

A marketing campaign is organised with a number of activities: leaflets, programmes, advertisements on the radio and in the press, website promotions, literary teasers...

An important element of the marketing campaign is the way the image and its contents are dealt with: all printed material uses an innovative and evocative image. (For example, the front cover of the general programme advertising the itineraries for 2003 featured a photograph of a teabag and the slogan, "It's not a book, but it could also help you relax". The itineraries are also advertised in the Library Agenda. This year's edition is devoted to a humorous piece entitled "Reader's quirks". Each month features a quirk, such as "The need to read absolutely everything", accompanied by a photograph of a lady reading the label of a jam jar...)

THE DEVELOPMENT

As mentioned earlier, we have been hosting these itineraries since 1998:

1998	*Lorca and Barcelona* (the poet's centenary)
1999	*Passing through.* Foreign writers who have made Barcelona their stage (George Orwell, Carmen Laforet, Cervantes, Italo Calvino...).

2000	*Sweet Angel of Death.* Walk through the cemetery of Montjuïc discussing the writers who are buried there.
2001	*Machado and Barcelona.* His experience of Barcelona during his stay in the civil war.
2002	*Writers of Barcelona.* Focusing on M. Rodoreda, M.A Capmany and Montserrat Roig. *Collserola, from the balcony of the City.* For families. Walk through a nature area and recital of poems that discuss the area.
2003	*Barcelona and the sea.* A walk along Barcelona's port and La Barceloneta (Barcelona's shipping district) to discover the authors that talk of the sea. *Orwell and Barcelona.* Part of a cycle of conferences about the author for the centenary of his birth.
2004	Dalí in Barcelona, to celebrate the artist's centenary.

For 2005, we have scheduled...

The Barcelonas of Carvalho, which pays homage to Manuel Vázquez Montalbán; Quixote in Barcelona, as part of the celebrations for the IV centenary of the publication of Don Quixote.

This literary itineraries project of Barcelona Libraries was presented with the IFLA/3M Marketing Award in 2003. The IFLA, regarded as the most important library federation in the world, chose the Barcelona Libraries project for this prize because of its creativeness, originality, tight budget and ability to attract new users.

BUDGET

The total budget is 11,100 euros, which is broken down as follows:

Preparation of actors	300
Preparation of guide	300
Preparation of expert	300
Guide	1,600
Actor performances	1,600
Hire of spaces, transport, technical needs	5,000
Promotional material (leaflets, pamphlets, guides...)	2,000

The source of financing of this programme is public, with contributions from publishing houses and radio stations (in exchange for other items, e.g. they publish leaflets and donate books in exchange for a presence in printed material...) or we are given free access to areas that normally charge an entrance or hire fee (e.g. the University of Barcelona features in the leaflets as a collaborator so we are not charged for using one of its classrooms for a stop along the way).

Users contribute to the costs of the itinerary with a payment of 6 euros each.

VIRTUAL ITINERARIES

Since November 2003, we have also offered the itineraries on our library website (www.bcn.es/biblioteques). An attractive design has been used and participants can obtain a map of the walk, photos, historical context and biographical information about authors and transcriptions of the literary texts with the reference works. Where available, the voices of the authors or video footage are also used.

EVALUATION BY THE ORGANISATION

After all these years of hosting literary itineraries, the organisation's evaluation is very positive. Year after year, the public wait anxiously for new itineraries and, because of its echo in the media, the initiative reaches other Barcelona residents who are not library users and, in some cases, not even readers. Other itineraries are held in Barcelona, but only those carried out by the Barcelona Library Consortium have a literary basis.

In 2002, we created an itinerary for families on Collserola, in a bid to promote reading among children. The walk was a success, which indicated a demand for this type of activity in this sector of the population. Each year, new itineraries are created for these users. The Quixote itinerary for 2005 has also been designed for younger children.

After the itineraries, many of the participants visit libraries and are surprised by what they have to offer (many of Barcelona's residents are not familiar with the services available at libraries or their collections), and they end up borrowing the books discussed on the walks.

Many participants of the walks also appreciate the possibility of discovering areas of the city, finding out about their history and being able to visit them. At the end of the walk, the participants have found out about writers, heard their works through the voice of professional actors at first hand (they act on the street without a stage) and they have discovered the history of that building, that bar or that street they always pass by, but never knew about.

We at the organisation believe that this is a good way of promoting libraries beyond their mere facilities and of encouraging reading. There is a clear link between the itinerary and reading, because users become potential readers of the authors discussed on the itineraries and very often visit the libraries afterwards.

Section - VI
DATABASES AND OTHER MARKETING LITERATURE

Section - VI
Databases and other Marketing Literature

Library and information science literature abounds with papers on marketing and there has been a steady growth of marketing literature in LIS over the years. LISA (Library and Information Science Abstract) introduced the key term "Marketing" for making searches in the database in 1969. A keyword "Marketing" search in LISA hits just 30 papers during the period 1970 to 1975 has increased to 1146 references for the period 1996-2000.

Literature on marketing of library and information centers is well reviewed. If we look at the international level, there are some reviews, such as Freeman and Katz (1978); Norman (1982 & 1989); Tucci (1988); Webber (1999); Cox (2000).

There is also good number of resources available on the web on the area of marketing of library and information services. The following table gives details of the some of the important resources available on web on the subject:

Bibliographies/ Databases/ Websites	Journals/Newsletters	Manuals	Tutorials/Online courses
Marketing in Public Libraries http:// www.slis.ualberta.ca/cap03/ jocelyn/homepage.html	Marketing Library Services www.infotoday.com/mls/ mls.htm	Marketing Tips for Information Professionals http://ip.lexis-nexis.com/ reference/ MarketingTipColor.pdf	Nebraska Library Commission's Market the library is a mini-course /www.nlc.state.ne.us/libdev/ mini-courses/outreach/sell.html
Marketing Our Libraries – On and Off the Web http:// www.librarysupportstaff.com/ marketinglibs.html	Marketing treasures www.chrisolson.com/ marketingtreasures/ index.html	Proactive Librarianship: Marketing and Public Relations A Manual for Workshop Presenters http:// www.inasp.info/pubs/pro-librarians/ INASPproactivelibrarian.pdf	Colorado Library Marketing Council www.clmc.org
Sheila Webber's Marketing library and information services www.dis.strath.ac.uk/people/ sheila/marketing/	Library Media & PR www.ssdesign.com/ librarypr/index.html	Principles directeurs pour l'enseignement du marketing dans la formation des bibliothécaires, documentalistes et archivistes www.unesco.org.web world.ramp.html	Dr Lutz's marketing class: www.cba.ufl.edu/classes/ MAR3023/index.html
Putting Your Library on the Map – Marketing Tools for Outreach / In Reach http:// www.dowling.edu/library/ papers/marje/ BibMarketcon.doc	IFLA M&M Section Newsletter (www.ifla.org/VII/s34/ #Newsletter)	Marketing and Public Relations in ARL Libraries. SPEC Flyer no. 240. Online: http:// www.arl.org/spec/ 240fly.html.	Ohio Library Foundation's course titled "Marketing the Library" http://www.olc.org/marketing/ index.html
Selected References on Marketing Special Libraries Online http://www.sla.org/ membership/irc/market.html	Shy Librarian http:// www.shylibrarian.com/	Marketing as if Your Library Depends On It– And It Does! http://www.semls.org/ PDF_files/ MarketBraintreeMay03.pdf.	ENSSIB's on line training on marketing strategy www.enssib.fr

This section covers contributions on theories of databases and database initiatives and important marketing literature published during recent times.

Monique Jucquois-Delpierre, in her paper *Databases as (Information) Resource, Language and Behaviour* emphasizes the language of new media, especially databases as information resource, and how it influences new media and discusses the behaviourial implications of the both: users and information specialists.

Angels Massisimo and Jorge Franganillo, in their paper The *"Matpromo" Database: An IFLA M & M Section Project* detail the - the online image database of library promotional materials- IFLA Management and Marketing Section's Project to facilitate ideas for promotional campaign for libraries world over.

(Late) Ashok Jambhekar, Dinesh K. Gupta, Abhinandan K. Jain and T. P. Ramarao, in their paper *Database of Marketing LIS Literature in India* shares experiences of developing database on the marketing literature published in India and by Indian writers outside.

Sueli Angelica do Amaral's paper *The Four Ps Concept in Library and Information Services: A Review of Literature* analyses four Ps (and addition Ps) concept as used in library and information sciences literature and tries to respond many important questions about the prominence of authors and their contributions.

Kathy Dempsy exposes the MLS Newsletter in detail. The Marketing Library Services (a bio-monthly newsletter started in 1988) gives specific coverage on marketing of library services and has offered tips, ideas and insights to librarians and others on how to promote and apply marketing tools to their information services and products. Originally published as a paper-based newsletter, select papers are freely available for download.

DATABASES AS (INFORMATION) RESOURCE, LANGUAGE AND BEHAVIOUR

Monique Jucquois-Delpierre

"*A library, a museum- in fact any large collection of cultural data is replaced by a computer....*"

Is Manovich's assumption true ?

Abstract *This paper is intended to emphasize a chapter of Lev Manovich's work « The Language of New Media ». It deals with the forms of the new media and especially the database. It reminds us of the latter's traditional functions of structuring and retrieving data and shows how the principles of new media (numerical representation, modularity, automation, variability and transcoding) influence a new language. It shows possible and existing implications in respect of users' and information specialists' behaviour. It does not take a commercial point of view but a cultural one, explaining how multimedia, new forms of spectatorship and information management, multiculturalism and reinforced security systems modify traditional modes of accessing information, transforming at the same time database forms and navigation systems. Taking up a suggestion by Manovich, this article concludes that "Information access is no longer just a key form of work but also a new key category of culture..."*

INTRODUCTION

I remember with slight nostalgia the wax-floor-polish smell of the Louvain University Library. The silence of the great reading room was only interrupted by someone whispering a question or coughing. A concert-hall atmosphere, scientific meditation that was almost religious. Sometimes the desk officer explained rather too loudly that a book that had been ordered had not yet arrived from the stores. The large shelves were full of precious dictionaries or encyclopedias often reached only with ladders. Readers copied studiously on to cards interesting sentences like monks in the middle ages. Photocopiers were rare if they existed at all. Today the smell of a library's spacious rooms has been replaced by a "humming" sound that informs you at what place in which catalogue the book you want is to be found. The noise of photocopiers indicate documents being extracted from books in free access, that of computer printers indicate data being downloaded from the magic internet. Readers have become computer users fascinated by a screen that is equivalent to the door of Ali Baba's cave. These users are disseminated in a virtual world. This world does not represent the death of libraries but on the contrary the multiplication of new forms of library and new media designed to access them. On the other hand, librarians and information specialists work to present, to structure and organize the data, to select and give the best access to the specific information requested by a user drowning under the gigantic universal library flowing in front of his eyes on a computer screen.

EVERYTHING ON THE WEB

Not on the web ? What information does not exist on the web ? Or on a CD? Today encyclopedias, lexica, dictionaries as corporate advertising , scientific articles, tour operators, databases for law or medicine, cinema and many other fields including even complete digital libraries exist on the web. Together these represent not so much a huge international « market » - the items are not always available for sale - but much rather a gigantic permanent exhibition of the knowledge existing in the world and an invitation to structure it, using other new tools.

In our contribution to the work of Gupta and Jambhekar (2003), "Information as a component of Internet marketing dynamics ", we started from a commercial context, namely how you can buy and sell (almost) everything on the Internet and the consequences of this for information specialists. We described how in this environment of free useful information and superficial advertising, in which troublesome copyright problems exist for authors and producers, marketing strategies were being designed to determine well in advance a community of interest of potential users (individualized customers), and new (electronic) forms of commerce.

Database : A Resource Vis-a-Vis Product

We studied in particular an e-enterprise, a movie producer, access providers and telecommunication enterprises and, last but not least, a producer of databases. And it is the latter product, databases, that takes all our attention today. The starting point of this present article is namely the analysis of Lev Manovich, media and visual arts specialist. His book « The Language of New Media » places these new media within the histories of the visual and media cultures of the last few centuries. It shows how categories and forms such as navigation, interface and database work alongside conventions with which we are already familiar. We would like to examine briefly the possible conclusions for librarians that can be drawn from the Manovich vision.

Since the arrival of the web (Tim Berners-Lee), the world appears to us «*as an endless and unstructured collection of images, texts and other data records*» (Lev Manovich). Side by side with traditional narrative forms, modelling databases to structure this collection of data seems therefore to be an activity that is necessary if we are to understand and explain our world. Moreover, databases are becoming no longer just a structured collection of documents but fundamental models of what the world (or parts of it) is or are like, as well as being guidelines for culture, science and technologies, and essential maps for libraries.

Especially in the chapter dedicated to the forms of the new media, Manovich underlines the existential importance of information and the part it plays in the total human experience, whether social or individual. He comes to the conclusion that "*Information access is no longer just a key form of work but also a new key category of culture*". Manovich finds that the dominance of the database form in new media is a corollary of the importance of information. He reports the results of George Legrady's exploratory work that defines a database as an « *information structure where stories / things are organized according to multiple thematic connections* » (personal communication, 16th September 1998, Manovich 221). Databases help to structure reality, creating virtualities and not telling stories like narratives; they do not have a beginning or an end ; they do not organise their elements into a sequence; every item contained in a database possesses the same significance as every other item. A data management system allows one to quickly access, sort, and reorganize millions of records; it can carry out multiple indexing of data, since each record besides data itself contains a number of fields with user-defined values (Peeters, Emile s. also Manovich 218) which take account of one or more kinds of classification.

As suggested by the title, databases are information resources, a modern language and imply new forms of behaviour. There are traditional information resources : every library catalogue is a database; every information specialist in the field knows - amongst others - The Financial Times, in medicine, Medline or Dimdi, in Philosophy , Francis, Booling Green or Philis, databases for (international) law or jurisprudence (in France : juripro.com, in Germany: Iuris), in Cinema (Allmovieguide or Internet Movie Database) or newspaper and journal documents (e.g. Le Monde, Rheinische Post or RP Online). There are different modes of access for different kinds of documents with different ways of paying (Le Monde, Rheinische Post or RP Online).

More and more frequently the databases are invisible due to interfaces and management systems as we will see in the following.

THE LANGUAGE OF NEW MEDIA

To become aware of the importance of a database as knowledge management and part of the culture, a quite different form of behaviour must be adopted from that for analysing possible marketing strategies within the Internet. Far from being an economic process, it must develop into a reflective, meaningful long-term strategy which understands each user's needs and interests. This form of behaviour will modify profoundly not only the information process but also cultural and scientific communication.

These modern structures and models, mostly databases following Manovich (27-48), are engraved in the new media language. This implies:

(1) All new media objects are composed in digital forms. Their representation is numerical. The media can be described using a mathematical function and are programmable. Most primary documents are digitalised. With the appearance of digital and virtual libraries, « grey » literature is disappearing, like numerous printed periodicals.

(2) New media objects are made up of elements which can exist independently of each other. This assures their modularity. The most common examples here are the Microsoft Office modules for databases, drawing, dictionaries, indexes and tool sets. For a long time now every software package has been composed of subroutines, functions, procedures and scripts. This is especially true of information retrieval software.

(3) The numerical coding of media and the modular structure of a media object permit many operations involved in media creation, manipulation and access to be automated. Thus human intentionality can be removed from the creative process, at least in part. Software package like 'Adobe Photoshop' can convert colour, can compare a coloured image and recreating exactly the same colour. Two traditional pillars of knowledge presentation, namely classification and indexing, can be automated. Automatic indexing is usually integrated in a database; one of many is the Filemaker data management system.

(4) A new media object is variable, is not something fixed once and for all, but something that can exist in a potentially infinitely large number of versions. An obvious example here are the multiple versions or sizes of the same software. Others are different cuts of the same film and different interfaces and applications for the same data.

(5) More than with older media, new media objects can be reproduced (Walter Benjamin) because of the transcoding principle. They follow the same rules as computer data and have the same potential to be converted into another format, and to be encoded without degradation.

Apart from these principles as systemised by Manovich but which in every case, every information specialist applies, sometimes automatically and unaware of this new reality, other trends are becoming apparent in the information world, changing thinking and behaviour patterns. These include (1) multimedia systems, (2) an increasing level of interactivity as well as other new forms of spectatorship, (3) explicit information architecture and navigable space design, (4) multiculturalism and globalisation and last but not least (5) reinforced security systems.

Multimedia Systems

A computer database can contain different media types, web-pages are images, text in pictures, more rarely sound. There are not only other kinds of collections, these different media types, image, new forms of texts, sound introduce also new forms of value, change deeply the way we think, see and dream.

Christ and Jordan (1995) introduced the term 'visuality', visual events and their discourses, what deals with perception and representation, to be seen, the act of seeing and its construction.

Too early, in 1982 or 1987, William J.T. Mitchell announced a 'pictorial turn' "*meaning not only the dominance and diversity of the visual in our culture but more particularly a paradigm shift in the way cultural discourses are organised.*" The visionary assumption of Mitchell at this time -in his mind the visual and the verbal could be regarded as equal- contrasted with the "denigration of vision " (Martin Jay, 1993) dominating the intellectual discussion with its textual forms and "linguistic-based concepts " (Brosch). This hegemony of the text is now contested as a result of 'visual culture' existing as a new field of theoretical inquiry. Images are multiplied like their importance.

For our information field it means new disciplines, new forms of publications, new journals, new genres of databases, and obviously software programms. Let us give some examples :

- Visual anthropology asks questions on the social production and exchange of signs, their function as a vehicle for social cohesion or rebellion.
- Cartoons like '*Persepolis*' by Marjane Satrapi are an artistic, political, social, religious and philosophical discourse in pictorial form. This Iranian emigrant in France received the price of the best cartoons of the year in the book fair of Frankfurt in October 2004.
- The Journal of Visual Culture was created in 2002. It increased acceptance of 'visual culture' as an interdisciplinary field of study reconceptualising images, and rejecting Western culture's tradition which privileged words and texts.
- Different genres of databases have arisen: biography, bibliography on CDs, collections of audio or video-works, databases of the users of libraries including their pictures and registration cards.
- Software programs for multimedia databases, image searching, scanning, scenario, image and film editing have become unavoidable tools for librarians and web content managers.

Our recent history (Iraq war) as well as an older one (Stalinist) shows examples of political manipulation through images. From recent pictures published by the Daily Mirror (2004) to the movie « Wag the dog » (Barry Levinson, USA, 1997, 97 min.) the impact of images is no longer in doubt.

David Freedberg's research (1989) demonstrated the iconic power that images have to change spectatorial attitudes when images moved from cult and magical to fetish and commercial since the Renaissance, the period when artist and also beholder attempted to seize power over the image. Jonathan Crary (2000) studied modes of visual attention which he considered attempted to create individual and social coherence in a fractured visual world.

Interactivity

Automation and digitalisation infer increasing interactivity and new forms of spectatorship. In the process of interaction the user can choose which elements to display or which paths to follow (Manovich, 55). He can choose pictures and film sequences in online databases (for example in the databases of the search engine Google).

The latest form of images in new media is interactive, the viewer has access to their production; computer technology permits a visitor to a website or virtual room to be present at the same time as hundreds or thousands of others, creating new forms of collective/individual spectatorship. The technology permits users to move about virtually in a library or a museum, e.g. in Bonn and its " Frauenmuseum", in Paris and virtually in Egypt, through the " Institut du Monde Arabe ".

Databases requires necessarily and traditionally navigable space, especially in media objects like simulation systems. A collection of documents and a navigable space, already traditional methods of organizing both data and human experience of the world itself have become two of the forms that today can be found in most areas of new media. The first form is a database, used to store any kind of data - from financial records to digital movie clips; the second is a virtual interactive 3-dimensional space, employed in computer games, motion rides, virtual reality, computer animation, and human computer interfaces (Manovich 213-221).

Content Management Systems have been developed and are being offered commercially for the creation and structuring of documents and particularly ones for the web.

The most important idea of a Content Management System is to separate content and form, to divide two processes, page layouting on the one hand and on the other hand the storing, integrating and archiving all kinds of data, image, sound and text

In these systems databases, mostly of the MySQL type, are not recognizable due to interfaces which are transparent for end users. Information about these one can be used by a computer program to customize automatically the media composition as well as to create elements themselves.

Content management systems should be constructed to meet specific business goals. They can present these requirements in 'narrative' format. The pages, "templates ", or "frames ", are stocked on the server - the data in a base. When a visitor reads a page, the CMS navigation engine joins page and content together.

This makes adding, updating and maintaining content as well as task sharing and multitasking easy and possible, and allows various, differenciated kinds of management of the whole or of parts of the work (links, articles, scenarios, description of business needs, etc...). In a nutshell a CMS creates "dynamic" as opposed to «static» web sites. The separation of content and form permits the required adhoc information to be inserted in the databases. Templates can be changed without influencing the content. But a Content Management Systems also acts as a Knowledge Management System, and integrates definitions of terms for a range of information systems where clear dividing lines must be drawn. It captures organisational knowledge and includes authoring tools, document management systems (DMS) and records management systems (RMS). It can provide a comprehensive guide on how to write CMS scenarios, as well as a detailed overview of the whole selection process. It must give a comprehensive starting point for identifying the business and technical requirements that will drive selection processes.

We can examine Plone as one of many examples of software content-managing systems. It is an intranet and extranet server, a document publishing system, a portal server and a groupware tool for collaboration between separately located entities.

Its interface has been translated into over 30 languages, and tools exist for managing multilingual content. It possesses traditional qualities of classification systems (standardisation, universal language) and uses best-practice web standards like XHTML and CSS. Plone is licensed under the GNU General Public License, the same license Linux uses. This gives users the right to use Plone without a licence fee, and to improve upon the product.

Modularity and transcoding are also observed by this program. Many add-on products provide new features and content types. It can be scripted using standard web solutions and Open Source languages. It can interoperate with most relational database systems, both open source and commercial, and runs on a vast array of platforms, including Linux, Windows, Mac OS X and Solaris. It is built using an object oriented application server and the language preferred by Google, NASA, and many others.

Multiculturism and Globalisation

Because of their universal use (amongst other things), all these features lead to multiculturalism and paradoxically at the same time to globalisation. Multiculturalism must be included in Information Architecture Processes. New forms of information exchange like global sourcing are being developed.

(Digital) library networks, general, common (digital) catalogues, interlibrary systems (for example Jason) have a very long tradition. Their free public access (re)assured their necessary users. Enterprises use the same body of information and share the same material but, unfortunately without any doubt, to maximise profit when sourcing globally.

The example of software development services could be taken (George L. Harris). Many organizations have decided to buy software services from companies in India. IBM has decided to open an office there and has staffed it with over 500 software engineers.

Why do organizations look to source globally? Amongst other things to reduce (transport) costs, and cycle times due to technology use, to achieve higher quality, to take advantage of core competence of particular suppliers and/or geographic regions, to fulfill local content requirements, etc…

These organizations have to find a balance between multiculturalism, profit and fair partnership. The obstacles are multiple : language differences, time and distance factors, business terms defined differently in different cultures (a business "relationship" or "partnership" will have many definitions), differences in legal terms and conditions, different standards and safety requirements, longer lead times due to transportation of products from international sources, local customs in regard to the use of labour and environmental protection requirements varying from country to country, more intermediaries, political and social climates in some countries posing a risk to buying organizations, risk in terms of supply continuity, countries being at different stages of development, protectionism, distance, lack of knowledge about local business, etc…

All these obstacles as enumerated by Harris are engraved in every multicultural project. The greater the desire for profit is, the greater are the risks for the human resources involved. Global sourcing requires that special attention is paid to intercultural communication, with value being attached not only to increasing profitability but also ethics and codes of conduct (for instance by Graham Packaging Company).

Global sourcing is typical of all processes integrating new media and depending on multiple partners and communication components - exactly like library procedures.

Attitudes and way of thinking change profoundly and rapidly. Forecasting this change is not possible. As early as 1988 we demonstrated difficulties « *Forecasting Information Manpower Needs* » (Jucquois-Delpierre). In 1989 Tim Berners-Lee invented the World Wide Web, starting a revolution the results of which are unpredictable.

His book "*Weaving the Web : the original design and ultimate* " (1999) was written to address the questions most people ask - These range from *What were you thinking of when you invented it?*" through , *So what do you think of it now?* to *Where is this all going to take us?*

From 2002 to 2004 some evil brutal « advertising » or virus attacked users, producers and scientists. Spams grow like an unavoidable cancer destroying filters and damaging the work climate.

Manovich was aware of both sides of the Internet. When discussing « totalitarian subjectivity », Manovich stated "*A Western artist sees the Internet as the perfect tool for breaking down hierarchies and bringing art to the people. In contrast, I, as a post-communist subject, cannot but see the Internet as a communal apartment of the Stalin era : no privacy, everybody spies on everybody else , always present are lines for common areas such as the toilet or the kitchen*."

Nevertheless new methods are being created to protect human, scientific, technical and even commercial data. Of course librarians also play a role here - finding methods to struggle against cyberterrorism and by adopting an Intranet.

Reinforced Security System

It has become obvious that new kinds of security systems, spam filters or killers are necessary. Nevertheless the open exchanging of information between cultures will never be without risk. Security systems and the respect of privacy in the Internet are two of the problems mentioned above.

CONCLUSION

In conclusion, every partner of the new forms of communication described in this short article, users and librarians learn together a new language. They must structure and use databases, learn new media expressions or tools, as information resources, as well as a new language - all of which implicitly requires new forms of behaviour.

All these information actors, one after the other, creators, producers or end users are immersed in an imaginary virtual world. From the Internet café at the seaside to the pub in the desert, differences between countries and between cultures inevitably transform the behaviour of these persons - whether with or without a computer - while at the same time changing the content and form of periodicals and other information products.

If they create much of their world out of the dialogue between verbal and pictorial representation they also copy, cut and paste images and texts. Using databases of photographs, movie clips, and audio recordings has become standard practice in modern media production and information processes. Media elements can be isolated, copied, and assembled in new combinations, images, can be scanned and superimposed, emphasis can be focussed on different parts.

Of course librarians play a role in structuring databases as well in the struggle against cyberterrorism, creating their intranet, making access to images simple or leading users through their library virtually. They enlarge their library to include the world, improve human communication and facilitate administrative processes. The humming we mentioned at the beginning of our article becomes a welcome for everyone, users and librarians, wishing to partake of the knowledge of the best world possible.

Nevertheless a large part of the world is missing from these new «spaces». And wisdom management does not exist. Internet communities are joining «invisible colleges» but are forgetting those who are obliged to collect, archive and interpret data in a traditional way.

Maybe this important part of the world appreciates better the treasure of human communication and could teach us that it is essential for every process including the WWW.

REFERENCES

1. Appadurai (A). Modernity at large: Cultural dimensions of globalization. Minneapolis: Minnesota University Press. 1997.
2. Benjamin (W). Das Kunstwerk im Zeitalter seiner technischen Reproduzierbarkeit: Drei Studien zur Kunstsoziologie. Ed.4. Frankfurt A. M: Suhrkamp. 1970.
3. Berger (J). Ways of Seeing. London: Penguin. 1983.
4. Berners-Lee (T). Original Proposals to the CERN - (retrieving 5.11.04) http://www.w3.org/History/1989/proposal.html -Page de Tim Berners-Lee au W3C (retrieving 5.11.04) http://www.w3.org/People/Berners-Lee/. Weaving the Web : the original design and ultimate. Harper San Francisco. 1999.
5. Brosch (R). Krisen des Sehens: Henry James und die Veränderung der Wahrnehmung im 19. Jahrhundert . Tübingen: Narr. 2000.
6 Visual Culture-http://www.ruhr-uni-bochum.de/britcult/DOFPBrosch.htm (retrieved in September 2004).
7. Crary (J). Suspensions of perception: Attention, spectacle, and modern culture. Cambridge, MA: MIT Press. 2000.
8. Christ (C T) and Jordan(J O), Eds. Victorian literature and the Victorian visual imagination. Berkeley: University of California Press. 1995.
9. Freedberg (D). The power of images: Studies in the history and theory of response. Chicago: Chicago University Press. 1989.
10. Graham Packaging Company. Key elements & philosophy of global sourcing 4 © 2004 Graham Packaging Company, www.grahampackaging.com (retrieving in september 2004).
11. Gupta (D K) and Jambhekar (A), Eds. An integrated approach to services marketing: A book of readings on marketing of library and information services. Mumbai: Allied Publishers Pvt. Ltd. 2003.
12. Harris (G L). The essence of global sourcing. Web: www.calyptusgroup.com (retrieved in september 2004).
13. JASON (Journal Articles Sent On demaNd) www.ub.uni-bielefeld.de/library/databases/dbf/jason.htm
14. Jay (M). Downcast Eyes : The denigration of vision in twentieth-century French thought. Berkeley : University of California Press, 1999.
15. Scopic Regimes of Modernity. *In,* Forster (H), Ed. Vision and Visuality. Seattle: Bay, 1988: 3-28.
16. Journal of Visual Culture. London, editorial board entre autres Mieke Bal and Martin Jay.
17. Jucquois-Delpierre (M). Problems in forecasting information manpower needs. *In,* Information manpower forecasting, Papers presented at the FID/ET seminar, Espoo,Helsinki, 24-27 August 1988. Unesco, PGI-91/WS/10. Paris. 1991.

18. Jucquois-Delpierre (M). Information as a component of the Internet marketing dynamics. *In*, Gupta (D K) and Jambhekar (A), Eds. An integrated approach to services marketing: A book of readings on marketing of library and information services. Mumbai: Allied Publishers Pvt. Ltd. 2003
19. Manovich (L).The language of new media. London, Cambridge: M I T Press. 2001
20. Mata-Toledo (R A) and Cushman (P K). Relationale Datenbanken. Bonn: mitp-Verlag. 2003
21. Mitchell (W J T). Iconology: image, text, ideology. Chicago: University of Chicago Press. 1987
22. Mitchell (W J T). The Surplus Value of Images. *Mosaic* 23 (2). 2002: 1-23.
23. Mitchell (W J T). Picture Theory. Chicago: The University of Chicago Press. 1994
24. Mitchell (W J T). The Reconfigured Eye. Cambridge, Mass : MIT Press. 1982
25. Peeters (E). Conception et gestion des banques de données. Paris, Les éditions d'organisation. 1984
26. Plone - CMS http://plone.org/ (retrieving in september 2004)
27. Satrapi (M) .Persepolis. Hamburg: edition moderne. 2004

THE "MATPROMO" DATABASE: AN IFLA MANAGEMENT & MARKETING SECTION PROJECT

Àngels Massísimo
Jorge Franganillo

Abstract *The "MatPromo" database was created in October 2002 as a project of IFLA's Management & Marketing Section. The objective of the project consists of creating a database of images of objects and documents designed for promoting all kinds of libraries in any country. The images are described and are accessible through a user-friendly interface for searching internationally. The aim of the database is to facilitate ideas for promotional campaigns of library services. The database is hosted on the project server of the University of Barcelona's Department of Library and Information Science (http://bidoc.ub.es/pub/matpromo/) and a link to it is made available from the web of IFLA's Management & Marketing Section (http://www.ifla.org/VII/s34/index.htm). This article attempts to introduce "MatPromo" and explain its technical characteristics, content, and usefulness for librarians around the world.*

INTRODUCTION

MatPromo is the name given to the on-line image database of library promotional materials that is currently being developed as a project of IFLA's Management & Marketing Section, agreed upon at the meeting of the Governing Board held in Glasgow in August 2002[1]. The immediate objective was to collect and describe images of objects of all types used by libraries of all types from any country in their promotional and dissemination activities, whether campaigns or isolated activities. The database offers a user-friendly interface for internationally based searches. The ultimate aim was to help librarians with ideas for promoting their centres and services, in keeping with one of the Section's objectives: to provide support for professionals in carrying out their management and marketing activities. Another aim was to increase the usefulness of the Section's web page and, at the same time, the number of visitors to it. It is worth remembering that the promotion of libraries, as an aspect of marketing, also contributes to disseminating their image and, therefore, to gaining social and financial support.

DESIGN OF THE "MATPROMO" PROJECT WITHIN THE FRAMEWORK OF IFLA

Over the years, through publications, seminars and awards such as the IFLA/3M International Marketing Award (This international prize, awarded this year for the third time, attempts to highlight the best marketing activities from all types of libraries in any country, regardless of budget.), IFLA's Management & Marketing Section has contributed to library development by stimulating the use of organisational techniques in libraries. In August 2002[2] during a satellite meeting conducted in Glasgow, several brainstorming sessions were held to come up with ideas to encourage marketing initiatives within the participants' organisations. One of the groups addressed the Management & Marketing Section itself and, among other proposals, suggested that more content be added to the web page to aid librarians around the world in management and marketing activities. Such an effort would also result in a greater number of visits to this web site.

Among the proposals was one for the creation of a database to gather and describe images of objects created by libraries for promotional purposes. Promotional initiatives generate much ephemeral material that is easily lost or else it is not well known and, therefore, little advantage is taken of it. Therefore, it was felt that it would be of value to gather images of promotional objects used in all types of libraries, anywhere in the world, and to structure this material so as to make it available through IFLA's web site to librarians around the world.

The idea was very well received by all the participants and, in particular, by the members of the Section's Standing Committee who suggested that it be proposed as a project to IFLA's management in the subsequent congress to be held later in the month. The outline of the project incorporated elements previously worked on under the Spanish project, Observatorio de la Imagen de las Bibliotecas (OIB), [Observatory of the Image of Libraries] [3], as well as adopting this project's collection of promotional images and draft database design.

From the start the still-unnamed project, as presented to IFLA, had the overall aim of creating and maintaining a database of images of library marketing and promotional tools of any type and from anywhere. Such a database would be made available to all visitors to the Management & Marketing Section's web page.

As such, various specific objectives were pursued:

- First of all, the intention was to make available a broad series of images of items used internationally for:
  - promotional campaigns for centres or networks as well as those aimed at attitudes and behaviour within L&Icentres (posters, bookmarks, postcards, etc.);
  - tools for the library's corporate communication and image (logos, membership cards, flyers, claim notes, etc.);
  - the full range of library merchandising objects;
  - images of libraries and books (book metamorphosis, etc.)

- Secondly, the idea was to structure these images in accordance with their characteristics, to describe them according to previously defined parameters, and to create a search strategy through fields that would help librarians in retrieving the images and also with descriptions of them.
- Thirdly, it was felt that the web should provide librarians with a "how-to-do-it" on creating promotional materials. This tool was envisioned as a theoretic complement to the practical focus of the database.
- Finally, and in addition to the obvious utility that the database would offer to anyone interested in promoting their library, another aim was to increase the number of visits to the Section's web page, and thus raise its profile and present it to an ever- expanding community.

In order to carry out the project we settled on the following steps

1. Redesign the aforementioned database prepared for the OIB project and adapt it to an international context. Once accomplished, all content from the database's fields should be translated into English, chosen as the official language of the project given the financing from IFLA and the need for international exploitation.
2. Classify the existing materials and digitise those that were not already in digital format: again we found many Spanish objects already digitised by Gómez-Hernández and Saorín[4], as well as a significant batch of images of logos and membership cards that were to be incorporated into the project.
3. Load the images into the database and prepare as complete a description as possible in each case, considering that depending on the country and the languages used, some data might be missing.
4. Clarify possible copyright problems that could prevent exhibiting some of the material on IFLA's web site.
5. Mount the database onto the web. IFLA accepted the proposal for the database to be housed on the project server of the Department of Library and Information Science of the University of Barcelona. At the same time a link would be made from the web page of the Management & Marketing Section.
6. Prepare a brief help guide in English on how to prepare library promotional material.
7. Load the guide onto the web after review by several experts.

At the same time this ambitious project entailed a series of other tasks that needed to be undertaken, for which funding was requested from IFLA. The budget was calculated in such a way as to reserve an important part of the funds for designing and adapting the database, and another part for the digitisation of the documents (undertaken in-house for the smaller sized material and by an image digitisation company for large formats). The total amount requested was 4,000 €.

It was agreed that once financed, the project would begin at the earliest in January. The timeframe foreseen was:

- Pilot phase:
  - 1st report on the organisation and start of work in the Section's winter meeting (Barcelona, February 2003),
  - 2nd report and pilot search in the database with approximately 300 images during the annual IFLA congress in Berlin (August 2003)
- Project completion and transfer of the database to IFLA:
  - 3rd report on the state of the loading procedure and open searching of the database during the Section's winter meeting (Budapest, March 2004),
  - Final report on the transfer and, if technically feasible, the loading of images onto IFLANet during IFLA's annual congress in Buenos Aires (August 2004).

In August 2002, IFLA's Board awarded 1,600€ for the project. Subsequently, the number of items to be digitised had to be reduced to a quarter of the originally projected amount. The funding was not obtained until well into 2003 which caused the digitisation of large format images to be reduced even further, since the cost of the service company was somewhat more expensive than at first calculated. Therefore, at present, we now have a fully developed and operational database, but with only 80 records loaded to date.

PROJECT DEVELOPMENT

The project team consisting of:

- Àngels Massísimo, of the University of Barcelona (member of the Section's Standing Committee), as project co-ordinator;
- Marielle de Miribel, of the University Paris-X (member of the Section's Standing Committee);
- José Antonio Gómez-Hernández, of the University of Murcia (Spain) and
- ANABAD Murcia; and Tomás Saorín, at that time the librarian and webmaster at the Regional Library of Murcia (Spain), Department of Culture.

It was agreed, in principle, to co-ordinate the project from Barcelona and implement it in the project server of the Library and Information Science Department of the University of Barcelona. Àngels Massísimo, as co-ordinator, began by obtaining the needed support from the Department and gathering new collaborators to contribute technological know-how to the project's progress. Two professors from the Department - Jorge Franganillo and Josep-Manuel Rodríguez-Gairín - joined with the initial team, together with Sergi Chávez, a student from the same Department who assisted in database maintenance tasks. These participants took charge of the design and maintenance of the database, the design of the web and search interface and technical assistance, respectively. With the team formed,

Àngels Massísmo took on the responsibility for redesigning the database – adapting the content of the fields for the new international focus and the subsequent translation into English. Once this work was completed through collaboration between the groups in Barcelona and Murcia, the efforts centred on the selection, description and comments of the images that were loaded into the database. José Antonio Gómez-Hernández and Tomás Saorín contributed some 300 previously digitised images from Spain, with their relevant descriptions. Àngels Massísimo has now taken charge of the final selection of images to be introduced and of the description of the new images. Throughout the project, the timing of the foreseen phases has been met without delay.

CONTENT OF THE DATABASE

The promotional materials digitised in MatPromo consist of a heterogeneous mix of images: posters, bags, pins, fans, coasters, cups, T-shirts and other objects. The criteria followed for including material reflects the dissemination efforts that were carried out internationally. As such, at present the database contains promotional objects coming from Spain, Great Britain, United States, South Africa, etc. There also is a great amount of Spanish material digitised, but not yet loaded, in order to maintain the international balance in the database contents.

The database will receive more contributions and will be increasingly enriched with material from many other countries. To this end there will be campaigns for collecting material via *IFLA Express* during IFLA's annual congress. The database interface also offers the possibility to load your images onto. It is hoped that these efforts will attract new objects to the database, whose content will evolve into a representative sampling of the large universe of library promotional materials, which can be adapted, free of border constraints, to different realities. The aim is to generate ideas for promoting libraries and their services, as well as to lead to increased library use as a result of these promotional activities.

The interest in the MatPromo project will undoubtedly persist for a long time. In fact, its objectives –both general and specific - are still valid, as recognised during the meeting of IFLA's Management and Marketing Section held in Budapest (February 2004), as well as by the executive secretariat of IFLA.

One valid criticism, recognised by the team, is the fact that the project is limited to a very specific area and there is a need, perhaps, to broaden the scope to include other types of content.

FEATURES OF THE DATABASE

The MatPromo database is implemented in PHP and MySQL. This combination was chosen because:

1. PHP is a free programming language and MySQL is a database management system available under a GPL license (that is, free for non-profit applications) and thus there was no direct charge for the implementation.

2. The two components are current models and, as such, there is a broad repertory of resources for developing applications (free documentation, free scripts, etc.).
3. PHP and MySQL are models conceived for one another and thus have specific functions for reciprocal communication.

A view of database has been given below:

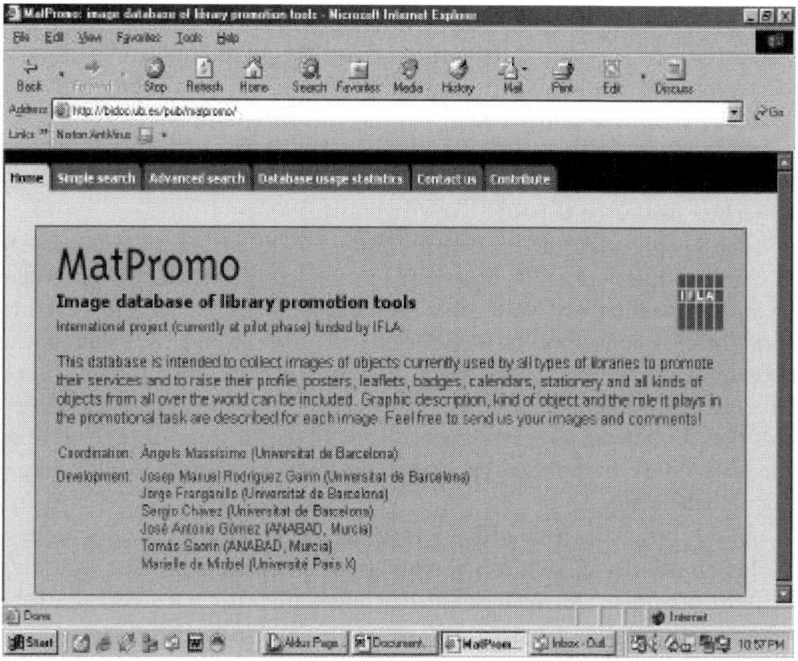

The database is structured on a record model that contains 17 fields, whose 15 are searchable: Title, Campaign, Slogan(s), Subject, Role, Date, Institution, Scope, Place, Summary description, Graphic description, Type of document, Physical description, Spread, File, and two internal fields that are not searchable. These latter fields serve for managing the thumbnails that are used as previews on the result page. Administrative tasks are handled through phpMyAdmin, a tool that allows the data and structure to be maintained through a navigator.

The basic principles of graphic design were applied to the layout of the MatPromo and it thus offers an organised, user-friendly, and functional interface. The visible spaces is organised into separate blocks, with uniform controls that help the user find the information needed and understand the functional conceptual model of MatPromo. In order to facilitate the activation of common actions, frequently used controls such as menus, search forms and navigational buttons are readily visible and easy to use. The information is distributed consistently and predictably in specific, uniform screen models so that the user can quickly locate the controls and information, independently of the context.

In order to speed up image downloads, the interface design economises on elements that do not contain relevant information and uses colour as a supplement for weighted information and for highlighting what is most significant. Since the screen is limited, as is the user's ability to grasp visual information, the economy of the design extends to other elements of the web. (Google's great popularity is owed, in part, to this concept of functional simplicity). MatPromo's design leaves out superfluous elements, does not overload the page, and seeks eloquence through simplicity, thus following the accepted wisdom that the best interface is the one that remains unnoticeable.

In order for information contained in MatPromo to be easily retrieved, intuitive navigation tools are provided: a tabbed menu allows access to sections of the web as described below:

The Simple search offers 2 modes through different search forms. The first, Field search, allows searching on any of 15 searchable fields as the access point. As an aid for locating key words, this form has an Index function that facilitates the insertion of search terms into the selected field, from an inverted index appearing in a pop-up window. The second mode, Keyword search, can efficiently execute global searches: without the need to specify search fields, the system recovers the records that contain the term introduced in any of the 14 searchable fields (except for the Date field). In both search modes, the user can sort the results, either by date or alphabetically.

The Advanced search offers a form for searching by a Field search, with the added possibility of Boolean combinations and results limited according to place (local, provincial, regional, national or international) or document type (object, poster, pin...).

Finally, the Contact page invites the user to communicate with the MatPromo team for contributing comments or suggestions, as well as for reporting any errors found. It also admits help requests on how to use the database. Communication between the user and MatPromo is not limited to issues regarding searching, but also includes instructions on how to contribute new items to the database through a tool available in the "Contribute" section. This feature allows librarians to add new material, with an appropriate description, through an assisted form.

REFERENCES AND NOTES

1. IFLA. Management & Marketing Section. *Newsletter* 12. February 2003. http://www.ifla.org/VII/s34/pubs/feb-03.pdf. [Consulted: 26 August 2004].
2. IFLA. Management & Marketing Section. *Newsletter* 12 (February 2003), p. 4. http://www.ifla.org/VII/s34/pubs/feb-03.pdf. [Consulted: 17 October 2004].

3. The "Observatorio de la Imagen de las Bibliotecas" was a project presented by 2 professors — Dr. José Antonio Gómez-Hernández and Dr. Tomás Saorín— of the University of Murcia to the Spanish Ministry of Education and Culture with the aim of gathering and describing images of promotional objects from Spanish libraries. Some of the images that served for the initial project were published in the book, *La información y las bibliotecas en la cultura de masas* (GÓMEZ-HERNÁNDEZ and SAORÍN, 2001).
4. Gómez-Hernández (JA) and Saorín Perez (T). *La información y las bibliotecas en la cultura de masas.* Valencia : Biblioteca Valenciana. 2001.

DATABASE ON LIS MARKETING LITERATURE IN INDIA

(Late) Ashok Jambhekar
Dinesh K. Gupta
Abhinandan K. Jain
T.P. Rama Rao

Abstract *Marketing in library and information services is a growing area of study and research in India. There is a good amount of researches in the country but are widely scattered in many sources of information. The present database attempts to collect literature on this subject at one place. It covers bibliographical details and abstracts of the literature published in India and published by Indian authors abroad. It also gives structural details of the database.*

INTRODUCTION

The 'knowledge' and 'Information Base' on marketing of information products and services from libraries are growing world-wide. The advent of modern 'Information Technology' (IT) has immensely facilitated documentation, access, dissemination, and sharing of vast knowledge and ever growing information base effectively as well as efficiently. Thus, the use of IT can play a vital role for libraries in design, development and marketing of information products and services. In a country like India this subject has got attention in only past 2-3 decades and the available literature is scattered and not readily accessible. It is therefore more critical to develop a database of literature on marketing of library and Information products and services. This paper describes the project dedicated to the design and development of a user friendly computerized bibliographic database of Indian literature on Marketing of Library and Information Products and Services. It reports the scope of the project, design of the database, web based system design consisting of software design and data structure design, and using the site by users and administrators. The research project was fully funded by Research and Publications Committee of Indian Institute of Management, Ahmedabad.

SCOPE OF THE PROJECT

The scope of the database includes documents in the form of papers published in journals, conference proceedings, edited books, books, encyclopedia, research reports, theses, monographs, etc., published in India and Indian authors abroad.

DATA BASE DESIGN

Identification of Sources and Collection of Documents

The steps followed in identification of sources and collections of data for the project were:

1. Literature survey was carried out on LISA (Library and Information Science Abstract) Database. The search was carried out using the terms" Marketing+India". This brought out 45 records in all. However, many records were not directly related with the subject.
2. Indian Library Science Abstract was also consulted and in which has very limited coverage on this subject.
3. A letter of request was put on the Indian List serves requesting LIS professionals to intimate about their publications on the subject. This resulted in a total of 20 items.
4. Literature was further identified from the citations made in articles/papers/ thesis/ books, etc.
5. Authors with more than two publications were also requested to send updated list of their publications on the area
6. Many authors were also requested to send a copy of each of their publications which could not be accessed through other sources.
7. Abstracts were not found in about 70 papers covered in the database for which abstracts were prepared and included in the database.

In addition, a provision has been made to receive contributions from database users and researchers and to incorporate the same into the database after a review.

Identification of Key words

Key words were selected from the abstracts and full text. Thereafter three-pronged approach was applied in finalizing key words of each paper/document on the basis of:

1. An alphabetical list of the key terms was prepared and same key words with different name were deleted.
2. To keep uniformity in terms, a list of key terms on the basis of marketing terminology was developed, and then
3. Key terms were identified in respect of subject, type of library/ service, location, etc.

Web Based System Design

A website for literature on Indian library and information services marketing was developed to create and retrieve the databases and to offer related services. The Homepage of the LILISM is shown here:

Home Page

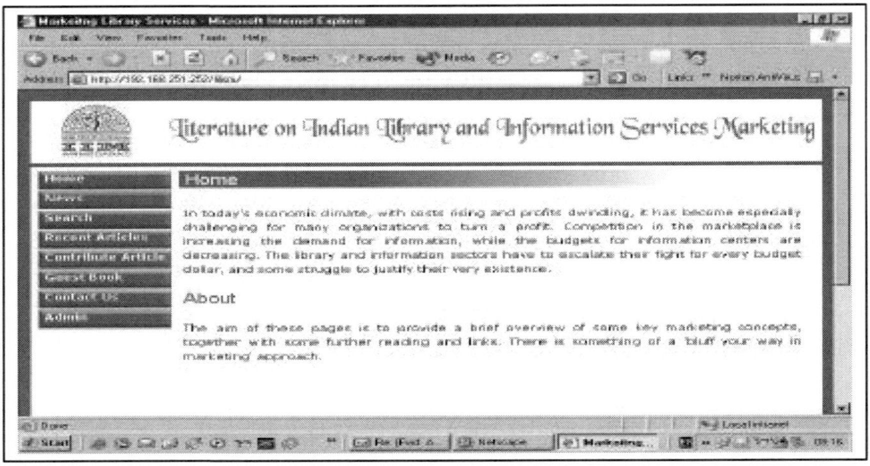

DEVELOPMENT OF DATABASE AND WEBSITE

The website, LILISM, was hosted on IIMA server and is accessible through any Internet browser, although, it is best viewed through Internet Explorer.

Software for this application was developed using Php 4.1.2-7.36. It has been hosted on a Linux (Red Hat, Release 7.3) server. The Web server software is Apache 1.3.27-4 (Win32) server and the database software is MySql 3.23.58-1.73.

The software is composed of several modules that create, maintain and search databases. Following sections give a brief overview of the databases and software modules.

Software Design

The LILISM software for this application was developed using Php 4.1.2-7.36. It consists of 184 files (html, php, shtml, sql, gif, jpg, txt, doc, xls, etc. types) in 11 directories and is organized into the following modules, each one performing a specific task.

Configuration Module

Software programmes in this module sets the system configuration parameters for the web server and SQL server. The configuration parameters are username, password, and database name. These parameters are transmitted to the SQL programs performing the user-friendly query operations.

This module consists of 4 php files namely: configadmin, configprojectrpcpu, functions, and configfinaltest

Administration Module

The software programmes in this module perform all activities related to uploading of articles and obtaining statistics on the usage of the website.

The software checks the user's authorization to perform editorial operations. It permits authorized members to create and edit entries of articles and books into the database.

This module consists of eight php files. These are: article entry, article edit, article delete, check article records, check record, edit author, edit journal, and index. In addition it also consists of an SHTML file check record, and HTML file article header.

Search Engine Module

The module provides for two types of search options: regular and advanced. The regular search option provides a dialog box to facilitate search into the database on marketing literature. It is a conventional search engine, offering search by Author, Title, and Any Field. The relational search expressions can be created using the AND, OR options (See Annexure-1). The scope of search could be all articles in the database or those that are published during the specified years. The advanced search feature collects complete information on the desired article to search the database (See Annexure-2). A drop down box is provided with the journal option to limit the scope of search

The search engine processes queries entered through Search Page and performs query operations on Books and Articles databases using mySQL. This module consists of four php files and one SHTML file. These are: search engine final, advance search for articles, advance search for articles, index and search engine (SHTML)

Recent Articles Module

The feature is offered to simplify the searching process. All the articles contributed during current month will be displayed here (See Annexure-3).

This module consists of three php files. These are recentar, recentardetails, and index.

Contribute Article Module

Users can contribute articles to the database using this module. The information on the contributor's, name, designation, organization, e-mail address of the contributor, in addition to the details of the article, are collected through a dialog box. The contributor is required to provide: title, author(s), source (journal), volume/issue number, year of publication, number of pages, keywords, and abstract of the article. The text of the article can be included as attachment (See Annexure-4).

After the details of contributed article are submitted through this option, the users are acknowledged and are informed that their contribution is registered and will be uploaded after the scrutiny by the editorial committee.

The software accomplishing these tasks consists of two php files (contribute and index) and one SHTML file (contribute)

News Module

News is a feature provided for bringing the latest news to the viewers of the site. Upload of news on the web site is performed through this module consisting of three software programs. They are newspage, newsdetail, index.

Guest Book Module

The Guest Book feature encourages the users to view the existing comments and to give their own comments (See Annexure-5).

This functionality is provided through three php programs and one SHTML file. These are: guestbook, guestbookview, index and guestbook (shtml).

Contact Us Module

This module enables the users to send a direct email to the editorial committee of the website.

This feature is accomplished through a shtml program called contact in the main lilism directory.

Images Module

It uses several images/ icons for offer improved and convenient interface of the website and database to the user. In all there are 130 images. These are stored as jpg, gif and psd files in the images12 directory. These images are displayed during the user interaction with the website.

Data Structure Design

The database tables which are designed to hold the literature data and offer user services, is given in the table-1 on the next page. The table presents the names of database tables, and for each table: a brief description on the nature of data, the names of the data fields and the fields on which the table is indexed (for faster access).

Using the Site

As of now, it is being used by the project research team only at IIM Ahmedabad. It has been populated with over three hundred entries and tested by the researchers. The decision to offer it to other users through internet is yet to be taken.

By the User

The home page provides brief introduction and self explanatory buttons to navigate through the web site. Each page displays detailed instructions to the user for accomplishing the tasks such as searching, contributing, sharing views, and contacting the site administration.

Table-1 : Data Base Structure

SNo	Database Table and Description	Fields	Indexed on
1.	articles Information on articles	article id, title, journal id, journal name, publisher, year, period, pages, keywords, abstract, hyperlink, source, volume, issue, and status	article id
2	Indexarticles Index for articles	title id, article id, author id, author name, title, journal name, year, keyword, volume, issue, and status, delete status	author name, title, journal name, and keyword
3	aauthor Authors of articles	author id, author name	both fields
4	atitle Title of article	title id, article title	both fields
5	books Information on books	book id, title, publisher id, publisher name, publisher locn, isbn, year, keywords, abstract, hyperlink, source, and status	book id, title, keyword
6	title Title of books	title id, book title	both fields
7	bauthorc Book-author data	Id, book id, author id	book id and author id
8	indexbooks Index on books	title id, book id, author id, author name, title, publ name, keyword, year, and status	title id, author, publ name, keyword
9	journal Information on journals	journal id, journal name	both fields
10	publisher Data on publishers	publisher id, publ name, publ location	publisher id
11	contribution Information on contributed articles	article id, contributor name, designation, organization, email, article title, author1, author2, author3, journal name, volume_issue, year, pages, keywords, abstract, upload flag, edit flag, new entry flag, hold flag, file path, and file name	article id
12	indexcontribution Index on contributed articles	article id, contributor name, designation, organization, email, article title, author id, author name, journal id,, journal name, volume, issue, year, pages, keywords, abstract, d status, em status, file path, and file name, reject flag	article id, author name, title, journal name, and keyword
13	aauthorc Contributed article-author data	id, article id, author id	article id, author id
14	guestbook Feedback by guests	feedback id, feedback message, email, date, name	feedback id
15	news News information	news id, news title, news matter, name, date, del status, display status	news id
16	user_table Data of authorized users	user id, password, session, authorized group, time stamp	user id

By the Site Administrators

Site administrators can access the site through a password and carry out the administrative tasks such as uploading new entries (from literature or contributors), editing, and obtaining web statistics. Detailed instructions are provided on the site itself.

The appendices provide the snap shots of interface pages of users and site administrators.

CONCLUSION

This database is an important tool for furthering researches in marketing of library and information services. It will be useful to researchers, teachers, and students of library and information services and will give a boost to library scientists to develop such databases in other areas of study and research in the domain of librarianship.

Annexure-I

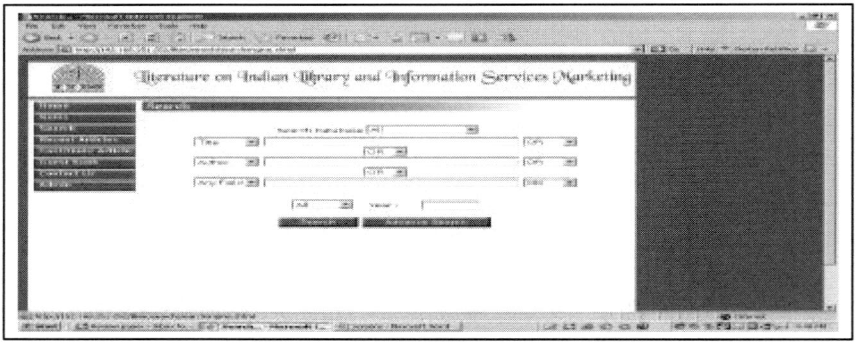

Annexure-II

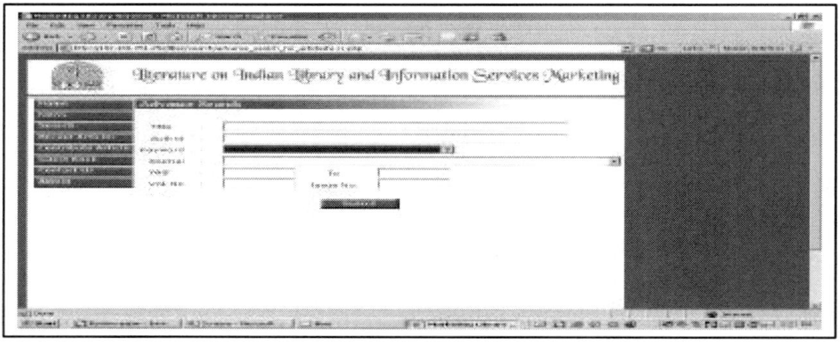

Annexure-III

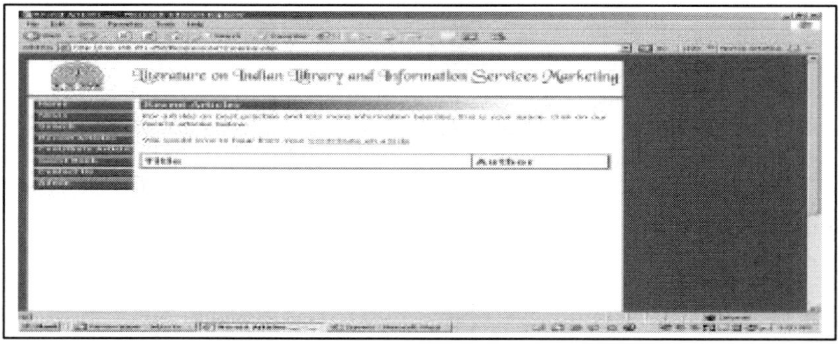

Annexure-IV

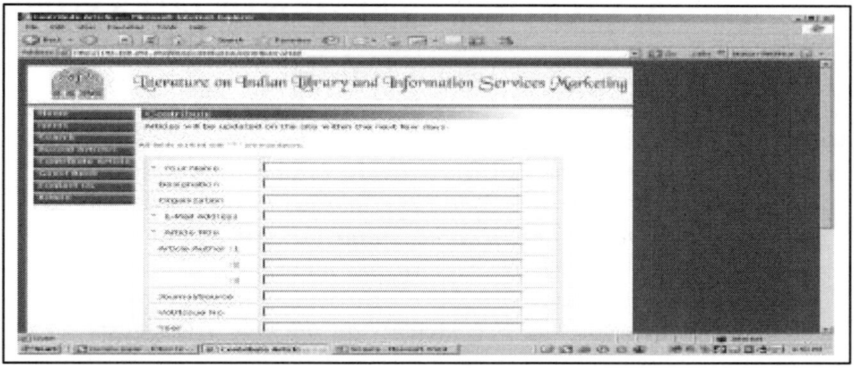

Annexure-V

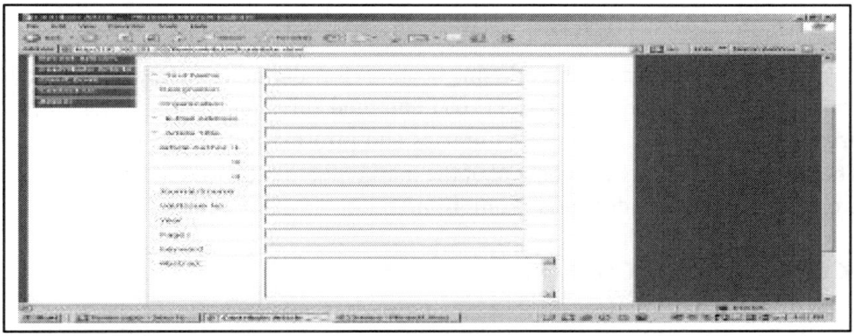

Annexure-VI

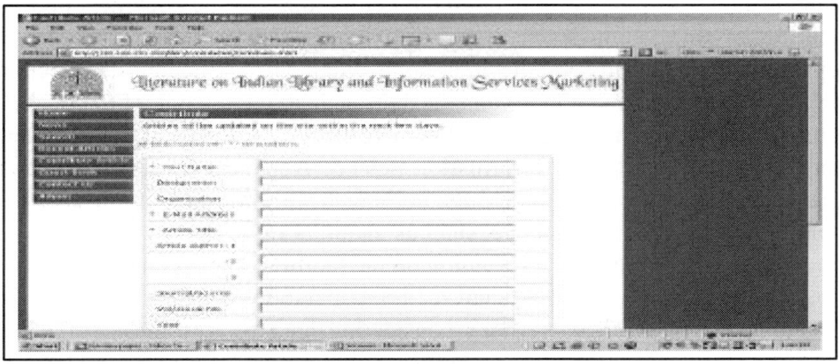

THE FOUR Ps CONCEPT IN LIBRARY AND INFORMATION SERVICES : A REVIEW OF LITERATURE

Sueli Angelica do Amaral

Abstract *The paper analyses 60 documents regarding the 4Ps of marketing mix in libraries in Information Science literature from 1975 to 1995, in order to know who and how many have written about this, and to answer questions such as: Who was the pioneer? Who was the pioneer to add Ps? It shows a chronology of the reviewed documents and it comments on the 4Ps. It suggests adopting the most completed addition proposal presented in order to guarantee library's future.*

INTRODUCTION

The initial concept of marketing began in for -the-profit organizations/sector. Only in 1969, Kotler and Levy (1969) enlarged this approach to the non-profit organizations/ sector, where the libraries and information agencies are included. This study will explore the concept of the marketing mix called four Ps. The four Ps are : Price, place, product and promotion.

SCOPE AND METHODOLOGY

To identify the four Ps in libraries and information agencies in library literature, it was necessary to check the original documents, because frequently the abstracts of the most important indexes did not mention this kind of approach. Sometimes the abstract does mention marketing mix, but the document does not mention anything about each one of the four Ps. These documents were not considered by this study. On the other hand, when the abstract does not mention the four Ps, the document mentions the approach about any one of them, and of course these documents were considered. The indexes used to find the documents analyzed were Library and Information Science Abstracts (LISA) and Library Literature, but only documents written in English were considered.The criteria to include other sorts of documents such as chapters in books encyclopedia, and proceedings was subjective, depending on the facility of accessing the item.

The aim of this work is to analyze library literature about marketing mix from 1975 to 1995. The period was chosen, considering that after 1995 the use of Internet had a great influence in all areas, including marketing and Information Science and the services, products started taking place in form and the whole marketing mantra has changed and started challanging the earlier theories with the new theories like

Internet marketing, database marketing, relationship marketing, etc.. The study aimed at finding answer to the following important questions about 4 Ps:

- Who were the pioneer to write about four Ps in libraries and information agencies?
- How many authors wrote about it?
- Who was the most productive author on this concept?
- Who was the pioneer to additional Ps?
- How many authors added Ps?
- Which was the most frequent conception of additions proposals?
- Which was the most complete addition proposal according the observed points focused on this paper?

The documents analyzed a sum of 60 items, including 37 articles, and 23 chapters of books, encyclopedia, proceedings,etc.

UNDERSTANDING THE FOUR Ps

Inspired by Cullington's ideas, approximately in 1950, Neil H. Borden (1965) started to use the phrase marketing mix in his teaching and writing. To Borden, the list of elements of the marketing mix "can be long or short, depending on how far one wishes to go in his classification and sub-classification of the marketing procedures and policies with which marketing management deal when devising marketing programs." In the beginning of his study, the elements of the marketing mix presented were: product planning, pricing, branding, channels of distribution, personal selling, advertising, promotions, packaging, display, servicing, physical handling, and fact finding and analysis. Later, he kept an abbreviated chart showing the elements and the forces of the marketing mix that, according to his opinion "provides an ever-ready check list as to areas into which to guide thinking when considering marketing questions or dealing with marketing problems."

In 1960, Jerome E. Mc Carthy (1978) in the first edition of Basic marketing: a managerial approach shows an innovative structure, using the marketing mix classification called the four Ps, that popularized product, place, promotion and price as its four elements.

Marketing mix is defined by Kotler (1980) as "the set of controllable variables and their levels that the firm uses to influence the target market."

To Mc Carthy (1978) a target market is "a fairly homogeneous (similar) group of customers to whom a company wishes to appeal." He states that "a marketing strategy specifies a target market and a related marketing mix." In his opinion, the customer is the center of the marketing mix that includes "some product, offered at a price, with some promotion to tell potential customers about the product, and a way to reach the customer's place."

Until now, many authors wrote papers changing Ps into Cs. In 1999, Evert Gummenson introduced total relationship marketing from 4 Ps to 30 Rs of relationship marketing.

THE FOUR Ps IN LIBRARY LITERATURE

About the four Ps in library literature, the questions to check the aim of the study will be answered one by one in order to present the obtained results.

Who was the pioneer to write about four Ps in libraries and information agencies?

In 1976, Weinstock (1976) included a topic about *marketing scientific and technical information service* in the Encyclopedia of Library and Information Science. He considers product, place, promotion, and price as "basic elements to provide answers to marketing research", but he did not call them as four Ps.

The first article about this topic was written by Bellardo and Waldhart, (1977). They comment on each one of the marketing mix elements, but according to the authors, "marketing mix consists of product design, pricing, communication and distribution". So, their conception did not include four Ps, because they used communication and distribution instead of promotion and place.

Among the reviewed texts, the first author that named four Ps in library literature was Moulton, (1981) in 1981, when he wrote an article about marketing and cooperatives. He stated that the four Ps are "a short term tool that helps with tactical planning."

Before Moulton, Dragon in 1979, and Edinger in 1980 also wrote about this theme, although they did not call it four Ps. Dragon (1979) stated that "price, product, promotion and place are traditional mechanisms to stimulate the market." Edinger (1980) defined that "marketing mix of product, place of distribution, price, and promotion factors is formulated in order to achieve the goals."

Table 1 shows the chronology to understand the reviewed texts. It presents information about the author; date and type of document (A = periodical articles, and C = book chapters or others). The table indicates if the author calls four Ps or not, and if he or she presents additions proposals to add Ps or not.

How many authors wrote about four Ps?

Forty seven authors wrote sixty analyzed documents, including nine in double authors.

Who was the most productive author in this topic?

The most productive author was Darlene E. Weingand. She wrote ten texts: three articles, and seven book chapters. One of the chapters belongs to a whole book about marketing written by her.

Cronin (1984; 1985) wrote three articles, and Virgo (1984) wrote two proceedings papers. Galvin ands Keiser (1994) wrote together a book and an article, although putting their names in different orders in each publication (1995).

All of the other forty four authors, including eight in double authors, wrote only one text each. This analysis proves Lotka's law about author's productivity: few authors producing a lot of papers, and a lot of authors producing few papers.

Table-1: Chronology of the Reviewed Documents

AUTHOR	DATE	TYPE	CALL 4PS?	ADD Ps ?
Weinstock	1976	C	NO	NO
Bellardo & Waldhart	1977	A	NO	NO
Dragon	1979	A	NO	NO
Edinger	1980	A	NO	NO
Moulton	1981	A	YES	NO
Condous	1983	A	NO	NO
Weingand	1983	A	YES	NO
Cronin	1984	A	NO	NO
Eisner, Joseph	1984	C	YES	NO
Mathews	1984	C	NO	NO
Simpson	1984	C	YES	NO
Virgo (A marketing approach ...)	1984	C	YES	NO
Virgo (The marketing audit ...)	1984	C	YES	NO
Weingand (Marketing: its ...)	1984	C	NO	NO
Weingand (The application)	1984	C	NO	NO
Weingand (Marketing with a smile)	1984	C	YES	NO
Wood, Douglas	1984	A	YES	NO
Bell	1985	C	NO	NO
Cronin (Improving your ...)	1985	A	YES	NO
Cronin (Information services ...)	1985	A	YES	NO
Freeman & O'Connell	1985	C	YES	NO
Fruitholf	1986	A	YES	YES
Leisner	1986	A	YES	YES
Warnken	1986	C	YES	YES
Weingand	1986	A	YES	YES
Wood, Elizabeth	1986	C	YES	NO
Weingand	1987	C	YES	YES
Char	1988	A	YES	NO
Montouri	1988	A	NO	YES
Strauss	1988	A	NO	NO
Dalton	1989	A	YES	NO
Norman	1989	A	YES	NO
Dean	1990	C	NO	NO
Eisner, Joe	1990	A	YES	NO
Kinnell	1990	A	YES	NO
Lett	1990	C	YES	NO
Wright & Nicholson	1990	C	YES	NO
Cooper	1991	A	YES	NO
Gallacher	1991	C	NO	NO
Weingand	1991	C	YES	NO
Yates-Mercer & Steward	1991	A	YES	NO
Amaral	1991	A	NO	NO
Simpock-Vieweg	1992	A	NO	NO
Collins & Glyptis	1992	A	YES	NO
Kinnell & McDougall	1992	A	YES	NO

AUTHOR	DATE	TYPE	CALL 4PS?	ADD Ps ?
Dijkstra	1992	A	NO	NO
McCarthy	1992	A	YES	NO
Morgan & Noble	1992	A	NO	NO
Smith & Saker	1992	A	YES	YES
Walters	1992	C	YES	NO
Weingand	1992	C	YES	NO
Booth	1993	A	YES	NO
Lindquist	1993	A	NO	YES
Galvin & Keiser	1994	A	NO	NO
Rowley	1994	A	YES	YES
Weingand	1994	C	YES	NO
Dimick	1995	A	YES	NO
Keiser & Galvin	1995	C	YES	NO
Powers	1995	A	YES	YES
Weingand	1995	A	YES	NO

The most productive year was 1984, when ten papers were published about the four Ps. Weingand's (1994) contribution was very significant. She wrote three papers and she had the responsibility of publishing the proceedings including three more documents, two of Virgo's (1984) papers and one written by Leisner (1984).

THE ADDITIONS PROPOSALS

Who was the pioneer to add Ps in library literature?

Considering the documents analyzed, in spite of the methodological restrictions mentioned, to determine who was the pioneer to add Ps in library literature was a difficult task.

In 1986, Weingand (1986) Leisner (1986) and Fruitholf (1986) wrote one article each, and Warnken (1986) wrote a paper included in a book. All of these texts presented additions proposals about the four Ps in library literature, and all of them were published in the same year. So, to determine the pioneer will depend on the considered criteria.

Darlene E. Weingand (1986) can be considered the pioneer, because her article was written in October; taking in consideration that Leisner's (1986) article was written in Fall, that begins in October, but finishes in December; and Fruitholf's(1986) article was published in a periodical title that did not mention the month of publishing. Finally, considering the kind of media of Warnken's (1986) paper, we have only the year of publishing, too;

Fruitholf (1986) can be considered as the pioneer, taking in consideration that the issue including his article was the first of the publishing year; or all of the authors can be considered pioneers, considering only the year of publishing.

In library literature, to determine who was the pioneer to add Ps will depend on the used criteria or point of view to analyze the documents. On the other hand, some similarities and differences can be found among the analyzed proposals in order to identify what do the proposals emphasize.

How many authors added Ps ?

Table 2 shows a summary of additions proposals' analysis in a total of ten papers. The table presents authors' names in a chronological file, including information about the type of analyzed document (A = periodical articles, and C = book chapters or others), and about authors' approaches (if they include comments on each P or not, if they call four Ps or not, and the additional P proposed). Nine authors presented suggestions adding Ps, considering that one of them Weingand(1986) and Weingand (1987) have presented her proposal as an article and later as a book. One of them was an article written by two authors.

Table-2 : Additions Proposals

AUTHOR	DATE	TYPE	COMMENTS	CALL 4Ps?	OWN	PROPOSAL
Fruitholf	1986	A	YES	YES	YES	Participants, Physical evidence, Process
Leisner	1986	A	YES	YES	YES	Politics Public policy
Warnken	1986	C	YES	YES	YES	Participation team
Weingand	1986	A	YES	YES	YES	Prelude Postlude
Weingand	1987	C	YES	YES	YES	Prelude Postlude
Montouri	1988	A	NO	NO	YES	Personal resources
Smith & Saker	1992	A	YES	YES	NO	People, Process Physical evidence
Lindquist	1993	A	NO	NO	YES	People
Rowley	1994	A	NO	YES	NO	Processing
Powers	1995	A	YES	NO	YES	Publics, Production

Cronin's (1985)articles of 1985 were not included in the table 2, but when he wrote his two articles, although he did not add Ps, he argued the adoption of four Ps by libraries and information agencies. In his opinion, "most textbooks on marketing make reference to the 4Ps, but a view has already been expressed about the assortment of products services on offer and the need, or a review of the producing to ensure that a socially appropriate melange is achieved.'

Which was the most frequent conception of additions proposals?

According to the table, Rowley (1984) Smith and Saker (1992) and Fruitholf(1986) suggested additions proposals, based on other authors, that presented their suggestions for profit sector.

Rowley(1994) showed her article as an addition proposal to add Processing, based on Beaumont's proposal presented for profit sector. She presented a figure about the five Ps of the marketing mix, where Processing means data collection, data analysis, and data presentation. Smith & Saker, based on Booms and Bitner, highlight that "as services are provided by People, the quality of the staff will go a long way to determining the quality of the service offered. Elements such as the recruitment and subsequent training of staff are vital to the provision of the service. This is reinforced by the Process or systems that are used by the staff. The final element is the Physical evidence which is "apparent to a customer, that make judgments about the quality of the service."Smith and Saker (1992)

Fruitholf, based on Bosman, emphasizes Participants, as "mainly employees of the organization and customers, Physical evidence, as the physical environment in which the service is rendered, and Process, as all aspects of the procedure employed in rendering the service." (Fruitholf, 1986).

Leisner (1986), Warnken (1986), Weingand (Weingand, 1986; Weingand, 1987), Montouri (1988), Lindquist (1993), and Powers (1995) presented their own approaches.

Three additions proposals (Montouri, 1988; Lindquist, 1993; and Powers, 1995)) did not call the marketing mix classification as four Ps. One of them was presented by Lindquist (1993) in a short article published in 1993. He did not comment about the four elements. He suggested to add the term People, considering organization, competency and capacity, as marketing variables, but did not explain his suggestion. The other proposal was presented by Montouri (1988). In his article, published in 1988, he commented on the importance of "professional librarians and support staff are the Personal Resources, assigned to the marketing effort." He suggests this addition, but he did not include explanations about the four elements, neither called them as four Ps. Powers (1995) did the same, when highlighting that "marketing audit also analyzes the Ps of marketing: product, Publics, price, place, Production, and promotion". In his opinion, "publics are the clients using the library". He emphasized that "meeting demand or Production of the product is essential to success of the product."

Among seven different proposals calling the marketing mix classification as four Ps, Rowley (1994) was the unique author who did not include comments on each P.

Among seven authors that presented their own approaches, Warnken (1986), Montouri (1988), Lindquist (1993), and Powers (1995) included aspects of human resources on their proposed P, and Leisner's approach (1986) mentioned Politics and Public policy. None of them mentioned specifically the focus on customers.

Warnken (1986), about design and promoting the right bibliographical program in a holistic approach, emphasized that "participation of all the team members like the program itself, as their total effort cannot be reduced to its separate components."

Montouri's (1988), Lindquist's (1993), and Powers' (1995) proposals were described above.

Leisner (1986) considered that "understanding of the public policy surrounding local activities can be a constraint on product or service changes. Politics and those with political interest are a constituency in themselves. Their agenda must be considered when planning change and usually library users are converted from mere statistics into voters when a presentation is made to a purely political interest."

In general, the additional proposals mention the importance of what is suggested, but sometimes the authors did not include sufficient information to justify their suggestion or indicate what and/or how to develop the proposal in libraries or information agencies, and this was essential to understand the proposal as a whole. None of them mentioned the meaning of or highlighted the benefits as an addition proposal's focus conception.

Which was the most complete addition proposal according to the observed points focused on this paper?

According this observation, Weingand's proposal (Weingand, 1986, and Weingand, 1987) can be considered the most complete among all the presented proposals. She presented her own approach to add Ps, first as an article published in 1986; and later, in her book edited in 1987. In Weingand's opinion, there are six elements to compound her vision of the marketing mix. She adds Prelude, and Postlude to the four Ps. In her article she states that we are living in a constantly changing environment and we need to look close at the needs, strengths, and limitations of our community and ourselves (prelude: the marketing audit); what we do (product); how much it costs to provide various services (price); the way we deliver service (place or distribution); the mechanisms we use to communicate with our community (promotion); and the results of our efforts (postlude: evaluation). Later, in 1987, she explained her proposal in other words:Prelude: the marketing audit consists of three parts:

1. evaluating the marketing environment of the organization (markets, customers, competitions, and macroenvironment);
2. evaluating the marketing system within the organization (objectives, programs, implementation and organization);
3. evaluating the major areas of marketing activities : the four Ps.Postlude: evaluation formative (process) and evaluation summative (final).

Weingand's proposal includes evaluation and considers the importance of environment in a marketing perspective. So, the proposal is completed, detailed, and it has all the information necessary to understand how to change the proposed plan into reality. Weingand adds two Ps, called by her Prelude and Postlude, that run along the process components of the marketing audit and evaluation, and provides an interface with the elements of planning that enables the library manager to successfully oversee today's operation and tomorrow's opportunities.

FINAL CONSIDERATIONS

The four Ps are an important set of principles working as a framework to transfer marketing concepts from the profit to non profit sector, showing the product in a whole view of its price, place, and promotion under a marketing perspective. This approach can help librarians to succeed using marketing techniques.

The four elements must be well interpreted as a whole and this kind of perception will be useful to facilitate understanding of these activities in the merged process of planning and marketing.

The four Ps can be an important tool to help librarians to understand information agencies as a "business" but more than to know the four Ps, librarians need to go out of the four walls of the information agencies to guarantee the future of these organizations.

REFERENCES

1. Amaral (S A). Marketing adoption in Brazilian Geoscience and Mineral Technology libraries: A study of library managers' opinions. *Infomediary*. 5 (2/3), 1991: 95-104.
2. Bell (J A). Marketing reference services: Translating selected concepts into action for a specific practice setting. *In,* Wood (M S), Ed. Cost analysis, cost recovery, marketing, and fee-based services: A guide for the Health Science librarian. New York : The Haworth Press. 1985: 127-142.
3. Bellardo (T) and Waldhart (T J). Marketing products and services.*Libri*. 27(3). Mar.1977: 181-194.
4. Booth (J). Marketing public library services: The gap between theory and reality. *Library Management* 14 (1). 1993: 9-23.
5. Borden (N H) The concept of the marketing mix. *In*, Schwartz (G), Ed. Science in marketing. Wiley: Chichester. 1965: 386-397.
6. Char (L K). Library marketing and its application to public libraries. *Singapore Libraries*. 18. 1988: 19-33.
7. Collins (M F) and Glyptis (S A). Marketing public leisure services in the UK. *Library Management*. 13 (4). 1992: 33-42.
8. Condous (C). Non-profit marketing- libraries' future? *Aslib Proceedings*. 35 (10). 1983: 407-417.
9. Cooper (S). Marketing strategies for growth in special libraries I. *New Zealand Libraries*. 46 (9). Mar. 1991: 16-19.
10. Cronin (B). Improving your I.Q. innovation quotient. *Information and Library Manager*. 5(3). Dec. 1985: 25-32.
11. Cronin (B). Information services marketing. *South African Journal of Library and Information Science* 53 (3). Sept. 1985: 115-119.

12. Cronin (B). The marketing of public library services in the UK: Practical applications. *The European Journal of Marketing*. 18 (2). Oct. 1984: 45-55.
13. Dalton (G M E). Marketing communication: A means to achieve a positive professional image. *South African Journal of Library and Information Science.* 57 (2). 1989: 184-190.
14. Dean (S). Part 1: definitions. *In,* Dean (S), Ed. Winning marketing techniques: An introduction to marketing for information professionals, a self-study program. Washington : Special Libraries Association, 1990: 7-23.
15. Dijkstra (J W). Factors in setting prices of journals. *Collection Management*. 15 (3-4). 1992: 533-540.
16. Dimick (B). Marketing youth services. *Library Trends.* 43 (3). Winter 1995: 463-477.
17. Dragon (AC). Marketing the library. *Wilson Library Bulletin*. 53(7). Mar. 1979: 498-502.
18. Edinger (J A). Marketing library services: Strategy for survival. *College & Research Libraries*. 41(4). July 1980: 328-332.
19. Eisner (J). The marketing budget: How much is enough? *The Bottom Line*. 4 (2). Summer 1990: 33-34.
20. Eisner (J). The fallacy of applying traditional market pricing theory to tax-supported public libraries. *In,* Weingand (D E), Ed. Marketing for libraries and information agencies. Nonwood, New Jersey : Ablex Publishing Corporation. 1984: 29-33.
21. Freeman (J K) and O'Connell (K A). The marketing of biomedical information service at the University of Minnesota: creative error correction. *In,* Wood (M S), Ed. Cost analysis, cost recovery, marketing, and fee-based services: a guide for the Healthy Science librarian. New York : The Haworth Press. 1985: 159-171.
22. Fruitholf (A C). Marketing in public library services in Belgium. *Mousaion* 4 (1). 1986: 38-64.
23. Gallacher (M). Marketing techniques applied to the development and presentation of a seminar programme. *In,* Wools (B),Ed. Continuing professional education: an IFLA Guidebook. A publication of the Continuing Professional Education Round Table (CPERT) of the International Federation of Library Associations and Institutions. Munchen: K.G.Saur(IFLA Publications, 55). 1991: 58-60.
24. Galvin (C K) and Keiser (B E). A market-driven approach for the library/ information center. *FID News Bulletin*. 44 (1). Jan 1994: 5-11.
25. Keiser (BE) and Galvin (C K). The marketing mix. *In,* Keiser (BE) and Galvin (C K). Marketing library services: a nuts-and-bolts approach. 4th ed. The Hague : FID. (FID Occasional Paper, n.9). 1995: 49-68.
26. Kinnell (M). Marketing first, promotion later: A review. *Outlook on Research Libraries*, Nov. 1990: 3-6.

27. Kinnell (M) and MacDougall (J). Libraries and leisure services marketing: Rhetoric and reality. *Public Library Journal*. 7(4). July/ Aug. 1992: .93-97.
28. Kotler (P). Marketing management: Analysis, planning, and control. Englewood cliffs : Prentice-Hall, Inc. 1980: 88.
29. Kotler (P). and Levy (S J). Broadening the concept of marketing. *Journal of Marketing*. 33 (1). Jan. 1969: 10-15.
30. Leisner (T). Mission statements and the marketing mix. *Public Libraries*, 25. 1986: 86-87.
31. Lett (B). Training for marketing and public relations in libraries. *In*: Prytherch (R), Ed. Handbook of Library training practice. Gower. 1990: 49-71.
32. Lindquist (M G). The marketing of information services. *FID News Bulletin*, 43 (11/12). Nov./Dec. 1993: 267-269.
33. McCarthy (E J). Basic marketing: A managerial approach. Ed.6. Richard D. Irwin, Homewood, 1978.
34. McCarthy (G). Promoting the in-house library. *Aslib Proceedings*, 44 (7/8). July/Aug. 1992: 289-293.
35. Mathews (A J). The use of marketing principles in library planning. *In*, Weingand (D E), Ed. Marketing for libraries and information agencies. Nonwood, New Jersey : Ablex Publishing Corporation. 1984: 3-14.
36. Montouri (C F). Marketing and public libraries: The commitment. *North Carolina Libraries*. 46 (3). Fall 1988: 148-150,152-153.
37. Morgan (P) and Noble (S). Marketing library and information services in the '90s. *The Australian Library Journal*. 41(4). Nov. 1992: 283-292.
38. Moulton (B). Marketing and library cooperatives. *Wilson Library Bulletin*. 55 (5). Jan. 1981: 347-352.
39. Norman (O G). Marketing library and information services: An annotated guide to recent trends and developments. *Reference Services Review*, 17(1). Spring 1989: 43-64.
40. Powers (J E). Marketing in the special library environment. *Library Trends*. 43 (3). Winter 1995: 478-493.
41. Rowley (J). Marketing information systems. *Aslib Proceedings*. 46 (7/8). July/Aug. 1994: 185-187.
42. Simpock-Vieweg (K). How to develop a marketing plan for a firm library. *Law Library Journal*. 84 (1). Winter 1992: 67-91.
43. Simpson (T). The marketing challenge in public library. *In*, Weingand (D E), Ed. Marketing for libraries and information agencies. Nonwood, New Jersey: Ablex Publishing Corporation. 1984: 21-28.
44. Smith (G) and Saker (J). Developing marketing strategy in the not-for-profit sector. *Library Management*. 13 (4). 1992: 6-21.
45. Strauss (D). Marketing fundamentals for librarians. *North Carolina Libraries*. 46 (3). Fall 1988: 132-135.
46. Virgo, (J A C). A marketing approach to identifying library services. *In*, Weingand (D E), Comp. Marketing public library services; new strategies.

(Proceedings of Public Library Association Frontiers Conference. Madison, WI, 1984). Madison : American Library Association. 1984: 17-27.

47. Virgo (J A C). The marketing audit in the public library. *In*, Weingand (D E), Comp. Marketing public library services: New strategies. (Proceedings of Public Library Association Frontiers Conference. Madison, WI, 1984). Madison : American Library Association. 1984:.33-45.

48. Walters (S). Marketing strategies. *In,* Walters (S). Marketing: A how-to-do-it manual for librarians. New York : Neal-Schuman Publishers,Inc. 1992: 37-49.

49. Warnken (P). Design and promoting the "right" BI program: a holistic approach. *In,* Kirkendall (CA), Ed. Marketing instructional services: applying private sector techniques to plan and promote bibliographic instructions (Papers presented at the 13th Library Instruction Conference held at Eastern Michigan University, May 3-4, 1984). Ann Arbor : Pierian Press, 1986: 55-63.

50. Weingand (D E). The application. *In,* Weingand (D E), Ed. Marketing for libraries and information agencies. Nonwood, New Jersey : Ablex Publishing Corporation, 1984: 99.

51. Weingand (D E). Distribution of the library's product: the need for innovation. *Journal of Library Administration*, 4 (4). Winter 1983: 49-57.

52. Weingand (D E). Marketing and financial management keys to fiscal accountability in the public library. *In*: Keeping the books. Fort Atkinson : Highsmith Press, 1992: 307-316.

53. Weingand (D E). Marketing continuing professional education. *In:* Wools, (B), Ed. Continuing professional education: An IFLA Guidebook. Munchen: K.G.Saur. (IFLA Publications, 55) 1991: 52-57.

54. Weingand (D E). Marketing: its relationship to the planning process. *In,* Weingand (D E), Comp. Marketing public library services; new strategies (Proceedings of Public Library Association Frontiers Conference). Madison, WI, 1984. Madison : American Library Association, 1984: 28-30.

55. Weingand (D E). Marketing: Phase two. *In*: Weingand (D E), Ed. Managing today's public library: Blueprints for change. Englewood : Libraries Unlimited, Inc. 1994: 132-148.

MARKETING LIBRARY SERVICES NEWSLETTER : AN OVERVIEW

Kathy Dempsey

Abstract *The newsletter MLS: Marketing Library Services was the brainchild of the principals of Riverside Data, Inc., a privately held publishing company that was originally developed to create, nurture, and then sell various print information products. The principals of U.S.-based Riverside Data, Inc. all worked on these creations part-time while holding their own information-related jobs. The present paper deals with emergence of the newsletter, its contents, coverage, and change over. Also discusses features of the newsletter in brief.*

HISTORY OF MLS NEWSLETTER

In 1987, *MLS: Marketing Library Services* was officially born. (ISSN: 0896-3908) The above-named people had been hearing that librarians wanted to increase their marketing expertise, so they created the newsletter and did test mailings to gauge reader interest. Having gotten positive results, Riverside Data, Inc. began regularly publishing *MLS* on a six-week cycle in January 1988. (Later, in its 1990 summary prepared for potential buyers of the *MLS* newsletter property, the principals claimed that "It was the first commercial newsletter devoted to information marketing.")

Principal Sharon LaRosa became the editor of *MLS*, writing most of the text as well as securing articles from others and putting the pieces together. LaRosa was well-suited to the task, possessing an M.L.S. from Simmons College in Boston and being the chair of the Marketing Management Committee of the Special Libraries Association.

In that same 1990 prospectus, it was written that "Since its inception, more than 750 information professionals (97 percent from the U.S. and Canada) have subscribed to the newsletter." It also called *MLS* "a highly-desirable property" in the new niche of marketing library and information services, "a topic that will be of greater interest to the targeted library market in the months and years ahead." That statement turned out to be correct, as did this one: "Budget pressure within libraries, increased competition from other information sectors, and the need for cost-recovery for information services—each of these factors will intensify in impact in the next decade."

CONTENT,COVERAGE AND CHANGE OVER

So the newsletter was created and tested in 1987. Riverside Data published it during its first full year of life, 1988 (volume 2), and through 1989 (volume 3) before putting it on the market in 1990. During each of those two years, eight issues were published during the winter/spring and fall/winter, with no summer issues. The issues varied between eight and twelve pages each. Initial prices were listed as $49 in the U.S. and Canada and $99 for subscribers elsewhere. Single sample issues were advertised for $12 each in the U.S. and $15 outside the country.

The January 1988 issue, vol. 2, no. 1, carried news that an editorial advisory board had been formed "to provide guidance and counsel to this newsletter." These were 9 members in 1988 on the editorial board.

The content in 1988 consisted of articles such as "Using Surveys for Market Research" (by Galvin, vol. 2, no. 1, p. 2), and "The Corporate Information Audit" (by LaRosa, vol. 2, no. 8, p. 4). News touched on such hot subjects as optical publishing and storage on CD-ROMs, videos for sale, library conference coverage, and *MLS* information such as prices and publishing schedules.

In the beginning, the newsletter layout was very unsophisticated. *MLS: Marketing Library Services* started out with news blurbs on the front page, different types of articles not clearly separated into sections, and plain white paper. However, by the end of 1988, it had arrived at the look that would last for more than a decade: a major feature on page one, clearly separated sections, cleaner columns of text, and that very distinctive robin's-egg blue on the outer edges of each page. (Interestingly, from the very first issue of 1998, that color was used for the logo/title on page one.) By the end of 1988, the overseas subscription price had changed from $99 to $70.

January 1989, vol. 3, no. 1, brought a similar look and feel to the new year. The light blue color continued throughout the newsletter, LaRosa continued as editor, and corporate-type feature stories still filled the cover and beyond. This second full year of publication saw articles such as "At Ingalls, A Winning Pitch Proves Value" about Ingalls, Quinn & Johnson PR agency (by LaRosa, vol. 3, no. 1, p. 1) and "A Primer on Pricing Library Services" (vol. 3, no. 1, p. 5). By this point, most issues contained the five basic types of information/sections that had been developed: (1) Case studies (2) How-to articles (3) Book reviews (4) News (5) Feature articles.

At the end of this year, all eight issues of *MLS* were indexed and that index was printed and sent with early 1990 issues. According to the index, some of the most-cited keywords were CD-ROM, customer service, Dialog Information Services, education, end-user searching, marketing objectives, marketing tools, online searching, planning, public relations, and training.

1990 was a year of transition. The publication was on the market and was eventually bought by Learned Information, Inc. The Medford, New Jersey-based publishing company was and is still run by Thomas H. Hogan, President and CEO, along with Roger R. Bilboul, Chairman of the Board. Learned Information had a number of other information-related serials at that time, including its flagship *Information Today* newspaper, *Searcher* magazine, and *Link-Up* newspaper. The company also published a small line of books and proceedings, and organized the annual National Online Meeting.

The first issue of *MLS* that Learned put out was vol. 5, no.1, February/ March 1991. Editor Sharon LaRosa had agreed to ride along with the newsletter property (and would continue her tenure there for two more years). A note in that issue said that purchase negotiations had put them behind schedule, and it spelled out the new publishing dates for the rest of 1991: April/May (no. 2), June/July (no. 3), August (no. 4), September (no. 5), October (no. 6), November (no. 7), and December (no. 8).

In Learned Information, Inc.'s first year of running *MLS*, the newsletter did not appear much different. The company kept the robin's-egg-blue color and layout style, and *MLS* still carried many articles by original principals and writers, Arnold, Galvin, and LaRosa.

By the end of 1991, Learned had changed the prices. U.S. subscriptions went from $49 to $59 per year, while Canadian fees rose from $49 to $65 and other countries' prices went from $70 to $80. Single-issue prices remained the same.

A sampling of content from volume 5 includes a cover story called "Fees for Service: The Silver Lining" (by LaRosa, no. 1), "Planning the Promotional Mix" (no. 4, p. 4), and a special feature called "Marketing Information in the Mid-90s" (by Arnold, nos. 7 & 8, p. 4). (Somehow the plan to publish separate issues in November and December 91 had gone awry, and the final issue of the year ended up being a 12-page issue that combined both months.)

After that, the next year and a half (1992 and the first half of 1993) was status quo. Volume 6 and half of volume 7 continued to come out with eight numbered issues per year; each one usually had eight pages.

Content-wise, the newsletter was shifting slightly from its previous focus on corporate libraries and including more articles on public and academic institutions. For instance, in August/September 1992, there was a major interview with Elliot L. Shelkrot, director of the Free Library of Philadelphia and newly elected president of the Public Library Association. Titled "PLA President Emphasizes Effective Communication" (by Suzanne M. Ward, vol. 6, no. 6, p. 4), it discussed communication training, lobbying public officials, and involving staff members.

The next issue, October 1992, carried a cover story about the Seattle Public Library and its 100th anniversary celebration (which later won a John Cotton Dana Award). And inside the same issue was the feature "Marketing the Academic Library: Current Trends" (by Katharina J. Blackstead, vol. 6, no. 7, p. 4), which stated, "Today's academic library has five essential targets on which to focus its marketing efforts: (1) Itself, including its own faculty, staff, and/or any other employees within its system; (2) The campus community, including students, faculty, administration, staff, advisory boards, trustees and the development office (if the latter is centrally administered by the university and not a part of the library);

(3) The area community, including the library's friends organization, off-campus users, and local area libraries; (4) The national community, including alumni and other academic libraries and universities; and (5) The international community." (This article concentrated on the first three market segments.) Interestingly, the marketing trends and segments here are still discussed in the current-day (2004) newsletter. So these particular ideas haven't changed over time.

MLS started the year 1993 in the same fashion it had been running, but then experienced a big change. During that year, Sharon LaRosa resigned as editor. The last issue bearing her name was June 1993, vol. 7, no. 4. Publisher Tom Hogan sought a replacement, but had difficulty finding someone who could commit the time that the newsletter demanded. Finally, in May 1994, he hired Kathy Miller to work in the New Jersey office, spending half her time on *MLS* and half her time editing books that Learned Information had recently acquired contracts for.

The first issue that Miller put together was vol. 7, nos. 5 & 6, published without a date because it did not appear until June 1994. Due to the lag in publishing during the search for a new editor, the newsletter had missed a number of issues. Hogan wanted to make up the lost issues and fulfill subscribers' needs, so he and Miller agreed on a double-time schedule to catch up on the missing issues and sent a letter to all subscribers explaining the situation. This started with the aforementioned vol. 7, nos. 5 & 6, 12-page issue to cover July through September 1993. It was followed by vol. 7, nos. 7 & 8, covering October, November, and December 1993. The series continued in 1994 with double issues through vol. 8, nos. 5 & 6, July/August and September. The following issue was back at its normal size and frequency; vol. 8, no. 7, October/November 1994.

Since the newsletter layout also came in-house at this time, the look was spruced up a bit. Art Director M. Heide Dengler took *MLS* under her wing initially, adding graphics to start each section and to separate columns, and polishing the overall appearance.

New editor Kathy Miller began compiling her first couple issues with advice and articles carried over from founder Steve Arnold, editorial board member Barbie Keiser, and former editor Sharon LaRosa. She quickly moved toward using writers she knew and topics that she had experience in—public libraries, printing and promotional items, and conference reports, all with a marketing spin. How-To articles appearing in the first several issues under this new editor included these: "No-Hassle Ways to Make More Money for Your Library" (by Miller, vol. 7, nos. 5 & 6, p. 7), and "Planning, Producing, and Printing a Promotional Piece" (by Joseph Kirschen, vol. 7, nos. 7 & 8, p. 6), followed up by the companion piece "A Quick Primer on High-quality Printing" (by Kirschen, vol. 8, nos. 1 & 2, p. 6).

Under Miller's stewardship, the newsletter also took on a less-corporate, less-academic tone as she encouraged authors to follow her own style of "informal, but informative." Marketing was a concept that had been more prevalent in libraries of corporations (which rely so much on marketing themselves), but Miller wanted to make it more accessible to public and academic libraries. She believed in the principals' original prediction that "Budget pressure within libraries, increased competition from other information sectors, and the need for cost-recovery for information services" would make marketing and promotion more necessary for all sorts of libraries in the years ahead, so she sought to include more case studies from leading-edge public libraries to serve as examples for them.

In fact, Miller revisited a library system that had been covered in the August/September 1992 article (mentioned above), the Free Library of Philadelphia, in the cover story of the April/May & June 1994 double issue. There was also a How-To on page 5 called "The Basics of Buying Promotional Products," demonstrating the new editor's penchant for seeking out practical articles over theoretical ones. Further evidence of that point came in the next issue, in an article full of tips on working with caterers and ordering food for receptions in the most efficient and economical ways ("Turn the Tables on Slow Business," by Miller, vol. 8, no. 7, October/November 1994, p. 4). Such information could be used by corporate or special librarians, to be sure, but could also be used by academic and public librarians, and contained insider information from an interview with a banquet chef.

By her sixth issue, Miller had hit her stride, producing a 12-page newsletter than ran the gamut of library types, contained practical information and expert tips, and also had program ideas, book reviews, and news. This July/August & September 1994 issue (vol. 8, nos. 5 & 6) carried this content:

- Cover Story: Big Success in a Small Library (fundraising at Navarro College, Texas)
- Special Report: ABB-CE Revisited (how ABB-Combustion Engineering in Connecticut works after transitioning to a profit center)
- Feature: Building Customer Loyalty in a Library (advice from a motivational-workplace consultant)
- How-To: You Oughtta Be In Pictures (how to create your own videos for effective communication)
- Ideas for Action: ideas for December that are not holiday-related
- Book Reviews: one on how-to-select-consultants book and another on a directory of information sources on the Internet
- News: highlighting a new directory, announcing upcoming conferences, telling readers where to get info and ideas for National Library Week

This would be the blueprint for *MLS* for the forseeable future. In fact, until the present day, the newsletter has continued to strive for this basic mix of case studies, ideas, news, and reports.

At the end of 1994 (vol. 8, no. 8, December), there was an index published that covered volumes 7 and 8. Miller built this keyword subject index by hand, including the past two years, which covered the end of LaRosa's editorship and the beginning of her own. Then again in the December 1995, Miller created and published a subject-based index that covered all of 1995.

MLS has had the same publisher and editor since 1994, although the names have changed: In 1995, Learned Information, Inc. changed its name to Information Today, Inc. to distinguish itself from its U.K.-based sister organization, Learned Information Europe Ltd. Then in 2000, editor Kathy Miller married and began using her new name, Kathy Dempsey. Different names, same players, continuing to build up this specialized newsletter on library marketing.

THE MOST RECENT DECADE OF MLS

Once the newsletter had a stable home and family, the changes that took place over its next 10 years were smaller ones. For instance, in 1996, Art Director Heide Dengler, who had since become Graphics Department Manager, stopped laying out the publication herself and assigned it to a newer graphic artist instead. Through the years, a number of artists have handled the layout and production of *MLS*, although the look and feel has remained consistent.

The content, however, has continued to shift. As mentioned earlier, by 1995 the focus of the articles had already morphed from very corporate (in topic and style) to less-formal language that also covered more public and academic library case studies. The Ideas for Action section had been added, which noted events and anniversaries from the popular reference book *Chase's Annual Events* and suggested how to build attention-getting library programs, events, and displays around them. But after 1995, the entire core focus of the newsletter expanded. Instead of sticking almost exclusively to the defined principles of marketing, Miller expanded the scope to include more promotion, advocacy, publicity, and programming. She did this for several reasons:

- It was difficult to keep getting case studies from corporate or special librarians who were often limited in what they could reveal for publication.
- She wanted to include other types of libraries in the mix.
- She realized that many libraries didn't have dedicated marketing or promotional staff, so it was important to publish case studies showing that smaller organizations could tackle smaller promo projects and still be marketing their services.
- She saw the need for all types of libraries to promote their services, and saw *MLS* as a good vehicle to help them do that.
- Covering a variety of projects, subjects, and library types would keep the newsletter more interesting to its readers.

MLS articles now covered topics like fundraising, political action, outreach, promoting oneself, marketing via electronic means (e-mail, electronic newsletters, Web site, intranets), using community or organizational partnerships, writing effective press releases and brochures, working with the media, and having cafes or snack bars in libraries. However, it didn't forget its roots at all: It still had articles about the more corporate side, like proving your worth to your management, positioning your library within an organization, measuring cost/benefit analyses, and quantifying your value.

While these topics have been the core of *MLS* since Information Today, Inc. bought it, others have surfaced briefly, been covered, and then quietly disappeared. For instance, at one time there was quite an outcry about outsourcing or co-sourcing library work, and*MLS* ran a controversial article about that ("Turning the 'O' Word into the 'Co' Word," by Linda Cooper, vol. 12, no. 3, April/May 1998, p. 1). In the early 1990s when CD-ROM database usage was really catching on in libraries, there were articles about how to promote those new-fangled resources to faculty and students. Ditto for when the Internet and online databases became something that patrons searched themselves; librarians needed to publicize this technology and train people to use it. *MLS* was there, and it continues to cover the marketing side of technology as it progresses (for example, "Why and How to Use Blogs to Promote Your Library's Services" by Darlene Fichter, vol. 17, no. 6, November/December 2003, p. 1).

THE NEWSLETTER GETS ITS FIRST COLUMNIST

At a conference in 2001, editor Kathy Dempsey enjoyed one particular session about marketing, recognized the expertise of the speaker, and approached her to write an article. So it was that Christie Koontz, a research associate at Florida State University, marketing speaker, and member of IFLA's marketing & management committee, published her first article in *MLS* (vol. 15, no. 7, October/November 2001, p. 4). "Marketing Research Is a Useful Tool for Libraries" filled a void that Dempsey had been noticing. As librarians had been rushing to discover more about marketing and to publicize their services, some of the basics had been forgotten. Many people had jumped into the field without much background, and without the ability to distinguish marketing from promotion from advertising. And many librarians weren't starting at the beginning, with good marketing research; they were simply promoting their products and calling that "marketing." Koontz' solid background in "real" marketing made her the perfect person to write a pointed article. What she published in *MLS* in Fall 2001 explained why public libraries needed to do marketing research, and how to gather and categorize data to glean useful information from it.

Dempsey knew that leading people in the library marketing field were starting to tell librarians that they needed to run their libraries like businesses, as far as marketing, cost-recovery, and customer service. Wanting to take *MLS* in that direction, and being pleased with Koontz' first article on market research, she arranged for Christie Koontz to become a regular columnist for *MLS*, starting in January/February 2002 (vol. 16, no. 1). Ever since then, the column Customer-Based Marketing has been published in every other issue of the newsletter.

Customer-Based Marketing explains essential tenants of marketing to make sure that librarians really realize what it means to be *marketing* library services. The first column in 2002 was called "Stores and Libraries: Both Serve Customers" and explained similarities between the two to help librarians think of their jobs the way businesspeople might. Columns since then have explained market segmentation and census data, and have gone on to explain how geographic information and segmentation can be extremely useful to librarians who want to understand their customers' behavior. Koontz is especially well-versed in that area, since she heads the GeoLib Program at Florida State. She and her colleagues have been developing the first-ever Public Library Geographic Database, using software to map the exact locations of 16,000 PLs and to combine that with census data and library usage statistics to allow better library decision-making (vol. 17, no. 5, September/October 2003, p. 6). Koontz' columns continue to enlighten subscribers about the nuances and new technologies of serious library marketing.

MLS OFFICIALLY CHANGES ITS FREQUENCY

Aside from beginning a regular column, 2002 brought another major change for the newsletter's subscribers: Its frequency changed from eight issues per year to six. This allowed the publisher and editor to create a simpler pattern of publication. After Information Today, Inc. bought the newsletter and got all the issues caught up, its eight-times-per-year publishing schedule had been very regular, but somewhat confusing: 1. January/February 2. March 3. April/May 4. June 5. July/August 6. September 7. October/November 8. December.

Changing the frequency to six times per year allowed the newsletter to come out on the simpler schedule of every other month : 1. January/February 2. March/April 3. May/June 4. July/August 5. September/ October 6. November/ December.

The whole change was explained as a special announcement on the cover of the March/April 2002 issue (vol. 16, nos. 2 & 3). From then on, some issues would have eight pages and some issues would have twelve, so that readers would still get the same 64 pages per year that they had always paid for and received.

WELCOMING OTHER SUBSCRIBERS

The biggest thing that happened in 2003 was not something that affected *MLS* itself, as far as content or stewardship. It did, however, affect hundreds of people who had subscribed to a quarterly marketing/promo serial called *The Shy Librarian*.

The owner/editor of *The Shy Librarian* approached Dempsey and Information Today, Inc. about taking over his newsletter in 2003. He had happy readers and enjoyed filling the newsletter with case studies, promotional tidbits, photos, and book reviews, he said, but he could not continue to finance the project. After months of negotiations, both parties reached an agreement saying that the *Shy* owner would turn over his subscription and mailing lists to Info Today in return for Info Today sending out issues of *MLS* to fulfill the remaining subscription obligations of *The Shy Librarian.*

Consequently, people who had subscribed to *Shy* got the September/ October 2003 of *MLS* in its place. That issue carried a welcome message to *Shy* subscribers explaining that they'd be getting *MLS* for the remainder of the issues they'd already paid for. Info Today also gave those readers an opportunity to switch to *MLS* at renewal time and get a discount on the price of *MLS* (which was more than the price of *Shy* had been). Within six months, a number of *Shy* readers had switched their expiring subscriptions to *MLS*, thereby boosting *MLS* circulation while keeping more librarians up-to-date on the latest marketing trends and ideas.

CURRENT STATUS OF MLS: MARKETING OF LIBRARY SERVICES

Today, in late 2004, *MLS* continues to publish regularly six times per year, with the same publisher and editor. It still delivers a mix of core marketing information, along with interesting publicity ideas, practical how-to articles, reviews of marketing-related books and tapes, news, its column, and of course, case studies of planning grand openings, winning bond issues, surviving budget cuts, and branding libraries.

Today's prices stand at $79.95 per year in the U.S.; $90 in Canada and Mexico; and $98 outside North America. A single back issue costs $14 or $18 outside North America. *MLS* does have a page on the Information Today, Inc. Web site (http://www.infotoday.com) where people can always find the Tables of Contents along with one full-text sample article from each issue, at no charge.

The Editor continues to seek out library marketing experts for articles and ideas. She is also sought out as a speaker herself, and the number of requests for appearances has grown over the past few years. The deep cuts in library budgets and hours has, unfortunately, been what it's taken for some librarians to realize the serious need for marketing and publicity. In the wake of these problems, more library associations have asked her to address their members about how to write marketing plans and how to convince the public that they are still essential, even when everyone is searching for his or her own information on the Internet.

CONCLUSION

Despite the great rise in the interest in this topic and the newsletter, subscription numbers have stayed about the same as always, fluctuating between 600 and 800 subscribers worldwide. One reason for the flat numbers is that, for every library that might start to subscribe, another library loses funding and can no longer afford the newsletter, or it closes down altogether. It is a painfully ironic situation when people do not have the money or time to read the professional journals that would help them to get more money and more time to do their valuable work.

But the *MLS: Marketing Library Services* newsletter continues to address a range of topics (advocacy, publicity, promotion, fundraising, partnering) and covering a range of library types (not only general corporate, academic, and public but specific types like medical, law, state, solo, and K-12 school). It continues to reflect its international readership by having a vast array of librarians and information professionals share their stories of success and failure. It covers the new IFLA/3M Marketing Awards to showcase best practices from around the globe. It aims to inform and to inspire, in the hopes that everyone will continue to believe in the value of libraries, and to respect the place they have long held in human society.